Hitler's Pope

Hitler's Pope

The Secret History of Pius XII

⚖

John Cornwell

Viking

VIKING
Published by the Penguin Group
Penguin Putnam, Inc., 375 Hudson Street,
New York, New York 10014, U.S.A.
Penguin Books Ltd, 27 Wrights Lane, London W8 5TZ, England
Penguin Books Australia Ltd, Ringwood, Victoria, Australia
Penguin Books Canada Ltd, 10 Alcorn Avenue,
Toronto. Ontario, Canada M4V 3B2
Penguin Books (N.Z.) Ltd, 182–190 Wairau Road, Auckland 10, New Zealand

Penguin Books Ltd, Registered Offices: Harmondsworth, Middlesex, England

First published in 1999 by Viking Penguin, a member of Penguin Putnam Inc.

7   9   10   8

Care has been taken to trace the ownership and obtain permission, if
necessary, for the photographs included in and on this book. If any errors
or omissions have occurred, they will be corrected in subsequent
printings, if notification is sent to the publisher.

Cornwell, John.
Hitler's pope : the secret history of Pius XII / John Cornwell.
p.   cm.
Includes bibliographical references.
ISBN 0-670-88693-9
1. Pius XII, Pope, 1876–1958.   2. World War, 1939–1945—Catholic Church.
3. Europe—Politics and government—1918–1945.   I. Title.
BX1378.C65   1999   99-28311
282'.092—dc21
[B]

This book is printed on acid-free paper. ∞

Printed in the United States of America
Set in Centaur
Designed by Betty Lew

"All successes [Pacelli believed] could only be attained by papal diplomacy. The system of concordats led him and the Vatican to despise democracy and the parliamentary system.... Rigid governments, rigid centralization, and rigid treaties were supposed to introduce an era of stable order, an era of peace and quiet."

   Heinrich Brüning, German chancellor 1930–32

"Pius XII and the Jews.... The whole thing is too sad and too serious for bitterness ... a silence which is deeply and completely in complicity with all the forces which carry out oppression, injustice, aggression, exploitation, war."

   Thomas Merton

"The cause of the beatification and canonization of Pope Pius XII, who is rightly venerated by many millions of Catholics, will not be stopped or delayed by the unjustifiable and calumnious attacks against this great and saintly man."

   Father Peter Gumpel, S.J., *relator* in the cause of Pius XII's canonization

Preface

～✣～

Several years ago I was at a dinner with a group of postgraduate students, some of whom were Catholics. The topic of the papacy was broached, and the party got contentious. A young woman asserted that she found it difficult to understand how any right-minded person today could be a Catholic, since the Church had sided with the most pernicious right-wing leaders of the century—Franco, Salazar, Mussolini, Hitler. Her father was Catalan; her paternal grandparents had suffered greatly at the hands of Franco during the civil war. Then the topic of Eugenio Pacelli—Pius XII, the wartime Pope—was raised, and how he had not done enough to save the Jews from the death camps.

In common with many Catholics of my generation, I was only too familiar with that allegation. It had started with Rolf Hochhuth's play *The Deputy* (1963), which depicted Pacelli—implausibly, most Catholics thought—as a ruthless cynic more interested in the Vatican's stockholdings than in the fate of the Jews. But Hochhuth's play sparked a controversy about the culpability of the papacy and the Catholic Church in the Final Solution, each contribution to the debate prompting a riposte from its opposite extreme. The leading participants, whose work I discuss at the end of this book, mainly focused on Pacelli's wartime years. Yet Pacelli's influence in the Vatican began during the first decade of the twentieth century and increased over a period of nearly forty years until he was elected Pope in 1939, on the eve of the Second World

War. It seemed to me that a fair appraisal of Pacelli, his deeds and omissions, required a more extensive chronicle than any attempted so far. Such a study would expand not only on Pacelli's earlier diplomatic activities but on the whole life, including the growth of his evident spirituality from childhood. I was convinced that if his full story were told, Pius XII's pontificate would be vindicated. Hence I decided to write a book that would satisfy a broad spectrum of readers, old and young, Catholics and non-Catholics alike, who continue to raise questions about the role of the papacy in the history of the twentieth century. The project, I realized, would be no conventional biography, since the impact of an individual pope on global affairs blurs the usual distinctions between biography and history. A pope, after all, believes, along with many hundreds of millions of the faithful, that he is God's representative on earth.

I applied for access to crucial material in Rome, reassuring those who had charge of the appropriate archives that I was on the side of my subject. Acting in good faith, two key archivists gave me generous access to unseen material: depositions under oath gathered thirty years ago for Pacelli's beatification, and also documents in the office of the Vatican Secretariat of State. At the same time, I started to draw together, critically, the huge circuit of scholarship relating to Pacelli's activities during the 1920s and 1930s in Germany, works published during the past twenty years but mainly inaccessible to a general readership.

By the middle of 1997, nearing the end of my research, I found myself in a state I can only describe as moral shock. The material I had gathered, taking the more extensive view of Pacelli's life, amounted not to an exoneration but to a wider indictment. Spanning Pacelli's career from the beginning of the century, my research told the story of a bid for unprecedented papal power that by 1933 had drawn the Catholic Church into complicity with the darkest forces of the era. I found evidence, moreover, that from an early stage in his career Pacelli betrayed an undeniable antipathy toward the Jews, and that his diplomacy in Germany in the 1930s had resulted in the betrayal of Catholic political associations that might have challenged Hitler's regime and thwarted the Final Solution.

Eugenio Pacelli was no monster; his case is far more complex, more tragic, than that. The interest of his story depends on a fatal combination of high spiritual aspirations in conflict with soaring ambition for power and control. His is not a portrait of evil but of fatal moral dislocation—a separation of authority from Christian love. The consequences of that rupture were collusion with tyranny and, ultimately, violence.

At the culmination of the First Vatican Council in 1870, Archbishop Henry Manning of Westminster welcomed the doctrine of papal infallibility and primacy as a "triumph of dogma over history." In 1997, Pope John Paul II, in his "Remembrance" document on the Final Solution, talked of Christ as the "Lord of History." The time is surely ripe for acknowledgment of the lessons of recent papal history.

Jesus College, Cambridge
April 1999

Contents

Preface   vii

Prologue   I

1
The Pacellis   9

2
Hidden Life   29

3
Papal Power Games   41

4
To Germany   59

5
Pacelli and Weimar   80

6
The Glittering Diplomat   96

7
Hitler and German Catholicism   105

8
Hitler and Pacelli   130

9
The Concordat in Practice   157

10

Pius XI Speaks Out   179

11

Darkness over Europe   193

12

Triumph   205

13

Pacelli, Pope of Peace   219

14

Friend of Croatia   241

15

The Holiness of Pius XII   268

16

Pacelli and the Holocaust   278

17

The Jews of Rome   298

18

Savior of Rome   319

19

Church Triumphant   336

20

Absolute Power   347

21

Pius XII Redivivus   360

Sources, the "Silence" Debate, and Sainthood   372
Acknowledgments   385
Notes   387
Select Bibliography   413
Index   419

Hitler's Pope

Prologue

During the "Holy Year" of 1950, a year in which many millions of pilgrims descended on Rome to show their allegiance to the papacy, Eugenio Pacelli, Pope Pius XII, was seventy-four years of age and still vigorous. Six feet tall, stick-thin at 125 pounds,[1] light on his feet, regular in his habits, he had hardly altered physically from the day of his coronation eleven years earlier. It was his extreme pallor that first struck those who met him. "The skin, tightly drawn over the strong features, almost ash-grey, unhealthy, looked like old parchment," wrote one observer, "but at the same time it had a surprisingly transparent effect, as if reflecting from the inside a cold, white flame."[2] The effect he had on otherwise unsentimental men of the world was often stunning. "His presence radiated a benignity, calm and sanctity that I have certainly never before sensed in any human being," wrote James Lees-Milne. "All the while he smiled in the sweetest, kindliest way so that I immediately fell head over heels in love with him. I was so affected I could scarcely speak without tears and was conscious that my legs were trembling."[3]

The Holy Year saw a host of papal initiatives—canonizations, encyclicals (public letters to the Catholic faithful of the world), even the declaration of an infallible dogma (the Assumption of the Virgin Mary)—and Pius XII seemed deeply settled in his pontificate, as if he had always been Pope and always would be. For the half-billion Catholic faithful in the world, he embodied the papal ideal: holiness, dedication, divinely ordained supreme authority, and, in certain circumstances, infallibility in his statements about faith and morals. To this day, elderly Italians refer to him as *"l'ultimo papa,"* the last Pope.

A man of monklike inclinations of solitude and prayer, he nevertheless met in audience a prodigious number of politicians, writers, scientists, soldiers, actors, sports personalities, leaders of nations, and royalty. Few failed to be charmed and impressed by him. He had beautiful tapering hands, which he used to great effect in his constant blessings. His eyes were large and dark, almost feverish behind gold-rimmed spectacles. His voice was high-pitched, a trifle querulous, with a tendency to overmeticulous enunciation. When he performed church services, his face was impassive, his gestures and movements controlled and elegant. Toward his visitors he was strikingly affable, putting them at ease, all assentation and eagerness, with not the slightest impression of pomposity or affectation. He had a ready and simple humor and would give a big silent laugh, mouth agape. His teeth, one observer noted, were like "old ivory."

Some spoke of a "feline" sensibility, others of an occasional tendency to "feminine" vanity. Before a camera there was a hint of narcissism. And yet he impressed most who met him with a sense of chaste, youthful innocence, like an eternal seminarian or monastic novice. He was at home with children, and they felt drawn to him. He was never known to gossip or speak ill of others. His eyes froze, harelike, when he felt assailed by overfamiliarity or a coarse phrase. He was alone—in a quite extraordinary and exalted sense.

How can one capture a sense of that unique solitude, that papal egotistical sublime, in which modern popes have chosen to live and have their being?

Overwhelmed by the solitude of his pontifical role, Paul VI, Pope in the 1960s and 1970s, confided a private note to himself that might just as well have been penned by Pacelli, whom Paul VI had served (as Giovanni Battista Montini) for fifteen years:

> I was solitary before, but now my solitariness becomes complete and awesome. Hence the dizziness, the vertigo. Like a statue on a plinth—that is how I live now. Jesus was also alone on the cross. I should not seek outside help to absolve

me from my duty; my duty is too plain: decide, assume every
responsibility for guiding others, even when it seems illogical
and perhaps absurd. And to suffer alone.... Me and God.
The colloquy must be full and endless.[4]

This vertiginous papal consciousness surely alters the man who shoulders the papal burden. It is a solitude attended by certain dangers—not
least the perils of increasing egotism and despotism. The longer the
papacy, the more entrenched the papal consciousness. The theologian
John Henry Newman, Britain's most famous convert to Catholicism in
the nineteenth century, delivered a devastating verdict during a previous
drawn-out pontificate: "It is not good for a Pope to live twenty years. It
is anomaly and bears no good fruit; he becomes a god, has no one to
contradict him, does not know facts, and does cruel things without
meaning it."[5] Within ten years of becoming Pope, Pacelli had elevated
the papacy to heights of unprecedented exaltation; there was certainly
no one to contradict him, and he adopted the manner of one destined
for canonization.

There is a striking picture of Pacelli at the zenith of his power, published in 1950. Photographed from above and behind his head and
shoulders, high over St. Peter's Square, he greets the seething multitudes
below like a colossus holding the entire human race in his embrace.
The picture is entirely apt for a bold initial assertion: *The ideology of papal
primacy, as we have known it within living memory, is an invention of the late nineteenth and early twentieth centuries.* In other words, there was a time, before
modern means of communication, when the pyramidal model of Catholic authority—whereby a single man in a white robe rules the Church in
a vastly unequal power relationship—did not exist. There was a time
when the Catholic Church's authority was widely distributed through the
great historic councils and countless webs of local discretion. As in a
medieval cathedral, there were many thrusting spires of authority. Certainly the tallest of these was the papacy, but Roman primacy for much
of two millennia was more a final court of appeal than a uniquely initiating autocracy.

That characteristic image of Pius XII—the supreme, albeit loving,
authoritarian floating above St. Peter's Square—suggests several contrasts
that distinguish the modern popes from their predecessors. The more

elevated the Pontiff, the smaller and less significant the faithful. The more responsible and authoritative the Pontiff, the less enfranchised the people of God, including bishops, the successors to the apostles. The more holy and removed the Pontiff, the more profane and secular the entire world.

This book tells the story of the career of Eugenio Pacelli, the man who was Pius XII, the world's most influential churchman from the early 1930s to the late 1950s. Pacelli, more than almost any other Vatican official of his day, helped to enhance the ideology of papal power— the power that he himself assumed in 1939 on the eve of the Second World War and held until his death in October 1958. But the story begins three decades before he became Pope. Among the many initiatives in his long diplomatic career, Pacelli was responsible for a treaty with Serbia which contributed to the tensions that led to the First World War. Twenty years later he struck an accord with Hitler which helped sweep the Führer to legal dictatorship while neutralizing the potential of Germany's 23 million Catholics (34 million after the Anschluss) to protest and resist.

Pacelli's goals and his influence as diplomat and Pope cannot be separated from the auspices and pressures of the office that gave impetus to his remarkable ambition. That ambition was no simple lust for power for its own sake; the popes of the twentieth century have not been self-seeking men of worldly pride, hubris, and greed. They have been, without exception, men of prayer and meticulous conscience, burdened by the checkered history of the ancient institution they embodied. Pacelli was no exception. That he nevertheless exerted a fatal and culpable influence on the history of this century is the theme of this book.

Pacelli was born in Rome in 1876 into a family of Church lawyers in the service of a papacy disgruntled by the sequestration of the papal states by the new nation-state of Italy. That loss of sovereignty had left the papacy in crisis. How could the popes regard themselves as independent of the political status quo of Italy, now that they were mere citizens of this upstart kingdom? How could they continue to lead and protect a Church in conflict with the modern world?

Ever since the Reformation, the papacy had been reluctantly readjusting to the realities of a fragmented Christendom amid the challenge of Enlightenment ideas and new ways of looking at the world. In response to the political and social changes that gathered pace in the aftermath of the French Revolution, the papacy had struggled to survive and exert an influence in a climate of liberalism, secularism, science, industrialization, an the evolving nation-state. The popes had been obliged to fight on two fronts—as primates of an embattled Church and as monarchs of a tottering papal kingdom. Caught in a bewildering series of confrontations with the new masters of Europe, the papacy had been attempting to protect the Church universal while defending the integrity of its collapsing temporal power.

Most of the modernizing states of Europe were inclined to separate Church from State (or, in the more complex reality of oppositions, throne from altar, papacy from empire, clergy from laity, sacred from secular). The Catholic Church became an object of oppression in Europe through much of the nineteenth century: its property and wealth systematically plundered; religious orders and clergy deprived of their scope for action; schools taken over by the state or shut down. The papacy itself was repeatedly humiliated (Pius VII and Pius VIII were held prisoner by Napoleon), and the papal territories had been in constant danger of dismemberment and annexation as the forces for Italian unity and modernization gathered strength.

Through the vicissitudes of this era, the Church had been riven internally by an issue fraught with consequences for the modern papacy. Broadly, the struggle was between those who urged an absolutist papal primacy from the Roman center and those who argued for a greater distribution of authority among the bishops (indeed, those who even argued for the formation of national churches independent of Rome). Both these tendencies found expression in France from the seventeenth century onward, although the antecedents of papal autocracy had an ancient lineage dating back to the eleventh century and the foundations of papal monarchism. Papal autocracy undoubtedly had been a principal cause of the Reformation itself.

The triumph of the modern centrists, or "ultramontanists" (a phrase coined in France indicating papal power from "beyond the mountains," or the Alps), was sealed at the First Vatican Council of 1870 against the background of the Pope's loss of his dominions. At that Council, the

Pope was declared infallible in matters of faith and morals as well as undisputed *primate*—supreme spiritual and administrative head of the Church. In some respects, this definition satisfied even those who had felt it inopportune: it was, after all, as much a statement of the limits as of the scope of infallibility and primacy.

In the first three decades after the Vatican Council, during the reign of Leo XIII, the ultramontanist Church waxed and grew strong. There was an impression of restoration; ecclesiastical Rome flourished with new academic and administrative institutions; Catholic missions penetrated to the farthest corners of the earth. There was a bracing sense of loyalty, obedience, fervor. The revival of the Christian philosophy of St. Thomas Aquinas, or at least a version of it, provided the perception of a bastion against modern ideas and a defense of papal authority. By the first decade of the twentieth century, however, the concept of the *limits* of papal inerrancy and primacy was becoming blurred. A legal and bureaucratic instrument had transformed the dogma into an ideology of papal power unprecedented in the long history of the Church of Rome.

At the turn of the century, Pacelli, then a brilliant young Vatican lawyer, collaborated in redrafting the Church's laws in such a way as to grant future popes unchallenged domination from the Roman center. These laws, separated from their ancient historical and social background, were packaged in a manual known as the Code of Canon Law, published and brought into force in 1917. The code, distributed to Catholic clergy throughout the world, created the means of establishing, imposing, and sustaining a remarkable new "top-down" power relationship.

As papal nuncio in Munich and Berlin during the 1920s, Pacelli sought to impose the new code, state by state, on Germany—one of the largest, best-educated, and richest Catholic populations in the world. At the same time, he was pursuing a Reich Concordat, a Church-State treaty between the papacy and Germany as a whole. Pacelli's aspirations for that accord with the Reich were frequently resisted, not only by indignant Protestant leaders but also by Catholics who believed that his vision for the German Church was unacceptably authoritarian.

In 1933 Pacelli found a successful negotiating partner for his Reich Concordat in the person of Adolf Hitler. Their treaty authorized the papacy to impose the new Church law on German Catholics and granted generous privileges to Catholic schools and the clergy. In exchange, the Catholic Church in Germany, its parliamentary political party, and its many hundreds of associations and newspapers "voluntarily" withdrew, following Pacelli's initiative, from social and political action. The abdication of German political Catholicism in 1933, negotiated and imposed from the Vatican by Pacelli with the agreement of Pope Pius XI, ensured that Nazism could rise unopposed by the most powerful Catholic community in the world—a reverse of the situation sixty years earlier, when German Catholics combated and defeated Bismarck's Kulturkampf persecutions from the grass roots. As Hitler himself boasted in a cabinet meeting on July 14, 1933, Pacelli's guarantee of nonintervention left the regime free to resolve the Jewish question. According to the cabinet minutes, "[Hitler] expressed the opinion that one should only consider it as a great achievement. The concordat gave Germany an opportunity and created an area of trust that was particularly significant in the developing struggle against international Jewry."[6] The perception of papal endorsement of Nazism, in Germany and abroad, helped seal the fate of Europe.

The story told in this book, then, spans Pacelli's youth, the years of his education, and his formidable early career before he became Pope. The narrative, moreover, finds a new center of gravity in Pacelli's fateful negotiations with Hitler in the early 1930s. Those negotiations, in turn, cannot be seen in isolation from the development of the ideology of papal power through the century, nor from his wartime conduct and his attitude toward the Jews. The postwar period of Pacelli's pontificate, through the 1950s, was the apotheosis of that power, as Pacelli presided over a monolithic, triumphalist Catholic Church in antagonistic confrontation with Communism both in Italy and beyond the Iron Curtain.

But it could not hold. The internal structures and morale of the Catholic Church began to show signs of fragmentation and decay in the final years of Pius XII, leading to a yearning for reassessment and renewal. The Second Vatican Council was called in 1962 by John XXIII, who succeeded Pacelli in 1958, precisely to reject the monolithic, centralized Church model of his predecessors, in preference for a collegial, decentralized, human community on the move. In two key documents, *The Church (Lumen gentium)* and *The Church in the Modern World (Gaudium et spes)*, there was a new emphasis on history, accessible liturgy, community, the Holy Spirit, and love. The guiding metaphor of the Church of the future was of a "pilgrim people of God." Expectations ran high, and there was no lack of contention and anxiety—old habits and disciplines died hard. There were indications from the very outset that papal and Vatican centrism would not acquiesce easily.

At the outset of Christianity's third millennium it is clear that the Church of Pius XII is reasserting itself in countless ways, some of them obvious, some clandestine, but above all in confirmation of a pyramidal Church model—faith in the primacy of the man in the white robe dictating in solitude from the pinnacle. In the twilight years of John Paul II's long reign, the Catholic Church gives a pervasive impression of dysfunction despite John Paul II's historic influence in the collapse of Communist tyranny in Poland and the Vatican's enthusiasm for entering the third millennium with a cleansed conscience.

In the latter half of John Paul II's reign, the policies of Pius XII have reemerged to challenge the resolutions of Vatican II and to create tensions within the Catholic Church that are likely to culminate in a future titanic struggle. As the British theologian Adrian Hastings comments: "The great tide powered by Vatican II has, at least institutionally, spent its force. The old landscape has once more emerged and Vatican II is now being read in Rome far more in the spirit of Vatican I and within the context of Pius XII's model of Catholicism."

Pacelli, whose canonization process is now well advanced, has become the icon, forty years after his death, of those who read and revise the provisions of the Second Vatican Council from the viewpoint of an ideology of papal power that has already proved disastrous in the century's history.

1

The Pacellis

⌇⌇⌇

Eugenio Pacelli was described routinely, during his pontificate and after his death, as a member of the Black Nobility. The Black Nobles were a small group of aristocratic families of Rome who had stood by the popes following the seizure of their dominions in the bitter struggle for the creation of the nation-state of Italy. The Pacellis, intensely loyal as they were to the papacy, were hardly aristocrats. Eugenio Pacelli's family background was respectable but modest, rooted on his father's side in a rural backwater close to Viterbo, a sizable town fifty miles north of Rome. At the time of Pacelli's birth in 1876, a relative, Pietro Caterini (referred to as "the Count" by members of Eugenio's own generation), still owned a farmhouse and a little land in the village of Onano. But Pacelli's father and grandfather before him, as well as his elder brother, Francesco, owed their distinction not to noble links or wealth but to membership of the caste of lay Vatican lawyers in the service of the papacy.[1] Nevertheless, from the 1930s onward, Pacelli's brother and three nephews were ennobled in recompense for legal and business services to Italy and the Holy See.

Pacelli's immediate family association with the Holy See dates from 1819, when his grandfather, Marcantonio Pacelli, arrived in the Eternal City to study canon, or Church, law as a protégé of a clerical uncle, Monsignor Prospero Caterini. By 1834 Marcantonio had become an advocate in the Tribunal of the Sacred Rota, an ecclesiastical court

involved in such activities as marriage annulments. While raising ten
children (his second child being Eugenio's father, Filippo, born in
1837), Marcantonio became a key official in the service of Pius IX,
popularly known as Pio Nono.

The quick-tempered, charismatic, and epileptic Pio Nono (Giovanni
Maria Mastai-Ferretti), crowned in 1846, was convinced, as had been his
predecessors from time immemorial, that the papal territories forming
the midriff of the Italian peninsula ensured the independence of the
successors to St. Peter. If the Supreme Pontiff were a mere inhabitant of
a "foreign" country, how could he claim to be free of local influence?
Three years after his coronation, it looked as if Pio Nono had ignomini-
ously lost his sovereignty over the Eternal City to a republican mob. On
November 15, 1849, Count Pelligrino Rossi, a lay government minister
of the papal states, famous for his biting sarcasm, approached the
Palazzo della Cancelleria in Rome and greeted a sullen waiting crowd
with a contemptuous smile. As he was about to enter the building, a man
leapt forward and stabbed him fatally in the neck. The next day, the
Pope's Quirinal summer palace above the city was sacked, and Pio Nono,
disguised in a priest's simple cassock and a pair of large spectacles, fled
to the seaside fortress of Gaeta within the safety of the neighboring
kingdom of Naples. He took with him Marcantonio Pacelli as his legal
and political adviser. From this fastness, Pio Nono hurled denunciations
against the "outrageous treason of democracy" and threatened prospective voters with excommunication. Only with the help of French bayo-
nets, and a loan from Rothschild's, did Pio Nono contrive to return to
the Vatican a year later to resume a despised reign over the city of Rome
and what was left of the papal territories.

Given the reactionary tendencies of Pio Nono, at least from this
period onward, we can assume that Marcantonio Pacelli shared his Pontiff's repudiation of liberalism and democracy. After the return to
Rome, Marcantonio was appointed a member of the "Council of Censorship," a body charged with investigating those implicated in the re-
publican "plot." In 1852 he was appointed secretary of the interior. The
papal regime during this final phase of its existence was not beneficent.
Writing to William Gladstone that same year, an English traveler characterized Rome as a prison house: "There is not a breath of liberty, not a
hope of tranquil life; two foreign armies; a permanent state of siege,

atrocious acts of revenge, factions raging, universal discontent; such is the papal government of the present day."[2]

The Jews were made a target of post-republican reprisal. At the beginning of his reign, Pio Nono had begun to promote tolerance, abolishing the ancient Jewish ghetto, the practice of conversionist sermons for Roman Jews, and the enforced catechizing of Jews baptized "by chance." But although Pio Nono's return had been paid for by a Jewish loan, the Roman Jews were now forced back into the ghetto and made to pay, literally, for having supported the revolution. Then Pio Nono became involved in a scandal that shocked the world. In 1858, a six-year-old Jewish child, Edgardo Mortara, was kidnapped by papal police in Bologna on the pretext that he had been baptized in extremis by a servant girl six years earlier.[3] Placed in the reopened House of Catechumens, the child was forcibly instructed in the Catholic faith. Despite the pleas of Edgardo's parents, Pio Nono adopted the child and liked to play with him, hiding him under his soutane and calling out, "Where's the boy?" The world was outraged; no less than twenty editorials on the subject were published in *The New York Times*, and both Emperor Franz Josef of Austria and Napoleon III of France begged the Pope to return the child to his rightful parents, all in vain. Pio Nono kept Edgardo cloistered in a monastery, where he was eventually ordained as a priest.

The juggernaut of Italian nationalism, however, was unstoppable; and Marcantonio Pacelli, close to his Pope, was present at events of great consequence for the modern papacy. By 1860 the new Italian state under the leadership of the Piedmontese king, Vittorio Emanuele II, had seized nearly all the papal dominions. In his notorious *Syllabus of Errors* (1864), Pio Nono denounced eighty "modern" propositions, including socialism, freemasonry, and rationalism. In the eightieth proposition, a cover-all denunciation, he declared it a grave error to assert that the "Roman Pontiff can and should reconcile himself with progress, liberalism, and modern civilization."

Pio Nono had erected about himself the protective battlements of God's citadel; within, he raised the standard of the Catholic faith, based on the word of God as endorsed by himself, the Supreme Pontiff, Christ's Vicar upon earth. Outside were the standards of the Antichrist, man-centered ideologies that had been sowing error ever since the French Revolution. And the poisonous fruit, he declared, had even affected the

Church itself: movements seeking to reduce the power of the popes by urging national Churches independent of Rome. Yet just as influential was a long-established tendency from the opposite extreme: ultramontanism, a call for unchallenged papal power that would shine out across the world, transcending all national and geographical boundaries. Pio Nono now began to prepare for the dogmatic declaration of just such an awe-inspiring primacy. The world would know how supreme he was by a dogma, a fiat, to be held by all under pain of excommunication. The setting for the deliberations that preceded the proclamation was a great council of the Church, a meeting of all the bishops under the presidency of the Pope. The First Vatican Council was convened by Pio Nono late in 1869 and lasted until October 20 of the following year.

At the outset, only half of the bishops attending the Council were disposed to support a dogma of papal infallibility. But Pius IX and his close supporters went to work on them. When Cardinal Guido of Bologna protested that only the assembled bishops of the Church could claim to be witnesses to the tradition of doctrine, Pio Nono replied: "Witnesses of tradition? *I* am the tradition."[4]

The historic decree of papal infallibility passed on July 18, 1870, by 433 bishops, with only two against, reads as follows:

> The Roman Pontiff, when he speaks ex cathedra, that is, when, exercising the office of pastor and teacher of all Christians, he defines ... a doctrine concerning faith and morals to be held by the whole Church, through the divine assistance promised to him in St. Peter, is possessed of that infallibility with which the Divine Redeemer wished His Church to be endowed ... and therefore such definitions of the Roman Pontiff are irreformable of themselves, and not from the consent of the Church.[5]

An additional decree proclaimed that the Pope had supreme jurisdiction over his bishops, individually and collectively. The Pope, in effect, was ultimately and unprecedentedly in charge. During the hour of these great decisions, a storm broke over St. Peter's dome and a thunderclap, amplified within the basilica's cavernous interior, shattered a pane of glass in the tall windows. According to *The Times* (London), the anti-infallibilists saw in the event a portent of divine disapproval. Cardinal Henry Manning, the archbishop of Westminster and an enthusiastic lobbyist for Pio Nono, responded disdainfully: "They forgot Sinai and the Ten Commandments."[6]

Before the Council could turn to other matters, the last French troops pulled out of the Eternal City to defend Paris in the Franco-Prussian War. In came the soldiers of the Italian state, and Rome was lost to the papacy, this time forever. All that remained to Pio Nono and his Curia, the cardinals who ran the erstwhile papal states, were the 108.7 acres of the present-day Vatican City, and that on the sufferance of the new Italian nation-state. Shutting himself inside the apostolic palace overlooking St. Peter's, Pio refused to come to an accord with the new state of Italy. He had already, in 1868, forbidden Italian Catholics to take part in democratic politics.

Marcantonio Pacelli might have been out of a job had he not helped found a new Vatican daily newspaper in 1861. L'Osservatore Romano became the "moral and political" voice of the Vatican, and the paper, now published in seven languages, thrives to this day. Meanwhile, following in Marcantonio's footsteps, Eugenio's father, Filippo, had also trained as a canon lawyer and was similarly appointed to the Tribunal of the Sacred Rota, eventually becoming dean of the consistorial advocates, lawyers to the Holy See.

Pacelli's parents were married in 1871. His mother, Virginia Graziosi, was a Roman and, as the phrase went, a pious daughter of the Church. She was one of thirteen brothers and sisters. Two of her brothers became priests and two sisters took the veil. Filippo Pacelli performed pastoral work in the parishes of Rome, distributing spiritual reading matter to the poor. He is chiefly remembered for his attachment to a book entitled *Massime eterne (Eternal Principles)*, a meditation on death by Alfonso Liguori, the eighteenth-century Catholic moralist and saint. Filippo handed out many hundreds of copies throughout Rome, and each year led a procession to a Roman cemetery, where the pilgrims under his guidance pondered their inevitable destiny.

The remuneration of Vatican lay lawyers was meager, and the Pacellis were not prosperous. After 1870, there is an impression of family hardship. In later years Pacelli recollected that there was no heating in the family apartment, even in the depths of winter, save for a small brazier around which the family members warmed their hands.[7] Whereas after 1870 many of their lay contemporaries entered the well-paid bureaucracies of the new Italy, the Pacellis remained faithful to their indignant rejection of Vittorio Emanuele's usurpation. It was the practice of the loyal papal bourgeoisie to wear one glove, to place a chair facing the wall in the principal room, to keep the shutters permanently closed, and to maintain the palazzo door half shut, in token of the Pope's confiscated patrimony. The Pacellis, although lacking an entire palazzo of their own, were of this staunch constituency. Eugenio Pacelli was thus raised in an ambiance of intense Catholic piety, penurious respectability, and an enduring sense of injured papal merit. Above all, the family was steeped in a wide scope of legal knowledge and efficacy—civil, international, and ecclesiastical. As the Pacellis saw it, their papacy and their Church, threatened on all sides by the destructive forces of the modern world, would survive and in time overcome through shrewd and universal application of the law.

The Church Oppressed

In the years following the First Vatican Council, Pio Nono surveyed a dismal scene of oppression from the upper stories of the apostolic palace, with its global perspective on the Catholic Church in the world. In Italy, processions and outdoor services were banned, communities of religious dispersed, Church property confiscated, priests conscripted into the army. A catalogue of measures, understandably deemed anti-Catholic by the Holy See, streamed from the new capital: divorce legislation, secularization of the schools, the dissolution of numerous holy days.

In Germany, partly in response to the "divisive" dogma of infallibility, Bismarck began his Kulturkampf ("culture struggle"), a policy of persecution against Catholicism. Religious instruction came under state control and religious orders were forbidden to teach; the Jesuits were banished; seminaries were subjected to state interference; Church property came under the control of lay committees; civil marriage was introduced in Prussia. Bishops and clergy resisting Kulturkampf legislation were fined, imprisoned, exiled. In many parts of Europe, it was the same:

in Belgium, Catholics were ousted from the teaching profession; in Switzerland, religious orders were banned; in Austria, traditionally a Catholic country, the state took over schools and passed legislation to secularize marriage; in France, there was a new wave of anticlericalism. The conviction had been widely and confidently expressed by writers, thinkers, and politicians across Europe—Bovio in Italy, Balzac in France, Bismarck in Germany, Gladstone in England—that the papacy, and Catholicism with it, had had its day.

Even Pio Nono's firmest supporters were beginning to suspect that the great longevity of this papacy lay at the root of all the problems. Reflecting on the matter in 1876, Westminster's Archbishop Manning dwelt gloomily on the Holy See's "darkness, confusion, depression ... inactivity and illness." Yet were things quite so universally and irredeemably bad? Had the obscurantism of the aging Pio Nono, in conflict with the unstoppable sweep of modernity, rendered the papacy, the longest surviving human institution on earth, moribund? Perhaps, on the contrary, the final passing of the Pontiff's temporal possessions, combined with the benefits of modern communications, had laid the ground for new power prospects as yet undreamt of. If such an idea occurred to him, Pio Nono betrayed no clear declaration of intent, save for his dying admission: "Everything has changed; my system and my policies have had their day, but I am too old to change my course; that will be the task of my successor."[8] After the death of Pio Nono on February 7, 1878, his corpse was eventually taken from its provisional resting place in St. Peter's to a permanent tomb at San Lorenzo. When the cortege approached the Tiber, a gang of anticlerical Romans threatened to throw the coffin into the river. Only the arrival of a contingent of militia saved Pio Nono's body from final insult.[9]

Thus ended the longest and one of the most turbulent pontificates in the history of the papacy.

Childhood and Youth in the "New" Rome

Against the background of the troubled end to Pio Nono's embattled papacy, Eugenio Pacelli was born in Rome on March 2, 1876, in an apartment shared by his parents and his grandfather Marcantonio on the third floor of Via Monte Giordano 3 (now known as Via degli Orsini). The building was a few steps from the Chiesa Nuova, with its ornate and gilded baroque interior; approaching the west end of Corso Vittorio Emanuele, one sees the portico set back a little from the street. From the door of the apartment building, it took just five minutes on foot to reach the Tiber at the Sant'Angelo bridge; fifteen minutes to arrive at St. Peter's Square. Eugenio was one of four children: his elder sister, Giuseppina, was four years old at his birth; his elder brother, Francesco, was two. A second sister, Elisabetta, was born four years later.

The Rome in which Pacelli was born and baptized had scarcely altered physically in two hundred years. More than half the area bounded by the Aurelian walls was resplendent with churches, oratories, and convents. Christian Rome stood alongside the ruins of classical antiquity and moldering villas shaded by evergreen oaks, orange trees, and splendid umbrella pines. Much of the city gave the impression of an ancient market town. Herds of goats and sheep assembled by the fountains and shared the streets and piazzas with pedestrians and carriages. All this was to change during Pacelli's childhood, as the city in the 1880s became the administrative capital of a new nation, and a modern world of technology, communications, and transport transformed its ancient languor.

The men from the north had arrived and they were building the new nation's capital in a hurry, cheaply and with scant regard for style or planning. Some of the new architectural and artistic innovations were designed to send hostile signals in the direction of the Vatican. The braggadocio "wedding cake" Emanuele monument was started in 1885 to glorify the unification of the country under its first king. A martial statue of Garibaldi seated upon his horse was raised on the highest point of the Janiculum hill, as if to dominate both the new capital and the Vatican City.

Aged five, Pacelli was enrolled in a kindergarten run by two nuns in what is now known as Via Zanardelli. By then the family had moved to a larger apartment in the Via della Vetrina, not far from where he was born. He graduated to a private Catholic elementary school in two rooms of a building in the Piazza Santa Lucia dei Ginnasi, close to the Piazza Venezia. This establishment was subject to the whims of its founder and headmaster, Signore Giuseppe Marchi, who was in the habit of making speeches from his high desk about the "hard-heartedness of the Jews."[10] One of Pacelli's contemporary biographers comments on this without irony: "There was a good deal to be said in favor of Signore Marchi; he knew that the impressions gained by small children are never lost."[11]

By the age of ten Pacelli was a pupil at the Liceo Quirino Visconti, a state school with a generally anti-Catholic and anticlerical bias. It was situated in the Collegio Romano, the former site of the renowned Jesuit university in Rome. Eugenio's brother, Francesco, was already two years ahead of him at the school. Filippo Pacelli evidently believed that his sons would benefit from gaining firsthand acquaintance with their secularist "enemies" while receiving the best classical education available in Rome.

Eugenio, according to the siblings who survived him, was headstrong. Spindly, constitutionally delicate, he showed impressive intelligence and powers of memory from an early age. He was capable of remembering at will whole pages of material and could recall entire lessons word for word after leaving the classroom. He had a flair for the classics and modern languages. His handwriting, in youth as in adulthood, was a painstaking, elegant italic script. He played the violin and the piano, and often accompanied his sisters, who sang and played the mandolin. He liked swimming, and during vacations rode at his cousin's farm at Onano.

Little has survived, anecdotally or in available literary remains, to give a sense of the personalities of Eugenio Pacelli's parents, except a testament to their "great rectitude" according to the younger daughter, Elisabetta. "Anything less than delicate expressions," she claimed, "never passed their lips." Virginia Pacelli led her children several times a day to pray before a shrine to the Virgin in their apartment, and the whole family said the Rosary each evening before supper. There is no evidence of childhood trauma or deprivation; with only three siblings, Eugenio clearly had much parental attention.

The beatification testimonies naturally focus on evidence of Eugenio's early piety. On his way home from school he regularly visited the picture of the Virgin, known as Madonna della Strada, close to the tomb of Ignatius Loyola in the Gesù Church. Here, sometimes twice daily, he poured out his heart to the Madonna, "telling her everything". Even as a child, he was said to have displayed an unusual sense of modesty. His younger sister remembered that he never entered a room unless fully dressed. He was independent and solitary; invariably appearing at meals with a book, he would solicit the permission of his parents and siblings and then lose himself in his reading. In adolescence he went eagerly to concerts and plays, keeping a notebook at the ready so as to write up critiques of the performances during the intermissions. Elisabetta recollected that he would compose spiritual bouquets (prayers decoratively recorded on a card), for the missions or the souls in purgatory. She also remembered that he imposed upon her his own self-denials (for example, forgoing treats such as fruit juices). While yet a child, he undertook to catechize the five-year-old son of the palazzo's janitor.

He was an altar boy at the Chiesa Nuova, assisting at the Mass of a priest cousin, and, like many boys destined for the priesthood, his preferred play was to dress up and act out the celebration of the Mass in his bedroom. His mother encouraged him in this, giving him a piece of damask which he could imagine a Church robe; she helped him set up an altar complete with candles set in tinfoil. One year he played out the entire Holy Week ceremonies. When a sick aunt could not go to Mass, the young Eugenio provided a substitute celebration, including a homily.

An important figure in Eugenio's life from the age of eight was an Oratorian priest, Father Giuseppe Lais. According to Elisabetta, their father asked Father Lais to care for Eugenio's spiritual welfare. Lais became a frequent visitor in the Pacelli household, where he made regular reports to the parents on Eugenio's religious progress. There are indications in this relationship of the sort of special friendship that frequently existed between a priestly role model and a pious youth who is considering a religious vocation.

Eugenio carried the influence of his parents and Father Lais with him into his secularized *liceo.* For an essay assignment on a "favorite" historical figure, Pacelli is said to have chosen Augustine of Hippo, prompting sneers from his classmates. When he attempted to expand a little on the history of Christian civilization, a theme absent in the curriculum, his teacher chided him, informing him that he was not employed to take the lesson.

Among Pacelli's scarce literary remains are a score or so of his school essays. A trifle priggish, they are nevertheless well structured and fluent. One entitled "The sign that what is imprinted in the heart appears in the face" dwells on the "evil of cowardly silence," relating the story of a venerable old man who, unlike other courtiers, refuses to flatter a tyrannical king.[12]

In another essay, entitled "My Portrait," the thirteen-year-old Pacelli writes a self-appraisal that manages to be both earnest and self-mocking. "I am of average height," he begins. "My figure is slender, my face rather pale, my hair chestnut and soft, my eyes black, my nose rather aquiline. I will not say much of my chest, which, to be honest, is not robust. Finally, I have a pair of legs that are long and thin, with feet that are hardly small." From this, he tells the reader, it is easy to grasp that "physically I am a fairly mediocre youth." Focusing on his moral nature, he concedes that his "character is rather impatient and violent." He hopes that "with education" he will "attain the wherewithal to control it." He ends by acknowledging his "instinctive generosity of spirit," and consoles himself with the reflection that "whereas I do not suffer contradiction, I easily forgive those who offend me."[13] A close schoolfriend of Pacelli's, later to become a cardinal, said that the boy Pacelli had "a sense of control over himself that was truly rare in the young."[14]

Among his youthful essays, only one, written when he was fifteen, reveals that Eugenio Pacelli might have experienced an adolescent setback. Written in the third person, it describes one who is "blind with vain and erroneous ideas and doubts." Who, he asks himself, "will give him wings" so that he can "rise from this miserable earth to the highest sphere and tear apart this evil veil that surrounds him always and everywhere?" In the conclusion, he talks of this person "tearing at his hair" and wishing that he had "never been born." He ends with a prayer: "My Lord, enlighten him!"[15] Was this evidence of an emotional crisis prompted by an excess of study and youthful asceticism? The dark episode passed, never, as far as we know, to return.

He developed a love of music, especially Beethoven, Bach, Mozart, and Mendelssohn, and he was interested in the history of music. Even as a boy he read the classics for pleasure and started his own classical library, which he kept all his life. He read Augustine, Dante, and Manzoni, and liked Cicero best of all.[16] His favorite spiritual reading was the *Imitation of Christ*, by Thomas à Kempis, the fifteenth-century monk. The *Imitation*, which was to enjoy widespread popularity among religious and even devout diocesan priests until the 1960s, was suited to the ascetic aspirations of enclosed monasticism: it encouraged an interiority that was funneled directly to God without social mediation, seeing human ties as imperfections and distractions. It nevertheless counseled cheerfulness, humility, and charity toward all—with special regard for those we like least. In time Pacelli knew the entire book by heart. Among other favorite religious authors was Jacques-Bénigne Bossuet, the seventeenth-century French bishop whose lofty and compelling eloquence Pacelli strived to emulate in years to come. Bossuet sat on his bedside table all the years of his life.

After Pacelli's death, his personal assistant of forty years, Father Robert Leiber, S.J., wrote that the Pope's spirituality remained essentially youthful. "In his own religious life he remained the pious boy of those days. . . . [He] had a genuine respect for any unpretentious, humble piety. He preserved a child-like love for the Mother of God from his youth."[17]

In the summer of 1894, having completed his education at the *liceo* at the age of eighteen with a diploma or *licenza "ad honorem,"* Pacelli went into retreat for ten days at the church of St. Agnes in Via Nomentana. For the first time (but not the last) he was guided through the *Spiritual Exercises* of St. Ignatius Loyola, a manual of spiritual meditation. The Ignatian exercises see life as a battle between Satan and Christ. Retreatants are called to make clear choices about their future: to follow the standard of Christ or the standard of the Prince of Darkness. Returning home, Pacelli informed his parents that he wanted to become a priest. According to Elisabetta, "The decision did not come as a surprise. As far as we were concerned, he had been born a priest."

Seminarian

The Almo Collegio Capranica, known simply as the Capranica, is a forbidding building situated in a quiet square in the heart of old Rome close to the Pantheon and no more than twenty minutes' walk from where the Pacellis lived. The Capranica, founded in 1457, was and still is famous as a nursery for Vatican highflyers. Eugenio Pacelli was installed there in November of 1894 and registered to take a philosophy course at Rome's nearby Jesuit university, the Gregorian.

Pacelli commenced his studies for the priesthood during the height of the papacy of Leo XIII, Pio Nono's successor, elected in 1878. Leo XIII was a conservative (he had collaborated in the writing of Pio Nono's *Syl-*

labus of Errors) and he was already sixty-eight years old when he was elected, but he nevertheless made strenuous efforts to come to terms with the modern world. The early years of his reign had been marked by a series of remarkable academic initiatives: the founding in Rome of a new institute for philosophy and theology, of scriptural study centers, and of a center for astronomy. The Vatican archives were opened to Catholic and non-Catholic scholars alike. Under Leo XIII, historical perspectives almost entirely neglected by Catholic scholarship in the past were actively encouraged.

As a nuncio Leo had traveled throughout Europe and witnessed the working and living conditions in the expanding industrial centers. In the 1880s Catholic labor groups, looking for guidance from the Church, descended on Rome in ever greater numbers. In 1891 Leo published the encyclical *Rerum novarum (Of New Things)*, the papacy's response, half a century on, to *The Communist Manifesto* and Marx's *Das Kapital*. While deploring the oppression and virtual slavery of the teeming poor by the instruments of "usury" in the hands of a "small number of very rich men," and while advocating just wages and the right to organize unions (preferably Catholic) and in certain circumstances to strike, the encyclical rejected socialism and was lukewarm on democracy. Class and inequality, Leo proclaimed, are unalterable features of the human condition, as are the rights of property ownership and especially those rights that foster and protect family life. Socialism he condemned as illusory and synonymous with class hatred and atheism. The authority of society, he taught, comes not from man but from God.

In 1880 he had written to the archbishop of Cologne that "the pest of socialism ... which so deeply perverts the sense of our populations, derives all its power from the darkness it causes in the intellect by hiding the light of eternal truths and corrupting the rule of life laid down by Christian morality."[18] Leo believed that the answer to socialism, this great evil of the modern world, was a Christian intellectual renaissance based on faith and reason. That renaissance, he declared, was to be rooted in the thought of the medieval philosopher and theologian St. Thomas Aquinas.

Thomism, or neo-Thomism as it came to be called following Leo's 1879 encyclical on the revival of Aquinas studies,[19] is an all-encompassing intellectual synthesis, bringing together the truths of Revelation and the realms of the supernatural, the physical universe, nature, society, family, and the individual. After a period of more than a century in which secular schools of philosophy throughout Europe and the United States had become ever more subjective or materialist, Leo's decision to rediscover the secure and abiding absolutes of Thomistic philosophy—rising, as the Pontiff thought, above the fogs of modern skepticism like a shining medieval cathedral—seemed inspired. Yet, much as Leo had energized Catholic academia after generations of intellectual aridity, the neo-Thomist revival, at the level of the average candidate for the priesthood, signaled an ominous swing toward conformity and a narrowing of the clerical mind. Neo-Thomism, at least as it came to be taught in seminaries in the 1890s, rejected much that was good and true in modern ideas. In 1892, two years before Pacelli arrived at the Gregorian University, Leo had decreed that St. Thomas's system was to be regarded as "definitive" in all seminaries and Catholic universities. And where Thomas had neglected to expound on a topic, teachers were urged to reach conclusions that were reconcilable with his thinking. Under the next papacy, of Pius X, neo-Thomism would acquire an orthodoxy tantamount to dogma.

Formed in Isolation

As Pacelli began his studies in the confident intellectual climate in ecclesiastical Rome, the arrangements for his priestly education took a strange turn in the summer of 1895. At the end of his first academic year, he dropped out of both the Capranica and the Gregorian University. According to Elisabetta, the food at the Capranica was to blame; his "fastidious" stomach would plague him for the rest of his life, suggesting a nervous, high-strung constitution. The whole family, she told the canonization tribunal, would troop along to the college every Sunday bearing special provisions to sustain him.[20] She goes on to state briefly that their father eventually managed to get Eugenio permission to live at home while continuing his academic studies. The effect of the new arrangement was that Pacelli returned to motherly protection, escaping the peer-group rough-and-tumble, the rigorous disciplines of seminary training as well as the fellowship of community life. An inability to cope with the hardship of the seminary would have spelled an abrupt end to the clerical ambitions of most candidates for the priesthood. The Pacellis, however, had powerful friends at court.

With the exception of a friendship with a younger cousin, as will be seen, his mother remained at the center of his emotional life. The mutual devotion between mother and son is everywhere apparent in the beatification testimonies. When he became Pope, he was to decorate his pectoral cross with her simple jewels.

In the autumn of 1895 he was registered for the new academic year to study theology and Scripture at the St. Apollinaris Institute, not far from his home, and simultaneously for languages at the secular university, the Sapienza, also close by. His association with these institutions, however, was merely academic. At home, Elisabetta said, he wore his soutane and Roman collar throughout the day and continued to "benefit from the influence of Father Lais," the figure who had hovered over his childhood spiritual progress. In the summer of 1896, at the age of twenty, he traveled to Paris with Lais to attend a "Congress of Astronomy."

There are no telling anecdotes to describe the course of his priestly education through the next four years. All that is known for certain is that he passed the necessary exams that qualified him to proceed to Holy Orders. On April 2, 1899, at the age of just twenty-three, he was ordained alone in the private chapel of an auxiliary bishop of Rome, rather than with the rest of the candidates of the Rome diocese in St. John Lateran. Once again he had eschewed his contemporaries. The following day he said his first Mass at the altar of the Virgin in the basilica of Santa Maria Maggiore, assisted by Father Lais.

Pacelli had completed his education in "Sacred Theology" with a doctoral degree (by today's standards, the degree was more accurately a licentiate) awarded on the basis of a short dissertation, now lost to posterity, and an oral examination in Latin. In the autumn he registered again at the St. Apollinaris Institute to study canon law. This marked the beginning of serious postgraduate research, during which he probably came under the influence of the Jesuit canonist Franz Xavier Wernz, an expert on questions of ecclesiastical authority in canon law.

But the influence of Rome's Jesuits, whom Pacelli regarded as his special mentors while he was a seminarian and throughout his life, is notable for other reasons. In 1898, as Pacelli was completing his studies for the priesthood, *Civiltà Cattolica*, the Rome-based Jesuit journal, was arguing the guilt of Alfred Dreyfus, the Jewish army officer accused of treason in France. The journal continued to proclaim his guilt the following year, even after he had been pardoned. The editor, Father Raffaele Ballerini, charged that the Jews "had bought all the newspapers and consciences in Europe" in order to acquit Dreyfus. In a chilling conclusion, he asserted that "wherever Jews had been granted citizenship" the outcome had been the "ruination" of Christians or the massacre of the "alien race."[21]

How Pacelli was affected by these opinions, published in a highly influential periodical in Rome, we do not know. But Catholic ordinands at the end of the nineteenth century were bound to be influenced by the long history of Christian attitudes toward Judaism.

Catholicism and Anti-Semitism

There were significant differences between nineteenth-century racism, inspired by perverted social Darwinism, and traditional Christian anti-Judaism that had persisted from early Christianity. Racist anti-Semitism, of the kind that was to give rise to the Nazi Final Solution, was based on the idea that Jewish genetic stock was biologically inferior in nature; hence the evil logic that their extermination would yield advantages on the path to national greatness. In the late Middle Ages, Spanish Jews were excluded from the "pure" community of Christian blood, and questions were raised during the period of European discovery of the Americas about the status of the indigenous "natural slaves" in the New World; but racist notions had never formed part of orthodox Christianity. Christians, on the whole, ignored racial and national origin in the pursuit of converts.

Christian antipathy toward the Jews was born out of the belief, dating from the early Christian Church, that the Jews had murdered Christ—indeed, that they had murdered God. The Early Fathers of the Church, the great Christian writers of the first six centuries of Christianity, showed striking evidence of anti-Judaism. "The blood of Jesus," wrote Origen, "falls not only on the Jews of that time, but on all generations of Jews up to the end of the world." St. John Chrysostom wrote, "The Synagogue is a brothel, a hiding place for unclean beasts. . . . Never has any Jew prayed to God. . . . They are possessed by demons."

At the First Council of Nicaea in 325, the Emperor Constantine ordained that Easter should not compete with the Jewish Passover: "It is unbecoming," he declared, "that on the holiest of festivals we should follow the customs of the Jews; henceforth let us have nothing in common with this odious people." An accumulation of imperial measures against Jews ensued: special taxes, a ban on new synagogues, the outlawing of intermarriage between Jews and Christians. Persecution flourished in successive imperial reigns. By the fifth century, Jews were routinely attacked during Holy Week and were excluded from public office, and synagogues were burned.

It may well be asked why the Christians did not exterminate all Jews in this early period of Christian empire. According to Christian belief, the Jews were to survive and continue their wandering Diaspora as a sign of the curse they had brought upon their own people. From time to time, popes of the first millennium called for restraint, but never for an end to persecution or to a change of heart. Pope Innocent III in the early thirteenth century epitomized the papal view of the first millennium: "Their words—'May his blood be on us and our children'—have brought inherited guilt upon the entire nation, which follows them as a curse where they live and work, when they are born and when they die." The Fourth Lateran Council, convened under Innocent III in 1215, laid down the requirement that Jews should wear distinguishing headgear.

Denied social equality, banned from owning land, excluded from public office and most forms of trade, the Jews had few alternatives to moneylending, which was forbidden to Christians under Church law. Licensed to lend at strictly defined interest rates, the Jews became cursed as "bloodsuckers" and "usurers" living off the debts of Christians.

The Middle Ages was an era of unprecedented persecution of the Jews, punctuated by occasional calls for restraint on the part of enlightened popes. The Crusaders made it part of their mission to torment and kill Jews on their way to and from the Holy Land; the practice of enforced conversions and baptisms, especially of Jewish boys, became widespread. One of the chief objectives of the new orders of preaching friars was to convert the Jews. A dispute flared between the Franciscans and the Dominicans over the right of princes to forcibly baptize Jewish

children as an extension of their lordship over slaves within their do-
mains. According to the Franciscans following the theologian Duns Sco-
tus, Jews were slaves by divine decree; Thomas Aquinas the Dominican
argued that, by the natural law pertaining to parenthood, the Jews had a
right to educate their children in the faith they chose for them.[22]

But the Middle Ages were also marked by the insidious development
that was later to be known as the "blood libel." Starting in England in
the twelfth century, the belief spread rapidly that Jews tortured and sacrificed Christian children. There was an associated myth that Jews stole
consecrated Hosts, the Communion bread that had become the "body
and blood" of Christ in the Mass, in order to perform abominable rites.
At the same time, allegations of ritual murder, human sacrifice, and
Host desecration gave impetus to a belief that Judaism involved the performance of magic aimed at undermining and ultimately destroying
Christendom.[23] Executions of Jews accused of ritual murder were accompanied by the destruction of entire Jewish communities accused of
employing magic arts to cause the Black Death and other calamities
great and small.

The advent of the Reformation saw a reduction in such ritual-magic
trials, as Jewish blood-libel myths gave way to the conviction that child
murder victims had been practiced upon by witches. But just as soon, a
Pope of the sixteenth century, Paul IV, instituted the ghetto and the
wearing of the yellow badge.

Through the eighteenth century, Jews gradually acquired freedom in
regions farthest from the Roman center of Catholicism—Holland, England, the Protestant enclaves of North America—but the papal states
persisted in repressive measures against Jews well into the nineteenth
century. In the brief flush of liberalism on his election, Pio Nono, as we
have seen, disestablished the ghetto, but he soon reestablished it after his
return from exile in Gaeta. It took the formation of the nation-state of
Italy to bring Rome's ghetto to an end, although the "ghetto area" survived as a residential district for the poorer Jews of the city until the Second World War. Meanwhile, anti-Judaism smoldered and occasionally
flared in Rome long into the reign of Leo XIII, when Pacelli was a
schoolboy. The most enduring form of antipathy focused on the "obstinacy" of the Jews, the theme of Pacelli's ranting schoolmaster, Signore
Marchi.

There was, in fact, a curious coincidence between Pacelli's birthplace and this myth of hard-heartedness, showing the importance of custom in the persistence of prejudice. On Via Monte Giordano, the street in which Pacelli was born, it had been the custom over many centuries for new popes to perform an anti-Jewish ceremony on their way to the basilica of St. John Lateran. Here the Pontiff would halt his procession to receive a copy of the Pentateuch from the hand of Rome's rabbi, with his people in attendance. The Pope then returned the text upside down with twenty pieces of gold, proclaiming that, while he respected the Law of Moses, he disapproved of the hard hearts of the Jewish race. For it was an ancient and firmly held view of Catholic theologians that if the Jews would only listen with open hearts to the arguments for the Christian faith, they would instantly see the error of their ways and convert.

The notion of Jewish obstinacy was a crucial element in the case of Edgardo Mortara. When the parents of the kidnapped Edgardo pleaded in person with the Pope for the return of their son, Pio Nono told them that they could have their son back at once if only they converted to Catholicism—which, of course, they would do instantly if they opened their hearts to Christian Revelation. But they would not, and did not. The Mortaras, in the view of Pio Nono, had brought all their sufferings upon their own heads as a result of their obduracy.

Jewish "hard-heartedness" was parallel and at points overlapped with the notion of Jewish "blindness," exemplified in the Good Friday liturgy of the Roman Missal, when the celebrant prayed for the "perfidious Jews" and asked that "our God and Lord would withdraw the veil from their hearts: that they also may acknowledge our Lord Jesus Christ."[24] This prayer, at which the celebrant and people disdained to kneel, continued until it was abolished by Pope John XXIII.

Raised in a family of canon lawyers (Marcantonio Pacelli was probably consulted on the Mortara case), Pacelli in all likelihood knew the Mortara story and the arguments defending the Pontiff's actions, just as he was surely influenced in the classroom by Signore Marchi's remarks about Jewish obstinacy. The importance of the allegation of Jewish blind obstinacy was its potential to reinforce the conviction, widely held by Catholics otherwise innocent of anti-Judaism, let alone anti-Semitism, that the Jews were responsible for their own misfortunes—

a view that was to encourage Catholic Church officials in the 1930s to look the other way as Nazi anti-Semitism raged in Germany.

And yet more extreme forms of anti-Judaism also erupted among Catholic intellectual clerics in Rome during the reign of Leo XIII, no doubt with an influence on ordinands in the pontifical universities. Allegations of blood libel were raised once more in a series of articles published between February 1881 and December 1882 in *Civiltà Cattolica*. Written by Giuseppe Oreglia de San Stefano, S.J., the articles claimed that the killing of children for the Paschal Feast was "all too common" in the East, and that making use of the blood of a Christian child was a general law "binding on the conscience of all Hebrews." Every year the Jews "crucify a child," and in order that the blood be effective, "the child must die in torment."[25] In 1890 *Civiltà Cattolica* again turned its attention to the Jews in a series of articles republished in pamphlet form as *Della questione ebraica in Europa* (Rome, 1891), aimed at exposing the activity of the Jews in the formation of the modern liberal nation-state. The author charged that "by their cunning," the Jews instigated the French Revolution in order to gain civic equality, and thence they insinuated themselves into key positions in most state economies with the aim of controlling them and establishing their "virulent campaigns against Christianity." The Jews were "the race that nauseates"; they were "an idle people who neither work nor produce anything; who live on the sweat of others." The pamphlet concluded by calling for the abolition of "civic equality" and for the segregation of Jews from the rest of the population.

While there is an arguable distinction between racist anti-Semitism and religious anti-Judaism, this material, published in Rome during Pacelli's school days, exemplifies a groundswell of vicious antipathy. That views such as these were promoted by the leading Jesuit journal, enjoying papal auspices, indicates their potential outreach and semblance of authority. Such prejudices were hardly inimical to the racist theories that would culminate in the Nazis' furious assault upon European Jewry in the Second World War. It is plausible indeed that these Catholic prejudices actually bolstered aspects of Nazi anti-Semitism.

2

Hidden Life

~∿~

There is a photograph in the papal archives depicting Leo XIII, Pope from 1878 to 1903, seated on a throne placed upon a dais in the Vatican gardens. He appears languid, emaciated (he was known by the American bishops as "bag of bones"), settled in his sense of absolute, monarchical authority. He is surrounded by close aides, but only one of them is seated—the stout figure of Mariano Rampolla del Tinaro, Cardinal Secretary of State and chief architect of Leo's international diplomacy. Rampolla sits on a simple chair, as if well satisfied with his lowly relegation, placed askew from the camera as if to avoid sharing the same viewpoint as his Pope.

There is a photographic portrait of Pacelli too at this time, as an appealing, gentle-eyed young priest. In 1901, two years before Leo XIII's death, he was recruited into the ambit of this powerful, intimate court to learn the ropes of Vatican bureaucracy and to become an instant and outstanding favorite. Was he, after five years' pontifical education and sheltered mothering *a casa*, a malleable factotum plucked for his pliancy from the hundreds of candidates in the great Roman seminaries? Or was he a strong and resolute personality who had arrived by long-laid strategy in his proper element? Events would soon reveal Pacelli's strengths, his potential to play a role in an administration in transition to the apotheosis of modern papal power.

For all his social compassion, Leo XIII was an authoritarian who established many of the twentieth-century standards of papal exaltation observed until the election of John XXIII. Catholic visitors were required to kneel at his feet during audiences, and throughout his reign he never spoke so much as a word to menial servants. He encouraged the cult of his own personality, cooperating in the creation of mass-produced full-color pictures of his personage and encouraging large pilgrim groups to the Eternal City. Yet, despite his propensity to personal absolutism, he strived to exert a direct and practical influence on the outside world from his Roman sanctuary. Through frequent encyclicals couched in flowery language, he established the modern practice of routine papal teaching from a lofty vantage point.

Papal influence was amplified by modern communications as missionary endeavors expanded, Catholic populations multiplied in industrial regions, and Catholic emigration to the New World increased apace. Leo recognized the need to keep abreast of a rapidly changing world and took measures to achieve outreach, to make a difference by strengthening lines of access and intelligence from the Roman center to the farthest reaches of the earth. Trained in diplomacy, Leo believed that the papal diplomatic service had a crucial role to play in both the implementation of internal Church discipline and the conduct of Church-State relations. In 1885, Spain and Germany appealed to him to mediate a dispute over the possession of the Caroline Islands in the Pacific. And in 1899 Czar Nicholas II of Russia and Queen Wilhelmina of Holland used his good offices in their attempts to establish a peace conference of European nations. Leo was eager to be seen as an independent arbiter, indeed a supreme judge, in world affairs. Pondering Vatican diplomacy with the aid of the works of Thomas Aquinas, he came to expound anew, in the encyclical *Immortale Dei* (1886), the relationship between the Holy See and nation-states. According to international law, secular states recognize mutual sovereignty not merely by treaties but in the exchange of accredited representatives. The papal nuncio, in Leo's view, was the representative of papal spiritual sovereignty as the ambassador is the representative of his nation's political sovereignty. Leo XIII saw the power of the stateless, otherworldly Holy See as a "perfect society"—perfect in its integrity and autonomy. Due to Leo's enthusiasm for the potential of papal diplomacy and a vigorous recruitment and training policy under the leadership of Rampolla, the permanent missions accredited to the Holy See were to increase from eighteen to twenty-seven.

Meanwhile, as a recently ordained priest, Eugenio Pacelli cared for the souls of pupils at the Cenacle Convent in Rome, and he was a frequent visitor at the Convent of the Assumption near the Villa Borghese, where he acted as celebrant for the chapel liturgies. No doubt under the influence of his grandfather, his father, and his brother Francesco, Pacelli was hard at work studying canon law in the expectation that he would receive a call to begin his "ecclesiastical career," as his father had termed it when he sought a place for Eugenio at the Capranica.

Details of how a high-level emissary headhunted the young priest have become legend.[1] Late one evening in early 1901, Pacelli was at home playing the violin, accompanied by his sister Elisabetta on the mandolin. There was an insistent rap at the door, and there stood Monsignor Pietro Gasparri, recently appointed undersecretary in the Department of Extraordinary Affairs, the equivalent of the Foreign Office within the Secretariat of State. Pacelli, according to his sister, could not disguise his amazement. A short, portly man of peasant stock, Gasparri, then fifty-one, was already famous in international circles for his brilliance as a canon lawyer, having held the chair in that discipline at the Institut Catholique in Paris for eighteen years. When the prelate invited Pacelli to join him in the Secretariat of State, the young priest at first protested that it had always been his ambition to work "as a pastor of souls." But after hearing out the monsignor on the importance of defending the Church from the onslaught of secularism and liberalism throughout Europe, he relented.

For the next thirty years, Gasparri and Pacelli, physically and socially at odds, were to work in tandem during a period in which canon law, and concordat law—the Holy See's scope of international relations—were to shape the growth of twentieth-century papal power. By 1930 Pacelli would succeed Gasparri as Cardinal Secretary of State, a post he would retain until he became Pontiff.

A few days after Gasparri's visit, Pacelli was appointed an *apprendista*, an apprentice in Gasparri's department. Not many weeks later (an indication of the favoritism he excited within the Vatican), Pacelli was chosen by Leo XIII himself, according to the official account,[2] to carry a letter of condolence to London for presentation at the Court of St.

James's to King Edward VII on the occasion of the death of Queen Victoria. He was just twenty-five years old and already singled out for the fast track of promotion.

In 1902, in addition to his Vatican post, he was appointed part-time lecturer in canon law at the St. Apollinaris. This was followed by a part-time post at the Academy for Nobles and Ecclesiastics, a college for young diplomats, where he taught civil and canon law. By 1904 he received his doctorate. The theme of his thesis[3] was the nature of concordats (special treaties between the Holy See and nation-states, monarchies, or empires) and the function of canon law when a concordat, for whatever reason, falls into abeyance. The importance of this research will become apparent later in this narrative, when we witness Pacelli embarking on a series of concordat renegotiations in order to bring Church-State treaties in line with the new Code of Canon Law.

He was soon promoted to the post of *minutante*, entrusted with writing digests of reports that were dispatched to the Secretariat from all over the world. In the same year, he was made papal chamberlain with the title *monsignor*, and he was promoted again during the following year when he received the title *domestic prelate*. Two years later, he was again favored with a trip to London, this time accompanying Rafael Merry del Val, the Spanish-Irish Cardinal Secretary of State, to a Eucharistic congress in London—an outdoor rally of religious and laity, where, resplendent in magenta, Pacelli processed through the streets of Westminster.

The beatification testimonies speak of his enormous appetite for work, his extreme love of order and discipline. His only recreation was a daily postprandial constitutional, breviary in hand, in the Villa Borghese. Just one story, however, suggests that Don Eugenio might have digressed a little from his well-regulated existence to court emotional danger during these early years of his priesthood.

Pacelli had a cousin, Maria Teresa Pacelli, the daughter of his cousin Ernesto, another Pacelli layman with "a certain influence within the Holy See." Maria Teresa's parents had separated (why, we are not told) and she was accordingly lodged with the nuns of the Convent of the Assumption from the age of five. In 1901 or thereabouts, Maria Teresa, then thirteen, was plunged into a *"silenzio sepolcrale"*—a sepulchral silence, or depression, as the result of a quarrel between her mother and one of the nuns, who had apparently made insulting remarks about the king of Italy during a lesson.

Ernesto Pacelli, without telling Maria Teresa, implored Don Eugenio to "draw her out of her psychological refuge," and thus began a relationship that appears to have persisted for five years. Every Tuesday the young priest and his cousin walked and talked alone in the vestibule of the convent chapel for at least two hours. They spoke of matters, she said, that were protected by the seal of the confessional. "He opened me up," she told the beatification tribunal, "and I confided in him." But much more than this: according to Maria Teresa, "our two souls came together, bound by God."[4] She found in him, she believed, "another Christ." Despite what she described as "their discretion and secrecy," her father became suspicious of the relationship during her eighteenth year and put an end to it. "My father," she recorded, "did not comprehend this discretion and secrecy, nor did he understand the noble integrity of Don Eugenio." Don Eugenio, Maria Teresa tells us, "mournfully accepted this humiliation, and I lost a unique support and moral and spiritual guidance." The next time she saw him, she says, was several years later at a special papal audience, when "he passed by me: his demeanor open, modest, humble, reserved but cheerful, and marked by simplicity as always. He had the purity of one who lives in the presence of God. And all the convent girls used to say—'Who could look at him and not love him!'"[5]

Apart from such glimpses, there are insufficient details to provide a narrative of the growth of his character. But a clearer account has emerged in recent years of a series of ecclesiastical shock waves that Pacelli witnessed silently from the Vatican epicenter. The fact that he remained an exceptional favorite through this crisis—known as the anti-Modernist campaign—and continued to be promoted while others were cast aside, tells us much about his discretion, his resilience, and his survival skills. That he was indelibly affected by the affair cannot be doubted.

Pope Pius X

In the first days of July 1903, Leo XIII, now in his ninety-third year, had finally admitted that he was dying. Over the next two weeks, flocks of prelates and Vatican hangers-on swarmed in the papal apartments, while multitudes gathered outside in St. Peter's Square. Still Leo clung to life, this skinny ancient with a palsied left hand who had been appointed a mere caretaker a quarter of a century earlier. Eventually, incredibly, the rumor spread that he had rallied and would soon go back to work. On the morning of July 20, he called for pens and paper and set about composing Latin verses in honor of St. Anselm. At four in the afternoon, however, he expired in a suffocating fit.

The body was not embalmed until the next day, and so, due to the heat, the ceremony of kissing the bare papal feet was on this occasion neglected. After the customary funeral the undertakers were obliged to give the casket a kick to shove it into place. The incident was observed by a horrified Giuseppe Sarto, Patriarch of Venice, who subsequently remarked to a colleague: "See. That's how popes end up."[6]

The cardinals went into the conclave the following month, from the first to the fourth of August, and it was widely expected that Rampolla, the man to have continued the policies of Leo XIII, would emerge as Pope. In the course of the conclave, the Emperor Franz Josef of Austria, who had a power of veto, expressed his displeasure with the erstwhile Cardinal Secretary of State. Support for Rampolla at first increased, in apparent reaction to this interference, but then it ebbed away. In the end, the triple crown went to Giuseppe Sarto, who had no insider experience of the Vatican and the Curia. He took the name Pius X. The secular world had intervened for the last time in modern papal elections, and the new Pope saw to it that outside influence would never again be countenanced. From one perspective, the Church as a sovereign society had at last attained the "perfection" for which Leo XIII had so devoutly strived. From another, the last taint of secular pluralism was removed from the election of popes.

Sarto, then sixty-eight, was the antithesis of his aloof and aristocratic predecessor. He was the son of a postman and a seamstress from Venetia. In choosing him, the conclave of cardinals had opted for a pastoral Pope, a man of prayer and singular piety who had spent much of his working life as a curate, a parish priest, a seminary spiritual director, and a diocesan bishop.

Sarto's ambition was to renew the spiritual life of the Catholic Church, to inspire genuine personal devotion rather than a mere outward show of piety, and to inculcate a sense of religious experience in the young. His motto was "to restore all things in Christ." In the course of his pontificate, from 1903 to 1914, he was to encourage the teaching of the catechism and regular attendance at Holy Communion as routi. features of parish life. He lowered the age at which children can receiv. the Eucharist from eleven to seven, which led to the popular celebration of First Communion with white dresses, sashes, presents, and family feasting. It also led to the practice of early regular confession.

Pius X had the aura of a pious, dedicated pastor, but he was suspicious of things intellectual and modern. His piety, so evident to all who came in contact with him, was matched by a holy anger. Where Leo XIII had seemed to engage and appease the modern world, Sarto set his face against it, promoting a reign of fearful conformity that would affect seminarians, theologians, priests, bishops, and even cardinals.

The Modernist Crisis

A few weeks after the coronation of Pius X, the academic year of 1903 had been marked in Milan's principal diocesan seminary with an inaugural address preached by a Father Antonio Fumagalli to the assembled ordinands and professors in the presence of the metropolitan cardinal archbishop.[7] All present, Fumagalli told them, must be on their guard against an intellectual poison that had erupted in France and was spreading throughout Italy. He was referring to a set of ideas, widely known as *"Modernism,"* linked with certain Catholic French scholars who, in contradiction to Thomas Aquinas, argued that there was an unbridgeable gap between natural and supernatural knowledge. The attempt, as Fumagalli described it, was to undermine Catholic orthodoxy and the beliefs of devout Catholics. Its evil effects were relativism and skepticism.

Revisiting the controversy after a century, it is fairer to describe the Modernist culprits less as progressives, liberals, modernizers than as writers and thinkers who were attempting "to re-engage Catholic life, thought and spirituality with the forces shaping contemporary culture."[8] Fear of modern influences in the Church had focused on a similarly disparate modernizing group in North America during the reign of Leo XIII. Known by its critics as Americanism, the transatlantic "modernists" had sought to bring Catholicism in line with democracy. Traditionalists in the United States, and the Curia in Rome, saw a danger of calls for democratization of the Church itself. Leo had stamped firmly on it in an apostolic letter in January 1899. "Religious

Americanism," the Pope wrote, "involves a greater danger and is more hostile to Catholic doctrine and discipline, inasmuch as the followers of these novelties judge that a certain liberty ought to be introduced into the Church."9 Americanism died a sudden death in the first cold blast of papal disapproval.

The "poison" of European Modernism had been identified, for example, in the teaching and works of Louis Duchesne, a Catholic professor in the 1870s at the Institut Catholique in Paris who questioned the notion that God acts in a direct way in the affairs of humankind. In the early 1890s Duchesne's pupil, the Catholic priest and scholar Alfred Loisy, went further by denying that every line of Scripture was literally rather than perhaps metaphorically true. In his book *The Gospel and the Church*, published in 1902, Loisy urged the importance of studying the Church from social, symbolic, and "organic" perspectives, precisely in order to counteract prevailing liberal Protestant ideas. But whatever his intentions, Loisy's work, like that of Duchesne, provoked the wrath of the Curia, which interpreted all such ideas, even in defense of the Church, as a dangerous challenge to Catholic orthodoxy and Roman authority. The book was nevertheless greeted with enthusiasm by a number of French seminarians and teachers who thus became tarred by the Modernist brush. It was also welcomed in Britain by the theologian Baron Friedrich von Hügel and the Jesuit George Tyrrell. Tyrrell attracted sufficient opprobrium from Rome to be denied a Christian burial. Five of Loisy's books were eventually put on the Index of Forbidden Books. Meanwhile, the "poison" that was deemed to be spreading throughout the Church had to be eradicated.

The man who ran Pius X's campaign to expunge Modernism, Umberto Benigni, worked in the very heart of the Vatican, in the same office as Pacelli: the Department of Extraordinary Affairs in the Secretariat of State. Benigni was a monsignor of enormous energy and charm who had won the confidence of his Pontiff and several highly placed cardinals. He was to hunt down suspect Modernists with fanatical zeal. Although he had studied Church history and had even held a part-time post in the subject at one of the Roman seminaries, he once condemned a group of world-class historians as men for whom "history is nothing but a continual desperate attempt to vomit. For this sort of human being there is only one remedy: the Inquisition."10

Benigni led a double life. In the mornings he worked in the Vatican department; during the afternoons and weekends he operated, from his private apartment, the secret service known as the Sodalitium Pianum ("Sodality of Pius"). Having managed a Catholic news service and newspaper, Benigni employed the most up-to-date media skills to run his espionage service, distributing anti-Modernist propaganda and gathering information on "culprits" through a network of stringers and correspondents. All this was done with the aid of modern copying machines and typewriters and the assistance of four staff members, two of them nuns. Benigni had his own secret code: Pius X, for example, was known as "Mama."

Countless seminarians, seminary teachers, curates, parish priests, and bishops were "delated," or reported, for doctrinal unorthodoxy, the details recorded in Benigni's bulging files. Even princes of the Church were not immune. The cardinal archbishops of Vienna and Paris were delated, as was the entire Dominican community at Fribourg University in Switzerland. The "offenses" ranged from favorable mentioning of "Christian democracy," to carrying a newspaper of liberal hue, to casting doubt on the truth of the translation by angels of the Holy House of Nazareth to the town of Loreto. A chance word in the refectory or in the seminary common room, being seen in the company of a suspected modernist, no less than preaching a sermon of unorthodox tendency, could lead to a denunciation followed by removal from a post of academic responsibility and banishment to a distant village curacy. And who could be trusted, when students and even old friends were known to cooperate with Benigni's espionage, perhaps out of righteous conscience, perhaps in hope of preferment?

In the absence of evidence, we can only speculate how Pacelli was affected by the anti-Modernist campaign that rocked the Church to its foundations and encouraged an intellectual narrowness and circumspection that would last for more than half a century. As the depositions for his canonization show, Pius X was ultimately responsible for this intellectual persecution. Pius X's attitude toward the Modernists in time became patently intemperate. "They want them to be treated with oil, soap, and caresses," he once said, referring to those who counseled compassion toward the alleged perpetrators. "But they should be beaten with fists. In a duel, you don't count or measure the blows, you strike as you can. War is not made with charity: it is a struggle, a duel."[11] Small wonder that he was prepared to endorse Benigni's remarkable measures to seek out and destroy the perceived enemy.

In his deposition for the canonization process of Pius X, Pietro Gasparri, Pacelli's boss and close confidant during these years, gave a condemnatory account of Pius X's personal initiatives in the campaign. "Pope Pius X," Gasparri told the tribunal, "approved, blessed, and encouraged a secret espionage association outside and above the hierarchy, which spied on members of the hierarchy itself, even on their Eminences the Cardinals; in short, he approved, blessed and encouraged a sort of Freemasonry in the Church, something unheard of in ecclesiastical history."[12]

As the persecution gathered pace, Pius X issued repeated warnings and banned more and more "Modernist" works. At length, on April 17, 1907, he delivered an allocution against these "rebels" who were attempting, he declared, to throw out Catholic theology and the decrees of the Church Councils, and to "adapt to the times." Their errors, he proclaimed in a catchall definition of Modernism, constituted "not a heresy, but the compendium and poison of all the heresies."[13] On July 3, 1907, he published the decree *Lamentabili*, condemning sixty-five Modernist propositions. One proposition to be especially lamented was the belief that "the Christ shown by history is much inferior to the Christ who is the object of Faith." Another was the belief that Catholicism can be reconciled with true science only if it is transformed into nondogmatic Christianity, that is to say, into a broad and liberal Protestantism. Two months later, Pius X issued *Pascendi*, his encyclical on Modernism.

Pascendi[14] is of crucial importance in the history of the twentieth-century Catholic Church, for it establishes much of the dogmatic and centrist tone of papal teaching until the Second Vatican Council in the early 1960s. At the same time, it further defines the power relations, the defining ideology of primacy, between the papacy and the entire Church, making it clear, and for all time, that intellectual questions within the Catholic Church are not a matter for scholarly peer-group discussion but a moral matter to be resolved by papal authority. As the saying went at the time, quoting Alfonso Liguori: "The Pope's will: God's will."

Meanwhile, Pius X had harsh words for the alleged errors of Americanism, which he believed to be still alive in the United States. Insinuating that Americanism had been a precursor of Modernism, the Pontiff declared that "with regard to morals, [the Modernists] adopt the principle of the Americanists, that the active virtues are more important than the passive, both in the estimation in which they must be held and in the exercise of them."[15] In their attempts to distance themselves from all taints of Modernism, the members of the American hierarchy now encouraged the Church in the United States to lapse into a "passive" intellectual torpor, from which it did not rouse itself for another thirty years.

Three years later, in an ultimate act of coercion, Pius X published a directive on September 1, 1910,[16] obliging ordinands, and priests in teaching and administrative posts, to swear an oath denouncing Modernism and supporting *Lamentabili* and *Pascendi*. Known as the Anti-Modernist Oath, sworn to this day in modified form by Catholic ordinands, it required acceptance of all papal teaching, and acquiescence at all times to the meaning and sense of such teaching as dictated by the Pope. As a recent commentator on papal authority, Father Paul Collins, puts it: "There was no possibility of any form of dissent, even interior. The conscience of the person taking the oath was forced to accept not only what Rome proposed, but even the sense in which Rome interpreted it. Not only was this contrary to the traditional Catholic understanding of the role of conscience, but it was a form of thought control that was unrivalled even under fascist and communist regimes."[17] This ambience of assumed mistrust was the predicament in which Pacelli found himself as he climbed the slippery ladder of Vatican bureaucracy.

The full extent of the detailed itemization of the Modernist conspiracy, as described by the Curia, was largely imaginary. What was not imaginary was the Pontiff's fear of the modern world, the terror of centrifugal breakup, that had driven Pius X into a posture of profound opposition to even the more moderate aspects of social and political modernity at the beginning of the new century, including the benefits of democracy.

It is impossible to say how the campaign affected Pacelli personally—whether he resisted suspicion by discretion or became a silent party to persecution. It is plausible, however, that the atmosphere of mistrust sharpened his skills in veiled language and circumlocution. Defenders of Pacelli's record on anti-Modernism point out that, many years later as

Pope, he found it in his heart to forgive Romolo Murri, an excommuni-
cated Modernist.[18] The fact, however, is that unlike his senior colleague
Gasparri who evidently deplored Pius X's behavior, Pacelli supported it.
It was Pacelli, as Pius XII, who canonized Pius X a great saint of the
Church on May 29, 1954, describing him as "a glowing flame of charity
and shining splendor of sanctity."[19]

3

Papal Power Games

Revered for his pastoral solicitude, deplored by liberals to this day for the anti-Modernist campaign, Pius X is less remembered for a project that constitutes arguably the most important event in the history of the Catholic Church in the modern era—the writing, promulgation, and publication of a Catholic legal manual known as the 1917 Code of Canon Law. Begun in strictest secrecy in 1904, the text, together with the Anti-Modernist Oath, became the means by which the Holy See was to establish and sustain the new, unequal, and unprecedented power relationship that had arisen between the papacy and the Church. Gasparri and Pacelli were its principal architects, with the support of two thousand scholars and the world's seven hundred bishops. The task was to absorb Pacelli for thirteen years.

Canon law, the body of internal laws of the Catholic Church, had been gathering over many centuries in a jungle of decrees, rules, and regulations. Principally organized (or disorganized) by date rather than by theme or topic, it was rich in local diversity. The idea of bringing order to this legal chaos was first suggested to the Curia by Pio Nono in 1864, but further decisions were postponed until the planned First Vatican Council six years later. As a result of the outbreak of the Franco-Prussian War and the suspension of the Council on October 20, 1870, a decision on the canon law project was neglected for another thirty years.[1]

The decision to create a code, rather than a mere compilation or collection of laws or canons in force, was critical. Codification involves abstraction, fitting laws to succinct formulae divorced from historical and social origins. Ever since the Napoleonic Code of 1804 (which played such an evident part in "modernizing" French society), codification had become fashionable—notably in Switzerland, Germany, and Italy. Ironic as it seems, Pius X, the anti-Modernist, employed the Code of Canon Law as a modernizing act: to create conformity, centralization, discipline.[2] The code was to be applied universally without local discretion or favor. It described lines of authority, and laid down rules, and penalties. It transformed the power of the papacy and thus the consciousness of what it meant to be a pope, and a Catholic. Via the most modern means of printing and distribution, it reached every Catholic priest in the world, across all cultural frontiers, its timelessness and universality lending eternity to a novel and unprecedented notion of supreme papal authority.

According to Ulrich Stutz, a distinguished Protestant canon lawyer of the period, the ideological significance loomed enormous for the future of the Catholic Church. "Now that infallibility in the areas of faith and morals has been attributed to the papacy," he wrote in 1917 with a frankness denied his Catholic counterparts, "it has completed the work in the legal sphere and given the [Catholic] Church a comprehensive lawbook that exhaustively regulates conditions within the Church, a *unicus et authenticus fons* [a unique and authentic source] for administration, jurisdiction, and legal instruction—unlike anything the Church has previously possessed in its two-thousand-year existence."[3]

At the apex of the pyramidal model of authority was the Pope, whose supremacy was described in Canon 218: "the supreme and most complete jurisdiction throughout the Church, both in matters of faith and morals and in those that affect discipline and Church government throughout the world." Under the auspices of this single head of authority, the code regulated and coordinated the entire life of the Church and its relations with the papacy and the Curia, which Pius X was simultaneously overhauling.[4]

In theory, the pontifical Commission on Canon Law had no powers to issue new legislation. But, as we shall see, there were to be significant nuances and new emphases as a result of the abstraction process. And while it was clear that Rome had declared unilateral independence from all secular influence, it was obvious that a transfer of authority from the local dioceses to Rome was also in progress.

Among the crucial new emphases was a blurring in Canon 1323 of the distinction between the ordinary and the solemn teaching authority of the Pope, confusion that the fathers of the First Vatican Council had strived to avoid.[5] It meant that there was now scope, in practice if not in theory, for papal encyclicals to be regarded with virtually the same authority as an ex cathedra dogma—"creeping infallibility," as it came to be called. At the same time, heresy and error were conflated in the terms of Canon 1324: "It is not enough to avoid heresy, but one must also carefully shun all errors that more or less approach it; hence all must observe the constitutions and decrees by which the Holy See has proscribed and forbidden opinions of that sort." In a standard edition used in seminaries until 1983, we find the following clarification: "Such are all doctrinal decrees of the Holy See, even though they be not infallibly proposed, and even though they come from the Sacred Congregations with the approval of the Holy Father, or from the Biblical Commission. . . . Such decrees do not receive the assent of faith; they are not *de fide catholica*. But they merit genuine internal and intellectual assent and loyal obedience."[6] Thus the Anti-Modernist Oath was absorbed into the code.

While tightening up assent to centralized Roman authority, the code also curbed peer-group ecumenical discussion in Canon 1325: "Catholics are to avoid disputations or conferences about matters of faith with non-Catholics, especially in public, unless the Holy See, or in case of emergency the [bishop of the] place, has given permission."[7] And under Canon 246, all judgments of theological orthodoxy were entrusted to the Holy Office (formerly the Roman Inquisition). Parallel with these disciplines were new regulations enforcing censorship. Under Canon 1386.1, no priest was allowed to publish a book, or edit or contribute to a newspaper, journal, magazine, or review, without permission of the local bishop. Every diocese would have its own censor (Canon 1393.1). Censors were obliged to make a special profession of faith (Canon 1406.1), and they were required to make sure that all work awarded the diocesan imprimatur should be in full accord with general Councils of the Church, "or in the constitution and prescriptions of the Apostolic

See" (Canon 1393.2). The name of the censor, moreover, was not to be divulged until the bishop had given a favorable judgment on the work (Canon 1393.5).

Above all, there was Canon 329.2, which endowed the Pope with the sole right to nominate bishops. The development of modern nation-states throughout the nineteenth century had seen the gradual and voluntary relinquishing of secular involvement in the nomination of bishops and the assumption of that right by the Holy See. Throughout much of the Church's history, popes had inherited the right to nominate bishops mainly within the papal states and areas in the East where dioceses owed direct allegiance to the Pope. Popes, in other words, exercised only an exceptional right to nominate bishops. Canon 329.2 took the recent historical circumstances and transformed them into a universal, absolute, and timeless law, supported neither by history nor by tradition. The late Garrett Sweeney, in his study on the question, has a powerful image to illustrate the effects of the regulation, which remains valid to this day. "If 'The Church' is conceptualized as a single machine, with divine assistance concentrated at the top, and nothing more is required of bishops than that they should operate the machine efficiently, it is entirely appropriate that they should be appointed from Rome."[8]

The nomination of bishops, moreover, was to have important implications for the exercise of infallible or definitive teaching by all the Catholic bishops when they teach in union with one another and the Pope. Clarified six decades later in a revised version of the Code of Canon Law, this idea of infallibility currently assumes collegial pluralism. And yet, as critics of the system point out, collegiality is a difficult ideal to attain when the Pope selects every bishop in the college after his own views and prejudices.[9]

In practice, the new ruling on the nomination of bishops was subject to challenge. There were in existence many concordats negotiated over the centuries between the Holy See and various governments and monarchies throughout the world, laying down local rules for the nomination of new bishops. The concordats typically allowed for secular involvement, as a well as measure of collegiality—for example, the wishes of the canons of the cathedral. It became clear to Gasparri and Pacelli that some major concordats would require renegotiation or rescinding if the code was to acquire due force."[10]

The complex task of tidying up concordat law was to prove more difficult than Vatican specialists had envisaged. In May 1917, when the full code was published, it was to be Pacelli's principal task to eradicate obstacles to its full implementation in the largest and most powerful Catholic population in the world: Germany.

Pacelli and French Church-State Relations

While facing the prodigious task of codifying canon law, Pacelli had also been entrusted with key projects in the field of international relations. The most important involved Church-State affairs in France, where anticlericalism was rampant. The issues and the history of the relationship between the Third Republic and the Holy See were to shape Pacelli's attitudes and policies on Church and State in years to come.

In view of the French government's antagonism toward the Catholic hierarchy and clergy because of their royalist tendencies, Leo XIII in the 1880s had attempted a gentle retrenchment from his own monarchist position. The French hierarchy, however, had no intention of swallowing republicanism, even if encouragement came from the Pope himself. Matters took a turn for the worse when the Catholic newspaper *La Croix* backed the wrong side in the notorious Dreyfus case. Dreyfus, a Jewish army officer, had been sentenced to hard labor on Devil's Island after he was accused of selling national secrets, an allegation the French bishops were disposed to believe in the light of their antisocialist prejudices. One Catholic cleric, Abbé Cros, proclaimed that Dreyfus should be "trampled on morning and night ... and should have his nose bashed in."[11] The Jesuit monthly *Civiltà Cattolica* proclaimed infamously: "The Jew was created by God to act the traitor everywhere," adding that France must now regret the 1791 Act that extended French nationality to the Jews, since the Jews were even now collecting funds for an appeal on behalf of Dreyfus within Germany. When Dreyfus was exonerated on June 20, 1899, the Catholic clergy came under attack from the socialists.

Taking advantage of yet another wave of anticlericalism across France, the ailing Waldeck-Rousseau government passed an act in 1901 forbidding the religious orders to teach. The Jesuits closed their schools and turned to other activities; whole communities of religious emigrated to England, Belgium, Holland, and the United States. In the following years the persecution was driven home by Waldeck-Rousseau's successor, Émile Combes, who boasted in September 1904 that he had closed 13,904 Catholic schools.[12]

Elected at the height of the French anticlerical persecution, Pius X made it clear that he wanted no appeasement of the French republic. Pius refused to approve certain candidates for dioceses proposed by the Combes government, and made an official protest to King Vittorio Emanuele III of Italy when President Émile-François Loubet of France announced a state visit to the Eternal City in 1904. The French government responded by cutting off diplomatic relations with the Vatican, then passed an act officially separating Church and State in France. A minor result of that split, but of great importance to Eugenio Pacelli, was the decision of Cardinal Secretary of State Merry del Val to commission from Gasparri a *libro bianco* (white book), an official report on the recent history of relations between the Holy See and France. Gasparri delegated the task to Pacelli, "one of my trusty staff in the Secretariat of State, in whom I had particular confidence."[13] Pacelli's report accused the French government of rabid sectarianism and alleged that government ministers were implicated in ordering a break-in of the Holy See's nunciature, or embassy, in Paris to steal the secret cipher for communicating with the Vatican.

Meanwhile, the crisis deepened. The French government attempted to control Church property by setting up joint lay-clerical administrative bodies (originally, these were to have included non-Catholic laity). In order to free the Church of any such secular influence, Pius X voluntarily handed over all Church property to the State in France, putting the *good* of the Church, as he expressed it, before her *goods*. The French responded by evicting the clergy and religious from their houses and monasteries. The government was determined to exert jurisdictional control over the Church it had set adrift from the State; Pius X was determined to exert untrammeled primacy over the Church as a spiritual, doctrinal, legal, and administrative entity. This was the clear-eyed papal vision of total separation of sovereignties: the Church with the Pope unquestioningly at its head, and the world mediated through the papal diplomatic service and the bishops.

The idea carried over into Pius X's attitude toward Catholic political parties in France, Italy, and Germany. He did not care for them because he could not control them. This anticipated Pacelli's future dealings with Catholic party politics in Germany in the 1920s and 1930s. Pius X once said of the German Catholic Center Party, the Zentrumspartei, "I do not like it, because it *is* a Catholic party."[14] The statement is all the more remarkable since Pius X was of an age to have remembered the role played by the Center Party in combating the persecution of the Catholic Church in Bismarck's Germany during the 1870s. The lessons learned during the Kulturkampf had certainly been absorbed within the Secretariat of State. "Let the French Catholics," said Cardinal Merry del Val, "follow the example of the persecuted Catholics in Bismarck's Germany. By uniting in their own defense, those German Catholics defeated the Kulturkampf." Yet Pius X preferred the demise of a Catholic political party precisely because he could see no role for lay-clerical pluralism within the pyramidal structure of papal power. Commenting on Pius X's view of political Catholicism, historian and journalist Carlo Falconi writes: "First, he believed the mixture of politics and religion to be the most hybrid and dangerous possible for the Church; secondly, because in general, and especially at that time, they [Catholic parties] fostered the participation of priests in politics; and lastly, because he thought them useless, for Catholics could always seek support for their religious claims from the lay parties favourable to the Church or at least not hostile to it."[15] The view was to be echoed, as we shall see, by Pacelli twenty years later, when as Cardinal Secretary of State he favored a quiescent, docile Church and collaboration with the Nazi Party over the continued existence of the Catholic Center Party, which represented the final obstacle on Hitler's path to dictatorship.

Pacelli had come of age as a specialist in Vatican foreign relations during the clash with the Combes government, while engaged on the lengthy toil of codifying canon law and occupied with the day-to-day tasks of the Department of Extraordinary Affairs. At the same time, hidden from the world, he busied himself year after year gaining the trust of his superiors, until in 1911 he rose to the level of undersecretary in the Department of Extraordinary Affairs,[16] replacing Umberto Benigni, who had resigned for reasons of health (possibly not unconnected with his exhausting double life as Vatican bureaucrat and spymaster).

The following year, in another sign of special favor, Pacelli was asked to travel to England yet again, in the company of Cardinal Gennaro Granito Pignatelli di Belmonte, to attend the coronation of King George V. It was on this visit that he attended the Spithead Review of the Royal Navy, an experience he often recollected in private audiences with English pilgrims after he became Pope. In the autumn of 1912 he was also appointed *consultore*, or adviser, to the Holy Office, indicating that not a scintilla of anti-Modernist suspicion had ever attached to his orthodoxy.

In his capacity as highly favored undersecretary, and as a coming figure in the world of international diplomacy and law, he now became involved in a series of negotiations that contributed significantly to the extreme tensions between Serbia and the Austro-Hungarian Empire in the period preceding the outbreak of the First World War.

The details of the story, anticipating his strategy in Germany a decade later, are contained in a quantity of files in the Vatican. The archive, known as Section for Reports with States, is divided according to Vatican activities with different nation-states. Within the boxes labeled "Austria-Ungheria 1913—Serbia—Belgrado 1913–1915" is a collection headed "Concordato tra la Santa Sede e la Serbia" ["Concordat between the Holy See and Serbia"], containing letters, deciphered top-secret memoranda, minutes of meetings between cardinals, drafts of treaties—all of them once in the keeping of Eugenio Pacelli and annotated in his scrupulous italic script.

The archival introduction states that the Serbian negotiator was a Signore Luigi Bakotic, assigned by the foreign minister of Serbia; that Serbia's special agent to the Holy See was a French-Italian priest, Denis Cardon; and that the negotiations were instigated in 1913 "at the invitation of Monsignor Eugenio Pacelli, undersecretary of the Sacred Congregation for Extraordinary Affairs."

The Serbian Concordat and the Great War

At precisely 11:30 on the morning of June 24, 1914, just four days before Archduke Franz Ferdinand of Austria was assassinated at Sarajevo, representatives of the Holy See and the government of Serbia sat down in the *salone* of the Secretariat of State to put their signatures to a treaty known as the Serbian Concordat. Present at the meeting were the principal Serbian negotiators, led by Milenko Vesnitch, Serbian ambassador in Paris, and Luigi Bakotic of the Serbian foreign ministry. For the Vatican was Cardinal Merry del Val and next to him the tall, sleek figure of the thirty-eight-year-old Monsignor Eugenio Pacelli. Pacelli had negotiated and drafted the document over the previous eighteen months.

Within the terms of the treaty, Serbia guaranteed that the Holy See had the right to impose the new Code of Canon Law on its country's Catholic clergy and subjects; that Catholics would have freedom of religion, worship, and education within its territories. Serbia also committed itself to paying stipends to the archbishop of Belgrade, the bishop of Üsküb (now Skopje), and clergy serving the Catholic communities. At the same time, the treaty implied the abrogation of the ancient protectorate rights of the Austro-Hungarian Empire over the Catholic enclaves in Serbia's territories.

The idea of the Vatican sanctioning a Catholic European country to act as protector of Catholics within another, non-Catholic nation-state was a familiar feature of the colonial era.[17] France in particular had exploited its protector status in the Far East and the Middle East until its break with the Vatican in 1905; Germany, Austria, Spain, and Belgium had at different times and in different parts of the world sought to exert the status for more or less political and commercial advantages. In the meantime, there had never been a question of a concordat with Serbia, since the numbers of Catholics there had been small—that is, until Serbia's success in the First Balkan War against Turkey in 1912 and its expansion into Macedonia, Epirus, and northern Albania. With these added territories, the number of Catholics within greater Serbia increased from about seven thousand to forty thousand, and Serbia, mostly Orthodox in religion, saw an advantage in making friends with them.

Austria-Hungary's protectorate rights, jealously guarded for more than a century, had been largely symbolic. But they carried the authority to nominate bishops and to educate Balkan priests of the Latin Rite in seminaries in Austria and Hungary, and even assumed a moral right on the part of the empire to invade the region if Catholic communities were deemed to be under threat. These symbolic rights were not negligible to the Austro-Hungarians. At a time when Serbia, encouraged by

Russia, was challenging Austria-Hungary's sphere of influence throughout the Balkans, Franz Josef was keen to use every means to maintain ties of loyalty to the empire. The Serbian Concordat signed in the Vatican that day in 1914 destroyed those links and the influence that went with them.

Serbia, for its part, had everything to gain by the concordat, for it removed doubts about its fierce sectarian partisanship of Orthodox Christianity and enhanced its imperialistic ambitions to be a focus for unity among the patchwork of Slavic peoples of both Latin and Orthodox background in the region. The Vatican also had much to gain, for the concordat proclaimed the end of centuries of antagonism between Rome and the Orthodox "schism," opening up the prospect of Catholic Latin and Eastern Rite evangelization toward Russia and Greece. Above all—and the documents reveal that this was Pacelli's motivating impulse— the concordat endowed the papacy with important features of authority, including appointment of bishops and prelates, later to be enshrined in the 1917 code, but up to this point enjoyed by the Austrian emperor under ancient usage. Only Austria-Hungary stood to lose, for the treaty threatened to increase the Serbian, pan-Slavic influence along its southern borders and to subject the empire to diplomatic humiliation.

The Serbian Concordat negotiations were conducted in a series of top-secret exchanges in a triangle between Vienna, Belgrade, and the Vatican. The Austrians, for their part, attempted to wreck the negotiations, but the Vatican, in the person of Eugenio Pacelli, had pressed the project to a conclusion despite all cautionary counsels, including solemn warnings from the papal nuncio in Vienna.

Vienna reacted to news of the concordat with outrage. "The Austrian press and people," wrote the Italian ambassador from Vienna on June 25, "consider the Serbian Concordat a major diplomatic defeat for their Government."[18] Under the headline "NEW DEFEAT," Die Zeit, the Viennese paper, proclaimed: "Now Serbian prestige will be inflated, and its bishops and priests will become an important factor in pan-Slav agitation.... Why in heaven's name should Austria have made such a vast financial outlay in these Balkan lands on behalf of our protectorate, which is not so much religious as political, only to throw it away in a matter of weeks, and without a struggle?" In an even more heated piece in the Arbeiter-zeitung on the day after the signing, the editorialist asked: "After this humiliation, will the voice of Austria ever be listened to again?" The government had dealt with the Serbs in a craven and incompetent fashion, proclaimed the press. The result was a sharp increase in anti-Serbian rhetoric and calls for action. When the archduke was murdered in Sarajevo only days later, emotions were already volatile. The Serbian Concordat undoubtedly contributed to the uncompromising terms that the Austro-Hungarian Empire pressed on Serbia, making war inevitable.

Pacelli's Secret Diplomacy

The starting point of the strange tale of the Serbian Concordat was a journey to Belgrade made by a country priest in the summer of 1912. Father Denis Cardon planned to "acquaint himself with the Balkan countries before returning to Vienna to attend a Eucharistic congress."[19] Cardon was a corpulent, bustling, meddlesome cleric, skilled in several languages, including Serbo-Croatian, who ran a small parish in a place called Taggia in the Alpes-Maritimes above Ventimiglia on the Mediterranean.

In his Belgrade hotel one evening, Father Cardon found himself in conversation with a Serbian government minister (unidentified in the Vatican documents). The priest suggested that a concordat might be of interest to both the Church and the Serbs. The minister said that he doubted whether the Serbian government could approach the Vatican directly because of the fierce opposition of Austria. Many people in high office, he told the priest, had tried and failed.

But Cardon spoke with such conviction on the merits of a concordat that the minister forthwith appointed this humble and apparently manipulable priest as Serbia's special agent to the Holy See. The next day Cardon was briefed by the *ministre des cultes* in the offices of the Serbian government, and in consequence the cleric eventually made contact with the Secretariat of State in the Vatican. "One wonders," wrote the editorialist of *L'Éclaireur de Nice*, the newspaper that told Cardon's story for the first time on June 26, 1914, "in fact, one *demands* to know, who really was the central negotiator of this crucial event!" It is clear from the files that it was none other than the undersecretary in the Department of Extraordinary Affairs, Eugenio Pacelli, reporting directly to the Cardinal

Secretary of State, Merry del Val. All dealings—with Cardon, with diplomats in Vienna and Belgrade, and with the Austrian ambassador to the Holy See in Rome—went through Pacelli. Pacelli drafted all the terms of the concordat, replied to every query, invariably writing in his own hand on behalf of Merry del Val and even redrafting his letters before encipherment, organizing and writing the minutes of curial meetings in which the final decisions were made.

For a whole year the Serbian negotiations did not include the Viennese diplomats in Rome, the papal nuncio in Vienna, or the appropriate Austrian government ministers. In a handwritten memorandum in French to Pacelli, dated January 10, 1913,[20] the Austrian ambassador to the Holy See complained that he was conscious of rumors—starting with a newspaper article in Belgrade the previous November—about the efforts of Serbia to reform the protection of Catholics within its territories. He warned the Vatican that the Austrian government regarded its Balkan protectorate, which it had held "since time immemorial," to be a matter "not of rights but of duties." The note poured scorn on the notion that Serbia was seeking to "emancipate the Catholics living in its territories, releasing them from the yoke of Austria, and replacing foreign priests with indigenous ones." He ended by seeking confirmation that the Holy See would see eye-to-eye with the Austrian government on the need to keep the protectorate in place.

A second note from the Austrian ambassador followed on February 4,[21] declaring that the parish priest of Üsküb had been approached by a civil servant in the Serbian ministry of religion, asking for numbers of Catholics in the diocese, reports on revenues and properties, and details of the archbishop's establishment. "Our consul in Üsküb has asked the parish priest to refuse these requests for information," wrote the ambassador, and he ended by reminding Pacelli that he had already asked for clarification, and was seeking it again.

Finally, in an aide-mémoire dated February 17, 1914,[22] the ambassador set out his government's determined response to the developments by stating the conditions under which Austria would countenance an alteration in the protectorate understanding. The conditions included prayers by name for Emperor Franz Josef and his family during every Mass; a seat of honor to be maintained for the emperor in every church; a special place for the emperor's representative during religious processions, "such representatives to be accorded special precedences during the ceremonial of incense, the kiss of peace, the *agnus dei*, reception of communion, etc."; the presence of the emperor's coat of arms; and the celebration of his birthday. All of seemingly trivial significance at this distance, but crucial symbolic matters in relation to cultural loyalty.

Another baffled and uninformed recipient of rumors was the Holy See's own nuncio in Vienna. In a letter dated February 15, 1913,[23] Archbishop Rafaele Scapinelli reported to Pacelli his recent encounters with Serbian diplomats. The nuncio had evidently not been briefed on the developments, but, guessing what was afoot, he took it upon himself to set out the advantages and disadvantages of such a treaty. On balance, he conceded, a concordat would open up new prospects for Catholic influence in the Balkans ("where Catholics are considered foreigners with no impact on the political and cultural life of the country"), but he concluded with a chillingly prophetic observation:

> Austria, however, appears determined to deal harshly with Serbia, and it is widely believed that there could be a war with that country in the spring, further complicating matters in the extreme. Would it not be better to leave [the concordat negotiations] for now rather than take risks in an uncertain and perilous set of circumstances that can only end with military humiliation for Serbia; for Serbia is a focus of attraction for the ambitions of the South Balkan states—all of which seems destined to threaten the integrity of the Austro-Hungarian Empire?[24]

Throughout the following twelve months, the Secretariat of State files show Father Cardon busily running between Rome and Belgrade, while Pacelli continued to play cat-and-mouse with the Austrian diplomats and the papal nuncio in Vienna. From the distressed notes of the Austrians, it emerges that Pacelli was determined, whatever the pleadings of Vienna, to end the protectorate status in the interests of centrist papal politics rather than the local benefit of Serbian Catholics. In the meantime, as a sop to the Austrians, he was promoting the idea of *patronatus* rights, "purely honorific rights as are compatible with canon law." The canonist Pacelli, it is evident, intended diverting the Austrians into the chaotic thickets of Rome's canon law, knowing full well, as the Austrians could not possibly have known, that the forthcoming 1917 code would grant them absolutely nothing in the way of "honorific rights." The Austrians were not to be assuaged, and yet there was nothing they could do to stop the Holy See, except to beg for clearly expressed rights of patronage in the concordat or at least a postponement.

Two curial meetings stood between the final negotiations and the signing of the proposed concordat. The first was called at 10:30 A.M. on May 3, 1914, a Sunday, reflecting the growing sense of crisis over the treaty. Cardinals Vannutelli, De Lai, Gotti, Ferrata, Gasparri, and Merry del Val were present. Pacelli was the meeting's secretary, taking the minutes in his own hand.[25] Serbia had threatened to withdraw from the negotiations in the event of the Vatican's conceding too much to Austria, or in the event, indeed, of further delay. The Curia was being rushed into a corner. Were Serbia to withdraw, the Curia believed, the plight of the Catholics in the region might now be worse than before the concordat was mooted. The cardinals were aware that the time had come to make up their minds, yet there is an impression in the meeting's minutes of their sleepwalking toward the inevitable.

Vannutelli started by urging his colleagues to sign, for he was convinced that the concordat would promote the interests of the Catholic Church in the East. He was aware, he said, of Austrian sensitivities, "But let's try to make them see the advantages rather than the disadvantages." He talked of keeping the Austrians happy with honorific entitlements, but had nothing definite to propose.

De Lai then spoke briefly, seconding everything Vannutelli had said, and asserting that they should proceed to a concordat because "it is the best concordat we have ever drafted," a flattering reference to Pacelli's efforts. Gotti followed, arguing that they should accept because it was not in their power to refuse any request for a treaty. He warned nevertheless that they should be "very careful about how we treat Austria," although he, too, had nothing positive to recommend. Then, engaging in a little casuistry, he raised the possibility of assuring Austria of its purely honorary status as "patron," adding that "there is no need to underpin this with a special agreement." In other words, the promise of honorary status need not be mentioned in the concordat.

Ferrata now came in, offering a note of caution: "Serbia," he asserted, "is not a country that inspires trust, and it is clear that it is seeking a concordat in order simply to eliminate the influence of Austria." Again, he suggested that the way forward was to keep Austria happy; but like the others he had nothing positive to suggest.

Gasparri, Pacelli's guide and mentor, was then credited with support-ing the concordat, like all the rest. As Pacelli wrote: *"E anch'egli, tutto consid-erato, per l'affirmativa"* ["He, too, all considered, was in the affirmative"]. But the rest of Gasparri's recorded comments are altogether sparse and noncommittal. "Austria now has no right to a protectorate status follow-ing the withdrawal of Turkey from the region," Gasparri said.

Now Cardinal Secretary of State Merry del Val spoke, marshaling the strongest arguments in support of the concordat. "To refuse," he began, "would be to give a pretext for the Slavs to hold the Catholics hostage even more. And we have to remember that the Serbs have come to us.... They are interested, therefore, in regularizing the situation. Such an op-portunity might never come again. In any case, the Austrian protectorate is no longer working or workable."

Making a point that Pacelli might well have remembered some twenty years later when dealing with Hitler, Merry del Val declared: "If we say that we cannot trust these Serbs, all the more reason for pinning them down with a concordat."

A final meeting of the cardinals in the Secretariat of State was called on June 7, 1914, at 10:30 A.M.[26] The cardinals discussed once again the issue of *patronatus* rights—now the Austrians' minimum conditions if they were to give the concordat their reluctant blessing. But, as the cardi-nals acknowledged, speaking one by one, the Serbian negotiators would certainly withdraw rather than grant any such rights in the treaty.

Toward the end of the meeting, Merry del Val offered the almost de-spairing reflection: "There will be grave consequences if we now break off negotiations. The Serbs will come down harshly on the Church, pro-claiming that we never did want a proper legal basis for what they were offering. At the same time, if the Catholic communities are then obliged to look to the Austrians for their defense, they will be doubly despised."

It was left to Gasparri, however, to echo the cautious observation made by Archbishop Scapinelli, the nuncio in Vienna, eighteen months earlier:

The principal reason Serbia had sought this concordat is to make overtures to those Slavic communities who owed allegiance to the Austro-Hungarian Empire, and to eliminate any obstacles that might arise from religious or cultural considerations. What they are trying to do is show that the kingdom of Serbia has cordial relationships with the Holy See and to offer Catholics guarantees of liberty and welfare.

It was the last word spoken on the matter by the Curia before going to Pius X for signature, and the single substantial objection in the final meeting among a chorus of yea-sayers. Gasparri, at least, had come to understand that the Vatican had been led into a trap, drawn by the Curia's desire to exert direct papal rule over Catholics in the Balkans and by the prospects of missionary success in the East. Serbia had drawn the Vatican into the legendary complexities of Balkan politics, and the Vatican had failed to consider the contribution the concordat would make to tensions in the region.

There is no evidence that Pacelli, who choreographed the entire process, questioned the wisdom of his conduct of these affairs, either at the time or subsequently. Nor is there any evidence that Gasparri grasped the extent of his protégé's initiatives in the matter.

The concordat, comprising twenty-two articles, was signed on June 24, bearing the hallmarks of Pacelli's future policy: the expansion of papal power over the Catholic Church at the local level, and, in particular, control of appointment of bishops. The virtual elimination of local discretion in the choice of bishops was to become a crucial issue within the Church to the end of the century.

Article 1 stated simply that "the Catholic and Apostolic Roman religion will be exercised freely and publicly in the kingdom of Serbia." Article 3 stated that the archbishop of Belgrade and the bishop of Üsküb would be "directly answerable to the Holy See for its ecclesiastical affairs," and Article 4 emphasized that "His Holiness would nominate the candidates for bishoprics," notifying the Serbian government lest any should be politically objectionable. Six other articles stressed the free exercise of the Catholic religion in harmony with the provisions of canon law, including the catchall Article 20: "If any difficulties arise in the interpretation of these articles ... the Holy See and the royal government will proceed, with common accord, to a solution that agrees with canon law."

The concordat contained generous government funding for the bishops, clergy, and teachers of the Catholic religion. Seminaries would be established within Serbia, and ordinands and catechists would be encouraged to teach the doctrines of the Catholic faith in the local language. Prayers would be said at Mass for the king of Serbia. There was no mention of Austria-Hungary, not a line to suggest that its ancient links with Catholicism in the region deserved residual consideration, no mention even of *patronatus* rights.

Austria's *Die Zeit* newspaper led with its "NEW DEFEAT" article the following day. Its expanded arguments set out the political dimensions of the concordat that Pacelli had ignored through eighteen months of negotiations. The Catholic hierarchy in the region, said the newspaper, now owed its allegiance to Serbia, as did the clergy, who would now be instructed in a seminary within Serbia. "This is a great loss of influence to which Austria must be acutely sensitive." It went on, "Austria has made tremendous sacrifices, all for nothing, down the centuries on behalf of the Balkan Catholics, including Albania—where we also stand to lose our protectorate status. This is a terrible blow to our prestige."

A third, most telling argument made by the paper that morning, and reprinted in newspapers across the world, was the most ominous. "The concordat is the very best propaganda instrument in favor of a Greater Serbia, for the only obstacle to a union of the Serbs and the Croats is the split between the Orthodox and Catholic religions. If in addition to military success [against Turkey] the Serbs can add a diplomatic success over Austria, Serbia must then become a focus for Slavs south of the Austrian borders. The pan-Serbian agitators regard the help of the bishops and clergy quite crucial in this struggle."

When Archduke Franz Ferdinand and his wife were gunned down by a pan-Serbian agitator in Sarajevo on June 28, the emotions prompted by the Serbian Concordat became part of the general groundswell of anti-Serbian anger. The concordat nevertheless represented a contribution to the tensions that led the Austrian government to overplay its hand by delivering a humiliating ultimatum to Serbia. There is no indication that Pope Pius X grasped the role of the Holy See in adding to the pressures that brought the Austro-Hungarian Empire and Serbia to the brink. The declaration of war, it is said, threw him into a profound depression from which he never recovered. He died on August 20, 1914—of a broken heart, it was said.

What is clear from the episode is the potentially negative impact of Vatican diplomacy on cultural and political relations, its power to provoke dismay and insecurity, its scope to further complicate and disrupt mounting tensions between countries. The Holy See, it is apparent, was no mere spiritual onlooker concerned exclusively with the spiritual welfare of Catholics in Serbia, but a player on the world scene with its own long-term ambitions and goals. In years to come, Pacelli's initiatives in international relations focused on the renegotiation of concordats that contradicted the new Code of Canon Law. There is no indication that Pacelli questioned the dangerous implications of the Serbian negotiations after the event. From this point of view, the episode marks the ominous beginnings of Pacelli's pattern of aloofness from the far-reaching political consequences of his diplomatic actions on behalf of the Pope.

4

To Germany

Benedict XV, Giacomo della Chiesa, was elected on September 3, 1914, two weeks after the death of Pius X. A Genoese aristocrat of diminutive proportions (his nickname was *picoletto*, "tiny one"), della Chiesa was saintly, modest, shrewd, and dynamic. A protégé of Rampolla, Leo XIII's Cardinal Secretary of State, della Chiesa had risen rapidly through the ranks of the diplomatic service to become undersecretary in the Secretariat of State to Cardinal Merry del Val. In the paranoid atmosphere of Pius X's pontificate, however, della Chiesa had fallen under suspicion—most likely because he had frequently and unwisely harked back to the happier days and counsels of Leo XIII. In 1907 he was removed from the Vatican to become archbishop of Bologna, an appointment deemed a demotion. In this post, he was not awarded a cardinal's hat, normally automatic for such an important diocese, until 1914.

On becoming Pope, he dismissed Merry del Val, barely giving the outgoing Cardinal Secretary of State time to clear his desk; at the same time, Benigni's spy network, Sodalitium Pianum, was hastily wound up (Benigni finished his days, appropriately, as an informer for Mussolini)[1] and the anti-Modernist witch-hunt brought to an end. All the same, the Anti-Modernist Oath, the censorship of books written by the clergy, and the strictures of the Code of Canon Law still in preparation, all remained in place to enforce consensus on the new ideology of papal power through much of the century.

Benedict now focused his attention on the task of coaxing the combatant nations of Europe to the peace table. He was tormented by the spectacle of Christians waging war against Christians, Catholics against Catholics. Immediately after his election, he published a protest to the world against the "horrible butchery." He was "stricken," he said, "with inexpressible horror and anguish before the monstrous spectacle of this war with its streams of Christian blood."[2] He was determined that a strictly neutral or, as he put it, impartial stance was the Holy See's best claim to influence. Given the potential for manipulating religious protest for purposes of propaganda, there was widespread pressure on Benedict to take sides. Benedict refused to join either side in condemnation of the enemy's atrocities and in consequence earned opprobrium from both. When Italy joined the Allies in May of 1915, it insisted at the secret Treaty of London that the alliance should prevent the representatives of the Holy See from taking any part in the arrangements for peace or the settlement of problems connected with the war. Italy, it seems, was not alone in thinking that the papacy was still capable of using the crisis of a world war to further its own aims in the still unresolved Roman Question, the antagonism between the Holy See and the Italian State.

Benedict appointed Pietro Gasparri as Cardinal Secretary of State, a post he would fill for the next sixteen years. Pacelli was now promoted to secretary in the Department of Extraordinary Affairs, where he focused on the plight of the vast populations of prisoners of war on both sides. Pacelli was a whirlwind of administrative activity, stretching to its limits the communications networks of the Catholic Church in the service of relief work. In every diocese where there were prisoner-of-war camps, bishops were required to enlist priests with appropriate language skills to set up links between prisoners and their families. Working with the International Red Cross and the Swiss government, Pacelli negotiated exchanges of wounded prisoners.[3] As a result of his efforts, an estimated 65,000 prisoners were sent home. Pacelli's department also busied itself with searching for news of the missing and the dead, and managed funds supplied by the Holy See for the purchase of medicine and food.

Through these first three years of the war, in which Pacelli is said to have declined even a day's vacation, he continued to work on preparations for the publication and promulgation of the Code of Canon Law. Through much of 1916, rumors circulated in the Vatican that Pacelli was to be appointed papal nuncio in Munich, but eventually the position went to Archbishop Giuseppe Aversa, who had been nuncio in Brazil. According to Baron Carlo Monti, an Italian diplomat and hanger-on at the papal court, Gasparri would not hear of Pacelli's leaving Rome until the new code had been published.

In the meantime, Pope Benedict had been awaiting the ideal opportunity to involve the powers in a Vatican-inspired peace plan. That moment seemed to have arrived in early spring of 1917, one of the grimmest periods of the war for the Allies. Bucharest had been occupied by the Germans; the U-boat war had devastated Allied shipping; the offensives on the western front had ground to a halt, while Russia was caught up in the chaos of revolution. The United States had not yet entered the war. Benedict believed that events had conspired to bring the belligerents to the peace table; but to whom should he entrust the delicate task of approaching the Germans?

As luck or providence would have it, no sooner had Archbishop Aversa installed himself at Munich than he died suddenly of appendicitis on April 3. Benedict decided that Pacelli was the ideal replacement. At a small private ceremony in the Sistine Chapel, Benedict XV personally consecrated Pacelli as archbishop of Sardi on May 13, 1917. Sardi, or Sardes, was not an actual diocese with a cure of souls, but one of the seven hundred dioceses of Eastern Christendom destroyed by the Muslim invasion, known in Rome as *in partibus infidelium* (in the regions of unbelievers). In the chapel that day, the celebrants formed a remarkable concentration of ecclesiastical power: Pope Benedict XV, Pietro Gasparri, and Achille Ratti, the Vatican librarian and diplomat, Pacelli's colleague and friend, who would be elected Pope himself five years later. Present, too, were Pacelli's mother and brother Francesco, but not his father, who had died of influenza the previous November.

Those with a mind to read significance into Marian dates would later note that Pacelli was made a bishop on the very day, Sunday, May 13, 1917, when three children were said to have witnessed a Lady all of dazzling light at a place called Fátima in Portugal. The apparition, later identified as the Virgin Mary, told them: "Come here on the thirteenth day for six months at this same time and then I will tell you who I am and what I want."[4] Following this event, there occurred the phenomenon of the spinning sun of Fátima, reportedly witnessed by thousands. In

1928 the surviving seer, Lucia, revealed the first of the famous Secrets of
Fátima, dealing with the prophecies of war and Communism throughout the twentieth century. Forty years later, as Pope, Pacelli himself witnessed in the Vatican gardens what he thought to be the phenomenon of
the spinning sun. The self-controlled, legalistic administrator had a
strangely mystical side to his character, which was to emerge in the fullness of time. The date of his consecration, May 13, was to become the
Feast of Our Lady of Fátima.

Negotiating the Peace Plan

On May 18, 1917, Archbishop Eugenio Pacelli set off in remarkable
style from Rome's Stazione Termini for Munich. Not only had Pacelli
commandeered his own private compartment, but an additional sealed
carriage had been added to the train to transport sixty cases of groceries
to ensure that his troublesome stomach would not be affected by the
food of wartime Germany. It was Baron Carlo Monti who imparted the
story of Pacelli's extravagance to Benedict XV on May 19.[5] Monti told a
scandalized Holy Father that, to satisfy Pacelli's travel arrangements, he
had been obliged to press into service no fewer than four ministries of
the Italian government, and that the cost of Pacelli's foodstuffs alone
had come to eight thousand lire, money that would have to be found by
the Holy See. The special wagon in which the foodstuffs were sealed had
been brought at high speed from Zurich, he told the Pontiff, and
Pacelli's private compartment, a concession unheard of during the war,
had to be specially requisitioned through the Italian state railways. What
was more, all the stationmasters from Rome to the Swiss border had
been placed on alert in the event that Archbishop Pacelli should require
assistance. Meanwhile, the foreign ministry had provided special passports, and the minister of finances had given special permission for the
enormous quantity of embargoed foodstuffs to be allowed to pass out
of Italy.

   According to Baron Monti, the Holy Father shook his head in wonder, remarking that, had he been sent to Munich himself, he should have
preferred to live like everyone else in Bavaria. Monti's account adds an
insinuating comparison by pointing out that this was a Pope who had

been shocked to learn that a chicken placed on the papal dining table had cost as much as twenty lire. "Here is a simple priest," wrote Monti, "who conducts himself without pomp or pretensions." Yet, as much as Benedict XV reportedly deplored Pacelli's extravagance, the young archbishop was held in highest regard by the Pope and the Curia and had been entrusted with a key role in the papal peace plans.

By May 25 Pacelli was installed at the nunciature in Munich, a neoclassical palace on the Brennerstrasse directly opposite what was later to become the Brown House, the cradle of Nazism. (Both buildings were destroyed by a large bomb during World War II.) The household was run by a small team of laypeople, and Pacelli had an *uditore*, or assistant, named Monsignor Schioppa. A grand automobile with painted papal crests on its doors stood in the garage.

Pacelli immediately set about promoting Benedict XV's peace proposal. Clear on principles, vague on details, it called for progressive disarmament, abolition of conscription, the substitution of arbitration for war, sanctions against nations refusing to accept the judgment of arbiters, and freedom of the seas. Crucially, it called for the return of occupied territories and laid down a protocol for discussion of disputed regions such as Alsace-Lorraine, Trent, and Trieste, including due consideration to be given to the wishes of the populations. Belgium, Benedict proposed, should be guaranteed independence, and Poland should be reunited and restored.

On May 28, three days after his arrival, Pacelli was taken by horse-drawn carriage to the royal palace, where he presented his credentials to King Ludwig III of Bavaria, attended by his foreign minister, Count Georg Friedrich von Hertling. More important meetings were to come, however, in Berlin, and later in Kreuznach, the military headquarters of Kaiser Wilhelm II.

He set out by train for Berlin on Monday, June 25.

In a letter to Gasparri relating the details of the trip, we hear the voice of Pacelli for the first time since those childhood essays. Crisp, almost journalistic, there is an impression of beady-eyed alertness to appropriate levels of deference.

> We arrived in Berlin at 7:20 in the morning. At the station, Deputy Erzberger [Matthias Erzberger, a prominent Catholic

leader of the Center Party] received me, and we drove in a splendid military automobile, which he put at my complete disposal during the whole of my stay in Berlin. He accompanied me to the Hotel Continental, one of the best in the capital, where I was lodged in a tolerably commodious apartment on the first floor as a guest of the imperial government. I impressed on Mr. Erzberger the need to discourage press coverage so as to avoid hostile comments against the Holy See on the peace plan in the newspapers, which in all probability will represent the Holy See as favorable to the German side. My request met with complete satisfaction: the newspapers were stopped by the Censor from making any comment on the matter.

Celebrated Holy Mass in the Catholic Church of Saint Edwige at 10 A.M.... At 11:30 A.M. started my meeting with the Imperial Chancellor [Theobald von Bethmann-Hollweg].... Signore Bethmann-Hollweg, a man of imposing physique, and of striking features, has a somewhat coarse exterior, but seems frank and ingenuous.[6]

Chancellor Bethmann-Hollweg told Pacelli that Germany "sincerely desired an end to this horrible war, which it had not provoked," and that it had demonstrated a willingness to treat with its enemies since the previous December. That offer, the chancellor continued, "had been interpreted as a sign of weakness, rather than a genuine wish to end the senseless slaughter, even though the Central Powers were militarily invincible." The time indeed had come to make peace, he asserted, and all that was preventing it was the bad will of Germany's enemies, "as can be demonstrated in the speeches of Lloyd George and Wilson."

With this, the two men got down to details. Pacelli informed Gasparri that the chancellor raised the issues of gradual and mutual disarmament, the independence of Belgium, and the question of Alsace-Lorraine and the border disputes between Austria and Italy. Bethmann-Hollweg, "not without hesitation," commented Pacelli, accepted that some movement was not impossible in these matters. Then the chancellor enlarged on a number of issues—speculating that Austria might give somewhat on the border dispute with Italy; gently chiding Pacelli for the tendency of French bishops to stir up anti-German hatred.

Reporting the honor that was paid to him at a dinner that evening, Pacelli expressed in a handwritten footnote his amazement that one of the principal heads of the Christian Workers Union was invited: "an indication," he added, "that the government actually intends encouraging workers' parties."[7]

Pacelli and the Kaiser

On the evening of Thursday, June 28, he left Berlin for the kaiser's Rhineland headquarters in a "sumptuous special imperial railway wagon" with his assistant Monsignor Schioppa.

He was transported to the residence of the kaiser in the castle of the ancient town of Kreuznach, where an "elegant apartment" had been put at his disposal. Pacelli was then led to an austere room with a few chairs, where the kaiser stood behind a desk, his withered left arm resting on the hilt of his sword and the Grand Iron Cross hanging from the collar of his army tunic. There was a field telephone on the desk, and maps of the front lined the high walls.

Pacelli reported to Gasparri that he read out to the kaiser the "revered letter of the pontiff, in conformity with my received instructions." The message contained the Holy Father's "anxious preoccupations over the prolongation of the war," the accumulated material and moral ruin, the suicide of European civilization built up over many centuries of human history. The Pope did not doubt, Pacelli proclaimed, that the German emperor wished to help him in the task of ending the war.

The kaiser apparently listened with "respectful and grave attention." When he responded, however, his voice, his gestures, his facial expressions, according to Pacelli, were "quite fanatical and not altogether normal [*esaltato e non del tutto normale*]."[8]

The kaiser told him that Germany had not provoked this war. "We were forced to defend ourselves against the destructive aims of England, whose belligerent power had to be smashed." With this, Pacelli observed, the kaiser punched the air with his fist. Germany had attempted to offer peace the previous December, the kaiser continued, but the Pope had failed to mention this. The rest of the monarch's reply, according to Pacelli, was mostly a harangue on the dangers of international socialism and the need for peace. What the Pope should do, Wilhelm eventually counseled the nuncio, was to solemnly command all the clergy and Catholic faithful to work and pray for peace. The Prussian army and the Catholic hierarchies should then form a united front against the threat of socialism.

According to Pacelli, the kaiser ranged over a number of disconnected themes: the treachery of the king of Italy, the importance of the Pope having his own territory with a corridor to the sea, the Russian situation and the scheme of England to support that country financially to keep it in the war; the future of Belgium. With this, Pacelli claimed, he intervened to plead vigorously "in the name of the Holy Father, and according to his majesty's promise, to stop the deportations of Belgians to Germany." (Some versions of the meeting, but not Pacelli's, record that the kaiser now grew conciliatory and promised that he would put an immediate stop to this practice.)[9]

The meeting over, Pacelli was led into lunch, and accorded "all the honors." During the meal, which was attended by various princes, "I was seated," he duly noted, "on the right of the kaiser, and Monsignor Schioppa on the left."

The kaiser was sufficiently struck by his meeting with Pacelli to leave his own detailed account of it in his memoirs, published in translation in 1922 and carried in *The New York Times*.[10] The kaiser's version, apparently written up from contemporaneous notes, is fascinating for its perspective on Pacelli's acquiescence and the comic relief of Schioppa, who felt that the nuncio was out of his depth and possibly struggling with the language.

The kaiser found Pacelli "a distinguished, likeable man, of high intelligence and excellent manners." He thought that the nuncio seemed to know German "well enough to understand it easily when he hears it, but not sufficiently to speak it with fluency." So they spoke in French, although the nuncio "occasionally employed German expressions of speech." Monsignor Schioppa, whom the kaiser refers to as "the Chaplain," spoke fluently and "took part—even when not asked—whenever he appeared to fear that the nuncio was becoming too influenced by what I said."

The kaiser claimed that when he turned to the question of peace between Austria and Italy, Pacelli intervened to say that it would be difficult for the Pope to interfere, since there were no relations between the Vatican and the Italian government and that Italy would not look with favor on even the suggestion of a conference if it came from the Pope.

Here, according to the kaiser's memoir, Monsignor Schioppa objected that such a step would be out of the question, as the Italian government would mobilize "the *piazza*," by which he meant a popular reaction. When the kaiser cast doubt on this, Schioppa, according to the monarch, became obstreperous. "He said that I did not know the Romans; that when they were incited they were simply terrible. . . . There was even a possibility of an attack on the Vatican, which might actually imperil the life of the Pope himself." Although the kaiser attempted to allay his fears, Schioppa "continued, unabashed, to expound on the terrors of the *piazza*."

Pacelli now retrieved the initiative by saying that it was difficult for the Pope to do anything really practical toward peace without giving offense and arousing opposition in lay Italy, which would place him in danger. In a peroration that echoed the old grievances of the unresolved Roman Question while anticipating his defensive silence as Pope, he went on to say "that it must be borne in mind that [the Pope] was, unfortunately, not free; that had the Pope a country, or at least a district of his own where he could govern autonomously and do as he pleased, the situation would be quite different; that as matters stood, he was too dependent upon lay Rome and not able to act according to his own free will."

Far from the kaiser's suggesting that the Pope regain his own territory (as Pacelli had reported), the monarch, in his own account, says that he exhorted Pacelli to consider the Pope's need for courage: "I remarked that the aim of bringing peace to the world was so great that it was impossible for the Pope to be discouraged by purely worldly considerations, from accomplishing such a task, which seemed created especially for him."

This, according to the monarch, made an impression on Pacelli: "He remarked that I was right after all." The kaiser's version of his own comments on socialism and Catholicism contrasts strikingly with that given by Pacelli to Gasparri.

> What must a Catholic soldier think [Wilhelm told Pacelli] ...
> when he heard always of efforts by the socialists only, never
> of an effort by the Pope, to free him from the horrors of war.
> If the Pope did nothing, I continued, there was danger of
> peace being forced upon the world by the socialists, which
> would mean the end of the power of the Pope and the Ro-
> man Church.

According to the kaiser, the argument struck home; Pacelli stated that
he would at once report it to the Vatican and give it his support, that the
Pope would have to act. At this point Schioppa again intervened to say
that the Pope would endanger himself by such a course of action, that
"the *piazza*" would attack him. But the kaiser replied that the Lord Jesus
Christ had never feared "the *piazza*."

"Was I now to believe," the kaiser apparently told the monsignor,
"that his Viceroy on earth was afraid of becoming a martyr, like his
Lord, in order to bring peace to the bleeding world; all on account of
the ragged Roman piazza? I the Protestant thought much too highly
of the Roman priesthood—particularly the Pope—to believe such a
thing."

With this, as the monarch remembered it, Pacelli grabbed him by the
hand and "with shining eyes" said in French: "You are absolutely right!
It is the duty of the Pope; he must act; it is through him that the world
must be won back to peace."

Thus Pacelli endorsed the mystical role of the papacy, the unique vocation of the Pontiff to influence the destinies of nations. Had he
understood, however, as evidently Monsignor Schioppa had done, the
kaiser's attempts to exploit that vision of unique responsibility to Germany's advantage? Whatever the case, here ended Pacelli's face-to-face
diplomacy on behalf of Pope Benedict XV.

The fate of Benedict's peace plan was largely predictable, considering
that both sides were still convinced that the war was winnable and that
the horrendous sacrifices could in some measure be justified to their
electorates. President Wilson's response to the papal proposals was
that they looked like a status quo ante peace. Replying for the United
States on August 27, he said, "We cannot take the word of the present
rulers of Germany sufficiently to trust their conciliatory disposition in a

peace conference," and that the real issue of the war had become "the deliverance of the free peoples of the world from the menace and actual power of a vast military establishment."

The French and the British were silent. They were still awaiting a response from the Vatican to inquiries about Germany's true intentions. By the same token, Germany was attempting to discover through Spanish channels how much the Allies were willing to concede.

The German and Austrian replies to the papal peace plan were finally published through a Swiss news agency on September 20. The Austrians announced that they welcomed the proposals and indicated that they were eager to talk peace. The German response merely made self-congratulatory noises about the kaiser's love of peace and expressed a pious hope that something would come of the proposals. A formal reply was made by Bethmann-Hollweg's replacement, Chancellor Georg Michaelis, on September 24. The statement, never published, said that "the situation was not sufficiently clear." In other words, the Germans were not prepared to be specific, for fear that they might end up with something less than they could get by continuing with the war.

In October 1917 Pacelli traveled briefly to Rome for a postmortem on the peace plan with Benedict and Gasparri before returning once more to Munich to devote himself to relief work.

The Pastoral Nuncio

Pacelli traveled tirelessly in Germany during the final twelve months of the war, bringing food and clothing to the starving "of all religions" on behalf of the Holy See.[11] Nazareno Padellaro, an early and reverential biographer, cites a prisoner of war who had witnessed Pacelli's arrival in a camp. "A shout goes up and echoes through the barracks. All the officers come to attention, as the austere figure of the nuncio approaches. . . . Men wave, weep, blow him kisses. He, correct and dignified, calm and serene, casts his sympathetic gaze, clouded with sadness, over this crowd of men whose inmost hearts he has touched."[12]

In the early autumn of 1917, however, Pacelli showed himself in a less than sympathetic light toward "all religions" when he refused to come to the assistance of Germany's Jews in a peculiar instance. The episode is described by Pacelli himself in a letter to Gasparri, which has lain buried in the files of the Secretariat of State until now.[13] On September 4, 1917, Pacelli informed Gasparri that a Dr. Werner, rabbi of Munich, representing the "Israelitic Community of Germany," had approached the nunciature begging a favor. In order to celebrate the Feast of Tabernacles, beginning on October I, the German Jews were in need of palm fronds, which normally came from Italy. Unfortunately, the Italian government had forbidden the exportation, via Switzerland, of a stock of palms that the Jews had purchased but which were held up in Como. "The Israelitic Community," Pacelli went on, "are seeking the intervention of the Pope in the hope that he will plead on behalf of the thousands of the German Jews. They are confident of a happy outcome to this request."

With an assurance characteristic of Pacelli's future dealings with his superiors, Pacelli now advised Gasparri as to how such a request should be handled in retrospect, for it was clear that he had already acted.

> It seemed to me that to go along with this would be to give the Jews special assistance not within the scope of practical, arms'-length, purely civil or natural rights common to all human beings, but in a positive and direct way to assist them in the exercise of their Jewish cult. I accordingly replied courteously to the aforementioned rabbi ... that I had sent an urgent report to the Holy Father on the matter, but I foresaw that in consequence of the wartime delays in communication that it was doubtful whether I should get an answer in time, and that the Holy Father would be delayed in explaining the matter in depth to the Italian government.

The letter went the slow route overland in the diplomatic bag. Gasparri replied on September 18 by enciphered telegram.

> I have thought carefully about the matter and I approve entirely of the way in which you have managed this delicate affair. The Holy See, evidently, cannot accede to the request of Professor Dr. Werner. Nevertheless, in making a further re-

ply to this gentleman—a reply in which I defer to your well-noted shrewdness [*destrezza*]—it should stress the fact that the Holy See has no diplomatic relations with the Italian government.[14]

So it was that Pacelli rejected a poignant plea of his Jewish brethren that might have brought spiritual consolation to many thousands. Unabashed, he wrote again on September 28, 1917, informing Gasparri that he had "communicated orally," employing "every delicacy," with Werner, "emphasizing, as your Eminence had advised, upon the fact that the Holy See has no diplomatic relations with the Italian government." Then he added, "Professor Werner was perfectly convinced of the reasons I had given him and thanked me warmly for all that I had done on his behalf."

Some Catholic canonists would defend his action to this day, arguing that he was under an actual obligation *not* to assist non-Christians in the practice of their religion. But the episode belies subsequent claims that he had a great love of the Jews and that his actions were always motivated by their best interests. That he was capable of implicating the Holy See in a diplomatic sleight of hand in order to frustrate the possibility of helping the German Jews, even in this minor liturgical matter, suggests that in his early forties he had little sympathy for the Jewish religion.

Pacelli nevertheless showed abundant evidence during this period of commendable works of corporal mercy, recorded in detail for the eyes of his superiors and especially the Pope himself. Again, his principal aim was to demonstrate the all-seeing, all-merciful beneficence of the Holy Father in Rome.

On October 17 he wrote to Gasparri from a prisoner-of-war camp in Puchheim, where he had visited some six hundred French and more than a thousand Russians, all of them "simple soldiers in the ranks."[15] Speaking in French, he delivered a homily, written out in full for Gasparri's benefit, in which he assured the bedraggled prisoners, most of whom were not Catholic, that Pope Benedict XV was concerned about their plight.

Having blessed these inmates, he distributed parcels specially shipped into Germany from the Vatican. "Each parcel," he records, "carried the coat of arms of the Pontiff and the legend 'The Holy Father offers his blessing,' and contained 200 grams of chocolate, a packet of biscuits, six packets of American cigarettes, 125 grams of soap, one tin of cocoa, 100 grams of tea, 200 grams of sugar."

He now toured the camp, passing down the files of miserable detainees, before proceeding to inspect the barrack quarters and the kitchen "where their daily ration of soup and adulterated bread is prepared." Finally, he stood meditating in the little cemetery, "where repose the poor prisoners who have died during their captivity."

As he left the prisoners, he informed Gasparri, he was conscious that the "compassionate and inexhaustible charity of the Holy Father had carried a soothing balm of faith and love into their terrible suffering."

Pacelli and the Bolshevik Jews

While Pacelli was thus engaged during his first twelve months as papal nuncio in Munich, Germany was sliding toward disaster. Having thrown away every opportunity to make a moderate peace with the Allies, the German military leaders increased the submarine raids in the North Atlantic, ensuring the entrance of the United States into the war. Finally they risked all in an ambitious but futile offensive on the western front.

By the end of the war, the toll in German lives had mounted to two million. It was difficult for the nation to accept that such a sacrifice had been in vain. Germany was ill prepared for the enormity of defeat, but one thing was clear in the final days: President Woodrow Wilson and the Allies were determined to make peace not with the kaiser and the old order but only with the representatives of the people. When the armistice was signed on November 11, 1918, the leader of the German commission was Matthias Erzberger, the Catholic Center Party deputy, who had been working for peace since the middle of the war. Kaiser Wilhelm II fled to Holland and abdicated; Prince Max of Baden, the last chancellor under the Second Reich founded by Bismarck, handed over his authority to the interim president, the Social Democrat Friedrich Ebert.

There was to be no smooth transition to democracy. The Allies had propelled Germany into a political vacuum, prompting profound revolutionary change and economic and social chaos, which in turn brought widespread starvation, riots, and strikes. For a time it seemed that the Bolshevik triumph in Russia would be repeated in Germany: workers' councils proliferated, a mutiny in the navy spread to spontaneous revolts throughout the country. In Munich, where Pacelli was now resident, the Independent Social Democrat Kurt Eisner, with a motley following of workers, demobilized soldiers, and peasants, overthrew the governing monarchy on November 8 and declared a socialist republic. In Berlin a council of "commissars" briefly proclaimed a new German government.

Yet these extreme left-wing groups did not have popular backing comparable to the moderate socialist groups that were to emerge as parties of government after the collapse of the Second Reich. The largest following was for the Social Democratic Party, led by Friedrich Ebert, from which the Independent Social Democrats had split in 1917 in a bid to stop the war and stake a claim for a "genuine" postwar socialism.

Pacelli was in the eye of the storm. Early in November, he sent three ciphered messages to Gasparri, reporting mounting tension and political chaos in the city, ending with the news that Eisner's provisional government would no longer allow ciphered messages to be sent to Rome. Was it not advisable, he asked, to leave Munich altogether?[16]

On November 13 Gasparri informed Pacelli that Benedict XV had granted permission for him to move the nunciature, but that he should first seek the advice of the archbishop of Munich.[17] A week later Pacelli responded that the archbishop had advised him to leave Germany for Switzerland. "Today," he reported in the same letter, "I depart for the time being to Rorschach.... The state of things looks uncertain and grave."[18] Until perhaps as late as February of 1919,[19] Pacelli watched events unfold from a tranquil Swiss sanatorium run by nuns. Meanwhile, Monsignor Schioppa, the redoubtable *uditore*, was left in charge in Munich.

Although Eisner, Munich's new socialist leader, saw himself as a democrat, he had no pretensions to democratically based authority save for an unelected ragtag of workers' council. A politically inexperienced dreamer, his utopian style of government was both ludicrous and doomed. A young war veteran and anti-Semitic nationalist named Count Arco-Valley shot Eisner in the head on February 21 as he traveled to the Landtag, the Bavarian parliament.

After a week or two of outlandish misrule, on April 12 a reign of terror ensued under the red revolutionary trio of Max Levien, Eugen Levine, and Towia Axelrod. To hasten the dictatorship of the proletariat, the new regime kidnapped "middle-class" hostages, throwing them into Stadelheim Prison. They shut down the schools, imposed censorship, and requisitioned people's homes and possessions. Food was denied those families judged to be bourgeois. The regime trespassed on extraterritorial properties of various embassies and consulates, confiscating food, furniture, and automobiles.

Back in Munich, writing to the Secretariat of State,[20] Pacelli had a tale to tell. Following these "deplorable events," there was a meeting of the diplomatic corps to decide how they should act. After a long discussion, it was decided to speak directly with Levien, head of the Munich soviet, so as to secure an unequivocal understanding that the Communist government should recognize the immunity of diplomatic representatives and the extraterritoriality of their residences.

"Since it would have been totally undignified for me to appear in the presence of this aforesaid gentleman," Pacelli wrote, "I sent the *uditore* [Schioppa], who was received there this morning along with the chargé d'affaires of Prussia, Signore Conte von Zech."

Schioppa returned from Levien's headquarters at the former royal palace with sufficient eyewitness detail for the nuncio to re-create the circumstances for Gasparri's benefit. Pacelli's account is larded with sentiments that he either garnered from Schioppa, and endorsed, or invoked on his own behalf. The typewritten letter is signed and occasionally annotated by Pacelli personally:

The scene that presented itself at the palace was indescribable. The confusion totally chaotic, the filth completely nauseating; soldiers and armed workers coming and going; the building, once the home of a king, resounding with screams, vile language, profanities. Absolute hell. An army of employees were dashing to and fro, giving out orders, waving bits of paper, and in the midst of all this, a gang of young women, of dubious appearance, Jews like all the rest of them, hanging around in all the offices with lecherous demeanor and suggestive smiles. The boss of this female rabble was Levien's mistress, a young Russian woman, a Jew and a divorcée, who was in charge. And it was to her that the nunciature was obliged to pay homage in order to proceed.

This Levien is a young man, of about thirty or thirty-five, also Russian and a Jew. Pale, dirty, with drugged eyes, hoarse voice, vulgar, repulsive, with a face that is both intelligent and sly. He deigned to receive the Monsignor Uditore in the corridor, surrounded by an armed escort, one of whom was an armed hunchback, his faithful bodyguard. With a hat on his head and smoking a cigarette, he listened to what Monsignor Schioppa told him, whining repeatedly that he was in a hurry and had more important things to do.[21]

Pacelli's constant harping on the Jewishness of this party of power usurpers is consistent with the growing and widespread belief among Germans that the Jews were the instigators of the Bolshevik revolution, their principal aim being the destruction of Christian civilization. But there is something else about the passage that is repugnant and ominous. The repeated references to the Jewishness of these individuals, amid the catalogue of epithets describing their physical and moral repulsiveness, gives an impression of stereotypical anti-Semitic contempt.

According to Pacelli, Monsignor Schioppa insisted that the mission of the nuncio merited special treatment, whereupon Levien said in an "exaggeratedly ironic tone" that the nuncio's main aim was to defend the Center Party. To which the good monsignor replied "that the nuncio was there to defend the rights of all Catholics, not only in Bavaria but in the whole of Germany."

After this exchange, Schioppa was taken to a fellow called Comrade Dietrich, responsible for foreign affairs, who told the monsignor roundly that if the nuncio did anything against the interest of the Republic of the Councils he would be "thrown in jail." He added that there was no need for a nunciature in Munich, since there was now a complete separation of Church and State.

After calming down a little, the comrade then insisted, according to Pacelli, that the extraterritoriality of the nunciature would be respected and a certificate was issued to this effect.

The Nuncio's Car

A week or so later, Pacelli was obliged to confront a Red mob that came to the nunciature to confiscate the official limousine. The incident has often been cited to explain his great hatred of communism and to illustrate both his courage in the face of personal danger and the mesmerizing power of his saintly personality.[22] His personal doctor claimed that Pacelli had recurring dreams about the episode for the rest of his life.

The principal source of the story, as recounted after Pacelli's death, was his housekeeper, Sister Pasqualina Lehnert who had joined the nunciature in March of the previous year at the age of twenty-three. Sister Pasqualina (later Mother Pasqualina) was to become a crucial figure in Pacelli's domestic life and a source of much hagiographical anecdotal material. A nun from Bavaria, she had been plucked from primary-school teaching duties in a "small Swabian village," as she described it, and assigned to "two months' stand-in duty" at the Munich nunciature. The "stand-in duty" never ended. She was to act as his housekeeper and substitute mother for the rest of her life. In her memoir of Pacelli, first published in 1959, a year after his death, she claimed to have been a witness and indeed a leading participant in the limousine episode.

In her account, two members of the Red Brigade entered the house, having been admitted by the butler. Then Pacelli, who had been visiting a local hospital for treatment, turned up at the front door. At the very sight of the nuncio, she wrote, the men were "stunned"; they appeared to "lose consciousness," then, "shaking off the spell, they put the gun to the nuncio's breast and shouted that they would leave with the nunciature's car."[23] On the nuncio's orders, she says, the garage was opened up and the revolutionaries departed in the limousine.

With the recent opening of the Secretariat of State archives we now have for the first time an account of the incident in Pacelli's own words, dated April 30, 1919. Writing to Gasparri, Pacelli reported that the commandant of the Red Brigade of the South, a man named Seyler, along with an "accomplice" called Brongratz and other soldiers "armed with rifles, revolvers, and hand grenades," came to the nunciature. The butler opened the door and they barged in, declaring that they wanted to impound the car—"a splendid carriage," Pacelli comments, "with pontifical coat of arms."

"Since the Monsignor Uditore was out of the house," Pacelli wrote, "I presented myself and made it clear to the commander that this violent entry into the nunciature and the request for the car was a flagrant violation of the international rights of all civilized peoples, and I showed him the certificate of extraterritoriality that had been released by the Commissioner of the People for Foreign Affairs." In response, Pacelli went on, the "accomplice pressed his rifle against my breast and the commander, a horrible type of delinquent, having given the order to his satellites to hold ready their hand grenades, told me insolently that talk was pointless and he must have the car immediately."

Protesting vigorously, Pacelli wrote, he asked the butler to conduct the party to the garage, whereupon a new drama ensued. It appeared that, "having anticipated such an event," the nunciature's chauffeur had immobilized the vehicle. At this, the commandant phoned the Ministry of Military Affairs and was told that if the car was not immediately put into service they should blow up the place and "the whole nunciature gang" would be instantly arrested.

Meanwhile, word had been got to Monsignor Schioppa, who set about halting the confiscation of the car by application to the Red Brigade headquarters. As a result, three "security agents" turned up and persuaded the commandant to desist. By six o'clock in the evening, Seyler and his brigade left the building empty-handed. "All returned to peace at the nunciature," wrote Pacelli, "but not for long."

The next day, April 30, the same crew was back again at nine in the morning, this time with a document of requisition signed by Supreme Head Egelhofer of the Red Brigade. This time Schioppa was in charge, and Pacelli was safely absent. "I was at the clinic of Professor Jochner," Pacelli explained to Gasparri, "having recently suffered a strong attack of influenza and suffering from a bad stomach for which I was undergoing a special treatment."

By pleading with the revolutionary executive committee and the Italian military mission in Berlin, Monsignor Schioppa managed to get the order for the requisition rescinded. Seyler was obliged to countermand the order—"but not," commented Pacelli, "without the bile dripping from his lips as he uttered threatening words to the effect that the whole nunciature gang should be thrown in jail!"

The incident of the car, he informed Gasparri, was conducted to the sound of gunfire, signaling "the fratricidal battle between the Red Brigade and the White Brigade struggling for the liberation of the capital of Bavaria, which is suffering under a harsh Jewish-Russian revolutionary tyranny." Pacelli's eyewitness account of the event gives no hint of heroism or mesmerizing charisma, although he comes across as reasonably intrepid under the circumstances. If there was a hero in these events, it seems that it was Monsignor Schioppa.

After a final three-week spasm of revolution in Munich, President Ebert had sanctioned the use of the Freikorps and Reichswehr troops, made up of returned veterans, to crush the Munich Soviet Republic, which they did brutally and with considerable loss of life. As the government mercenary force fought pitched street battles to take over the city, there was one last insult to the nuncio's Munich palace before it was all over.

Late in the evening, five days after the car incident, Pacelli was again safely at a distance, spending the night at Professor Jochner's clinic. Monsignor Schioppa, despite suggestions that he, too, should sleep away, was in the building and had just finished his supper. Pacelli wrote another report for Gasparri from Schioppa's eyewitness account.[24] Apparently Schioppa had switched the light on in his bedroom and a cry went up from a platoon of militia patrolling the street outside. Believing that they were about to be fired upon, they sprayed the upper stories of the building with machine-gun bullets before assaulting the front door of the nunciature and demanding to make a search.

Schioppa led the party of militiamen through every room in the house and they found nothing. Leaving two guards on duty outside for the rest of the night, the platoon departed. Investigating the upper stories, Schioppa found devastation. The next morning he counted more than fifty holes in the masonry of the building's facade. "It was a miracle," Pacelli commented, "that one of the shells did not strike the gas pipe, which would have prompted an immense explosion."

This unnerving attack past, the Munich crisis was over, at least as far as Pacelli was concerned, and he could begin to contemplate the true purpose of his mission to Germany.

5

Pacelli and Weimar

Germany's economy was close to collapse, its alliances in tatters, its military might vanquished, its society vulnerable to revolution and civil war. Shamed, pressed by harsh peace terms at Versailles, Germany was in desperate need of friends and allies with moral influence. By coming to Germany's aid, the Holy See's nuncio could expect a special hearing when he argued for the legitimate interests of the Catholic Church. Already *L'Osservatore Romano*'s editorialists had pointed out, in February and again in April 1919, that the Allies should moderate their demands at the Versailles peace conference. And there was more that the Holy See could do on Germany's behalf, from bringing pressure to bear over disputed borders and territories to encouraging diplomatic links with former enemies and neutral countries. By the same token, the Holy See could only benefit by assisting Germany's return to economic and political health.[1] Before the war, Germany had donated more funds to the Holy See than all the other nations of the world put together. The longer it took Germany to revive its economy, the longer the Vatican would suffer fiscally.

The lay Catholic political leadership in Germany also saw the nation's new situation as a striking opportunity, but from a rather different perspective. Having shown unquestioning loyalty throughout the war, German Catholics trusted that their days of inferiority, their days of being regarded *Reichsfeinde* (enemies of the Fatherland), had at last ended. Catholics accounted for about a third of the German population in the postwar era. (In Hitler's Greater Reich—including the Saar, the Sude-tenland, and Austria—this would rise to almost half the population.) Catholics boasted a powerful web of social and political associations—trade unions, newspapers, publishing houses, youth groups, women's groups, schools, colleges—many of them originally developed and strengthened in reaction to Bismarck's persecution of the Catholic Church in the 1870s, and maintained and extended through four decades.

At the level of national politics, the Catholic Center Party emerged from the war as a major force with a nationwide network of offices and experienced parliamentary representatives. The party had yielded its leading position in the Reichstag to the Social Democrats in 1912, but it had nevertheless gained in influence during the war, pulling off a signifi-cant coup on April 19, 1917, by forcing the repeal of the anti-Jesuit laws of 1872. From that point on, the Society of Jesus was free to enter Germany and found communities, schools, and colleges, which it did with great energy.

In the election of mid-January 1919, the Center collected 6 million votes and 91 seats, second to the Social Democrats, who gained 11.5 million votes and 163 of the assembly's 421 seats. The Center Party thus became a key player in this and subsequent Weimar coalition gov-ernments, power-broking between the Social Democrats and the parties that accounted for the remaining 73 seats. Between 1919 and 1933, no less than five Catholic Center Party members became chancellors in ten cabinets.

The determination of Catholics to play a positive role in the creation of a postmonarchist, democratic, and pluralist Germany owed little or nothing to papal social teaching or papal encouragement. On the con-trary, the Center Party was repeatedly obliged to turn a deaf ear to the urgings of Pacelli—and Pope Pius XI, elected in 1922—to shun al-liances with the majority Social Democrats, with whom it was con-strained to form a partnership in government or else retreat into the political wilderness. All the same, the Catholic leadership, excluding a re-actionary element that harked back nostalgically to the days of princes, might have taken a crumb of comfort from the long-dead Leo XIII who had grudgingly conceded, citing the case of the United States, that re-publican democracy might offer one unobjectionable political system among others.[2]

A sense of the aspirations of the Catholic political leadership can be gleaned from the political and religious ideas of Max Scheler, the most prominent German Catholic philosopher and political scientist of the period. Scheler, an exact contemporary of Pacelli, and the product of a Protestant father and a Jewish mother, was to become a seminal influence in European Catholic thought throughout the century. In the 1950s, when Karol Wojtyla, the future John Paul II, labored over his thesis on the human person at Kraków seminary, the works of Scheler never left his elbow. Scheler, who by 1916 had shed an embarrassing earlier attachment to German nationalism (and who would one day leave the Catholic Church, having divorced and remarried), believed that Christian ethics could provide societies, communities, and individuals with guidance in concrete social and political situations. In other words, he believed Christianity to be a social religion. Scheler was opposed to an account of the individual that denied solidarity with others.[3] By the same token, he was against a communist style of collectivism that denied the responsibility and dignity of the individual.

Scheler's importance at this juncture is the extent to which he defines, by contrast, the growing influence of Eugenio Pacelli upon German Catholic affairs. In the darkest days of the Great War, Scheler proclaimed that Catholics should offer Germany and Europe neither strict Roman Catholic orthodoxy nor apologetics nor papal power from the Vatican, but a beneficent, self-determining influence rising from the smallest groups and communities. This influence he characterized as "generous and gentle rather than harsh," "concrete rather than abstract," "rooted in people and lived tradition rather than ahistorical principles," "more attached to the organic than artificial elites." These comparisons indicated the gulf that lay, in his perception, between social Catholicism and the pyramidal ideology of papal supremacy that saw the Pope as an initiating doctrinal and ecclesiastical autocrat. Scheler saw the future of the Center Party and Catholic unions, moreover, as rallying points for Christian democrats of every complexion; nor were Jews to be excluded.[4] Catholic influence, he insisted, must not merely stand alongside something called Germanhood—"rather, it must be woven into it and be evident in international relationships."[5]

This idea of an imminent Catholic "moment," combining internal reconciliation and international outreach, was endorsed by Matthias

Erzberger, the influential Catholic Center Party deputy. From 1916 onward, Scheler and Erzberger had collaborated as peace activists. Scheler had made frequent journeys to Switzerland, Holland and Austria, as an emissary of armistice and disarmament. It was Erzberger who represented Germany at the signing of the Treaty of Versailles, earning him in time the slur of a "November criminal" and his eventual assassination.

As early as 1917, Erzberger sought to persuade Archbishop Michael von Faulhaber of Bavaria that, win or lose the war, a "great Catholic renaissance" was in the offing. In the year of the four hundredth jubilee of Luther's antipapal Wittenberg Theses, Catholicism should be seen as a focus of a Christian cultural and intellectual revival, he told the prelate. Its natural center, he suggested, should be Munich, the heart of Catholic Bavaria, but its benefits should be shared with the entire nation.

Erzberger was typical of those Catholic politicians who were urging a new political pragmatism on the part of Catholics in postwar Germany. No longer was Germany synonymous with Protestantism: a spirit of conciliation and tolerance was needed on both sides of the great religious divide. Erzberger urged that Catholics, who had traditionally failed to enjoy a proportionate share of places in higher education, the professions, and civil service, must now take their rightful place in the community and make their presence felt.

At the very point, however, when German Catholics were aspiring to make a difference by becoming part of the warp and woof of German culture, society, and politics—at the very moment when even Protestant politicians were talking of forging new links with the Holy See—a historic Vatican initiative was about to subvert the entire process. Pacelli's mission as papal nuncio was the negotiation of a Church-State treaty that would recall the four hundredth anniversary of Luther's Reformation in an altogether different fashion from that envisaged by Erzberger. It was on December 10, 1520, at the Lestertor in Wittenberg, that Luther and his students burned the corpus of canon law in token of their break with Rome. The act symbolized not only Luther's defiance of papal authority but his conviction that Rome "exalts its own ordinances above the commands of God." The volumes of canon law, Luther had complained, "say nothing about Christ." That historic act of apostasy, sacred to German Protestantism, lent immense import to

Pacelli's ambition—the bid, after four centuries, to achieve official government recognition of, and indeed acquiescence in, the imposition
upon German Catholics of the 1917 Code of Canon Law. That new
code, as we have seen, was a work dedicated to the concentration of
Church authority in the person of the Pope. Here, in this act of supreme
summitry and centralization, as far as Pacelli was concerned, lay the future source of Catholic unity, spirit, culture, and authority—in striking
contrast to the pragmatic, pluralist, communitarian Catholicism urged
by Scheler and Erzberger.

Pacelli's Concordat and Hitler

The acquiescence of the German people in the face of Nazism cannot
be understood in its entirety without taking into account the long path,
beginning as early as 1920, to the Reich Concordat of 1933, Pacelli's
crucial role in it, and Hitler's reasons for signing it. The negotiations
were conducted exclusively by Pacelli on behalf of the Pope over the
heads of the faithful, the clergy, and the German bishops. (When Hitler
became Pacelli's partner in negotiations, the concordat thus became the
supreme act of two authoritarians, while the supposed beneficiaries were
correspondingly weakened, undermined, and neutralized.) Diplomatic
correspondence of the period, to the end of 1929, shows Gasparri and
Pacelli signing most of the documents, with the pontiff playing Moses
to Gasparri's Aaron.[6] But, as will be apparent, the strategy and the style,
particularly from 1930, were shaped and directed by Pacelli himself.

For centuries, Vatican concordats had enshrined a variety of agreements between the Holy See and secular governments, securing rights to
define doctrine; conditions of bestowing sacraments; rights to worship
and education; laws concerning property, seminaries, clerical and episcopal appointments and salaries; marriage and annulment law. The terms
of concordats before the First World War varied from country to country and even, as with Germany, from regional state to regional state, each
treaty being tailor-made to local circumstances, customs, and secular
patronage.

In the light of the 1917 code, however, the Vatican's concordat policy
was transformed. Thenceforward the concordat was to become an in-

strument of consensus by which the lives of bishops, clergy, religious, and faithful were regulated, top-down, everywhere and anywhere in the world on an equal basis. In addition, the concordat assumed the papacy's right to bind the faithful, without consultation, to whatever conditions it saw fit for them to embrace in the course of local negotiations.

Thirteen years on, one man, Adolf Hitler, was to stand between Pacelli and his dreams of a super concordat that would impose the full force of canon law equally on all Catholics in Germany. Anticipating that final negotiation, the principal condition imposed by Hitler in 1933 was to be nothing less than voluntary withdrawal of German Catholics from social and political action as Catholics, including the voluntary disbanding of the Center Party, by then the sole surviving viable democratic party in Germany. This abdication from political Catholicism was to be implemented by Pacelli himself (who had risen by that time to Cardinal Secretary of State in the Vatican), using the considerable powers of persuasion at his command.

Pacelli's remarkable agenda was impelled, as we have seen, by an almost messianic conviction through three generations of the Pacelli family, that the Church could survive and remain united in the modern world only by strengthening papal authority through the application of law. Pacelli's concordat policy focused not so much on the interests of the German Church but on the pyramidal model of Church authority that had been in the making since Pio Nono. Unlike Scheler and Erzberger, Pacelli was not concerned about the fate of parallel faiths, religious communities, or institutions, or about human rights and social ethics. Complaints against the Nazi regime by the German episcopate, when they came, were mostly preoccupied with transgressions against Catholic interests cited in the terms of the concordat, and were funneled through the Vatican.

Nothing could have been further from the notion of strength through organic, self-determining, pluralist Catholicism acting as a rallying point for interconfessional Christian democracy. Nothing could have been better designed to deliver the powerful institution of the Catholic Church in Germany into the hands of Hitler. In the immediate aftermath of the Great War, however, the contrasting aspirations of Rome on the one hand and the German Catholic leadership on the other, and their remote consequences, had yet to be grasped.

Pacelli's Concordat Strategy

From the outset, Pacelli confronted a series of obstacles arising from the long and checkered history of Germany's relationship with the papacy. With no help from Pacelli, some of these difficulties began to crumble after the drawing up of a new constitution at Weimar, a small and ancient city in Thuringia that gave its name to the series of governments that ruled Germany until Hitler's accession to power.

In 1872 Bismarck had grandiloquently ruled out for all time the notion of a Reich Concordat with the Vatican in a notorious speech to the Reichstag. "I do not believe," he said, referring to the dogma of papal infallibility and primacy, "that after the recently expressed and publicly promulgated dogmas of the Catholic Church it is possible for a secular power to arrive at a concordat without that power to some degree or in some manner losing face. This the German Reich cannot accept at all."[7]

The occasion of that speech was the dissolution of a Reich legation to the Holy See, effectively leaving Germany, Prussia, and the Vatican without mutual representation and with no written understandings to protect the rights of Catholics in Prussia save for the papal bull of 1821 *De salute animarum*,[8] to which the Prussian king had given his grudging "permission and sanction." In 1882, as Bismarck's anti-Catholic persecutions came to an end, a Prussian legation to the Holy See was restored in Rome, but there was still no Reich legation. And that remained the case in 1918. The problem was, then: how could Pacelli begin to negotiate a Reich Concordat without a nunciature in Berlin at the level of an embassy, and likewise without a Reich embassy at the Holy See in Rome?

Putting this matter to rights was one of Pacelli's priorities.

With the ratification of the constitution in Weimar on August 11, 1919, he realized that the new republic's decision to separate Church and State appeared to open the way to Prussia's acceptance of the crucial canon endowing the Pope with sole power to nominate new bishops. Article 137 of the new constitution seemed to sweep away State prerogatives over ecclesiastical matters by declaring that religious associations would govern their own affairs "without the involvement of the state or the civil community," thus returning governance to the churches, or, as Pacelli read the matter for Catholics, to the Pope in person. There was a snag, however, since the article was only an outline regulation, the details being left to individual regional states. Hence the urgency, as Pacelli judged the matter, of negotiating concordats with the states one by one, while at the same time probing the feasibility of a Reich Concordat.

In another Weimar provision, Pacelli saw a useful ambiguity that would aid his overall strategy. Article 78 asserted that "the maintenance of relations with foreign states is exclusively the business of the Reich"; but since the Holy See was, strictly speaking, a foreign sovereign, as Pacelli saw it, and not strictly a foreign state, this suggested a way of establishing links with both the regional states and the Reich, with rich potential for playing one off against the other.

Another article of supreme importance to all German Catholic parents no less than to Pacelli, the new constitution reserved for the Reich extensive powers over religious education, especially over school inspections, the structure of curricula, standards of qualification, and the hiring and firing of teaching staff. Since the seedbed of Catholicism was the schools, Pacelli was determined that this article of the constitution must go, at least for Catholics—although he had no intention of challenging the constitution's obligation to underwrite the funding of religious schools and religious education in state schools. Far from it. Starting with the regional state of Bavaria, Pacelli aimed to introduce correctives on the schools question in all the regional states of Germany, with the ultimate intention of making a final deletion for the entire nation-state in a future all-embracing Reich Concordat.

The state of Bavaria in the south of Germany, with its large Catholic population and historic links with the Church of Rome, was an obvious starting point for his first state concordat. In the meantime, the predominantly Protestant state of Prussia, which shared its capital with the seat of the Reich government, could wait a while. Catholic Bavaria, with its sense of cultural independence from the north, was always eager to test the extent of its regional autonomy, and Pacelli thus had an opportunity to set a precedent by creating a model concordat with a pro-papal state.

The Question of Bishops

Pacelli, however, had another reason for treating the Protestant state of Prussia with circumspection at this early stage. On November 11, 1919,

the great and ancient See of Cologne, within Prussia, fell vacant with the
death of Cardinal Archbishop Felix von Hartmann, thus putting to the
test the crucial new canon of the 1917 code reserving the nomination of
a new archbishop to the Pope himself. Since time immemorial, the
nomination in Cologne had been reserved to the canons of the cathedral
in a free election, according to local and ancient precedent, confirmed in
the papal bull of 1821. This first test of the new code raised passionate
issues of centrist papal absolutism versus local discretion.

On the very day of Hartmann's death, the nine principal canons of
the chapter of Cologne, two of them auxiliary bishops, signed a letter to
the Holy Father seeking his blessing, "since it is now incumbent on us
to elect a new archbishop."[9] This prompted an "urgent" enciphered
telegram from Gasparri to Pacelli on November 17: he must inform the
canons that "regarding the name of the archbishop they will await instructions from the Holy See."[10] A week after Hartmann's demise,
Pacelli wrote to the canons of Cologne that they should by no means
proceed to an election but "await instructions on the nomination of an
archbishop, which the Holy See will not fail to send."[11] The canons,
however, were not inclined to surrender their ancient rights, and the
Prussian government was determined not to remain neutral in the matter.

On December 2 Pacelli received a letter from the Prussian chargé
d'affaires expressing the firm opinion of his government that the
Weimar constitution did not alter the provision of the papal bull *De
salute animarum*.[12] In other words, Pacelli's interpretation of the new constitutional split of Church and State in the Vatican's favor was being vigorously challenged in Prussia, at least as far as the selection of new
Catholic bishops was concerned. Any attempt to interfere in the election of the Cologne bishop, the charge went on, "would have the gravest
consequences for relations between the Holy See and German
Catholics." And there was worse to come. In an enciphered cable dated
December 15, Pacelli warned Gasparri that the canons of Cologne
had told him in their reply that they had reason to believe the Prussian
government would withdraw the appropriate episcopal salary and ex-
penses for the archbishopric if the Holy See unilaterally altered the election procedure. "Do you want to maintain your previous instructions?"
Pacelli cabled Gasparri.[13]

In the meantime, in the first week of December, the papal nuncio in Switzerland, Luigi Maglione, had learned from the Prussian minister at the Holy See, Diego von Bergen, that the Prussian government, the German bishops, and the canons of Cologne were all in agreement that the present bishop of Paderborn, Monsignor Schulte, was the best candidate for the vacancy. Maglione's consequent suggestion to Gasparri exemplifies the subtle machinations of papal diplomacy of the era.

"If perhaps he was also acceptable to the Holy Father, as I think it to be the case," wrote Maglione, "then filling this most important vacancy would proceed with the great satisfaction of everyone in Germany."[14] Maglione then pointed out, with the utmost delicacy, that a German emissary had given him to understand that the government would be reasonable about the choice of Schulte (this "excellent" candidate "in the eyes of all concerned") if there were some indication that he might be made a cardinal in the next consistory. Maglione then ventured to point out that there were no Germans named in the next consistory (the announced nomination of new cardinals by the Pope), and yet Poland, "this state of recent constitution," had two cardinals already named, one of them the "archbishop of Gnesen and Posen—a region torn away from the homeland of Germany."

Doubtless under the suave tutelage of the Swiss nuncio, the German emissary had distanced himself from any scintilla of complaint or moral blackmail. Maglione could report that the emissary had added: "I only wish to inform the Holy See that our people have been made all the more sensitive and more susceptible as a result of the many sufferings that they have come through; so much so that they are loath to suspect that they do not enjoy the august benevolence of the Holy Father." In other words, if the Holy Father wants to show that he is sincerely not anti-German, he had best give us a cardinal.

On December 17 Gasparri sent another enciphered cable to Pacelli, modifying his previous instructions in the light of the agreement on the candidate. "Your Excellency should proceed to Berlin where the government will not oppose the appointment [of Schulte], since it has now been consulted. Your Excellency will then go to Cologne and tell the chapter that just on this occasion they can have the bishop of Paderborn, since the consent of the government is already in place."[15]

So Pacelli swept down to Cologne by train and told the assembled canons that on this occasion, and this alone, they could elect a new arch-bishop according to their ancient privileges, but they were to understand that this was not to be a permanent arrangement for the future.

Pacelli's acquiescence in 1919 was made easier since he and the Curia were of one mind on the canons' nominee;[16] but there were other reasons for Pacelli to feel sanguine about his wider strategy and his conviction that he would get his own way eventually with the Reich, even while he seemed to be failing with Prussia.

Berlin-Munich Machinations

On September 27, 1919 Foreign Minister Hermann Müller announced that the Prussian legation in Rome was to become a fully fledged German embassy to the Holy See, and that Diego von Bergen, with the agreement of the Vatican, was to be its first ambassador, representing the entire Reich as well as the state of Prussia. Matthias Erzberger, who had been promoted to *Reichsminister*, now saw no obstacle to a Reich Concordat, a complete restructuring of Church-State relations between the Vatican and Germany "to be conducted by all states in concert, under the leadership of the Reich,"[17] and he announced as much at a banquet given by the president and the chancellor in Pacelli's honor in Berlin after Christmas.

There were, however, inherent difficulties in the Vatican embassy arrangement, involving complex and ancient rivalries between Bavaria and Prussia, Munich and Berlin, Catholic Germany and Protestant Germany. But Pacelli was about to resolve these problems with the astuteness of a wily poker player, to the congratulatory satisfaction of the Pope and Curia in Rome. As far as the ministers in Berlin were concerned, the decision to establish a Reich embassy to the Holy See in Rome was made on the assumption that the existing Bavarian legation would be closed. But that was not at all to Pacelli's liking. He did not intend dealing exclusively with the traditionally Protestant Reich if there was a possibility of playing divide-and-rule by simultaneously negotiating with Catholic Bavaria. Hence he proceeded to reap the advantage of the divisions and rivalries between national and local government in Germany, throwing in an item of diplomatic blackmail for good measure.

He would prefer, Pacelli told the state and Reich governments in Berlin, "a Reich embassy to the Vatican [in Rome], with a papal nunciature for German affairs (excluding Bavaria) in Berlin, and a Bavarian legation to the Vatican in Rome, with a papal nunciature in Munich." But if the Reich government could not see its way to accepting this arrangement, he went on, the Holy See would wish "to maintain the *status quo ante*." In other words, he would refrain from sanctioning a mutual diplomatic representation between the Reich and the Holy See, with the consequent loss to Germany of the Vatican as an eloquent ally on the world stage. Whatever the case, the nuncio was saying, the Holy See was determined "to maintain the nunciature in Munich."[18]

A measure of its desperation, the Reich gave in and Prussia agreed that its own representation in Rome should become a division of the Reich embassy to the Vatican. In the meantime, Gasparri told the German ambassador in May 1920 that the nuncio to the Reich would take up residence in Berlin and that Pacelli would fill that appointment. The Holy See announced, however, that for the time being the new nuncio to the Reich would continue as nuncio in Munich, representing Bavaria, and that he would commute between the two cities as he saw fit. Pacelli now held all the reins in his hands, and his diplomatic skills could be seen in every detail of these remarkable arrangements. Matters had come a long way since early 1917, when Matthias Erzberger advised Pacelli's predecessor in Munich, the late Archbishop Aversa, that the kaiser would never agree to a Bavarian nuncio's being subsequently accredited to the Reich or to Prussia, since this would be tantamount to making the Reich play second fiddle.[19]

Yet, skillful as it seemed, this diplomatic sleight of hand delayed the negotiation of a Reich Concordat. And the consequence of that failure, in the view of German Church historian Klaus Scholder, "created the fatal starting point from which in 1933 Hitler was to force the capitulation of German Catholicism within a few weeks."[20] In other words, Pacelli could have achieved a Reich Concordat in the early 1920s without compromising Catholic political and social action. A decade later, Hitler cunningly saw the concordat as an opportunity to secure the *voluntary* withdrawal of political Catholicism, confrontation with which he was determined to avoid.

Pacelli the Diplomatic Doyen

On June 30, 1920, Pacelli presented his credentials to the Reich, the first
diplomat to do so under the Weimar government. Thus he became the
senior diplomat in the capital, an honor that he was to grace with outstanding charm and distinction.[21] Having warmly welcomed the nuncio,
President Friedrich Ebert solemnly announced that his duty was to order, "with the proper authorities, the relations between Church and State
in Germany [so] that they correspond to the new situation and to contemporary conditions." Pacelli responded: "For my part, I will devote
my entire strength to cultivating and strengthening the relations between
the Holy See and Germany." (Thirteen years later, Hitler used the selfsame phrase, word for word, when he promised an immediate readjust-
ment of relations between Berlin and the Holy See in exchange for the
Center Party's acquiescence in the Enabling Act that awarded him dictatorial powers.)[22]

Having pronounced these glowing phrases, Pacelli now turned almost
exclusively to the negotiation of a concordat with the Bavarian government, with which he had already lodged an outline treaty that amazed
ministers for its audacity. On the schools question, for example, he insisted that the state would be bound by any and all proposals of the local bishop regarding teachers of religion, and that the state would be
obliged to fire such teachers if the bishop so demanded. Meanwhile, the
state would be required to meet all financial obligations and at the same
time guarantee the application of canon law to the faithful.[23]

The reaction in Munich to Pacelli's shopping list of demands was not
so much dismay as shock, even among those who were warmly disposed
to a concordat. In September 1920 the civil servant in charge of Vatican
affairs at the Foreign Office in Berlin, Professor Richard Delbrück,
recorded the "ill feeling" prompted in Munich by Pacelli's "excessive demands." He also observed that "the most striking thing about Pacelli
is that he seems to have little awareness of what is possible in Germany
and that he negotiates as if he were dealing with Italians."[24]

Delbrück also discovered the lengths to which Pacelli was prepared to
go. The nuncio would secure his demands by open threats of diplomatic
reprisal. Unless his terms were met, Pacelli told the Bavarian government,
there would be no concordat; and if there were no concordat, then the

Holy See could not see its way to assist in the event of territorial disputes with Germany's neighbors, "for example, in the question of the Saar diocese, which could be an acute issue at any time. With deep regret it would have to yield."

Pacelli was referring to the delicate issue of former German territories annexed or demilitarized by the Allies at the end of the war. Many of these territories, both east and west, were inhabited by Catholics. Should these territories remain within their old German dioceses? And if not, were the clergy at least to come from German seminaries, thus giving Germany a continuing influence?[25] Clearly it was in the interest of the German government to maintain German cultural and religious influence over these separated subjects, something that Pacelli himself could influence with the stroke of a pen. But with extraordinary nerve he informed the Bavarian government, and hence the Reich, that this cooperation came at a price: namely, surrender on the schools question.

Such was the Reich's anxiety over the border issue that approval of the Bavarian outline concordat, including the requirements on education, was granted in November 1920: an apparent triumph for Pacelli. The question remained: what impression was this giving to Protestant Germany, and Prussia in particular? In December Pacelli granted an interview to Le Temps in Paris, expanding on his plans to pursue an identical concordat with the rest of Germany or with Prussia. Once again he was keeping his options open as to which way he would jump: Prussia first? Or the Reich? In the meantime, he was being lobbied by both parties: by the Reich and separately by the regional Prussian government, which feared that the Reich would be a pushover for Pacelli and hence wished to set its own criteria for a concordat in advance.

A Domestic Drama

Pacelli was drawn into a domestic storm at this time, prompted by a below-stairs power struggle between Sister Pasqualina, his young housekeeper, and the lay staff.[26] It appears that a clique among the permanent staff, resentful of the advent of the sister, set about making life difficult for her. As beatification witnesses have testified, she could be a troublesome woman, especially when her work companions lacked her sharpness. She had what one beatification witness described in Italian as *"snellezza,"* her agility.

With the permission of Pacelli, Pasqualina eventually took on the entire household management of the nunciature, including the cleaning, cooking, and laundry, effectively making her antagonists redundant. Thenceforward she was supreme in her domain. According to Pacelli's sister, Elisabetta, however, the household enemies responded by spreading a rumor in Munich that the nuncio had cast more than priestly eyes on her.

Pacelli was naturally stung by the accusation, as his sister Elisabetta told the beatification tribunal fifty years later, and insisted on an investigation of this *"orribile calunnia"*—this horrible slander—at the highest level in the Vatican. He later wrote to her, Elisabetta said, expressing his satisfaction with the verdict of the *inchiesta,* declaring that he had "found peace and tranquillity of spirit once more—of which he had great need so as to carry on the heavy burden of his work."[27]

At about this time, Pacelli began to enjoy the benefit of an ideal assistant in the Jesuit Robert Leiber. Leiber, a quiet and diminutive man, is described in one beatification testimony as a "melancholy and sad type, always sighing, but who was a great worker and thought in complete unison with the nuncio on the problems of the Church." The two worked together long hours, side by side. Father Leiber is reported to have said of Pacelli in those days: "He is a born monarch." Leiber had a view, too, of Sister Pasqualina: "The nuncio should send her packing, but he doesn't want to because she knows the domestic economy of the house extremely well."[28]

The Black Shame

A significant instance of the national and international problems facing Pacelli during this period was the dispute between Germany and France over the use of black troops in the occupied Rhineland. As early as April 1920, responding to requests of German bishops and lay petitioners, Pacelli had informed Gasparri that France's black troops were routinely raping German women and children in the Rhineland and that the influence of the Holy See should be employed to bring pressure on the

French government to remove these soldiers forthwith. On December 31, 1920, Cardinal Adolf Bertram of Breslau wrote a letter (in Latin) to Gasparri, declaring that "France preferred to employ African troops, who in the savage absence of culture and morals have inflicted unspeakable assaults on the womenfolk of the region in a situation that has come to be known as the 'Black Shame.'"[29] The French were planning, Bertram claimed, to send even more black troops to the area. In the meantime, a German government inquiry had produced plentiful evidence of "the crimes committed by these troops: a catalogue of sadistic abuse, rapes, and horrendous assaults on women and cruelty to children, among other things."

In a reply to Gasparri on January 16,[30] the French ambassador to the Holy See vigorously dismissed Pacelli's and Bertram's allegations, describing them as "odious propaganda" inspired by Berlin. The facts were, he asserted, that there was only a handful of North African troops in the region, most of whom were of "an old civilization and among whom there were many Christians." In the meantime, an international campaign had now been whipped up against the black troops and their alleged atrocities. In the United States, under a barrage of patently racist petitions, the House of Representatives commissioned an investigation,[31] which disproved the German charges. The committee advised that the United States should take no action on the complaints coming from the German government and the Holy See.

But Pacelli, who was in receipt of the investigation, remained unconvinced. On March 7, 1921, he again wrote to Gasparri, urging the Pope to intervene on behalf of molested German women and children. Gasparri made no further representations to the French government, but allegations of the "Black Shame" continued to reverberate until the territories were eventually liberated. For Pacelli, however, the episode was a shaping experience in his attitude to race and war. Twenty-five years later, when the Allies were about to enter Rome, he asked the British ambassador to the Holy See to beg the British Foreign Office that "no Allied colored troops would be among the small number that might be garrisoned at Rome after the occupation."[32]

6

The Glittering Diplomat

In the course of 1921, Pacelli continued to maneuver himself between the Reich and Prussia, seeking the most advantageous negotiating posture in pursuit of his concordat policy. To his aid and service at this time came an unusual individual: Ludwig Kaas, an expert in canon law, representative of the Catholic Center Party in the Reichstag, and (strange for a full-time politician) a Roman Catholic priest. Five years Pacelli's junior, dapper, bespectacled, and invariably accompanied by a smart walking stick, Kaas, known as "the prelate," became an intimate collaborator of Pacelli's on every aspect of the concordat negotiations. Ominously, as it turned out for the German people, while he was officially a "spokesman for the Reich," Kaas was increasingly devoted to Pacelli.

Kaas haunts the story of Pacelli's concordat policy and the eventual involvement with Hitler, his ambiguous position waxing ever more extraordinary. It was Kaas who was to succeed as leader of the Center Party when ex-chancellor Wilhelm Marx resigned in October 1928. Kaas was the first priest to assume leadership of the Center Party in its long history, and at a time when there was a growing gulf between the interests of the Vatican and those of German Catholicism. Encouraged by Pacelli, he slipped in as a compromise candidate as a result of a vote split between left- and right-wing lay candidates. As it turned out, Kaas's pretense to represent the party that held the balance of power in Germany to the very last was belied by the facts: by 1931 he was, to all intents and purposes, Pacelli's private personal assistant, his friend, confidant, and beloved companion. He represented the interests of Pacelli and the papacy from first to last.

Like Pacelli, Kaas was convinced that the new Code of Canon Law was the central feature of any future concordat. Kaas, moreover, consistently encouraged Pacelli to believe that a comprehensive and overriding Reich Concordat was necessary to prevent individual regional states from invoking measures characteristic of the Kulturkampf. It was this conviction, in part, that was to lead Pacelli into the noose set by Hitler, who would offer many reassurances on that score in 1933.[1]

Meanwhile, through the summer of 1921 the Reich government, now under the chancellorship of Joseph Wirth, a left-wing Center politician, was exerting pressure on Pacelli to conclude an early Reich Concordat in the hope that it would assist Germany in a bitter territory dispute with Poland. Poland had laid claim to Upper Silesia; Wirth was convinced that closer ties with the Vatican could help. Pacelli dragged his feet, possibly because he disapproved of Wirth's leftist tendencies.

In the autumn, hoping to lure Pacelli into talks, Wirth asked the nuncio to at least give him in writing a list of points to which the Holy See attached special importance. What Pacelli gave him in return was more or less a draft of the Bavarian Concordat, with conditions relating to the schools question that for Prussia constituted an insult.[2] Once again Pacelli astonished ministers by adding open threats. At a meeting in the *Kultusministerium* in December 1921, he told both the minister Otto Boelitz and Secretary of State Carl Heinrich Becker that he would assist Germany by making a rapid appointment of a German bishop to Trier in the Saar region, an area under territorial dispute with France, only if the government would cooperate on the schools question in the concordat. Then he added his usual rider, informing them blandly that the Holy See would think itself better off without a concordat if it could not get its own way over the schools. The ministers observed at the end of the meeting that the problems of German politics appeared beyond Pacelli's grasp.[3] All the same, following intensive negotiations, on January 6, 1922, in exchange for a speedy appointment of a German bishop in Trier, Pacelli wrung from Prussia an agreement that it would at least discuss the schools issue "at the request of the Reich."[4]

Having drawn an equivalence between the schools question and menacing territorial issues, Pacelli boasted about his triumph to Cardinal Adolf Bertram, adding that his success in the matter was owed not to any talents of his own but to God. Cardinal Bertram and Archbishop Schulte, the leading Catholic prelates in Prussia, were aghast. Writing to Bertram on January 9, Schulte described the deal as "a most extraordinary risk," since it would only tend to encourage the French to greater acts of territorial aggression. In the fullness of time, reflected Schulte, it would work against the interests of the Vatican in Germany. As a result of these exchanges, Bertram implored Pacelli not to overreach himself, as the Prussian state's jurisdiction in education was sacrosanct. Pacelli, however, knew better than his German hierarchy.

Thus he proceeded, turning a deaf ear to the advice of his brother bishops, ignoring German social and political realities, so obsessed with winning on the schools question that he disregarded other serious implications: a characteristic mixture of persistence and recklessness that would make him an eminently suitable negotiating partner from Hitler's point of view a decade later.[5]

A New Pope

On January 22, Benedict XV died after a short illness and was succeeded on February 6 by Achille Ratti, who became Pius XI. Ratti, the sixty-four-year-old son of a silk-factory manager near Milan, was a scholar, an expert palaeographer, and an archivist; he was also an enthusiastic mountaineer. After a stint at the Vatican library, he had been sent to Poland as nuncio, where he distinguished himself as a skillful and courageous diplomat. In 1921 he was appointed archbishop of Milan and created a cardinal. Short and thickset, with an Alpine climber's physique, he had a broad, high forehead and penetrating eyes. He exuded smiles when greeting pilgrims or receiving visitors, but he could be stern. A prelate commented that preparing for a meeting with Ratti was like preparing for an examination. His cross-questioning was fierce, and woe betide a cleric who did not have the answers. He was to become one of the most self-willed pontiffs in the recent history of the papacy.

For the first time since 1870 the blessing *urbi et orbi* was given from the loggia above St. Peter's Square, indicating that Pius XI was determined to resolve the Roman Question. The rector of the English college, watching the new Pope as he stood looking out over St. Peter's, recollected that "he was as calm and self-possessed as when he stood on the summit of Monte Rosa or spent the night on that rocky ledge in the Alpine storm."[6]

Pacelli and Ratti were well known to each other, and of one mind in their hatred and fear of Bolshevism. To Pacelli's considerable advantage, one of Ratti's first decisions was to retain Pietro Gasparri as Secretary of State. There would be no change in the concordat policy.

While pursuing the concordat renegotiations with the regional states, Pacelli was also absorbed through 1923 and 1924 with the bitter domestic and international crises sparked by the French occupation of the Ruhr Valley and the collapse of the German mark.

On January 11, 1923, claiming that coal and timber deliveries had been withheld, French and Belgian troops occupied the heavily industrialized Ruhr region. In retaliation, Berlin halted reparations payments and called for passive resistance and strikes, obliging the government to pay compensation to the resisting workers. Terrorist groups struck at railways and other industrial assets with the help of the German army. There were waves of arrests, executions, expulsions, and harsh measures against civilians. The mark went into free fall against the U.S. dollar, first to 18,000, then to 160,000 by July 1. By November the rate was four billion marks to one dollar, and thereafter the figures multiplied into trillions.

The French bitterly complained that the Vatican was favoring Germany. Gasparri turned a deaf ear. Benefiting from Pacelli's reports, the Cardinal Secretary of State on numerous occasions warned of the threat of a Communist takeover in the region if Germany were made desperate by French measures. Under pressure from the German ambassador to the Holy See, and as a result of Pacelli's reports, which also harped on the threat to his concordat prospects, Pius XI published an open letter in *L'Osservatore Romano* on June 28, condemning the harsh reparations terms and criticizing France for its occupation of parts of western Germany. The Germans were overjoyed. The French were furious. Largely due to Pacelli's diplomacy, the two sides were drawn together, although the French remained suspicious of Vatican intentions.[7] Meanwhile, Gasparri, acting in concert with Pacelli, and through the mediation of "secret unofficial missions," issued warnings to French prelates that France was playing a dangerous game in the Ruhr: he had received reports that

Russia was about to take advantage of the turmoil in Western Europe. Thus, via private meetings, coded dispatches, and whispered suggestions in both French and German ears, the Vatican used its good offices to bring both sides together.

Bavarian Concordat

Pacelli's efforts to conclude a Bavarian Concordat finally bore fruit in March of 1924, when the document was ready for the signatures of both sides. Pius XI and Pacelli had sat together in the apostolic palace, going over the German text of the treaty word by word in early January 1924. A few days later, it was passed in the Bavarian parliament by 73 votes to 52. It had been a long and arduous business, stretching over five years. Gasparri was well satisfied, and especially with his protégé Pacelli, to the point of extolling him to the Bavarian legate in Rome as being "one of the best nuncios, if not *the* best."[8]

The concordat ensured that the new Code of Canon Law would be recognized by the Bavarian state as the norm for appointing archbishops, bishops, monsignori, and canons. It gave Pacelli all the powers he had demanded for religious schools and indeed for religious instruction throughout the entire educational system. It achieved, besides, recognition, protection, and advancement of the Catholic Church and all its associations and institutions for all time. In return, in Article 13, the Church conceded that because the Bavarian state was paying the salaries of the clergy, only those with Bavarian citizenship or the citizenship of another state within Germany would be employed.[9]

Pacelli's success with the Bavarian Concordat, however, immediately created problems for the prospects of a Reich and a Prussian Concordat. Prussian ministers were all the more suspicious, since Pacelli was publicly boasting that he planned to use a Reich Concordat to impose his will on them. On November 27 the Prussian government informed the Reich that since Bavaria had negotiated its own concordat, Prussia must emphatically have one special to itself as well. It was unacceptable for the largest German state to have its Church-State policies dictated in Rome rather than in Berlin, ministers insisted. At the same time, they declared that there could be no Reich Concordat without the consent of the Prussian government.

Pacelli the Accomplished Host

Pacelli formally moved to Berlin on August 18, 1925, and settled into a splendid nunciature residence surrounded by parklike grounds at Rauchstrasse 21 in the Tiergarten quarter. Tall, elegant in his purple silk cloak, he became a familiar figure in the capital, arriving in his limousine at the Reich and Prussian ministries, or sweeping into receptions at the embassies.

He began to throw parties for the diplomatic and official elite of the capital, acquiring a reputation as an accomplished host. President Ebert was a regular guest at the nunciature, as was Field Marshal Paul von Hindenburg, Foreign Minister Gustav Stresemann, and other members of the cabinet. Pacelli became known as a delightful dinner guest, famed for his amusing repartee and ability to talk on any topic in virtually any language. Lord D'Abernon, British ambassador in Berlin from 1930 to 1936, thought Pacelli the "best-informed diplomatist in Berlin."[10] According to the American journalist Dorothy Thompson, Pacelli was indeed "the best-informed diplomat in Germany."[11] Pacelli began to relax and enjoy himself a little, abandoning his customary asceticism in the interests of oiling the wheels of diplomacy. There are stories of him exercising horses on the estates of the wealthy outside Berlin. According to Sister Pasqualina, Berlin friends purchased for him a mechanical horse that worked by electricity. He rode it, she claims, wearing jodhpurs and a hacking jacket.

Writing after his death, Pasqualina recollected that "he won everybody's hearts by his refined, noble modesty ... everywhere he revealed himself as the superior and yet the humanly warm Prince of the Church." She recalled, in her characteristically saccharine fashion, that despite his high calling as the Berlin nuncio, "his gaze did not miss the flower that graced his table, or the little gesture meant to make his simple meal more enjoyable, even the cat that had crept in and affectionately sat by his feet." He loved all animals, she went on, with the exception of flies, "against which he had a particular aversion."[12] In the privacy of the nunciature, she went on, "he was just as dignified and unassuming wearing a simple cassock as in his full ornate robes." Returning from a walk in the Tiergarten one morning, a delighted Pacelli reported to Sister Pasqualina that a small boy had approached him and asked if he was "Almighty God."

Did the polished, self-disciplined, austere prelate ever truly relax? A small hint of playfulness in his character turns up in an anecdote provided by an aristocratic Berlin neighbor. Hans-Conrad Stahlberg described an "odd ceremony" that involved greeting Pacelli each morning as they sharpened their razors while looking out at each other from distant but adjacent bathroom windows. "One day," Stahlberg told his son, "Pacelli surprised me by lowering his razor in a rapierlike greeting."[13]

Prussian Concordat

During this period of socializing as the doyen of the diplomatic corps in Berlin, Pacelli continued to concentrate on coming out on top in the concordat negotiations with Prussia. Prussian ministers, influenced by generations of Protestant pluralism, instinctively believed in the preservation of the traditional rights of local cathedral chapters, even for Catholics. For his part, Pacelli saw Protestant resistance on the nomination of bishops as evidence of anti-papal prejudice. As the months passed, the issues were aired in public and passions rose. Pacelli whipped up Catholic anxieties about an imminent threat to Catholic schools. The Protestants saw themselves holding a standard for liberalism against Romish dogma. Was not this Italian nuncio attempting to instigate a Counter-Reformation in the heartland of Protestantism? The more Pacelli tacked and veered, the more the Prussians followed suit.

By the autumn of 1928, the central problem of the schools question remained unresolved. It was time to be blunt. The Prussian prime minister, Otto Braun, told Pacelli that "no provision of whatsoever nature about the schools could be included in the concordat." Pacelli responded that he could not "go back to the Holy Father in Rome with a draft concordat that did not mention the schools." Braun retorted, "And I can't go to parliament with a concordat that does mention the schools without exposing myself to certain defeat."[14]

It was Pacelli who eventually gave way in the spring of 1929. In the final negotiation the two sides reached agreement on a new diocese of Berlin in accordance with Pacelli's wishes. On the matter of the nomination of bishops there was a temporary compromise: the cathedral canons were allowed to select a list of names, with the Holy See choosing three from which the canons would make their final choice. An extra clause allowed the Prussian government the right of veto where a sufficiently grave objection arose. All clergy must be citizens of the German Reich and have reached degree level in education. On the matter of schools: silence.[15]

The concordat was signed on June 14, 1929. A month later it was approved in the Prussian parliament by 243 votes to 171. On August 5, Pacelli sent an official note to Braun informing him that the apparent compromise on the schools issue had been made under pressure. He was obliged to declare, he wrote, that he had not renounced "the fundamental principles" he had appealed to, and indeed had secured in other concordats on the schools question.[16]

Pacelli had not given up on a Reich Concordat, but the time remained inopportune as the Reich once again became embroiled in perilous external and internal crises.

The end of October 1929 saw the collapse of the New York Stock Exchange and the beginnings of a world economic slump. Three weeks earlier, Gustav Stresemann had died, exhausted from years of attempting to restore Germany to its prewar eminence. Stresemann had brought Germany into the League of Nations; he had negotiated the Dawes Plan and the Young Plan, reducing reparations to a feasible level. It was Stresemann who had been one of the principal architects of the Locarno Pact, which had brought a measure of peace to Europe. With his passing, and with the gathering economic and industrial storm clouds, the days of the Weimar Republic were numbered. Following the Wall Street crash, the flow of loans from the United States ceased and the old ones were called in. As world trade slumped, Germany became incapable of exporting sufficient products to pay for imports of raw materials and food. Unemployment rose, businesses failed. Bank collapses were imminent.

While these events were in progress, Pacelli was summoned back to Rome. The call came by telegram in November while he was resting at his favorite retreat, the Rorschach convent sanatorium where he had stayed at least twice each year since 1917. Cardinal Secretary of State Pietro Gasparri, almost eighty years of age, had at last been retired. His protégé and favorite of almost a quarter century had been chosen to replace him. Pacelli hurried back to Berlin to clear his desk and say his farewells.

Among the many farewell celebrations was a lunch given by Hinden-burg, now president of the republic. Toasting Pacelli, he declared: "I thank you for all you have accomplished during these long years in the cause of peace, inspired as you have been by a high sense of justice and deep love of humanity; and I can assure you that we shall not forget you and your work here."[17]

On December 10 Pacelli left Berlin. The government had provided him with an open carriage in which to proceed to the Anhalter station. Rauchstrasse was lined with tens of thousands of young members of Catholic Action holding torches above their heads. Flags were lowered in Pacelli's honor, hymns were sung, and the people cried out as he passed. On the platform, a band played the papal anthem. The barriers that kept back the crowds were almost knocked down. Pacelli blessed the crowds repeatedly.[18]

By Christmas, Pacelli had been awarded the red hat. According to Sis-ter Pasqualina, he never wanted the job and was displeased to get it. In reality, she wrote, "his heart's desire was to dedicate himself to the care of souls."[19] By February 7, 1930, however, he had taken up his new ap-pointment as Cardinal Secretary of State, the most powerful post in the Catholic Church next to the Pope. He was not yet fifty-four years of age.

7

Hitler and German Catholicism

❧

Adolf Hitler recognized at an early stage the potential for Catholic resistance to National Socialism. In *Mein Kampf*, he wrote that a confrontation with the Catholic Church in Germany would prove disastrous. During his vagabond days in Vienna, he recalled, he had pondered the futile consequences of the Kulturkampf and had seen the importance of drawing a strict distinction between political Catholicism and religious Catholicism. "Political parties," he wrote, "have nothing to do with religious problems, as long as these are not alien to the nation, undermining the morals and ethics of the race; just as religion cannot be amalgamated with the scheming of political parties."[1] After his release from prison for his part in the Beer Hall Putsch, he reiterated this view in the party newspaper *Völkischer Beobachter* on February 26, 1925, declaring that the National Socialist movement would not be "dragged into religious disputes." Two years later, in a party circular distributed in 1927, he declared that all statements about religion were forbidden for tactical reasons.[2] There would be no new Kulturkampf in his battle with the Catholic Center Party, he promised, but he would take on the party purely on the basis of "political perceptions."

Hitler, in fact, had two views on the churches—public and private. In February of 1933 he was to declare in the Reichstag that the churches were to be an integral part of German national life. Privately, the following month, he vowed to completely "eradicate" Christianity from

Germany. "You are either a Christian or a German," he said. "You cannot be both."[3] In the meantime, he was bent on careful manipulation of the power of the churches to his own ends.

During 1927, Hitler conducted a significant private correspondence with a Catholic Nazi sympathizer called Father Magnus Gött, a troublesome young cleric posted by his superiors to a rural backwater called Lehenbuhl. Gött had written several contentious but adulatory fan letters to Hitler, which elicited two replies.[4] In the first, Hitler characterized the Catholic Church as "an immense technical apparatus" which "dwarfs" the National Socialist Party. It is not the task of the party, he went on, to appeal to loyal Christians, "but to win back for the nation all the elements of itself and its moral and spiritual culture which were lost." In a second letter, written from Munich in March, Hitler declared, "I always and under all circumstances take it to be a misfortune when religion, regardless in which form, is joined to political parties." The politicization of religion, he continued, is "pernicious," and he accused the Catholic Center Party of waging a bitter conflict against the national idea since the end of the Great War. He ended with the generalization that political Christianity had "won no new church members, but it has lost millions." This opinion eerily echoed the sentiments of Pius X in relation to France, and of Pius XI in relation to Italy and the Catholic Popular Party (Partito Popolare). In time, the same view would be endorsed by Eugenio Pacelli in the case of Germany and the Center Party.

As it happened, bolstered by the strength of the Center Party during the postwar period, there was an unprecedented growth of German Catholic life and activity—religious and cultural as well as political. There had been a proliferation of Catholic associations, workers' unions, religious vocations, and publishing, as well as a striking increase in public fervor. The numbers of Catholic diocesan clergy rose from 19,000 to 21,000 in the course of the 1920s. Monastic foundations for men almost doubled, from 366 to 640, members of religious orders increasing from 7,000 to 14,000. Women religious expanded their numbers from 60,000 to 77,000. The Catholic population in Germany was about 23 million by 1930, about 35 percent of the nation, having risen by almost 2.5 million since before the Great War despite the considerable loss of territory heavily populated by Catholics.[5]

True to Scheler's and Erzberger's vision, Catholic writers, poets, artists, and journalists made a vital contribution to the mold-breaking cultural activity of the Weimar era. Under the influence of thinkers like Romano Guardini and Pieter Lippert, Catholic thought acquired a reputation for energy and originality. Chairs in Catholic ideas were endowed in Frankfurt am Main, Breslau, and Berlin. Catholic professional and academic clubs and societies flourished, and there were frequent conferences and seminars on Catholic topics in every part of Germany. Although Catholicism was a minority faith, compared with the Protestant churches, it was better organized. Some 700,000 individuals belonged to the Protestant youth groups by 1933 but Catholic Youth alone numbered 1.5 million. Even after the rapid success of the Nazi organizations, up to 1933 Catholicism remained the largest single social institution in the country.

Catholic publishing both reported on and gave impulse to the associations. By the end of the 1920s, there were some four hundred daily Catholic newspapers, representing about 15 percent of national daily circulations. In addition, there were some 420 Catholic periodicals in Germany, thirty with circulations above 100,000. Two Catholic news and feature services syndicated material nationwide, and a Catholic cinema review, *Film-Rundschau,* strongly influenced the expanding German cinema industry.

Rallies of Catholic workers, boy scouts, and other youth groups were held frequently in every part of the country, as were outdoor services. One outdoor Mass at Dortmund in 1927 was attended by eighty thousand.[6] Released from the strictures against religious assembly by the Weimar constitution, Catholic processions became popular where they had never been seen in living memory. On the Feast of Corpus Christi, the Eucharist was carried in an emblazoned monstrance down Unter den Linden in Berlin, with Catholic politicians following, invariably led by a Catholic chancellor of the day.

When Hitler's party, against the background of soaring unemployment (3.2 million in January 1930), made its spectacular leap in the Reichstag election on September 14, 1930, the Catholic Church in Germany was still a formidable force. To what extent had Hitler managed to assuage Catholic fears of National Socialism through the 1920s? To what extent was Hitler's initial success a result, even, of the beginnings of a Catholic slide toward National Socialism?

Hitler's triumph in the polls of September 1930 took his party from a 2.6 percent share of the vote to 18.3 percent and increased his seats in the Reichstag from 12 to 107. The Nazis became the second-largest party after the Social Democrats. The swing appeared to owe much to the attractions of an ideological party of the Right for Protestants in search of radical solutions for the dire economic situation. There is even evidence of Catholic workers' associations, in the Black Forest region for example, leaning toward National Socialism as a result of local anticlericalism and disillusionment with the Weimar government.[7] Yet while the liberals had been decimated and the Social Democrats had slipped by 5 percent, the Catholic Center Party, relying on its traditional vote in Catholic areas, held its own—actually increasing its seats from 62 to 66, or 14.8 percent of the vote.

By the turn of the decade, in fact, Catholic criticism of the National Socialists was vehement and sustained in the press and from the pulpits. The Catholic journalist Walter Dirks, writing in the August 1931 edition of the journal *Die Arbeit,* described the Catholic reaction to Nazism as "open warfare." The ideology of the National Socialists, he asserted, "stood in blatant, explicit contrast to the [Catholic] Church."

Among the reports from Nazi activists collected by Theodor Abel in 1934, there are vehement complaints of combative Catholic resistance to National Socialism in the early 1930s. "The [Catholic] Church made life difficult for us. The consolations of religion as well as burial in consecrated ground were denied to murdered National Socialists," wrote one witness.[8] Another, writing of the "persecution" conducted by the Center against the Nazis, complained that "at a local mission we were barred from the sacraments because we refused to leave the Party. A letter to the bishop was without avail."

How was it, then, that Catholic antagonism to Nazism failed to materialize in the form of the confrontation Hitler so greatly feared?

An instructive starting point is a correspondence after the 1930 Reichstag elections between the National Socialist *Gauleitung* (area command) in Hessen and the Catholic bishop's office in Mainz. The *Gauleitung's* press officer wished to know whether the bishop shared the views of a certain parish priest at Kirschhausen, who had given his parishioners the following guidance:

1. No Catholic may be a card-carrying member of the Hitler Party.

2. No member of the Hitler Party may participate in [parish gatherings] at funerals or any other events.

3. So long as a Catholic is a card-carrying member of the Hitler Party he may not be admitted to the sacraments.[9]

The *Gauleitung's* inquiry elicited prompt confirmation from the vicar-general of Mainz that the parish priest of Kirschhausen had indeed been speaking in accordance with diocesan thinking. The prelate drew attention, moreover, to the "Hitler's Party's" policy of "racial hatred," which, wrote the vicar-general, was "un-Christian and un-Catholic." Then he pointed out that while Hitler had made appreciative noises about Catholic institutions in *Mein Kampf*, this could not disguise the fact that "the religious and educational policy of National Socialism is inconsistent with Catholic Christianity."

The Mainz affair, much discussed at the time, troubled the Catholic bishops in Germany. Had not Mainz spoken out of turn? Should the bishops publish a united view? Some privately grumbled that the Mainz policy lacked tactical prudence: after all, had not National Socialism championed "positive Christianity" against atheistic Marxism? Yet the Catholic bishops failed to produce a single agreed-upon document when they gathered for their conference at Fulda in the late autumn. Instead, Cardinal Bertram of Breslau, president of the conference, made a New Year statement, warning the Catholic Church in Germany against political extremism and the insanity and wickedness of racism.

In February 1931, however, the Bavarian bishops made a more specific directive for the clergy in their region. Avoiding the outspokenness of the Mainz position, they took a more pluralist, grassroots approach, arguing that priests should be allowed to judge each situation locally on its own merits: "As guardians of the true teaching of faith and morals, the bishops must warn against National Socialism, so long and so far as it proclaims cultural and political opinions that are incompatible with Catholic teaching."[10] The following month, Catholic archbishops in three other regions—Cologne, Paderborn, and the upper Rhine—stated in the clearest terms that National Socialism and Catholicism were incompatible, and repeated the key sentence of the Bavarian bishops' letter.

Hence, in the critical years before 1933, as Hitler grew closer to his moment and the Nazi movement burgeoned and spread, these episcopal initiatives were symptomatic of a united, forthright response from the Catholic Church. Exceptions were few: the Benedictine abbot Alban Schachleitner, who supported the Nazis for what he deemed tactical reasons against the Lutherans; the unhinged Father Wilhelm Maria Senn, who believed Hitler had been sent into the world by divine providence; Hitler's Catholic pen friend, Father Gött.

Could there be any lingering doubt in the mind of the average thinking Catholic about National Socialist ideology and its likely consequences? In his study on the popularization of Catholic attitudes to the Nazis, Klaus Scholder, the German Church historian of the period, cites two key tracts and a powerful press campaign.

In the spring of 1931, a Catholic Reichstag representative, Karl Trossmann, published a best-selling book entitled *Hitler and Rome*, in which he described the National Socialists as a "brutal party that would do away with all the rights of the people." Hitler, he declared, was dragging Germany into a new war, a war that "would only end more disastrously than the last." Not long after, the Catholic author Alfons Wild published a widely distributed essay entitled "Hitler and Catholicism," in which he proclaimed that "Hitler's view of the world is not Christianity but the message of race, a message that does not proclaim peace and justice but rather violence and hate."

Meanwhile, two Catholic journalists, Fritz Gerlich and Ingbert Naab, excoriated National Socialism in the pages of the Munich-based periodical *Der Gerade Weg* [*The Straight Path*], characterizing the movement as a "plague." In the issue dated July 21, 1932, the writers declared that "National Socialism means enmity with neighboring countries, despotism in internal affairs, civil war, international war. National Socialism means lies, hatred, fratricide and unbounded misery. Adolf Hitler preaches the law of lies. You who have fallen victim to the deceptions of one obsessed with despotism, wake up!"[11]

This vehement and united front of the Catholic Church in Germany, however, was not at one with the view from inside the Vatican—a view that was being increasingly shaped and promoted by Eugenio Pacelli.

Pacelli on Home Ground

Ensconced in the Vatican as Cardinal Secretary of State, Pacelli had responsibility for foreign policy and state relations throughout the world during a period when Pius XI was plagued by illness and entrusting more and more to his favorite cardinal.

Pacelli was back on home territory in more senses than one, since he had served in the Secretariat for sixteen years, from humble clerk to undersecretary. As he settled himself into the task of overseeing the Church's vast and complex relations on every continent, he was drawn into yet another domestic drama involving his housekeeper nun, Sister Pasqualina.[12]

When he said his good-byes to the people of Berlin in December, he also made his relieved farewells to Pasqualina and her two assistant nuns, who had become part of the household. There was no plan to take them with him to Rome. According to Pacelli's sister Elisabetta, he had formed a poor opinion of Pasqualina, whom Elisabetta described as "bossy" and "extremely cunning" (*scaltrissima*). On arriving in Rome, he lodged temporarily on Via Boezio with his brother, Francesco, before establishing himself in the Vatican apartment of the Cardinal Secretary of State above the loggias of the apostolic palace. Just before the move, he asked Elisabetta to manage his new Vatican household. Elisabetta reminded him that she was a wife and mother and had certain obligations, but Pacelli was not to be deflected. He would ensure, he told her, that the arrangement would not affect her family duties.

A day or so after this conversation, Elisabetta told the beatification tribunal, Sister Pasqualina turned up in Rome, without warning and without permission either from her congregation or from Pacelli. First she took rented rooms in a convent in Via Nicolo V, then, pleading poverty and inability to speak Italian, she entreated Elisabetta to take her in, quickly making herself at home and resuming her usual commanding role in all things. Elisabetta reported that she endured the nun out of regard for her brother, but added that she could not understand why he did not send her packing. Elisabetta eventually contrived to oust Pasqualina from the house, and, she hoped, from Rome, with a drastic measure. "I was so fed up with her that I eventually told her that we were going to shut up the apartment because we were going to Lourdes."

Elisabetta was as good as her word, but no sooner had Elisabetta left the city than Sister Pasqualina moved into Pacelli's Vatican apartment on the pretext of furnishing it and organizing the redecoration. Having insinuated herself into these new quarters, she then summoned her two former nun assistants from Germany. Pacelli was back in the hands of Pasqualina and the sisterhood, a circumstance that would persist until the day of his death nearly thirty years later.

The Red Triangle

From the moment that he took over in the Secretariat of State, Pacelli had been absorbed in German affairs, not the least of his concerns being the rise of Hitler's Nazi Party. Yet for all Pacelli's distaste for the explicit racism of National Socialism, his fears were overshadowed by the known aggression and goals of Communism in what the Vatican came to call the "Red Triangle"—Soviet Russia, Mexico, and, by 1933, Spain. The Holy See's attitude toward Hitler was ambiguous: if it came to comparisons, the Nazis had not vowed to destroy Christianity; in fact, they had made soothing gestures toward the Catholic Church. From the Secretariat of State's view of the Church in the world, the threat of Communism was an altogether different matter.

Lenin, and Stalin after him, had never concealed their intentions. They had declared war on religion itself, and the Orthodox Church in Russia had suffered widespread murderous persecution at the hands of the Communists since 1917. Bishops and priests were jailed and murdered; churches were despoiled and destroyed or turned into atheist museums; the schools and the press were exploited as a means of vilifying religion. It became a crime to teach children under sixteen about God. Although Roman Catholics in Russia numbered no more than 1.5 million and offered no threat to the regime, the Catholic Church was no less a victim of Bolshevik persecution. In 1923 the administrator of the key Catholic archdiocese of Mohilev and its vicar-general were arrested along with thirteen priests, charged with having "fostered the counter-revolution." The vicar-general had his ear ripped off and was tortured until he collapsed. He was executed on Good Friday of that year. Not long after, the exarch of the Byzantine Catholic Church in Russia was imprisoned for life. Meanwhile, many hundreds of bishops, clergy, and laity were rounded up and transported to a gulag at Solowki on the Black Sea. By 1930 there were no more than three hundred Catholic priests in Soviet Russia (compared with 963 in 1921), of whom a hundred were in prisons.[13]

On March 19, 1930, a month after Pacelli formally took office, Pius XI led a ceremony of expiation in a packed St. Peter's, during which the saints of Holy Russia were invoked and a *De profundis* sung for the souls of the recent martyrs.

In Mexico, Catholics had likewise suffered persecution, since the latter half of the nineteenth century, in successive waves of indigenous communist-style revolutions owing little or nothing, even after 1917, to Marxism or the Comintern. In 1924, however, coinciding with the presidency of Plutarco Elías Calles and the unleashing of yet another merciless persecution, Mexico became the second Western nation to recognize the Soviet Union. According to Catholic sources, some 5,300 Catholic priests, religious, and members of the laity were murdered during the four years of Calles's presidency and the seven further years of his influence. The very presence of a priest in Mexico under Calles was a capital offense and the Church went underground, its priests, as later depicted in Graham Greene's *The Power and the Glory*, traveling the country in disguise and saying Mass in barns and stables.

In 1926 Pius XI had denounced the Calles regime in his encyclical *Iniques afflictusque*, proclaiming that "in Mexico anything called God, anything resembling public worship, is proscribed and trampled underfoot." In a move aimed at fomenting resistance, he encouraged the Mexican hierarchy to sanction an *interdict*, a complete suspension of religious ceremonies and the sacraments throughout the country. The persecutions continued unabated; but so did resistance at every level, including the militant activities of the formations known as *Cristeros*. In the view of Church historian H. Daniel-Rops, this resistance achieved the eventual defeat of the antireligious elements in Mexico's governing elite.[14]

The Lateran Treaty and Its Aftermath

Pius XI and Pacelli realized that no accommodation could be made with
Communism, anywhere in the world. In the case of totalitarian movements and regimes of the Right, it was a different matter. In Italy the
Holy See had signed a pact with Mussolini in February 1929, fore-
shadowing Pacelli's 1933 deal with Hitler. Negotiated and drafted by
Pacelli's brother, Francesco, and his predecessor as Secretary of State,
Pietro Gasparri, the accord, on the face of it and for the time being,
ended the antagonisms that had existed between the Holy See and Italy
since 1870.

According to the terms of the Lateran Treaty, Roman Catholicism
became the sole recognized religion in the country. Crucially, the agreement acknowledged the right of the Holy See to impose within Italy the
new Code of Canon Law, the most significant expression of which, for
Pius XI, was Article 34, in which the state recognized the validity of
marriages performed in church. The papacy was awarded sovereignty
over the tiny territory of Vatican City (just 108.7 acres) along with territorial rights over several buildings and churches in Rome and the summer palace at Castel Gandolfo on Lake Albano. In compensation for the
loss of lands and property, the Vatican was given the equivalent at the
time of eighty-five million dollars. The powerful democratic Catholic
Popular Party (the Partito Popolare), in many respects similar to the
Center Party in Germany, had been disbanded and its leader, Don Luigi
Sturzo, exiled. Catholics had been instructed by the Vatican itself
to withdraw from politics as Catholics, leaving a political vacuum in
which the Fascists thrived. In the March elections following the Lateran
Treaty, priests throughout Italy were encouraged by the Vatican to sup-
port the Fascists, and the Pope spoke of Mussolini as "a man sent by
Providence."

In the place of political Catholicism in Italy, the Holy See was allowed, under Article 43, to encourage the movement known as Catholic
Action, an anemic form of clerically dominated religious rally-rousing,
described ploddingly by Pius XI as "the organized participation of the
laity in the hierarchical apostolate of the Church, transcending party
politics."[15] Article 43 stipulated, however, that Catholic Action would
be recognized only so long as it developed "its activity outside every
political party and in direct dependence upon the Church hierarchy for

the dissemination and implementation of Catholic principles." In a second paragraph, the article declared that all clergy and all those in religious orders in Italy were prohibited from registering in and being active in any political party.

In Germany in the late 1920s, well ahead of the Reich Concordat, Pacelli had also promoted Catholic Action, announcing its establishment at a Eucharistic rally in Magdeburg in 1928. As we have seen, Pacelli's distaste for political Catholicism—dating back to the era of Pius X and turbulent Church-State relations in France—was profound, if at this stage muted. His interest in the Center Party and indeed any Catholics within government in Germany, as became increasingly apparent, focused on the extent to which he could exploit them as negotiating counters to achieve a Reich Concordat favorable to the Holy See. The Lateran Treaty, drafted and negotiated by his elder brother, Francesco, with all its measures designed to cripple political and social Catholicism, contained all that Pacelli yearned for in a Reich Concordat.

Ironically, and ominously, one key figure in German politics who had taken similar comfort and delight in the signing of the Lateran Treaty, and who similarly entertained hopes of an identical agreement for his future regime, was Adolf Hitler. A few days after the signing of the Lateran Treaty, Hitler wrote an article for the *Völkischer Beobachter,* published on February 22, 1929, warmly welcoming the agreement. "The fact that the Curia is now making its peace with Fascism," he wrote, "shows that the Vatican trusts the new political realities far more than did the former liberal democracy with which it could not come to terms." Turning to the German situation, he rebuked the Center Party leadership for its recalcitrant attachment to democratic politics. "By trying to preach that democracy is still in the best interests of German Catholics, the Center Party . . . is placing itself in stark contradiction to the spirit of the treaty signed today by the Holy See."

The conclusion of his rant contained a gross distortion as well as a remarkable intuition of future opportunities: "The fact that the Catholic Church has come to an agreement with Fascist Italy," he went on, ". . . proves beyond doubt that the Fascist world of ideas is closer to Christianity than those of Jewish liberalism or even atheistic Marxism, to which the so-called Catholic Center Party sees itself so closely bound, to the detriment of Christianity today and our German people."

Despite Hitler's confident assertions, the Vatican was by no means inclined toward the Nazi Party; the Holy See endorsed neither the implicit nor the explicit racism of National Socialism, and warned of its potential for establishing an idolatrous creed based on pagan fantasies and spurious folk history. The fact was, however, that from the days of Pio Nono the Vatican did indeed encourage a distrust of social democracy as a precursor of socialism, and thus of communism. Hence, pragmatically, the Vatican's estimation of any political party was colored by how it stood in relation to the communist threat. In this sense, quite ludicrously, even the Nazis' nominal association with socialism was enough to raise doubts about the party among certain naive Vatican monsignori. In *L'Osservatore Romano*, October 11, 1930, the editorialist declared that membership in the National Socialists was "incompatible with the Catholic conscience," adding, "just as it is completely incompatible with membership of socialist parties of all shades."

At the end of the day, however, Pius XI and Pacelli judged movements on the basis of their anti–left-wing credentials, which had led the Holy See to forbid the Partito Popolare to make approaches to the socialists in 1924, thus neutralizing its attempts to thwart Mussolini. After 1930, when the Center Party in Germany had more need than ever of creating stability by collaborating with the Social Democrats, Pacelli was pressuring the Center Party leadership to shun the socialists and court the National Socialists. Insofar as the National Socialists had declared open war on socialism and communism alike, Pius XI and Pacelli were inclined to ponder the advantages of a temporary and tactical alliance with Hitler, a circumstance that Hitler would exploit to the full when his moment came. How much this potential alliance with the devil of Nazism was a result of fears for the future of the Church in Germany, and how much it was a tactic to further the aims of papal power, will become apparent.

Kaas's Double Life

Pacelli's close and continued involvement in German affairs after his return to Rome was facilitated by the political double life of Ludwig Kaas, his closest confidant and disciple, and leader of the Center Party since 1928. No sooner had Pacelli settled in the Vatican than Kaas began to neglect his German political responsibilities and to shuttle to and fro between Rome and Berlin at the Cardinal Secretary of State's bidding, spending weeks at a time in Pacelli's apartments. If the political fate of Germany depended to any extent on the views and actions of the Center Party, Kaas's position as both party leader and intimate of Pacelli was remarkable.

What brought the leader of the Center Party to Rome to sit in private conference with Pacelli for weeks on end? Barely had Pacelli entered his new office at the beginning of February 1930 than he and Kaas resumed work on the Reich Concordat while continuing negotiations on a Baden Concordat.[16] In the meantime, Pacelli informed his successor at the Berlin nunciature, Archbishop Cesare Orsenigo, that these matters of high diplomacy were for him, Pacelli, and Kaas alone to treat.

As was his custom in negotiations, Pacelli had found a useful means of diplomatic leverage. In 1930 it was the question of army chaplains, an issue of crucial importance at the time. Should Catholic chaplains report to a specially appointed military bishop, or should they be under the jurisdiction of the local bishop in whose diocese they were resident? The army had opted for the former in order to eliminate potential conflict of interest and to exert control. The German Catholic diocesan bishops naturally tended toward the latter; Pacelli, however, saw the issue as an important trump card in the concordat negotiations.[17]

Hence, on March 9, the Bavarian diplomat to the Holy See, Baron von Ritter, informed Munich that Kaas was in the Vatican and that Pacelli had asked for a meeting on the army bishop question that perhaps could be expanded into discussions on "a concordat relationship with the Reich in order to secure the fulfillment of the modest wishes of the Holy See as a quid pro quo from the Reich."[18] When the Reich envoy to the Holy See, Diego von Bergen, became fully apprised of Pacelli's quid pro quo, his response was brusque: "Cardinal Secretary of State mentions possibility of solving question military chaplaincy in the framework of a Reich Concordat. Transfer of matter to this base rejected."[19]

Meanwhile, in Berlin, the Reich government had other things on its mind than an accord with Pacelli and quid pro quos that could only increase their difficulties. While Kaas and Pacelli brooded on the furtherance of the concordats in Rome, parliamentary democracy was under acute threat in Germany due to the economic crises that worsened after the 1929 Wall Street crash, leading eventually to the September 14, 1930, elections that saw the huge success of Hitler's party.

The dismantling of German democracy, moreover, was being furthered by a coterie of powerful military figures, notably General Kurt von Schleicher, a veteran who had insinuated himself into a position of influence over President Hindenburg. A protégé of another machinator, General Wilhelm Groener, Schleicher (his name in German means *prowler* or *sneak*) helped organize the Freikorps after the First World War and became a rising star in the new Reichswehr, the resurrected German army. By 1928 he had control of the intelligence services and was the chief liaison officer between the Reichswehr and the government. By 1930 he was regarded as the most powerful man in Germany, with a network of spies, the authority to tap telephones, and influence over the press.

The Rise of Brüning

On March 27, 1930, the grand coalition under Hermann Müller broke up as a result of cabinet and Reichstag disagreements over dole payments for the unemployed. Once again the Center Party became the power broker when one of its most popular deputies, Heinrich Brüning, a devout Catholic who had risen through the trade-union wing of the party, was chosen by Hindenburg as chancellor. This soft-spoken forty-five-year-old bachelor and war hero had been greatly affected by his experience in the trenches in the Great War. He was determined to strengthen the unity of the country, resolve the burden of reparations payments to the Allies, and make Germany economically dominant again in Europe. Unfortunately, his personal courage was matched by acute myopia in the art of the possible. Known as the "Hunger Chancellor," Brüning proposed a series of austerity measures designed to balance the national budget. When the Reichstag failed to vote in his package by July 1930, he introduced the measures again, invoking Article 48 of the Weimar constitution, which enabled the government to rule by presidential decree. Under the same article, however, the Reichstag could declare such presidential decrees invalid. The decrees were voted down by 236 to

222, automatically triggering a new election. Precipitating a general election when the economy was in disarray proved a serious miscalculation. On September 14, 1930, the Nazi vote increased eightfold, from 800,000 to 6.4 million, making the National Socialist Party the second largest and thus destined for major power-sharing against the background of the worsening economic crisis.

Brüning's fate was to run a shaky minority government by presidential decree for almost two years, blocking the large minority Socialist and Nazi representations in the Reichstag, and administering ever more stringent medicine to an ailing economy. When he first came to office in January 1930, the unemployment figures stood at 3 million. By December of that year, the figure was 4,480,000; by the end of 1931, it was 5,615,000.[20] With Hitler waiting in the wings, the retreat from parliamentary democracy smoothed the way for public acceptance of a dictatorship in 1933. And yet Brüning, in both character and purpose, was the very antithesis of a demagogue. Brüning's political formation had drawn significantly on the notions of solidarity explored by Scheler and Erzberger, emphasizing the delegation of regulatory powers to voluntary associations of management and unions, but entrusting ultimate political control to a parliament based on universal suffrage. In urging such a program, he stood in striking contrast to the devout Catholic industrialist Fritz Thyssen, who crusaded against workers' unions and promoted a corporatist political model. Citing Pius XI's encyclical *Quadragessimo anno* (1931), written to celebrate the forty years that had lapsed since Leo XIII's *Rerum novarum*, Brüning later criticized Pius XI for encouraging Thyssen in the view that the papacy was soft on Italian Fascist-style corporatism.[21] Brüning later claimed that his secret strategy for Germany was to lead the country to a British-style constitution, a parliamentary democracy with a constitutional monarch. Arguments over the accuracy of his account of these years, published in his memoirs in 1970, continue to this day, as do the debates over the alternatives to his harsh deflationary policies.[22]

The background to Brüning's chancellorship—the economic crises and impending portents of political catastrophe—makes Pacelli's dealings with him all the more extraordinary. As far as Pacelli was concerned, Brüning's agonizing responsibilities as chancellor of a great nation in crisis were of less significance than his status as a malleable Catholic whom he could shape to his will in the interests of achieving a Reich Concordat favorable to the Holy See.

In March of 1931, amid growing economic and political turmoil in Germany, Pacelli was badgering Berlin with his concordat demands, including the insistence that the Reich should surrender on the schools question—the very condition he had failed to secure in the concordat with Prussia. In return, Pacelli hinted, he was prepared to let the Reich have its way on the issue of army chaplains and their allegiance to the military bishop.

Not surprisingly, there was no appetite for Pacelli's deal in Berlin, not even among the most loyal leaders of the Catholic Center politicians, excluding of course Ludwig Kaas. Matters came to a head at Easter when several party members, led by Joseph Wirth, then minister of the interior, visited Rome. Wirth informed Pacelli that, given the volatile state of German politics, the Holy See's demands were out of the question. At another Vatican meeting, Wirth clashed with Pius XI when the Pontiff attempted to persuade him that the Center Party should sever its coalition with the majority Socialists in the Landtag in Prussia. The discussion grew so heated that Wirth stormed angrily from the audience.[23] Undismayed, Pacelli decided to bide his time until he could meet Chancellor Brüning face-to-face. The opportunity for such an encounter arose in August, when Brüning came to Rome for talks with Mussolini.

Brüning arrived in the Eternal City in the midst of a major German bank crisis sparked by the failure of the Darmstadt and National Banks on July 13, which led to a rush of withdrawals from savings deposits throughout the country and the suspension of banking business. When normal business resumed on August 5, the bank rate was 15 percent and the deposit rate not less than 20 percent. With 4.5 million unemployed, and industrial output and exports plummeting, Brüning had hoped to persuade Mussolini to support Germany in the matter of reparations payments.

Pacelli Clashes with the Reich Chancellor

When Brüning called on Pacelli, before a scheduled audience with the Pope on the morning of August 8, 1931, he reflected irritably on the time-wasting protocol that obliged him to shuffle at a snail's pace through endless chambers with guards of honor snapping to attention. This was "nothing for fast-traveling politicians, who have to make every hour count." The chancellor eventually spent forty-five minutes alone with Pacelli in his office.

The conversation began "very amiably," according to Brüning, until Pacelli began to exhort him to actions that could only aggravate the political situation in Germany. According to Brüning, Pacelli had a poor grasp of his visitor's predicament and mood.[24] As Pacelli rehearsed his quid pro quo—the notion of trading the military chaplaincy issue for the Vatican's tough conditions on a Reich Concordat—Brüning was nonplussed. He had already committed the Reich to a policy that obliged army chaplains to report to the military bishop, and had hoped for Pacelli's unqualified support in the matter. So much for Ludwig Kaas's backroom preparation for this Vatican meeting. In any event, Brüning was adamant that there could be no scope for a Reich Concordat that favored the Catholic Church on the schools question. "Given the crisis in Germany, as a Catholic chancellor it was out of the question, I told him, to even raise the issue. Most of the great German states had concordats and there were promising negotiations with the remainder. If I tried to press the issue of a Reich Concordat at this point I would spark Protestant rage on one side and total bafflement on the part of the Socialists."[25]

Ignoring the political realities that were being explained to him, Pacelli plowed on. Lecturing Brüning on how he should conduct the future of his government, he advised him to "form a right-wing administration precisely in order to achieve a Reich Concordat, and that it should be a condition that the treaty be concluded at once."[26] The inference was that if the price of a Reich Concordat was to draw the Nazis and Hitler into his minority cabinet, he should seek an agreement with them without delay.[27]

Once again the chancellor told Pacelli brusquely that he "misunderstood the political situation in Germany and, above all, the real character of the Nazis." Doubtless Brüning was remembering his meeting with Hitler on the preceding October 5 to sound out the Nazi leader on future cooperation. Hitler had ranted at the chancellor for an hour while brownshirts marched to and fro outside the supposedly secret venue.

Brüning was struck by the number of times Hitler had used the word *vernichten* (annihilate), and concluded that Hitler's principle would always be "first power, then politics."[28]

Tempers flared between Pacelli and Brüning when the question of a series of Church-State treaties with the Protestants was raised. Successive Weimar governments had welcomed agreements with the other confessions in Germany, modeled on Pacelli's concordats, a policy that Brüning was determined to continue. Pacelli told him roundly that he thought it incredible that a Catholic chancellor should sign a Protestant concordat.[29]

"I told him angrily," records Brüning, "that in the spirit of the nation's constitution, to which I had sworn an oath, I was obliged to study the interests of the Protestant church on an equal basis with all other religions."[30]

It appears that Pacelli now gave vent to a remarkable tantrum, condemning the chancellor's "entire policy" and resorting to a threat that appears as ludicrous at this distance as it evidently was to Brüning at the time.

Rounding on the German chancellor, Pacelli told him that, in view of his lack of cooperation, Ludwig Kaas had now been put in an invidious position, that his standing in the Vatican was destroyed. Pacelli said that he would have to insist that Kaas resign his presidency of the German Center Party and accept a minor ecclesiastical post in the Vatican.[31]

An astonished Brüning replied that, since Kaas was a priest as well as a leading German politician, "I could hardly contradict him." He went on to say that, nevertheless, he "must oppose any attempt on the part of the Vatican to influence his political decisions or to interfere with the stance of the Center Party."[32]

According to Brüning, there now followed a curious exchange in which the chancellor raised the issue of Mussolini's ominous infringements of the articles of the Lateran Treaty, pointing out the intrinsic weakness of such concordats with totalitarians.

In the previous weeks, just two years after the signing of the Lateran Treaty, Mussolini had been attacking the innocuous nonpolitical Catholic Action movement, accusing the Church of conducting politics under the guise of its religious associations, especially the youth movements. In May of 1931, copies of *L'Osservatore Romano* carrying criticisms against the regime had been burned. Fascist bully boys had beaten up the newspaper vendors. Three weeks before Brüning's arrival in Rome, Pius XI had published his encyclical *Non abbiamo bisogno* (*We Have No Need*), a fierce denunciation of the Fascist government for its unfair treatment of Catholic Action. Significantly, however, Pius chose as the ground of his argument the unacceptable claim of Italian Fascism over the totality of a citizen's life. The grotesque political realities of Fascism, however, were not rebuked. Within two or three years, the same constrained papal protests against the Nazi regime in Germany would be similarly selective.

Reflecting on the crisis between the Vatican and Mussolini's government, Brüning told Pacelli that "it was obvious to all that the Fascist leadership laughed at the feebleness of the Vatican's denunciations in the face of constant infringements of the Lateran Treaty." He said that he "saw great dangers for the Church in too close an identification between the Vatican and Italian Fascism in the long term."

According to Brüning, Pacelli nevertheless insisted that the German Center Party should reach an understanding with the Nazis. "I explained to him," wrote Brüning, "that up till now all acceptable attempts to come to an understanding with the extreme Right in the interests of democracy had failed. [Pacelli] misunderstood the nature of National Socialism. On the other hand, whereas the Social Democrats in Germany were not religious, they were tolerant. But the Nazis were neither religious nor tolerant."[33] By this time, Brüning, being late for his appointment with the Pope, had to leave.

During the papal audience, which Pacelli did not attend, Brüning listened as Pius XI "spoke almost without pause, with an admirable power of recollection, about personal experiences and relationships that linked him to Germany." Then Pius dropped a bombshell. "After my conversation with Pacelli, I could not believe my ears when the Pope suddenly congratulated the German bishops on their clear and courageous stance against the erroneous tenets of National Socialism."

Brüning relates that he now began to speak against the advisability of concordats with totalitarian regimes, and that the Pope allowed him to run on. "Experience has shown," Brüning told the Holy Father, "that concordats always carried the risk that, step by step, the Church would be obliged to concede more and more ground in areas where the concordat was ambiguous. It would only come to a real clash when every single

Catholic grasped instinctively that it must take the Vatican's side. Disagreements over questions that were less clear would be difficult." Brüning felt that his remarks "made a strong impression on the Pontiff."

At a second meeting with Pacelli that evening, in an encounter that
was to end all future dealings between the two men, Brüning told the
Cardinal Secretary of State what had passed between him and the Pope.
He informed him "sharply" that he had reflected on their morning's
conversation and as a result had decided to drop the issue of the army
chaplains and the Reich Concordat altogether and leave the matter to his
successor as chancellor.

Brüning's parting shot was the ironic observation—chilling from
hindsight—that he trusted that "the Vatican would fare better at the
hands of Hitler . . . than with himself, a devout Catholic."[34] Brüning, or
his editor, however, was to leave his most devastating characterization of
Pacelli unpublished. His manuscript reflection, cut from the published
memoirs, states:

> All successes [Pacelli believed] could only be attained by papal
> diplomacy. The system of concordats led him and the Vati-
> can to despise democracy and the parliamentary system. . . .
> Rigid governments, rigid centralization, and rigid treaties
> were supposed to introduce an era of stable order, an era of
> peace and quiet.[35]

That evening Brüning took the sleeper train for Germany. "Exhausted
and agitated, I did not sleep that night," Brüning wrote. "At the Brenner
Pass, it was pouring with rain. It seemed freezing cold. Kaas boarded the
train at Innsbruck, very apprehensive, and asked about my conversations with Pacelli. Due to my physical exhaustion, I perhaps failed to
convey the full force of Pacelli's demands. I arrived in Berlin tired and
anxious."[36]

Despite Brüning's quarrel with Pacelli, and his warning to Pius XI of
the calamitous consequences, Pius XI and Pacelli continued to encourage the Center Party leadership to explore the advantages of cooperation
with the Nazis. The catalyst was Ludwig Kaas, increasingly in Pacelli's
company and increasingly voicing Pacelli's opinions. Questions had sur-
faced about Kaas's loyalties during the year, to the point where he had

offered his resignation as party leader. The gesture, taken as a signal of allegiance to his party, appeared to expel doubts and the offer was declined. But in November of 1931, Kaas was declaring a view, already espoused by Pacelli and clearly rejected by Brüning, that right-wing and left-wing groups that "had never cooperated" should now collaborate "for a particular purpose over a limited time."[37] By late December, the Pope was repeating the suggestion to Baron von Ritter, the Bavarian envoy to the Holy See: that a cooperation between the Church in Germany and the National Socialists "perhaps only temporarily and for specific purposes" would "prevent a still greater evil."[38] Ritter made it clear in his dispatch that the Holy Father's recommendation was purely pragmatic. After all, how should the Center Party react to the Nazis should they continue to grow and eventually form a government? As events would show, the idea of such a cooperation, originating within the offices of the Cardinal Secretary of State, was very far from the minds of the Catholic bishops, the clergy, or the faithful in Germany.

In the meantime, thwarted in his attempts to press Brüning into a Reich Concordat in August, Pacelli was presented with another opportunity to push forward his concordat policy in the provinces. This time it was Baden, where matters were still unresolved, and where Archbishop Carl Fritz of Freiburg, always openly cool toward Pacelli's concordat ambitions, died on December 7, 1931. Pacelli immediately seized the opportunity to exploit the episcopal selection process. The Baden government at this time was an uneasy standoff between a Center Party–led coalition and the Social Democrats. Convinced that pressure to conclude a concordat would upset the fragile status quo, Baden's Center Party chairman, Peter Fohr, begged Pacelli to exercise discretion. Traveling to Rome, Fohr explained to Pacelli in person that the best way to preserve the coalition, and the Center Party's ruling position, was to postpone the concordat indefinitely. He asked Pacelli to confirm old understandings, allowing for local and secular discretion in the selection of a new bishop, agreed upon between Baden and the Holy See in the previous century.

Pacelli was not inclined to take the least notice of such German local advice. In a haughty letter to Fohr, in which he rebuked the Baden government for its "attitude and intentions," he declared that satisfactory relations between Church and State could be achieved only with a new concordat. In a more forthright letter to Baden's *Kultusminister* (minister of public worship and education), Pacelli then issued a familiar item of moral blackmail: "Should the government decline to comply with the proposal to conclude a concordat as speedily as possible, the Holy See would have no option but to proceed to the appointment of a new bishop of the diocese of Freiburg in accordance with Canon 329, Paragraph 2, of new canon law."[39]

The negotiations dragged on into the spring of 1932, by which time Pacelli was as good as his word. He dealt with the appointment of a new bishop by papal fiat without reference to the rights or wishes of the diocese. As it happened, the choice, which Kaas imparted to Fohr in the Reichstag building in mid-April, was Konrad Gröber, bishop of Meissen, who was well liked in Baden. More important for the long term, Gröber, later known as the Brown bishop for his Nazi sympathies, was an enthusiastic supporter of Pacelli and his concordat policy. Gröber immediately set about pressuring the Baden government for an early conclusion of a concordat.

The pressure and the negotiations continued right through to the autumn, when Pacelli finally got his way. But Fohr was proved right about the political fallout. Following the initialing of the new treaty in Pacelli's office in August 1932, a series of fierce political battles resulted in a break between the Social Democrats and the Baden coalition that had maintained stability in the state since 1918. A new coalition of the Center Party, the German People's Party, and the Economic Party managed to pass the concordat only with the deciding vote of the Landtag's president.

The Fall of Brüning

Even as Pacelli pursued the Baden Concordat, the basis of democracy was disintegrating in Germany against the background of 5 million unemployed and a host of unmitigated economic woes. Largely due to Schleicher's plotting, partly due to Hindenburg's disillusionment with him, Brüning, the "Hunger Chancellor," resigned the chancellorship on May 30, 1932. Schleicher and his Reichswehr cronies had persuaded Hindenburg to appoint Franz von Papen in Brüning's place.

Aristocratic, charming, a right-wing Catholic Center Party deputy,

Papen was a socialite who moved easily in a milieu of senior military officers, industrialists, and landed gentry. Under the tutelage of Schleicher, he brought together a cabinet dominated by unrepresentative aristocrats and plutocrats, Schleicher himself securing the Ministry of Defense. At the same time, with no standing in the Reichstag, Papen immediately alienated his own party, the Catholic Center. Ludwig Kaas, still chairman of the Center, had already told him that he would not succeed Brüning as chancellor, and Papen had given Kaas his word that he would not appoint a cabinet. Kaas, at the hour of his party's greatest need, sulkily took himself off to a retreat in the Alto Adige to write an essay on the Lateran Treaty. Meanwhile, Papen's first act was to dissolve the Reichstag, scheduling new elections for July 31. His second act was to lift the ban that had been imposed on the SA, Hitler's brownshirts.

It was a violent summer in the approach to the new elections. In June there were hundreds of clashes across the country and scores of deaths in running fights between the Nazis and the Communists. Blaming the Communists for the worst of the violence in Prussia, Papen made a scapegoat of the state government and had Hindenburg authorize the ousting of the Prussian minister, assuming executive powers himself as *Reichskommissar.* Two weeks later the Nazis won a resounding victory in the Reichstag elections, gaining 37.4 percent of the vote against the majority Socialists' 21.6 percent and the Center's 16.2 percent. The Communists received 14.5 percent of the vote. Germany was now in theory ungovernable, since the two parties committed to the overthrow of the Weimar constitution—the Nazis and the Communists—formed almost a majority of the seats in the Reichstag. The stark reality, moreover, was that the Nazis were now the single largest political force in Germany, with 230 seats, a voting strength of 13,700,000 electors, and a private army of 400,000 brownshirts and blackshirts.

After the July elections, the German hierarchy repeated its denunciation of the Nazis and repeated their condemnation in the published minutes of the Fulda bishops' conference in August. "All the diocesan authorities have banned membership in this party," declared the document. The Nazis' official program, said the bishops, contains "false doctrine" and the declarations of numerous representatives are "hostile to the faith." Finally, they said, the collective judgment of the Catholic clergy was that if the party achieves the monopoly of rule in Germany that it so ardently desires, "the interests of Catholics will prove extremely bleak."[40]

For the right-wing Papen, however, a coalition with Hitler seemed the best prospect for the survival of his chancellorship. A coalition that included the National Socialists also appealed to Pacelli in Rome, although for rather different reasons. Once again he was attempting to sell the idea of a coalition to block the socialists and prevent the Bolshevizing of Germany. Would not the Center Party "do well to take its bearings from the Right," he asked Baron von Ritter, "and to look there for a coalition that would correspond to their principles?"[41] As it happened, more to sustain constitutional government than to embrace Nazi policies, the Center Party was finally considering negotiations for a coalition with Hitler throughout August and September, a process the Catholic *Der Gerade Weg* characterized as "a fairy tale of wolves and sheep." Hitler, however, was playing for higher stakes, refusing to settle for anything less than full control. He wanted the chancellorship and the key cabinet posts for his party. Hindenburg, however, held back from the brink, chiding Hitler for his contempt for the constitution.

Meanwhile, as Germany's democratic structures approached collapse under Papen's chancellorship, Ludwig Kaas was completing his essay on the political significance of the Lateran Treaty. He believed that his ruminations on the question had significance for Church-State relations not only in Italy but closer to home.[42] Considering the intimate relationship between Pacelli and Kaas, the essay elucidates Pacelli's thinking at this time.

Kaas argued that the treaty with Mussolini was an ideal agreement between the modern totalitarian state and the modern Church, a treaty in which the central issue was the acceptance by the state of the Code of Canon Law for Catholic citizens. "The authoritarian Church," he reasoned, "should understand the 'authoritarian' state better than others." Mussolini ordered things on the basis of a hierarchical concentration of power under the unlimited will of the Duce, and yet, Kaas explained, it would have made no sense for the Duce to interfere in the details of canon law. "Nobody would have better understood the claim to comprehensive law, such as that demanded by the Church, than the dictator who in his own sphere had established a radical, unchallenged and unchallengeable, hierarchical Fascist edifice."

Nowhere had the ideology of papal primacy, legislated just fifteen years earlier in the 1917 Code of Canon Law, been so clearly compared with the fascist *führer-prinzip*—leadership principle—or the necessity for withdrawal from social democracy more frankly urged. It is inconceivable that the article was written without prior consultation with Pacelli or indeed his close supervision and approval, since according to the code itself Kaas required his immediate superior's permission to publish. Pacelli's spirit, in fact, breathes through every line of this manifesto on the relationship between the Holy See and the Fascist state, published, as it was, at the very point when decisions about the fate of the Catholic Church in Germany were being made entirely by Pacelli in the Vatican.

8

Hitler and Pacelli

Only a dictator could have granted Pacelli the sort of concordat he was seeking. Only a dictator of Hitler's cunning could have seen the concordat as a means of weakening the Catholic Church in Germany. After it was all over—when Pacelli and Hitler had reached their fateful accord in July 1933—both men expressed their separate views of the treaty's significance. The gulf between their aims was remarkable.

Writing to the Nazi Party on July 22, Hitler declared: "The fact that the Vatican is concluding a treaty with the new Germany means the acknowledgment of the National Socialist state by the Catholic Church. This treaty shows the whole world clearly and unequivocally that the assertion that National Socialism is hostile to religion is a lie."[1] On July 14, during a cabinet meeting following the initialing of the concordat, he declared to his ministers a crucial implication of that moral approbation: "An opportunity has been given to Germany in the Reich Concordat," the cabinet minutes record Hitler as saying, "and a sphere of confidence has been created that will be especially significant in the urgent struggle against international Jewry."[2]

As soon as he had been made aware of the July 22 letter, Pacelli responded vehemently in a two-part article on July 26 and 27 in *L'Osservatore Romano*. First he denied categorically Hitler's assertion that the concordat implied moral approval of National Socialism. Then he went on to state what had been the true purpose of his concordat policy. Here was the single aim that ran through Pacelli's diplomatic policy from the Serbian Concordat negotiations in 1913 to the conclusion of the Reich Concordat in 1933. It was to be stressed, he wrote, "that the Code of Canon Law is the foundation and the essential legal presupposition of the concordat." This involved "not only official recognition [by the Reich] of the legislation of the Church, but also the adoption of many provisions of this legislation and the protection of all Church legislation." The historic victory in the accord, he was saying, was entirely the Holy See's; for the treaty emphatically did not mean the Holy See's approval of the Nazi state, but, on the contrary, the total recognition and acceptance of the Church's law by the state.

The dramatically contrasting goals of Pacelli and Hitler were the tragic subtext of the concordat negotiations conducted in great secrecy over the heads of the episcopate and lay Catholic leadership through six months as Hitler rose to power.

Hitler's Rise

Hitler's path to power was paved through the formation of successive cabinets that became ever more remote from parliament and thus increasingly remote from democratic government. At the first meeting of the Reichstag on September 12, 1932, Franz von Papen, the socialite and closet Nazi admirer, was confronted with a vote of no confidence and immediately called fresh elections for November 6. Meanwhile, he continued as chancellor, attacked on both sides by the Nazis and the Communists, who were united in nothing but their contempt for democratic politics.

The new elections, the fifth that year, saw the Nazis again emerging as the largest party; yet there was a decline of two million in their vote and a significant drop in party membership, indicating that they were perhaps losing momentum. Late in 1932 an overall Nazi majority appeared as elusive as ever, and while Hitler remained reluctant to seek a coalition representative of a parliamentary majority, Hindenburg was equally loath to give him the chancellorship. At the same time, neither the Reichswehr nor the industrialists were prepared to accept another socialist-dominated government. Thus the Catholic Center Party found itself stranded, incapable of finding a partner in government; uncertain as to its next move but determined to support the constitution.

On December 2 President Hindenburg accepted Papen's resignation and the arch-plotter Schleicher briefly became chancellor with the declared ambition of splitting the Nazis in the Reichstag and creating a new coalition to include a segment of the National Socialists without Hitler. For all his machinations, however, Schleicher proved no more capable of forming a viable government than had Papen.

In the new year, after talks with Hitler, Papen approached Hindenburg with a formula that was to grant Hitler the chancellorship while he, Papen, had it in mind to emerge as the real power behind the scenes in the office of vice-chancellor. Hindenburg remained skeptical about Hitler, but Papen's scheme, it appeared, sheltered Hindenburg from exposure in a lurking scandal involving the misappropriation of aid to landowners and the evasion of estate taxes. On such tawdry bases was Hitler ushered into power.

Hitler was sworn in as chancellor on January 30, 1933, along with Hermann Göring, who doubled as minister of aviation and Prussian minister of the interior. Göring now controlled the police in Prussia and thus had wide-ranging potential for coercion, which he would exploit in the coming weeks as he set about purging the party's opponents. The new minister of defense, with crucial influence in the army, was General Werner von Blomberg, a Nazi sympathizer who had become captivated by Hitler's charisma. Alfred Hugenberg, the leader of the ultra-conservative German National People's Party (DNVP), took the dual role of minister of economics and minister of agriculture. Hitler, however, was not to be tamed into any kind of power-sharing. Immediately he called new elections for March 5, and set about using his chancellorship to control the media, to oppress the opposition democratic parties, and to begin the persecution of Jews and "leftists."

February 27 witnessed the Reichstag fire, which Hitler immediately claimed had been set by a Dutch Communist. In the resulting anti-Communist hysteria, Hindenburg granted Hitler authority to suspend the civil-liberties clauses of the Weimar constitution, measures Hitler exploited to further his electoral campaign in pursuit of an overall majority to back a mandate for dictatorship.

In the March 5 elections, however, Hitler still failed to obtain an absolute majority for the National Socialists. But with temporary allies in the form of Hugenberg's right-wing nationalists, he scraped together a majority of 52 percent, securing 340 out of 647 seats in the Reichstag. In a turnout of 88.7 percent, the Nazis obtained more than seventeen million votes. The socialists dropped to 18.3 percent of the vote, and the Catholic Center, which had conducted a courageous campaign in the face of widespread Nazi intimidation, remained impressively solid at 13.9 percent, actually gaining three more Reichstag seats.

Right up until March 1933, then, German Catholicism, with its 23 million faithful, still comprised an impressive, independent democratic constituency that, together with the Catholic hierarchy, remained steadfast in its condemnation of National Socialism. While the Center Party had no viable allies to form a coalition, and therefore no purchase on power, Hitler feared a reaction from the bastion of political Catholicism as a whole, a group that was naturally much larger than the Center Party vote, with extensive links and associations on many levels throughout the country. Because of his long-standing determination to avoid a new Kulturkampf and the attendant risk of a successful Catholic noncooperation or resistance, Hitler was not inclined to tackle the bishops head-on. Something nevertheless had to be done to neutralize them, and it was here that Pacelli's Reich Concordat ambitions came to Hitler's aid.

From Hitler's point of view, the ideal solution to the Catholic threat was precisely a summit agreement with the Vatican in all respects similar to the Lateran Treaty, which had outlawed Catholic political action in Italy and effectively integrated the Church into Fascist Italy. As Hitler saw it, such an agreement would grant the Catholic Church freedoms restricted to religious practice and education in exchange for Catholic withdrawal, on the Holy See's own insistence (and on definitions to be dictated by the Nazi regime), from social and political action.

There could be no Reich Concordat, however, without the bishops reversing their denunciation of National Socialism. Nor could there be a Reich Concordat unless the Center Party, before its demise, gave legal force to the passing of the Enabling Act that would grant Hitler powers of dictatorship. Throughout the period of the Weimar Republic, no government had got close to accepting Pacelli's terms for a concordat. Only by dictatorial fiat, with the Führer dealing directly with Secretary of State Pacelli in the name of the Pope, could such a treaty become a reality.

In his first cabinet meeting after the elections, on March 7, Hitler revealed his anxiety about the power of Catholicism when he told ministers that the Center Party would be defeated only if the Vatican could be persuaded to ditch it.[3] When Hitler raised the matter of the Enabling Act, Papen spoke of his conversation the previous day with Ludwig Kaas. According to Papen, Kaas, who made no initiatives without Pacelli, had offered "a clear break with the past" and the "cooperation of his party." Events would show the extent to which Kaas, or more accurately, Pacelli, drew an equivalence between support for the Enabling Act and the commencement of negotiations for a Reich Concordat. At the same time, these developments would reveal the extent to which the strings were being pulled in the Secretariat of State at the Vatican.

An indication that Pacelli was putting out feelers toward Hitler came on March 13, a week after Hitler's first cabinet meeting. In a note to Germany's Vatican envoy, Pacelli brought to the Führer's attention recent words of praise uttered by the Pope for the Reich chancellor's anti-Bolshevist crusade. The envoy commented, "In the Secretariat of State it has been suggested that these comments should be taken as an indirect endorsement of the action of the Reich chancellor and the government against Communism."[4]

Despite these flattering signals from Pacelli's office, the German bishops were in the main as opposed to Hitler as they had ever been. Cardinal Michael von Faulhaber of Munich, who had been present in the Vatican when the Pope made his remarks at a consistory of cardinals, recorded that everybody present had been startled: "The Holy Father interprets this from afar. He does not understand the actual implications, but only the final goal."[5] So anxious was Cardinal Faulhaber at the prospects for Catholics under Hitler that on March 10 he wrote to President Hindenburg, telling of the "fear that besets wide circles of the Catholic population."[6] On March 18, moreover, when Papen visited Cardinal Bertram to inquire whether there had been a change of heart among the bishops, the hierarchy spokesman told Papen that nothing whatsoever had changed; in fact, the prelate added, if there was any alteration to be made it should be on the part of "the Führer of the National Socialists."[7] Which only served to confirm Hitler's anxieties. But the way forward for Hitler lay in neither his dealings with the bishops nor the Center Party collective leadership but in the party's chairman, Ludwig Kaas, as Pacelli's unofficial representative in Germany.

In the days following the March elections, although he was the leader of a great parliamentary party heading for breakup, Kaas became curiously inactive and unreceptive. At a party meeting in Cologne a week after the election, Heinrich Brüning, the former chancellor, urged the party not to collaborate with anything so unconstitutional as the Enabling Act. According to a witness who took minutes on the discussion, Kaas, who had declined to express an opinion on the matter, pounded the table and yelled, "Am I the leader of the party? If not, who is?" The writer then raised the question: "Had Kaas in his negotiations with Hitler perhaps made promises to the latter so that he had to stand firm?"[8]

As historian Owen Chadwick has commented, Kaas's "role in making the party vote for Hitler's Enabling bill of March 1933 is still one of the most controversial acts of Germany history."[9]

Kaas was indeed deep in negotiation with Hitler, as well as in close communication with Pacelli in Rome, and the talks appeared to be prospering in the view of both parties. So much so that by the cabinet meeting on March 15, Hitler announced that he now anticipated no difficulty reaching a two-thirds majority in support of the Enabling Act. Five days later, Goebbels noted in his diary that "the Center Party will accept [the Enabling Act]." (In 1937 Goebbels stated in his newspaper *Der Angriff* that Kaas had agreed to the Enabling Act in exchange for the government's agreement to negotiate a Reich Concordat with the Holy See.)[10]

When Kaas eventually faced the members of the parliamentary Center Party in Berlin on March 22–23, before the critical Reichstag vote on the Enabling Act, he pleaded with them to support a "yes" vote in order to exert a moral hold over the Führer and his stated promises to the Catholic Church—promises he was confident Hitler would deliver in writing (although the written promises failed to materialize). Brüning declared that he could never vote in favor, since the act was "the most monstrous resolution ever demanded of a parliament." In his speech to the Reichstag, Hitler had gone out of his way to declare his determination to seek accommodation with the Vatican. He set the highest store, he said, on "further cultivating and strengthening friendly relations with the Holy See." According to Brüning, Kaas declared Hitler's pledge "the greatest success that had been achieved in any country for the last ten years [in state relations]."[11] The phrase echoed precisely and hauntingly, as if written into the speech, the words spoken by Pacelli fourteen years earlier when he presented his credentials to Reich President Ebert: "I will devote my entire strength to cultivating and strengthening the relations between the Holy See and Germany." Hitler's declaration was a clear indication of an agreed-upon adjustment of relations with Catholicism, to be negotiated from the summit by corresponding authoritarians in Berlin and Rome.

After the speech, a minority led by Brüning pleaded passionately against handing Hitler the legal means of conducting a dictatorship. But in a straw poll, only fourteen of the seventy-four delegates stood out against the act. Kaas then pleaded with the minority on the score of the probable threat to their personal safety, whereupon Brüning spoke of resigning his deputyship, and Wirth, in tears, offered to join him. Eventually, after listening to differing Catholic unionist views in the partly ruined Reichstag building, Brüning was persuaded that a split in the Center Party would destroy any prospect of a future Catholic resistance to religious persecution.[12] In order to make a disciplined and united stand as a party, the minority eventually fell in with the majority. They joined their colleagues and marched through the battalions of jeering storm troopers to the Kroll Opera House to take the vote.

The Center Party's endorsement of the Enabling Act, it appears, was in recognition that Kaas, who had been in close contact with Hitler all along, was in the best position to judge the issue.

The act, passed later that day by 441 to 94 votes (only the Social Democrats opposed), gave Hitler a comfortable majority vote to pass laws without the consent of the Reichstag and to make treaties with foreign governments (the very first of which was to be his treaty with Pacelli). The legislation declared that the powers of the president would remain inviolable, but the precise terms of the document rendered the clause meaningless.

The next day, without informing anyone within his party as to his destination or purpose, Kaas took the train to Rome for secret discussions with Pacelli. Two years later, Kaas was to confirm in a letter to the German Vatican envoy the precise link between his endorsement of the Enabling Act and a future Reich Concordat: "Immediately after the passing of the Enabling Act, in the acceptance of which I had played a positive role on the basis of certain guarantees given to me by the Reich chancellor (guarantees of a general political as well as a cultural political nature), on March 24 I traveled to Rome.... In order to develop the views I put forward in the Reichstag on March 23, I wanted to explain the situation created by the Reich chancellor's declaration and to investigate the possibilities of a comprehensive understanding between Church and State."[13]

In the meantime, Hitler's cunning statement to the Reichstag, with its promise of close ties with the Holy See, indeed with the broad hint of ties already initiated, did not fail to embarrass the German Catholic bishops, who had been thrown into a quandary in the previous weeks by a series of government blandishments and reassurances. Broadcasting to the country, Hitler had appealed to God and assured the population that Christianity would be the basis of his reconstruction of the nation. On March 21, Hitler had published a note declaring his "great distress" at not being able to attend a religious service of reconciliation on Potsdam Day as a result of the Catholic bishops banishing the Catholic Nazi leadership from the sacraments. The bishops were thus put under pressure to make some kind of answer to the new chancellor; but while some believed that it was opportune to revoke the denunciation of the party, a number of prelates, including Cardinal Schulte of Cologne and the bishops of Aachen, Limburg, Trier, Münster, and Paderborn, urged that the denunciation should be renewed and strengthened. Hitler's Reichstag statement on March 23, however, and the acquiescence of the Center Party together with extravagant government reassurances had weakened the resolve of key bishops. In addition there were those signals from Rome, emanating from Pacelli's office.

Cardinal Faulhaber on March 24 sent a letter to the bishops of his conference in the south of Germany: "I must after what I have encountered at the highest places in Rome—which I cannot communicate to you now—reserve to myself, in spite of everything, more toleration towards the new government which today is not only in a position of power—which our formulated principles could not reverse—but which has achieved this power in a legal fashion."[14] A reference to the constitutional legality of Hitler's government had first been noted in L'Osservatore Romano. Hence the legality that Hitler had sought, and that Kaas, with the prompting of Pacelli, had granted, now became the very stimulus that was to persuade the Catholic bishops to endorse Hitler's regime.

The same day Cardinal Bertram, hierarchy spokesman, distributed the draft of a conciliatory statement for the bishops' consideration. The breakneck speed with which the bishops were required to respond remains baffling to this day. Ludwig Volk, a Jesuit historian of the period, intimated in his original exploration of these events that the pressure had come "from other quarters," meaning the Vatican. Papen, he argued, had spent a crucial weekend persuading Bertram that a public statement of conciliation from the bishops could aid the process of a Reich Concordat, whereas the lack of one would only hinder matters. By this stage Papen had scheduled a meeting with Pacelli in Rome, who was at work with Kaas on a prospective Pacelli-Hitler agreement.

On March 26 the Protestant churches across Germany formally acknowledged their acceptance of Hitler and his regime. The Protestants, having watched the Vatican negotiating a concordat with Hitler, now sought, and were to achieve, a similar agreement of their own on the Catholic model.

An agreed Catholic bishops' statement conciliatory to the Nazis was hurriedly published on March 28 throughout the country. It contained reservations, but it indicated, despite its evident ambivalence, a devastating acquiescence on the part of the bishops.

> Without revoking the judgment made in our previous declarations in respect to certain religious-ethical errors, the episcopate believes it can cherish the confidence that the designated general prohibitions and warnings need no longer be considered necessary. For Catholic Christians, to whom the voice of the Church is sacred, it is not necessary at the present moment to make special admonition to be loyal to the lawful government and to fulfill conscientiously the duties of citizenship, rejecting on principle all illegal or subversive behavior.[15]

The Nazi press welcomed the statement as an endorsement of Hitler's policies, giving no clue to the ambiguity intended by the hierarchy. Center politicians were appalled, for it appeared that the bishops were saying that the Nazis were preferable to the Catholic Center Party. The reaction of the Catholic faithful was one of widespread perplexity and betrayal. A typical response was that of Father Franziscus Stratman, senior Catholic chaplain at Berlin University, who wrote to Cardinal Faulhaber on April 10: "The souls of well-disposed people are in a turmoil as a result of the tyranny of the National Socialists, and I am merely stating a fact when I say that the authority of the bishops among innumerable Catholics and non-Catholics has been shaken by the quasi-approval of the National Socialist movement."[16]

After returning from consultations with Pacelli at the beginning of April, Kaas published an editorial welcoming Hitler's Reichstag speech as the logical development of the "idea of union" of Church and State. He declared that the country was in an evolutionary process in which the "undeniably excessive formal freedoms" of the Weimar Republic would give way to "an austere and, temporarily no doubt, excessive state discipline" over all walks of life. The Center Party, he went on, had been obliged to cooperate in this process as "sowers of the future."[17]

As if to exculpate the extraordinary ease and suddenness of the hierarchy's affirmation of the regime, and to underline Pacelli's role in it, Faulhaber wrote on April 20 that the bishops had been put in this tragic situation "because of the position of Rome."[18] Rome, however, in the person of Eugenio Pacelli, had far from completed its acquiescence in the face of Hitler's determination to destroy political Catholicism in Germany.

The Jewish Boycott

Following the bishops' statement, Hitler at short notice had convened a working committee on Church-State relations for March 31, prompting Kaas to hurry back from Rome to lobby for the protection of Catholic education.

The timing of the committee was significant, for on April 1 the Nazis began their boycott of Jewish businesses across the country. It was not the first indication of the persecutions in store. A week earlier, thirty brownshirts had broken into Jewish homes in a small town in southwest Germany, herded the occupants into the town hall, and beaten them up. The attack was repeated in a neighboring town, resulting in the deaths of two men. The boycott, however, was something different. As Saul Friedländer has commented, it was "the first major test on a national scale of the attitude of the Christian Churches toward the situation of the Jews under the new government."[19] Yet, even as Hitler deliberated with Christian representatives on future relations between his regime and the Churches, there was no word of protest as a result of this first systematic and nationwide persecution of the Jews, neither from Germany nor from Rome.

Cardinal Faulhaber of Munich, referring to the Nazi attacks on the Jews, wrote at length to Pacelli, confirming that protest was pointless since it could only extend the struggle to Catholics. "Jews," he told Pacelli, "can help themselves." All the same, he went on, it was "especially unjust and painful that by this action the Jews, even those who have been baptized for ten and twenty years and are good Catholics ... are legally still considered Jews, and as doctors or lawyers are to lose their positions." There is no record of a reply from Pacelli, and no indication from his future directives that he disagreed with the cardinal. In response to a plea for intervention in defense of the Jews that same week, Cardinal Bertram pointed out that there were "immediate issues of much greater importance: schools, the maintaining of Catholic associations, sterilization." In conclusion, he repeated the same reflection: "The Jews," he declared, "are capable of helping themselves."[20]

Among the many thousands of individuals affected by the Jewish boycott was Edith Stein, a German-Jewish philosopher who had been influenced by Max Scheler at the University of Freiburg, where she researched a doctorate entitled "On the Problem of Empathy." An atheist from her teens, Stein was initially drawn to Christianity emotionally, but felt a different kind of attraction after reading the autobiography of St. Teresa of Ávila, the sixteenth-century Carmelite mystic. She wrote that her "return to God made me feel Jewish again," and she thought of her conversion to Christianity as existing "not only in a spiritual sense, but in blood terms." She became a Catholic in 1922 and by April 1933, when the boycott came into operation, she had been accepted for a philosophy post at the German Institute for Scientific Pedagogy in Münster. The April decree against the Jews deprived her of the appointment.

By October 1933 she had entered the Carmelite convent at Cologne, taking the name Sister Teresa Benedicta of the Cross. From the cloister she wrote a passionate letter to Pius XI, begging him to "deplore the hatred, persecution, and displays of anti-Semitism directed against the Jews, at any time and from any source." Her letter drew no response. Four years were to pass before he came to issue the tardy encyclical on anti-racism, *Mit brennender Sorge*.

Papen and Kaas in Rome

Meanwhile, the discussion at Hitler's working committee on Church-State relations had by April 2 progressed sufficiently for the papal nuncio in Berlin to inform Pacelli that Papen, the vice-chancellor, wished to come to Rome to see him for discussions before Easter. As we have seen, Pacelli had been fully informed by Faulhaber of the persecution unleashed against the Jews at the very point when he was to enter into substantive negotiations for a concordat with its perpetrators. The Reich Concordat, moreover, was now to take those issues of "greater importance" out of the hands of German Catholics and place them in the hands of Pius XI, or more precisely his trusted Secretary of State. Small wonder, therefore, that the Catholic bishops felt so little responsibility for the fate of the Jews when the Holy See entrusted them with scant responsibility for the fate of their own Church.

On the evening of April 7, Papen left for the Eternal City, having confided to the chief of Vatican affairs in the Foreign Office that he "intended to demand as one of the chief concessions the acceptance of a provision which was also contained in the Italian concordat [the Lateran Treaty], according to which the clergy were forbidden to be active for, or to join, any political party." With its traditional but minority clerical membership and its multilevel reliance on parish networks, such a clause could only spell the end of the Center Party, as well as social and political action on the part of all Catholic associations in Germany.

The following morning, April 8, in the dining car of the Munich–Rome Express, Papen "by chance" met Ludwig Kaas, also returning to Rome. The notion that they were both headed for Pacelli's office without prior knowledge of each other's intentions, as Kaas suggested at the time, seems implausible. As it was, Kaas recorded that they agreed that the chances of a Reich Concordat were now a distinct possibility. Papen told Kaas in outline the basic requirements of the treaty from the Reich's point of view: "the safeguarding of religious rights for Catholics in exchange for the depoliticizing of the clergy and the disbanding of the Center Party."

According to Kaas, as the two men discussed over breakfast the ideal relationship between Germany's 23 million Catholics and Hitler's regime, Kaas reassured Papen that "some evidence had to be given of the creation of adequate cultural-political guarantees. If the latter were the case, then I certainly should not be petty."[21] As a result of their conversation, Kaas, who had no official status in the negotiations, would become a key figure in the talks. As the Italian countryside rolled by, he offered to "be available" to Papen in the negotiations ahead, and Papen graciously accepted. Kaas thus assumed the role of mediator while remaining principally loyal in mind and soul to Pacelli.

Just how intimate Kaas had become with Pacelli is evinced by a series of remarks in Sister Pasqualina's autobiography after the death of both men. She tells us that Kaas, who "regularly accompanied Pacelli on holiday to Rorschach," was linked to Pacelli in "adoration, honest love and unconditional loyalty." She goes on to describe tensions between Kaas and Father Leiber as a result of "mutual jealousy when Pacelli favored the one or the other, which even Pacelli's genius as a diplomat could not easily soothe." She also wrote of an episode when Pacelli was deeply upset by Kaas's sudden departure for Germany.[22]

Pacelli and Papen met in the cardinal's office on the Monday of Holy Week, April 10, and set a working schedule whereby Papen and Kaas would produce a basic draft for a meeting by Holy Saturday. During the fullest week in the Church's liturgical calendar, the men worked at furious speed, drafting articles that in other circumstances would have taken years to reach fruition. Pacelli and Kaas spent Easter Sunday and Easter Monday going through the draft point by point.

The German hierarchy and clergy had not been involved, nor had the Catholic Center Party or the German laity as individuals or at large. The bishops were even denied information about the *fact* of the negotiations. Yet they could not help hearing rumors. When Cardinal Bertram, president of the bishops' conference, petitioned Pacelli with a series of anxieties about the rumored negotiations on April 18, Pacelli did not deign to respond for two weeks. He merely confirmed that "possible

negotiations had been initiated." Three weeks later, when the final
points were being argued, Pacelli patently lied when he informed Cardinal Faulhaber of Munich that there had been merely talk of concordat,
but nothing concrete.[23]

Meanwhile, the Center Party was made all the more impotent by
virtue of the absence from Berlin of its chairman, Ludwig Kaas, now
based permanently in Eugenio Pacelli's apartments in the Vatican. It had
been suggested to Kaas that he should resign, but he refused, arguing
that "it would upset things in Rome"—the clearest indication that one
of the last great democratic parties in Germany was now being run at
the whim of Pacelli. In a letter to the vicar-general of Passau at this
time, Franz Eggersdorfer of Munich University observed tartly: "The
future of German Catholicism appears to be decided in Rome. A result
of the progressive centralism."[24]

What was driving Pacelli to conclude an early draft in such unseemly
haste and secrecy? The Center Party, in Pacelli's view, had to go. But
before its final dissolution, the circumstance of its continued existence
(according to Pacelli's tactic of two decades) offered a bargaining
counter in his negotiations with Hitler. Time was of the essence. For
his part, Hitler nourished two principal aims in this helter-skelter rush
to an agreement. First, as we have seen, he was determined to separate religious Catholicism from political Catholicism, by legal measures and
without delay. Second, there was the prospect of a bold international
propaganda coup. As he had commented on the conclusion of the Lateran Treaty in 1929: "If the Pope today comes to such an understanding
with Fascism, then he is at least of the opinion that Fascism—and therefore nationalism—is justifiable for the faithful and compatible with the
Catholic faith."[25] While the Holy See for centuries had been in the habit
of signing treaties with monarchs and governments inimical to its beliefs
and values, the terms of the Lateran Treaty had indeed established the
semblance of an unprecedented integration of Catholicism and the cor-
porate state. Hitler saw with great clarity that the concordat could be
presented as a papal endorsement of the Nazi regime and its policies.
Realizing the impatience of Pacelli and the inherent weakness of the
Cardinal Secretary's aims, preoccupied as they were with the power of
the Holy See, Hitler could dictate the pace of the negotiations and manipulate them entirely to his own considerable advantage.

The German Bishops Capitulate

Papen returned to Berlin on the Tuesday of Easter Week. After a "general" discussion with Hitler, he could inform Pacelli that the Führer was ready "to grant far-reaching guarantees in the matter of the schools" but that the wording of the depoliticizing article was "quite inadequate."[26] In a flourish of diplomatic hubris, despite his personal preference for depoliticization, Pacelli had attempted to fob off Hitler with a newly expanded article in the Code of Canon Law requiring episcopal permission for a Catholic priest to hold office in a political organization.

What had motivated Pacelli to muddy the water when it came to the depoliticizing clause? Had he been assailed by the last-minute scruple that he was about to undermine the Church in Germany? No such thought seems to have occurred to him. Rather, it was a negotiating ploy. How well these two men seemed to understand each other. The negotiations continued into May, until, in the third week of that month, Hitler upped the stakes by penning into his draft that *all* political activity by the Catholic clergy was to be categorically forbidden.

In the meantime, during the critical months of April and May, the Catholic Center Party, leaderless, neglected by Rome and the hierarchy alike, was floundering, its once faithful supporters abandoning hope by the hundreds of thousands. And at the same time, the Nazis were growing ever more loud and confident, convinced of their victorious destiny as the exclusive party of the state, the party to bring full employment and prosperity to a country racked by economic crises and foreign humiliation. The desertion of Catholics to the National Socialists, at first a trickle, now became a great river in the chasm created by the collapse of the once great Center Party.

Finally, the leadership insisted on Kaas's resignation, which he granted grudgingly over the telephone from the Vatican. Heinrich Brüning was elected his successor on May 6. But the Hitler juggernaut was by now unstoppable, as were the forces for voluntary dissolution of the Center Party. Against all odds, Brüning pleaded with the party members to stay united and autonomous.

And now, with the negotiations on the concordat far advanced, Pacelli decided to bring the German bishops into the picture. The occasion was an *ad limina* visit to Rome by Bishop Wilhelm Berning of Osnabrück and Archbishop Gröber of Freiburg on May 18. Pacelli's choice of emissaries left nothing to chance. Both were Nazi sympathizers. The time had come, Pacelli told the two prelates, for all the German bishops to consolidate their view of the concordat.

As it happened, a meeting of the German bishops had been scheduled for the end of May to review the standpoint of the episcopate toward the Third Reich. When they came together, however, the issue of the concordat, successfully stage-managed by Pacelli's two envoy bishops, dominated their deliberations. Berning and Gröber assured the assembled prelates that the concordat was virtually complete and that the remaining focus of negotiation was the depoliticization clause.[27] The Cardinal Secretary of State wanted their support, Berning told the bishops, and speed was of the essence.

The fragmentary notes of Ludwig Sebastian, bishop of Speyer, indicate that there were fierce disagreements at this critical meeting. Cardinal Schulte of Cologne objected that under the Nazi government "law and right" were nonexistent and "no concordat could be concluded with such a government." Bishop Konrad von Preysing distributed a memorandum to the conference reminding the bishops that the view of the world held by the National Socialist Party was completely at odds with that of the Catholic Church. "We owe it to the Catholic people to open their eyes to the dangers for faith and morals which emerge from National Socialist ideology." He asked for a pastoral letter setting out the errors of Nazism to be addressed to all Germany. It was essential, he said, to have such a letter to refer to "in a conflict which is probably coming."[28] All too little, and too late.

The objectors were a minority. The fact that Pacelli was involved in direct negotiations with Hitler inspired the bishops with a measure of confidence. All the same, they evidently saw the dangers of the depoliticization clause, Article 31, since the provision could ban any and every species of social action performed under the auspices and in the name of the Catholic Church. Rushed into a corner by Pacelli's envoy bishops, the hierarchy did not make their suggested revision a condition of acceptance. Following a persuasive plea by Archbishop Gröber, the German bishops endorsed the concordat, passing the responsibility back to Pacelli.

As a result of the bishops' decision, a pastoral message drafted by Gröber was published on June 3 announcing the end of the hierarchy's opposition to the Nazi regime, provided that the state respected the rights and freedoms of the Church—notably in relation to Catholic schools and associations. On securing the agreement of the bishops, Gröber wrote to Kaas: "Praise God, I succeeded in getting approval for the accompanying pastoral. . . . A series of wishes were expressed but I could easily reject them because they demand the impossible."[29]

Cardinal Faulhaber brought the matter to a close by informing Papen that he was willing to yield on Article 31 because "the concordat as a whole is so important, for instance [in the matter of] confessional schools, that I feel that it ought not to fail on this point."[30] From Pacelli's point of view, the bishops' decision was a victory, since he judged it not so much a surrender to Hitler as a capitulation to the will of the Holy See, leaving him free, with their apparent backing, to bring the concordat to a successful conclusion by his own criteria.

Pacelli's complacency on June 3, however, was short-lived. During the week in which he received the bishops' unhappy and reserved acquiescence, news reached Rome that made it impossible for him to ignore the savage realities of Nazi rule and the true nature of his negotiating partner. The occasion was a rally of Catholic apprentices in Munich scheduled for June 8–11, drawing 25,000 young Catholic visitors from all over Germany. Originally banned by Heinrich Himmler and Reinhard Heydrich, the SS leader and his deputy, the rally was allowed to go ahead on condition that the marchers walked with banners furled. After sporadic attacks on individuals by brownshirts during the first two days, the Nazi uniformed thugs organized a series of violent attacks on larger groups on Saturday evening. Catholic youths in their hundreds were beaten up and chased off the streets, their distinctive orange shirts ripped from their backs. The rally at the open-air Mass planned for Sunday morning was canceled. If Pacelli had entertained any lingering illusions as to what the Nazis understood by "political Catholicism," he was now disabused. It was now plainly evident that the ban on political activity on the part of the Catholic clergy, and the ban on all but purely religious associations, as referred to in Article 31 of the proposed concordat, extended to any and all Catholic public activities that the Nazis in their sole discretion defined as political.

The reaction of the Catholic hierarchy was everything the SA instigators could have hoped for. Faulhaber wrote to the Bavarian bishops, counseling them to discontinue rallies of Catholic youth associations, "since we do not want to risk the lives of our young men and a government ban on youth organizations." He further insisted that stern action must be taken "against clergy who speak imprudently." Here, from the outset, was Pacelli's centrist policy for German Catholicism in the early summer of 1933: paralysis through self-policing. The concord had not even been signed and the Nazi police state had hardly got under way.

A mighty Church with dedicated pastors and a host of lay social and political organizations was in a state of self-imposed inertia, looking to the Vatican for the next move, the next idea, the next directive. In the meantime, Hitler was taking full advantage of that inaction to outlaw and destroy every vestige of social and political Catholic capacity and identity. Throughout June, Center Party deputies and members were subjected to a wave of terror: house searches, arrests, intimidation. In Munich, Fritz Gerlich, the courageously outspoken Catholic editor of *Der Gerade Weg*, was beaten almost to death in the magazine's offices, then thrown into a concentration camp (he was murdered a year later). In Bavaria, where the Center's local counterpart, the Bavarian People's Party, had enormous traditional strength, some two thousand supporters and officials were jailed. The Nazi press justifications claimed that there was evidence that "Catholicism aims in every way to sabotage the orders of the government and to work against it."[31]

On June 22 Papen met with Hitler to discuss the state of the concordat negotiations as a prelude to the vice-chancellor's meeting in the Vatican for a final session with Pacelli. Hitler's definitive position on Article 31 was now this: "In consideration of the guarantees afforded by the conditions of this treaty, and of legislation protecting the rights and freedom of the Catholic Church in the Reich and its regional states, the Holy See will ensure a ban on all clergy and members of religious congregations from party political activity."[32] The clause acknowledged the Holy See's power to control and coerce Catholic clergy in Germany with efficient sanctions through canon law. It was the ultimate authoritarians' Church-State charter.

The Final Negotiations

Papen arrived in Rome on June 28, and Article 31 was placed on the table for Pacelli, the Curia, and the Pope to ponder while news of fresh acts of persecution and suppression of the Church in Germany were relayed to the Secretariat of State by the hour. Pacelli may well have been reminded of that final meeting in June of 1914, when the cardinals saw no retreat from the Serbian Concordat, which he himself had sought so assiduously, that did not spell greater suffering for the Catholics in the region.

The concordat text was finalized on Sunday morning, July 1, 1933, and Pacelli went over it with Pius XI that day. The dogged Pontiff, fully apprised of the acts of violence against Catholics across Germany in the previous weeks, had a new and final stipulation. Pacelli noted at the end of their meeting that the Pope had insisted that there should now be "guarantees of restitution for acts of violence." The Holy Father had had enough of "alternating abuse and negotiation." Like a bride-to-be battered by her fiancé and vociferously insisting on restitution in her wedding contract, Pius XI was asking Hitler to "make a declaration on reparations or there would be no signature."[33] On July 2 Pacelli and Kaas put the finishing touches on the terms of the treaty. But there was a crucial item of unfinished business that still threatened to unravel everything.

Back in Germany, Brüning, the new head of the shattered Center Party, had been attempting to salvage what he could of a demoralized political organization, in preparation for the persecutions that he knew lay ahead. Papen had been telling Pacelli and Kaas that it was Brüning's refusal to dissolve the party that prevented completion of the concordat and laid the Church open to renewed attacks. The German bishops warned Pacelli that he should not trust Papen's version of events. But the die was cast; Pacelli and Kaas now understood that the Center Party *must go* in order to smooth the passage of the article on Church associations in the Reich Concordat. With the encouragement of Pacelli, Kaas on July 2 called the Center Party left-winger Joseph Joos and shouted indignantly into the telephone: "What! Haven't you dissolved yourselves yet?" Joos was to remember for the rest of his life the order from the Vatican insisting on the sacrifice of the Center Party to ensure the success of Pacelli's diplomacy.[34]

Since Papen already had Hitler's authority to make a full settlement, and since the definition and delay of restitution was sure to be an endless process, he saw no problem with the final papal demand. On July 3 he forwarded the text to Hitler by special courier with a self-congratulatory covering letter. That evening the concordat document was dispatched to Berlin.

The Center Party Disbanded

The next day, July 4, after many Center politicians had threatened to defect to the National Socialists, Brüning agreed with bitterness in his heart to dissolve the party. It was the sole remaining democratic party in Germany, and the fact that it had gone into voluntary rather than enforced liquidation was to have immediate and far-reaching consequences. The party's complicity with its own dissolution, along with the bishops' apparent approval of the one-party state, was a circumstance that boosted the spirits of the Nazis and drove Catholics in ever greater numbers into the bosom of National Socialism.

Monsignor Ludwig Kaas, who was to remain in the Vatican for the rest of his life, was much to blame for the pathetic implosion of the party. His opportunism, his divided loyalties, his absences for months on end in the service of Pacelli, had been incompatible with the responsibilities of a chairman of a great democratic party. But Pacelli surely bears the principal blame, for he had been Kaas's mentor, religious superior, and close personal intimate, and he had never deviated from his animosity toward Catholic political parties independent of the Holy See's control.

Almost thirty years later, Robert Leiber claimed that Pacelli had said, on hearing of the dissolution: "A pity that it had to come now."[35] Pacelli's apologists have exploited the phrase in an attempt to exculpate him from any responsibility in the party's tragic end. Elsewhere, however, Leiber admitted that this was no pang of regret but an expression of irritation at the loss of a bargaining chip before closure. "[Pacelli] wished," wrote Leiber in 1958, "that [the party] could have postponed its dissolution until after the signing of the concordat. The mere fact of its existence, he said, might have been of use at the negotiation stage."[36] In 1934 Pacelli denied that the voluntary disbanding of the party had been a quid pro quo for the concordat; but as Klaus Scholder comments: "Given all that we know, this is untrue."

Ex-chancellor Heinrich Brüning, who observed the entire process, had no doubts about the connection. In 1935 he was quoted as saying:

Behind the agreement with Hitler stood not the Pope, but the
Vatican bureaucracy and its leader, Pacelli. He visualized an
authoritarian state and an authoritarian Church directed by
the Vatican bureaucracy, the two to conclude an eternal
league with one another. For that reason Catholic parliamentary parties, like the Center, in Germany, were inconvenient
to Pacelli and his men, and were dropped without regret in
various countries. The Pope [Pius XI] did not share these
ideas.[37]

Hitler now held all the cards and he played them with ruthless brilliance. Just when Pacelli thought that closure was a matter of hours away,
Hitler once again called a halt. Summoning Rudolf Buttmann, a legal
expert in the Ministry of the Interior, Hitler now insisted that the civil
servant go through the document with a fine-tooth comb. As an indication of the importance Hitler attached to the treaty (Hitler, according
to Scholder, spent more time and effort on the concordat with Pacelli
than on any other treaty in the entire era of the Third Reich), on July 5
he asked Buttmann to set out a critique of the document in the presence
of the minister of the interior, the foreign minister, and the finance minister. That same day, Buttmann flew from Berlin to Munich and from
Munich to Rome, where he joined Papen and then went on to meet with
Pacelli to explain Hitler's last-minute queries and demands. The points
in dispute involved the distinction in nature between religious and political Catholic associations. Hitler also wanted greater precision on the issue of restitution for Nazi attacks.

On July 7, a day of protracted wrangling, Pacelli became irritable and
openly spoke of detecting a "spirit of distrust" on the German side.
Given the attitude of the Reich negotiators, he declared, it seemed unlikely that they could reach a conclusion.[38] In Buttmann, however, the
Cardinal Secretary of State had met his match. The civil servant responded smoothly that it made so much more sense to iron out everything at this stage than to run into difficulties after the document had
been signed. He also asserted, to Pacelli's extreme annoyance, that comparing the Lateran Treaty with the Reich Concordat was not to compare
like with like, since in Germany there were other confessions, including
the "overwhelming Protestant majority."

The sticking point remained the issue of Catholic associations. Buttmann was arguing that only those associations that could be characterized as purely "religious, cultural, and charitable" could be protected. All others would have to be disbanded or merged with civil or Nazi associations. But how should the distinction between the two categories—religious and civil—be decided, and by whom? Since Pacelli was not prepared to accept Buttmann's formula without a formal definition of the distinction, both sides eventually agreed on the inclusion of a proviso to seek a joint definition at some future date. This turned out, as events were to prove, a remarkably irresponsible decision for Pacelli to have made. The precise wording of Pius XI's restitution clause also created difficulties, which were only resolved by Hitler himself in the course of a marathon telephone conversation with Buttmann on the evening of July 7.

The following day, Saturday, July 8, at the stroke of six in the evening by the bells of St. Peter's, the two sides came together in the salone of the Secretariat of State for the initialing ceremony. Pacelli and Papen sat side by side. Pacelli was attended by Monsignor Giuseppe Pizzardo of the Secretariat of State and Ludwig Kaas, while Papen was attended by Buttmann. Pacelli was evidently on edge, since he had received news that day of a parish priest who had been dragged barefoot out of his house in Königsbach and beaten up.[39]

As the initialing proceeded, Pacelli, normally meticulous in matters of protocol, mistakenly wrote out his full signature on one of the pages. Kaas saw the lapse and suggested that the copy should be kept for the Secretariat. When they had finished, Pacelli raised the matter of the beaten priest. It was the diplomatic Buttmann who responded. He suggested that it was probably a cleric with a high political profile. In any case, he added, the people of the region were very volatile.[40]

Hitler Hails the Concordat

On Monday the press throughout Germany carried news of the concordat in banner headlines, and Hitler sanctioned a statement agreed by Pacelli the previous Friday. It contained the two crucial concessions upon which the Vatican had insisted, but the published statement was

introduced by a sentence that had not been agreed upon and that made
the concessions seem a historical triumph for National Socialism:

> The conclusion of the concordat seems to me [wrote Hitler]
> to give sufficient guarantee that the Reich members of the
> Roman Catholic confession will from now on put themselves.
> without reservation at the service of the new National Social-
> ist state.

> Therefore I am ordering as follows:
> 1. The disbanding of such organizations as are recognized by
>   the present treaty, and whose disbanding occurred with-
>   out the order of the Reich government, is to be rescinded
>   immediately.
> 2. All coercive measures against the clergy and other leaders
>   of these Catholic organizations are to be revoked. Repeti-
>   tion of such measures in the future is not allowed and will
>   be punished on the basis of existing laws.[41]

The treaty was formally signed in the Secretariat of State on July 20
by Papen and Pacelli. A photograph of the ceremony shows the participants stiff and unsmiling. Afterward there was an exchange of gifts.
Pacelli received a Meissen Madonna, Papen a papal medal; Buttmann
was presented with a photograph of the Pope in a silver frame. The
German embassy in Rome donated 25,000 lire to the Holy See for
charitable purposes.[42]

As far as the Reich was concerned, the remarkable affair of the concordat had been brought to a conclusion at a cabinet meeting on July 14,
when Hitler refused to debate the issue with his ministers, insisting that
"only the great success should be noted." Listing the advantages of the
treaty, he emphasized the Vatican's recognition of "the one nationalist
German state," and the withdrawal of the Church from political organizations. The disbanding of the Center Party, he noted, "could be
regarded as final."[43]

At this meeting Hitler expressed the chilling opinion that the concordat had created an atmosphere of confidence that would be "especially
significant in the urgent struggle against international Jewry." There is
no record of further explanation, but the statement can be understood

readily from two points of view. First, the very fact that the Vatican had signed such a treaty indicated both at home and abroad, despite Pacelli's disclaimers on July 26, Catholic moral approval of Hitler's policies. Second, the treaty constrained the Holy See, the German hierarchy, the clergy, and the faithful to silence on any issue the Nazi regime deemed political. To be specific, since the persecution and elimination of the Jews in Germany was by now a stated policy, the treaty had legally bound the Catholic Church in Germany to silence on outrages against the Jews.

Also adopted at the July 14 cabinet meeting was the Law for Prevention of Genetically Diseased Offspring. This called for the sterilization of those suffering from hereditary mental or cognitive diseases, including blindness and deafness. Some 320,000-350,000 patients would be sterilized in the Third Reich, many without their own or their families' consent.[44] Such a public sterilization policy, a form of "racial cleansing" that complemented in spirit the gradual formation of the Final Solution, ran counter to Pius XI's recent elucidations on the sanctity of life in his encyclical *Casti connubii* (December 30, 1930). The concordat, as it soon became apparent, had trapped the Catholic Church into accepting such a policy and its practice as a borderline political matter, arguably off-limits even for debate let alone complaint.

German Catholics, moreover, had been placed in an immediate moral dilemma by the concordat's provisions on Catholic education, the most important area of advantage to the Church in the treaty.[45] In the terms of Article 21 of the concordat, Hitler was to protect and underwrite the cost of educating Catholic pupils and students in every kind of institution, from the primary level up to the end of secondary education. The Catholic diocesan authorities were granted the right to examine religious instruction in schools and to appoint and dismiss teachers. More important still, according to Article 23, Catholic parents could demand the provision of Catholic schooling where it did not exist, depending on local conditions. Thus Hitler had promised Catholic education a carte blanche for expansion of facilities and places for students. At the very point, however, when Hitler and Pacelli were involved in the negotiation of these educational benefits for Catholics, the Nazi government, on April 25, 1933, passed with much trumpeting its Law Against Overcrowding of German Schools and Universities, aimed at reducing the number of Jewish pupils allowed into these institutions. The act laid down a strict quota (1.5 percent of school and college enrollments) deemed appropriate for the size of the non-Aryan or Jewish student population. Hence the selfsame government with which Pacelli had negotiated favorable educational rights for Catholics had simultaneously trampled on the educational rights of the Jewish minority. Inescapably, the papacy, the Holy See, and German Catholics were being drawn into complicity with a racist and anti-Semitic government.

Another example of Catholic complicity with the regime began on April 25 when thousands of priests across Germany became part of an anti-Semitic attestation bureaucracy, supplying details of blood purity through marriage and baptism registries. This was part of the red tape that accompanied the quota systems for Jews in schools and universities and in the professions, notably law and medicine. These attestations would in time implement the Nuremberg Laws, the Nazi regime's system for distinguishing Jews from non-Jews. Catholic clerical compliance in the process would continue throughout the period of the Nazi regime and would connect ultimately the Catholic Church, and the Protestant Churches, too, with the death camps.[46] In the case of the Holy See, however, there was far greater culpability, because the outreach and coercion implicit in centralized application of canon law, which Pacelli had spent so much of his career enhancing and strengthening, was not employed to defy the process. In fact, the very reverse seems to have been the case. As Guenter Lewy writes: "The co-operation of the Church in this matter continued right through the war years, when the price of being Jewish was no longer dismissal from a governmental job and loss of livelihood, but deportation and outright physical destruction."[47] Some brave priests exploited their control of baptismal registries to thwart the Nazis, but these were isolated cases.

This was the reality of the moral abyss into which Pacelli the future Pontiff had led the once great and proud German Catholic Church. And by now Pacelli was under no illusions as to the violent nature of the Nazi regime. In early August 1933, Ivone Kirkpatrick, British minister at the Vatican, had a "long conversation" with Pacelli in the Secretariat of State in which the cardinal "made no effort to conceal his disgust at the proceedings of Herr Hitler's government."[48] Writing to Robert Vansittart at the British Foreign Office, Kirkpatrick described Pacelli as deploring the Nazi "persecution of the Jews, their proceedings against political opponents, the reign of terror to which the whole nation was subjected." Pacelli now felt moved "to explain apologetically [to Kirk-patrick] how it was that he had signed a concordat with such people." No mention was made of his earlier contention, expressed in *L'Osservatore Romano*, that the concordat had been a triumph for canon law, a victory for the Holy See, nor did he mention that he had sought just such a Reich Concordat for years. "A pistol," he said, "had been pointed at his head and he had had no alternative." Then came an extraordinary admis-sion. "The German government," Kirkpatrick reported Pacelli as saying, "had offered him concessions, concessions, it must be admitted wider than any previous German government would have agreed to, and he had to choose between an agreement on their lines and the virtual elimina-tion of the Catholic Church in the Reich." Pacelli seemed to have quickly forgotten Brüning's warning about the intrinsic weakness of con-cordats with totalitarians.

Pacelli told Kirkpatrick, who relayed it to London, that "the Church ... had no political axe to grind. They were outside the political arena." Pacelli then made this parting comment: "If the German govern-ment violated the concordat, and they were certain to do so, the Vatican would have a treaty on which to base a protest." Pacelli then said, appar-ently with a smile: "The Germans will probably not violate all the arti-cles of the concordat at the same time."[49]

Brüning Flees

And what of Heinrich Brüning, the former conservative chancellor whom Pacelli had made look like a radical liberal? Without a political base, he spent his time lobbying the bishops to stop the ratification of the Reich Concordat, which took place on September 10. He traveled throughout Germany, reading out reports of physical torture inflicted upon Jews and Social Democrats, warning that Hitler's ultimate aim was to destroy the Church. According to the Jesuit resistance organizer Fa-ther Friedrich Muckermann, it was Brüning who shook him out of the moral inertia that had resulted from the view that the Vatican approved of Nazi policies, a principal effect of the concordat of which Pacelli seemed oblivious. Brüning preached the need for resistance everywhere he could.

In October 1933, worn down by constant police surveillance, Brüning's health finally broke. The hospital in which he received treatment for a heart condition was threatened. He began to change his lodgings every two or three days. By the spring of 1934, Father Muckermann recalled in his personal story of the resistance, *Im Kampf,* that Brüning looked like a hunted animal—on edge, exhausted, waiting for the "final bullet." He at last allowed Muckermann's brother to drive him across the Dutch border on May 21, 1934, to begin a new life in exile with no more than he could put in a suitcase.

Brüning lived to influence the postwar formation of the Christian Democratic Party in Germany, "an interconfessional socially progressive party, conservative in tempo." He also supported the growth to leadership of Konrad Adenauer as the Christian Democrats' leading politician and the most viable candidate for chancellor in the Federal Republic.

9

The Concordat in Practice

The signing of the Reich Concordat marked the formal beginning of German Catholicism's acceptance of its obligations under the terms of the treaty which imposed a moral duty on Catholics to obey the Nazi rulers. Thus Catholic critics fell silent. A great Church, which might have formed the basis of an opposition, confined itself to the sacristy. There were to be notable exceptions, as for example Cardinal Faulhaber's Advent sermons in defense of the Old Testament in the fall of the year, but these were individual (and, as it turned out, qualified) acts of defiance. There was to be nothing remotely resembling a concerted act of protest from within Germany, even over issues connected with the infringements of the terms of the treaty itself.

The signing of the concordat did not result in an end to the attacks on Catholic associations and societies that were, by the Church's own criteria, nonpolitical. Nazi officials across Germany did not feel bound by the spirit of the treaty, since, through Pacelli's impetuosity, it was still incomplete in relation to the definition of "political" associations. Sporadic persecution of Catholic associations continued and increased. Bans and intimidation tactics against Catholic groups, in particular the Catholic press, were frequent in Bavaria, the traditional homeland of German Catholicism, where Himmler and Heydrich were most active. On September 19 a circular distributed by Bavaria's political police banned all Catholic meetings with the exception of choir practices and gatherings of the St. Vincent de Paul charity.[1] But the centralized process of Vatican "protection" found the German Church in a state of self-imposed passivity. Loath to complain in any direct or public fashion for fear of breaking the terms of the concordat and offending Rome, the hierarchy looked to Pacelli to act as a conduit for complaints against infringements. But there was little that Pacelli could do without a definition, or a proposed list of those organizations meriting protection. As long as no list existed, the perpetrators of bureaucratized Nazi terror could declare that the associations were unprotected; delay was thus in the Nazis' interest; given time, the targeted associations would dissolve themselves under pressure.

Early August found Pacelli exhausted and vacillating over the last act, the decision to ratify the concordat. Hesitant to take the entire responsibility for the final irreversible decision, he asked the German hierarchy to reconvene a full conference of bishops to proffer a joint opinion. Although their meeting at Fulda in the last week of August 1933 expressed fears for the survival of German Catholic newspapers, among other things, the moment for withdrawal from the treaty had passed. They voted to ask Pacelli to ratify the concordat without delay, in the tenuous belief that ratification might improve matters; but they also asked him to convey to the regime a list of their grievances, among them a pathetic request on behalf of Jewish converts to Catholicism. The fact that they now saw it necessary to ask Pacelli to speak on behalf of Jewish converts indicated the abject weakness of Pacelli's policy, involving long delays between acts of persecution and reaction in Rome.

The bishops' plea to Pacelli went as follows: "Would it be possible for the Holy See to say a heartfelt word for those Christians who had converted from Judaism, who themselves or their children or grandchildren, because of non-Aryan descent, were suffering great hardship?"[2]

The ratification of the concordat was due to be completed at a ceremony in the apostolic palace of the Vatican on September 10, with the last-minute details to be settled by Pacelli and Counselor Eugen Klee of the German embassy. Again, Pacelli had failed to clarify the distinction between religious and political associations, which could have been achieved by an agreed-upon list of organizations. After direct contact with the Reich government, he had been assured that the current attacks against Catholic bodies throughout Germany would cease only on the speedy ratification of the concordat. Pacelli therefore responded swiftly in the vain conviction that it would produce results.

In the ratification parlays, Klee treated Pacelli with an arrogance bordering on contempt. When the Cardinal Secretary handed Klee a memorandum of complaint that cited treatment of Jewish converts to Catholicism, the envoy refused to accept it. So Pacelli rewrote the document, mentioning the Jewish converts to Catholicism in a *pro memoria*. Again Klee refused to accept it, declaring that the Secretary of State would have to preface the document with a sentence stating that "the Holy See has no intention of interfering in Germany's internal affairs." Klee then insisted that only complaints referring to articles within the concordat could be accepted, and that the sentence about Catholics of Jewish descent would have to be deleted altogether.[3]

In the end, Pacelli withdrew the *pro memoria*, submitting it later in the form of a note to the embassy in which he indeed granted that "the Holy See has no intention of interfering in Germany's internal affairs." Then he went on to make his entreaty "on behalf of those German Catholics who themselves have gone over from Judaism to the Christian religion or who are descended in the first generation, or more remotely from Jews who adopted the Catholic faith, and who for reasons known to the Reich government are likewise suffering from social and economic difficulties."[4] The very fact of making such distinctions betrayed, of course, Pacelli's diplomatic collusion with the overall anti-Semitic policy of the Reich.

The final act of ratification left Pacelli in a state of nervous collapse. By September 9, the eve of the official ceremonial exchange of signed documents, he had departed for his sanatorium hideaway at Rorschach in Switzerland. When Buttmann asked whether he might follow him there to discuss the outstanding points of contention, the request was denied. The German side argued later that if only Buttmann had been able to meet with Pacelli in Switzerland the outstanding concordat differences might have been resolved speedily and easily.[5]

The following week, the ratification of the concordat was celebrated in Germany with a service of thanksgiving at St. Hedwig's Cathedral in Berlin with papal nuncio Orsenigo presiding. Nazi flags mingled with traditional Catholic banners; at the culmination of the rousing service, the "Horst Wessel song" was sung inside the church and relayed by loudspeakers to the thousands outside. Who could now doubt that the Nazi regime had the blessing of the Holy See? In fact, Archbishop Gröber went out of his way to congratulate the Third Reich on the new era of reconciliation. And yet it was evident from the very first day of ratification that in various parts of Germany, not least in Bavaria, the failure to distinguish religious from political associations was being exploited to suppress Catholicism.

Protesting via Rome

The German hierarchy now began the routine and lame procedure of carrying their complaints not to the perpetrators but to the Pope, or more specifically to Pacelli. On a German bishops' *ad limina* (a periodic visit of national bishops "to the threshold" of the Pope) on October 4, 1933, Cardinal Bertram brought a catalogue of protests that aptly characterizes the extent of the continuing and expanding Nazi persecution of the Christian Churches in Germany, and the Catholic Church in particular. His complaints included "the totalitarian claims of the state" with its consequences for family and public life; the suppression of Church associations, including even Catholic "sewing circles for winter relief "; restrictions on the Catholic press, which the cardinal believed to be worse than anything carried out during Bismarck's Kulturkampf; the firing of Catholic civil servants and the widespread discrimination against Jewish converts to Catholicism. Finally, he anticipated a serious conflict over the sterilization law.

Despite Gröber's and Papen's attempts to play down Bertram's protests, the unhappy German bishops were putting pressure on Pacelli. What were the bishops really telling him? It is clear from Pacelli's next move that at least some of them were suggesting a strong protest by the Pope and even the ditching of the concordat—a step toward retrieval of initiative and potential opposition that might have had unpredictable consequences for Hitler even at this late stage. On October 12 the German ambassador to the Holy See, Diego von Bergen, alerted the Foreign Office in Berlin that Pacelli had informed him that the Pope had indicated his intention to protest "against the steadily increasing infringements of the concordat and pressures against Catholics in spite of the official German promises." Pacelli added that the Pope planned to make a public stand in an address "against the things that had happened in Germany."[6]

There now began a protracted diplomatic game of hide-and-seek. Pacelli's chief ploy was the "threat" of a papal denunciation, while the Reich negotiators attempted to stave off official papal protests by seeming to remain in a negotiating stance. Pacelli's approach proclaimed that the Holy See was prepared to acknowledge Hitler's Reich, whatever its offenses against human rights, whatever its offenses against other confessions and other faiths, provided that the Catholic Church in Germany was left in peace.

Hitler at this time was approaching Reichstag elections, as well as withdrawing from the League of Nations and seeking a plebiscite on the issue. Hence a papal protest therefore might have been damaging to the Führer's interests. Buttmann, the chief negotiator of the final stages of the concordat, was hastily dispatched to the Vatican, where Pacelli handed him a *pro memoria* listing the bishops' complaints. Pacelli then met Buttmann for prolonged talks on October 23, 25, and 27, and the two men sought once again to address what constituted a "political" Catholic organization. The arguments went to and fro, as they had done early in July. At one point, when Buttmann suggested that all Catholic youth, sport, and occupational organizations should be incorporated into National Socialist groups, Pacelli was sufficiently annoyed to declare that "this would be a violation of international law [and] international law supersedes Reich law."[7]

Buttmann's visit to Rome had forestalled a papal denunciation indefinitely, and he now retreated to Berlin to busy himself with other issues involving Church-State relations, including a conference to discuss the sterilization law. Even here, despite an invitation for a contribution from the bishops, the Catholic view played no part in the final implementation of the ordinance. Buttmann meanwhile was in no hurry to return to Rome to make good the outstanding disagreements. But while he dangled the promise of a resolution, Pacelli restrained the Pope from making a worldwide protest.

In the meantime, from the pulpit of St. Michael's Church in Munich, the largest in the city, Cardinal Faulhaber issued a qualified protest on behalf of all German Christians, indicating, in isolated and therefore altogether tragic fashion, the untried potential for protest. Between the first Sunday of Advent and the New Year, he preached a series of five sermons against the Nazi denunciation of the Old Testament. The sermons were heard by large congregations (loudspeakers were installed in two neighboring churches) and distributed throughout the country (in 1934 they were published in New York in English under the title *Judaism, Christianity and Germany*).[8]

Speaking on behalf of Protestants as well as Catholics—"we extend our hands to our separated brethren, to defend together with them the sacred books of the Old Testament"—Faulhaber was reiterating, for those who cared to read between the lines, what he had said three years earlier: that National Socialism was a heresy. In his fourth sermon, the cardinal declared that a dangerous storm was brewing; the Nazis were threatening to abandon the Old Testament because its books were Jewish. Faulhaber proclaimed that Christ rejected "ties of blood" and replaced them with "ties of Faith." In the final sermon, he declared: "We may never forget: we are not saved by German blood. We are saved by the precious blood of our crucified Lord."

Faulhaber's sermons were outspoken, but there was little here to comfort Germany's Jews, certainly nothing to defend the Talmud, and a good deal, as Saul Friedländer has commented, of "common clichés of traditional religious anti-Semitism." Faulhaber was in fact defending any Jews who had become Christians, not all Jews. The sermons were directed principally against theological anti-Semitism,[9] and Faulhaber himself admitted that it was not his intention to comment on contemporary aspects of the Jewish issue: "I defended the Old Testament," he was to say. "I did not take a position in regard to the Jewish question of today."[10]

All the same, a secret situation report by Himmler's security officer charged that Faulhaber was "generally considered the spiritual leader of the Catholic resistance to the National Socialist state, especially the foreign press. . . . His occasional admonitions to the clergy to 'cooperate with the state' did not outweigh the disruptive effect of his Advent sermons about Judaism and especially his New Year's Eve sermon on Germanhood."[11]

Was it possible that Cardinal Faulhaber, at the moment when political Catholicism appeared to have surrendered, was about to test the mettle of a last-ditch resistance? If he was, he soon allowed the moment to pass. In his own words, he did not wish "in any way to set out on a course of fundamental opposition."

In any case, the Holy See was now, for better or for worse, in control of Catholic Church-State policy in Germany, a policy aimed at securing a balance of interests through conciliation.

Pacelli Continues to Appease

By the end of November, Pacelli had become increasingly agitated by the lack of response from Buttmann. He became even more alarmed on hearing that Vice-Chancellor Papen was planning to integrate Catholic youth groups into the Hitler Youth. Pacelli could not have been more upset by this development than the German bishops themselves, but he insisted that the matter could be resolved only between himself and Berlin, and he entreated the bishops to stand solidly behind him by remaining silent and supporting his negotiating stance. Justifying Pacelli's claim for centrist summitry in the crisis, Kaas commented to Archbishop Gröber: "In the state there is the leadership principle; at the Vatican the same holds. If parliamentarianism continues to rule in the episcopate, the Church will be the one to suffer."[12]

Sensing that the pressure on Pacelli might have unpredictable results, Buttmann was persuaded by Germany's Vatican envoy to make another trip to Rome. He spent much of December 18 with Pacelli, who told the Reich's negotiator yet again that the Pope was disturbed and would soon lose patience. "[Pius XI] would definitely have to speak about Germany in his Christmas address allocution," Pacelli told Buttman. Then he added, exposing the tragic weakness of his underlying tactic: "If I could only present something pleasant to His Holiness, I believe the disposition of the Pope would be improved."[13] Protest had thus become a mere commodity in Pacelli's gambits, to be threatened and withdrawn according to the state of diplomatic play.

In consequence, Buttmann telephoned Hitler and the very next day Pacelli had in his hands a note of intent telegraphed from the Reich government. Its contents, however, hardly amounted to a positive step toward a resolution of the German Catholic complaints. There was a

promise of "oral negotiations in the near future," a decision to allow the
Holy See its way in the selection of a bishop, military service exemption
for ordinands. But there was no word on the persecution of Jewish converts to Catholicism; no constructive progress on the issue of associations. All the same, this was sufficient for Pacelli to dissuade the Pope
from criticizing the Hitler regime in his Christmas sermon.

But no sooner had the Reich government got beyond the danger of
papal reproof than it switched again to the offensive. The German ambassador to the Holy See advised the Foreign Office in Berlin that since
Pacelli liked to get his teeth into documents, a point-by-point response
should be sent to the Vatican answering all the Holy See's protests to
date. At the same time, the minister of foreign affairs, Konstantin von
Neurath, attempted to protest over alleged political interference by
Catholic priests, particularly clergy in Austria. Could the Church not be
restrained in its unjust attacks on the elected government?

Thus, well into April 1934, Pacelli's time was absorbed in penning one *pro memoria* after another in preparation for successive meetings
with Buttmann, none of which came to anything. The sticking point
was the youth organizations. Buttmann argued that, provided Catholic
youth were allowed time to fulfill their religious duties, surely there
could be no objection to absorbing all Catholic youth into the Hitler
Youth. On Hitler's express orders on March 29, Buttmann was told to
press this compromise in the next round of talks with Pacelli scheduled
for the second week of April. Pacelli, however, refused to agree to limit
Catholic youth organizations to mere "prayer societies" for fear that
young Catholics would be swamped by Nazi neopagan culture. In February, in fact, citing its anti-Christian racism, the Holy See had put on the
Index of Forbidden Books *Myth of the Twentieth Century*, by Alfred Rosenberg, Hitler's new head of Nazi ideological education.

As the months passed and the two parties got no closer to a resolution of the impasse over Catholic associations, Pacelli became specifically frustrated by the fact that the apparent holdup was the Reich's
stated obligation to consult with the regional state governments. On
May 14 he wrote an extraordinary note to Buttmann that apparently
caused astonishment in the Wilhelmstrasse and no doubt some amuse-
ment. Pacelli reproached the Reich for failing to use the dictatorial powers at its command to order the recalcitrant regional states to fall into

line on concordat provisions. In a summary of Pacelli's note sent to Hitler, it was observed that "the repeated keynote of the *pro memoria* was that the causes which gave rise to the complaints of the Church should not be permitted, particularly in an authoritatively led state [*Führerstaat*]. The Reich government had methods of exerting influence and physical power to a degree that formerly was unknown."[14]

Was it possible that Pacelli was upbraiding Hitler for failing to be sufficiently dictatorial? Or was this a gesture of heavy irony, indicating his awareness that delays on account of local recalcitrance were merely a ploy? Perhaps both propositions have a measure of truth. Whatever the case, it was now Pacelli's turn to be recalcitrant.

On June 27 three German bishops (Gröber, Berning, and Nikolaus Bares) met with Hitler, having been appointed by Pacelli to liaise between the hierarchy and the Reich government on Church-State relations. Hitler reassured them that on completion of the current negotiations over the association problem he would issue a statement on the freedom of the Catholic Church to engage in activities "in her own sphere." On June 29, without reference to Rome, the three bishops and their Reich negotiators completed a draft that, on the face of it, formed a reasonable basis for reconciling outstanding differences. Many Church organizations were recognized as religious, including those youth societies that were confined to moral and religious education. Sport and labor organizations were to be merged into the purely religious auspices of Catholic Action, but physical training, it was acknowledged, must be the preserve of the state. The bishops promised that Catholic youth would not wear uniforms or go camping.

Allowing for the fact that any agreement with the Reich government seemed by this stage to be worth little, it appeared preferable to none whatsoever, given the perilous predicament in which the Catholic Church increasingly found itself. But the conclusion of the accord was halted in a characteristic act of centrism that revealed once again that the Holy See was not going to allow the German bishops local discretion under any circumstances. Before the draft could be sent to the Ministry of the Interior in Berlin, Cardinal Bertram submitted it to Pacelli for endorsement, and it was turned down, reportedly by the Pope himself, on account of the blood purge of June 30, 1934.

To this day, it is difficult to be certain how many lost their lives on

the orders of Hitler on that "Night of the Long Knives." Among the es-
timated eighty-five victims were figures who had been crucial to the rise
of Hitler: Ernst Röhm, Kurt von Schleicher, Karl Ernst, and Gregor
Strasser. In the course of that night, however, Catholic opponents to
Hitler's rise were also murdered, including Erich Klausner, the head of
Catholic Action; Dr. Edgar Jung, also prominent in Catholic Action;
Adalbert Probst, leader of the Catholic sports organization; and Fritz
Gerlich, editor of the Catholic weekly *Der Gerade Weg*. In all cases, denials
and alibis were concocted by the murderers.[15]

The deadly nature of the Nazi gangster regime was plain for all to
see. To the German hierarchy's shame, and to the deeper shame of
Pacelli, who continued to constrain them, the Catholic bishops uttered
not a word of protest at this massacre of courageous lay Catholic leaders. The Pope and his Secretary of State, however, were moved to the
minimal protest of declining to conclude the negotiations to incorpo-
rate the bishops' resolution into the incomplete Article 31 of the concordat. Within three weeks, Pius and Pacelli were even less enthusiastic
about accepting the resolution, after the assassination on July 25 of
Chancellor Engelbert Dollfuss of Austria, who in the previous month
had signed a concordat with the Vatican favorable to the Catholic
Church. In the meantime, since the resolution on Article 31 had not
been endorsed in Rome, Hitler declined to publish his statement granting the Catholic Church immunity from attack in Germany.

On September 2 Pacelli informed the German bishops that the
concessions made by the German government were "below the degree of
religious freedom guaranteed by the text of the concordat."[16] The two
sides—the Reich negotiators and the German bishops—did not definitively end the negotiations, but further progress was postponed indefinitely as Pacelli, the key figure in the fate of Germany's Catholics,
departed on a protracted visit to the other side of the world. It was to be
the first of several that would take him away from his office as darkness
gathered over Europe.

To South America

During the four years that Pacelli had served as Secretary of State in the Vatican, he had made a deep impression on the autocratic Pius XI. While temperamentally the two men were at odds, a crucial basis of the Pope's admiration for Pacelli was their shared conviction that the Church was a "perfect society, supreme in its own order." This notion, developed by Leo XIII and transformed, as we have seen, into the model of a centrist bureaucracy controlled by canon and concordat law, was pushed to its ultimate conclusion in Pius XI's encyclical *Quas primas* (1925), in which he declared that the Church "not only symbolizes the definitive reign of God over the universe, but actuates, if by gradual degrees, the sovereignty of Christ in the world, including men and peoples to its law of justice and peace." That same year, Pius established the feast of Christ the King, who, according to Pius XI, held sway over not only Catholics but also all other men, and over not only individuals but also societies. By comparison with Christ's universal principality, such secular projects as the League of Nations, in his view, were of no consequence. With the storm clouds of war on the horizon, the only hope for human societies was to submit to the Church and the Vicar of Christ the King upon earth.

Pius XI evidently had such universal spiritual and moral monarchism in mind in 1934 when he asked Pacelli to travel in his name and to present himself as the representative of Christ's Vicar on earth abroad. But he had another motive. By his own admission, the Pontiff wanted to show off his favored protégé to the bishops of the world. In 1936 he told the then Monsignor Domenico Tardini, "I make him travel so that he may get to know the world and the world may get to know him." After a pause, he added: "He will be a splendid Pope."[17] In view of this and other remarks, it is clear that as early as 1934, Pius XI was attempting to influence the outcome of the next conclave by loading the dice in Pacelli's favor.

Despite Pacelli's pressing responsibilities during this period of mounting danger in Europe, Pius XI dispatched him in the autumn of 1934 as papal legate to Buenos Aires for the scheduled International Eucharistic Congress. Other trips would follow in quick succession. The mission to Argentina had both religious and political dimensions. In the

light of an anticlerical communist regime in Mexico and frequent up-
heavals throughout the continent, Pius XI looked favorably on Argentina's traditional Catholicism under a benign military president with
a semblance of republican democracy. There had been elections in the
previous year. Was not Argentina the true voice of Church-State harmony in this revolution-torn region? The visit of the papal legate would
be a sign that the world had not yet apostatized, a living witness of the
presence of Christ in the Eucharist held in the hands of the legate of
Christ's Vicar on earth. The triumphalist arrival of Pacelli in Latin
America was unprecedented in the history of the Catholic Church, and
it was to anticipate the global trips of two later Popes—Paul VI and
John Paul II.

    Pacelli's orchestration of the trip was remarkable, every aspect of it
extravagantly stage-managed for maximum public impact. With the papal flag snapping from the masthead, he sailed from Genoa on September 24 on the Italian liner Conte Grande to peals of the city's bells, the
playing of bands, and the cheers of crowds that thronged the dockside
to receive Pacelli's blessing as if it were the benediction of the Pope himself. His quarters in the stern of the ship included a private chapel, an
office, a drawing room, and two further staterooms. His office was fitted
out with a huge desk and a portion of his personal library. A radio-
telephone had been installed so that he could remain in touch with the
Secretariat. Quartered in other parts of the ship were a retinue of secretaries, four bishops, various Latin American diplomats, and representatives of religious orders. As well as Monsignor Kaas, who had become a
factotum in the extensive ambit of the Secretariat of State, he had
brought along his niece Elisabetta's daughter. The press described the
vessel as a "floating cathedral."

    According to reports of the voyage,[18] Pacelli never showed himself
once to the passengers, still less mixed with them, except for the day
when the ship reached the equator. Instead of the usual ribald crossing-
the-line carnival, Pacelli decreed a religious service. Emerging from
below in robes of gold cloth, he processed the length of the ship
with all his prelates and acolytes and paused to bless the four quarters of
the Atlantic.

    As the ship approached Buenos Aires after a voyage of two weeks, the
Argentine president, General Agustín Pedro Justo, came aboard from the

battleship *25 de Mayo* to greet Pacelli thus: "Your Eminence, I salute in the person of a papal legate the foremost sovereign of the world, before whose spiritual authority all other sovereigns prostrate themselves in veneration."

Drawn in a ceremonial coach and showered with flowers from every balcony, Pacelli entered the city like an emperor. In the five days that followed, he impressed the citizens of Argentina's capital with his El Greco–like visage and concentrated piety. Conversations about the politics of the region with various government and diplomatic officials punctuated protracted processions and services conducted in the Parco Palermo, where see-through bulletproof screens sheltered the altar and Pacelli's throne. A wheeled contraption drawn by hundreds of priests in white robes bore Pacelli through the streets of Buenos Aires as he knelt before the exposed Eucharist.

A revealing incident occurred on an evening when Pacelli was invited to attend a performance of Refice's *Cecilia* at the Colón theater. Pacelli at the last moment decided instead to take a flight in an airplane over the city. As photographs of the incident attest, he sat bolt-upright during the flight reading his breviary. The following evening he repeated the experience, this time in a military aircraft, which he preferred for its speed.

On this highly visible trip the pious demeanor that marked his appearances in later years as Pope was already evident: as Carlo Falconi was to put it, his general bearing was "compounded of asceticism and religious inspiration"; whenever he appeared among groups of local, civil, or ecclesiastical authorities, his invariable pose showed him with "hands joined as if taking part in a liturgical ceremony."[19]

On the return journey, he stopped at Montevideo to bless the faithful multitudes on the dockside, then proceeded to Rio de Janeiro, where he was greeted as a visiting head of state by the president and government. Escorted to the summit of the hill above Rio on which stands the Redemptore statue—its arms outstretched, a posture Pacelli would emulate in years to come—he blessed the land of Brazil in the name of the Holy Father. His departure for home was attended by gun salutes from shore batteries, aerial fly-pasts, and squadrons of naval escorts sounding their horns.

Instead of heading straight for Genoa, the *Conte Grande* docked on November 1 at Barcelona, where Pacelli had talks with General Domingo

Batet, the military governor of Catalonia. The city had been in turmoil throughout the month of October following the proclamation of an independent Catalan state by the separatist leader Luis Companys.

The general organized a reception for Pacelli to meet prelates and military and civil dignitaries from various parts of Spain. Dispensing hospitality with imperial aplomb, Pacelli threw a gala dinner on board the ship for members of the Madrid government and the archbishop of Tarragona. How could Pacelli have predicted, any more than General Batet, the explosion of violence and carnage that would soon erupt in Spain, or the thousands of clergy and religious who were to lose their lives? General Batet himself was to be executed two years later for failing to inflict the violence Franco regarded as essential to the conduct of the civil war.[20]

Pacelli reached Genoa on November 2, and by the next day he and his entire suite were received in audience by the Pontiff, who showered praise and gratitude upon his favorite cardinal. For his part, Pacelli could report: "I have never before seen an entire nation, rulers and ruled together, bow the head and bend the knee so devoutly before Him who said: 'I am a King ... but My kingdom is not of this world.' "[21] The apostolic palace had not witnessed such scenes or heard such sentiments since the high period of the baroque papacy.

The next evening, according to a hagiographer,[22] a secretary went to Pacelli's room with an urgent telegram. The room was dark, but in the dim light from the windows the startled underling saw a tall figure hoist himself from the marble floor where he had been lying spread-eagled in prayer. As the lights came on, Pacelli received the telegram and, seeing the cleric's agitation, said with smile, "Do not be worried. After so much glory and splendor, it is necessary to lie close to the earth to know that we are nothing."

Pacelli had returned to a Europe on the brink of conflict. As he arrived in Buenos Aires on October 9, King Alexander of Yugoslavia and the French minister of foreign affairs had been assassinated by a Croatian nationalist in Marseille. The origin of the "plot" had been traced to Hungary, and there were strong pressures for Yugoslavia to retaliate. In the complex alliances of Europe, Italy and France were consequently in danger of being drawn into military conflict.

Meanwhile, in the final weeks of 1934, Hitler had been concentrating all his efforts on preparing for the plebiscite in the disputed Saar region. The vote was held in January 1935 and resulted in an overwhelming mandate, aided by the Catholics who were a majority in the region, for a return to the Reich. Not long after, Hitler announced the introduction of compulsory military service. The British government's white paper on the failure of the disarmament conference and Göring's announcement of the establishment of the Luftwaffe combined to increase the state of tension in Europe.

At the same time, Mussolini had openly expressed his ambition to create an empire by force of arms. On February 1, 1934, the Duce had announced that he intended conquering Ethiopia in pursuit of that dream and in fulfillment of the Fascist culture of domination and power. Mussolini was convinced that Britain was unlikely to interfere, but he was uncertain of the disposition of France, which had invested in a railway from Addis Ababa, the capital of Ethiopia, to the port of Djibouti in French territory.

Pacelli and France

Pierre Laval, France's new minister of foreign affairs, arrived in Rome on January 5, 1935, for talks with Mussolini in the hope of easing Franco-Italian tensions. The visit was a success, resolving Mussolini's fears about the Yugoslav situation and the possibility of French intervention in Ethiopia. Laval informed the Duce of negotiations for a pact between France and the Soviet Union and opened the way to special understandings between France and Italy.

The Vatican was not neglected during this visit. On the afternoon of January 7, Laval had talks with Pacelli in his office in the Secretariat of State. They spoke about the rising danger of Germany and the likelihood of an Anschluss with Austria. They met again later that day at a dinner given for Pacelli at the residence of the French ambassador in the Palazzo Taverna. Pacelli was invested that evening with the grand cross of the Legion of Honor. Under the suave diplomatic influence of the Cardinal Secretary of State, Laval's visit had created opportunities for drawing France and French Catholics closer to the Holy See.

Since the beginning of Pius XI's accession, the Church in France had been riven by the extreme right-wing movement and newspaper known as *L'Action française*, under the leadership of Charles Maurras. The movement—which had many Catholic sympathizers and followers, more for its antirepublicanism than for its peculiar prejudices—preached primacy of the Church over the "Hebrew Christ," the subjection of man to society, the exaltation of nationalism, and the return of the monarchy. Anti-Semitic and at the same time committed to the strange goal of de-Christianizing Catholicism, *L'Action française* was for Pius XI a dangerous cuckoo in the Catholic nest. Resolved on suppressing it, Pius condemned both the newspaper and the movement. The bishops fell in line. Many lay and religious members of the movement were disciplined. By 1926 *L'Action française* had capitulated and Pius XI attempted to gather France, the "elder daughter" of the Church, to his breast and heal the rifts within French Catholicism.

Pacelli was now chosen to represent the Pontiff in France on a pilgrimage to the shrine of the Virgin at Lourdes. An enthusiast for the patronage of Mary, Pius XI continued the modern papal tendency to draw an equivalence between papal infallibility and the dogma of the Immaculate Conception, the sinlessness of Mary, dogmatically proclaimed by Pio Nono in 1854. "All true followers of Christ," wrote Pius XI in 1928, "will believe the dogma of the Immaculate Conception of the Mother of God with the same faith as they believe the mystery of the august Trinity, the infallibility of the Roman Pontiff, and the Incarnation."[23] Mary's obedience symbolized collective and individual submission to the Holy See; just as her status was founded on papal dogma.

Before he was due to depart for France, Pacelli was called to the deathbed of his brother, Francesco, the distinguished Vatican lawyer who had negotiated the Lateran Treaty. Pacelli was so overcome by the demise of his brother that he considered abandoning the journey. "But that," reported an early biographer, Nazareno Padellaro, with evident approval and no further explanation, "would have been too human a decision."

Pacelli departed for France on April 25 and was received at the station at Lourdes the next day with messages from the president of the republic and the honors appropriate for a visiting head of state. Amid a quarter of a million pilgrims, Pacelli prayed and processed at the grotto for three days. In a typical sermon, he spoke of the enemies of the Church. "With the illusion of extolling new wisdom," he said, "they are only lamentable plagiarists who cover old errors with new trumpery. It matters little that they mass around the flag of social revolution. They are inspired by a false conception of the world and life." Excoriating the superstitions of race and blood, and false conceptions of the social and economic world, he declared that the Church "does not consent to form a compact with them at any price"—precisely what he had spent half of 1933 doing with Hitler.

On the final day, a Sunday, he expounded on the Woman of the Apocalypse clothed with the sun, the ransoming of the human race, and of Golgotha—"the center of the history of mankind." Then he spoke of the "superstition of race and blood" in Germany and how the Church would choose the blood of Calvary rather than betray her spouse, in striking contrast to the realities of appeasement he had encouraged in recent years in Germany.[24]

During his stay in Lourdes Pacelli spent much of the night in prayer; declining to sleep in a proper bed, he slept only on a chaise longue. One afternoon, according to Falconi, Pacelli allowed himself a small break from the ceremonial in order to visit the valley of Labigorre near Saint-Savin. A priest sat with him in a horse-drawn carriage to act as his guide. But once they had gained the countryside, Pacelli opened his breviary and started to read, giving the passing view not a single glance. After an hour or so, Pacelli said: "And now, Monsignor, let us go back." On the return journey Pacelli sat with his eyes shut as if in a mystical trance. When they arrived at his lodging, he merely said to his companion, "Excuse me!" and hurried into the house.

But the visit to France had been a success, and there was talk even before his departure of a second visit. On any subsequent sojourn, opined the French press, nothing less than the Palace of Versailles should be put at the legate's disposal.

Pacelli returned to France on July 9, 1937, arriving in Paris to military bands and a ceremony of official welcome. He said Mass in the basilica of Sacré Coeur before taking the train to Lisieux in Normandy. Crowds lined the platforms of every station on the way. The town of Lisieux greeted him with military honors, more bands, flags, and a cavalry escort. No fewer than three hundred thousand pilgrims, it was said, lined the route to the bishop's palace. One newspaper correspondent compared Pacelli to a figure on the Royal Porch at Chartres.

Pacelli's principal task in Lisieux was to consecrate the new basilica built above the tomb of St. Thérèse, the Carmelite nun who had entered the convent of Lisieux at fifteen in 1888 and died of tuberculosis in 1897. The act was a significant endorsement of a spirituality that emphasized interiority over community, submission over social action, silence over speaking out. St. Thérèse was famous for the reflection: "I wish to spend my heaven doing good upon the earth." Her legacy was a posthumous spiritual autobiography, *Story of a Soul*, which revealed a sanctity based on the lowly routines in an enclosed convent.

By 1925, when Pius XI canonized her a saint of the Church, Thérèse's cult had become an important focus of popular Catholic piety throughout the world. Pius declared her the patron of the missions, and she was especially popular among diocesan priests. Daniel-Rops, the French Catholic historian, argued that her "little way" contained the century's answer to the two great apostasies of the age, which had led to communism and Nazism. "To the assertions of Nietzsche and Karl Marx, the saint opposes the sole irrefutable answer.... 'God is dead,' said the prophet of Sils-Maria. [But] for Thérèse ... when everything might have persuaded her of His annihilation, she still knew that nothing could destroy Him, because He is the sole Reality."[25]

Pius XI's personal devotion to St. Thérèse knew no bounds. He asked Pacelli to bring back with him three roses from Lisieux, "three special graces which We implore from the beloved little saint." The roses were duly produced by the guardians of the shrine, but Pacelli, according to Padellaro, "avoiding all sentimentality, studied the three roses with the precision of a botanist."[26]

Before leaving France, Pacelli traveled back to Paris to preach in French at Notre-Dame to a packed congregation of ecclesiastical and civil dignitaries. It was reported that he seemed a little nervous on entering the pulpit. But he soon warmed to his theme, crying out *"Vigilate fratres!"* ("Be on your watch, brothers!") He reminded France of its vocation to observe the "law of love," since it was the law of love that demanded "a just and Christian solution to the capital question of the proletariat." The drift of his argument, developed through a series of generalizations, was a rejection of those "false prophets" who had returned the world to a new dark age comparable to the darkness of the pre-Christian era. In his peroration he declared that "the sooner everyone fully realizes that there is a definite correlation between the mission of the Church of Christ and the progress and greatness of nations, the sooner will come the harmony which God desires."[27] Uncharacteristically for the reception of a Catholic homily, the congregation rose to its feet and applauded.

The following week, Diego von Bergen, the Reich ambassador to the Holy See, could report to Berlin that Pacelli vehemently insisted on the "purely religious nature" of his sermon. The French trip had "served no political purpose; the Vatican had never thought of even an indirect demonstration against Germany."[28]

Pacelli in the United States

The socialist victory in the Spanish elections of February 1936 had culminated that summer in widespread violence and the outbreak of civil war. The Catholic Church, identified with the reactionary side of the ideological divide, was exposed to some of the worst atrocities, committed in the main by the anarchists. According to Catholic sources,[29] during the thirty-month period of the war, more than seven thousand priests and religious were slaughtered. Pacelli was, of course, hardly unaware of the atrocities being committed on Franco's side, but the Caudillo had declared that "Spain shall be an empire turned toward God." By September, receiving a group of Spanish pilgrims, Pius XI denounced the "satanic enterprise" of Marxism that had prompted the war, and blessed those who were defending "the rights and honor of God against a wild explosion of forces so savage and so cruel as to be well-nigh incredible."[30]

Despite Pacelli's many speeches throughout the year on the theme of justice and peace, Mussolini's attack on Ethiopia on October 3, 1935, was not condemned by the Holy See. Nor did Pius XI restrain the Italian hierarchy from war enthusiasm. "O Duce!" declared the bishop of Terracina, "today Italy is Fascist and the hearts of all Italians beat together with yours. The nation is ready for any sacrifice to ensure the triumph of peace and of Roman and Christian civilizations.... God bless you, O Duce."[31] Such sentiments appeared to welcome an alliance between the Holy See's vision of the Church as a universal "sovereign society" and Mussolini's fantasy of a temporal empire in the making.

Although Pius XI had told a friend in September that war with Ethiopia would be "deplorable,"[32] his statements on the issue, after the fact, were so convoluted and vague as to carry no clear denunciation.

Against this background, Pacelli, accompanied by Enrico Galeazzi and Sister Pasqualina, sailed from Naples for North America in the luxury liner *Conti di Savoia* on October 8, 1936. It was the first time a papal Secretary of State had ever visited the United States. An early visitor on board ship after it docked in New York Harbor was the thirty-seven-year-old bishop Francis Joseph Spellman, a friend of Pacelli's destined to be cardinal archbishop of New York. Spellman had brought Pacelli a black clerical suit of jacket and trousers, but the secular-style apparel was at once declined.

Spellman, a former Vatican bureaucrat of enormous energy, efficiency, and ambition, was auxiliary bishop of Boston. Despite the attempts of his superior, William O'Connell, the cardinal archbishop, to thwart him, Spellman had organized most of Pacelli's trip. Throughout Pacelli's thirty days in the country, which involved 6,500 miles of travel, mostly by air, Pacelli stood on his clerical dignity, gliding in his soutane and silken cloak across the thresholds of countless Catholic colleges, convent schools, monasteries, and parish churches.

An unspoken quid pro quo of the visit was an exchange of favors between Pacelli and President Roosevelt. Roosevelt wanted help in quelling the Catholic radio priest Father Charles Coughlin, who preached weekly and subversively to an audience of fifteen million Americans. Coughlin, pastor of a church dedicated to St. Thérèse in the Detroit suburb of Royal Oak, was anti–New Deal and blamed America's ills on Roosevelt, the Jews, the communists, and the "godless capitalists." Roosevelt wanted Coughlin muzzled. For his part, Pacelli was concerned that the United States had three years earlier recognized the Soviet Union. Now he hoped for reassurance from Roosevelt in the form of formal U.S.–Vatican diplomatic links.

Pacelli was not to meet Roosevelt in person until the very end of his stay, on November 6, after the elections were decided and the president had been returned to office. After their visit at Roosevelt's estate at Hyde Park it became clear that Pacelli had secured an undertaking to forge the U.S.–Vatican ties he was seeking. The United States had supported a diplomat at the Holy See until the Senate withdrew the stipend in 1867, when Pius IX, following the antidemocratic *Syllabus of Errors*, became extremely unpopular with both democrats and liberals. In 1870 the Pope had lost his temporal power and with it, in the view of the US government, the constitutional basis for diplomatic links. By 1929 the Lateran Treaty had reestablished a case for statehood on the part of the Holy See, but the U.S. Senate remained reluctant to foot the bill for representation. Such a decision could only anger a Protestant majority. It appears that Roosevelt assured Pacelli that he would get around this by appointing a personal representative who would not require payment. The appointment was not in fact made until 1940, when Myron Taylor became accredited to the Holy See.

In the meantime, although Pacelli never breathed a word of what had been said or how it had been done, Father Coughlin announced on November 8 that he was making his final broadcast. He was as good as his word. Although there was wide coverage of the visit, the American press never managed to interview Pacelli on these or any other sensitive issues during his stay, largely due to the expert protection afforded by Spellman.

For the rest, Pacelli was on a nonstop roller coaster of liturgical services, lunches, dinners, speeches, and lectures in virtually every major city in the United States, excluding the southern states. He was, among many places, in Boston, Philadelphia, Baltimore, Washington, South Bend, Cleveland, St. Paul, Cincinnati, Detroit, Chicago, San Francisco, Los Angeles, and St. Louis. He went to the top of the Empire State Building, and gazed on the Boulder Dam and the Grand Canyon. He saw a movie being made in Hollywood and received honorary degrees from various colleges. Everywhere he arrived, there were enthusiastic crowds on the streets, reminiscent of the multitudes that would gather to greet traveling popes later in the century. By all accounts, Pacelli relished the road-show fanfare, including the speed of his motorcades and the wailing sirens of the outriders. Dubbed "the Flying Cardinal" by the press, he developed a taste for airplanes, and seems to have been moved by the aerial view of the country's mountains, plains, deserts, and forests. On his way back to New York City, he stopped at Niagara Falls. He stood silently for a while at the very brink, looking out at the awesome scene. He made to leave; then turned back once more. In a characteristic gesture, Cardinal Pacelli blessed the falls.[33]

In New York, before his return to Europe, Pacelli stayed at Inisfada, the Long Island estate of Mrs. Nicholas Brady, a rich Catholic who had been granted the papal title of duchess for her generosity to the Holy See. Duchess Brady threw a grand reception in her Georgian-style mansion for Pacelli. Flares illuminated the driveway to the front door; Pacelli and the duchess received their distinguished guests to the sound of an electric organ installed for the occasion in a rose-filled hall in which the fireplaces were fueled with unsplit tree trunks.

Before leaving the United States, Pacelli entrusted the ever-helpful Spellman with $113,000, gifts pressed upon him by wealthy Americans during the trip, to invest for him personally. Mrs. Brady died not long after Pacelli's departure and left the Cardinal Secretary of State a personal legacy of $100,000.[34]

10

Pius XI Speaks Out

Following Pacelli's veto of the German bishops' recommended compromise on Article 31 of the concordat, relations between Catholics in Germany and the Nazi regime had continued to deteriorate through the summer of 1935. On August 28 the Catholic bishops of Germany issued a joint pastoral letter to be read from the pulpits of all Catholic churches. It was tragic in its failure to translate ideal into action, ironic in its contrast between word and deed. Repudiating the principle that "religion has nothing to do with politics," the bishops reminded the faithful, quoting from the Gospel of Matthew, that "the messengers of Christianity are to be 'the salt of the earth' and 'the light of the world,' and 'should let their light shine before the people.' The Church should be as 'a city on the hill,' visible from afar in the life of the people." Hollow exhortation was the fullest extent of the bishops' protest. In the meantime, they continued to look to Pacelli, who controlled both their own avenues of complaint as well as that of the Pope.

In response to the bishops' pastoral letter, Hitler declared at the Nazi congress in Nuremberg on September 11 that he was not against Christianity in itself, "but we will fight it for the sake of keeping our public life free from those priests who have failed their calling and who should have become politicians rather than clergymen."[1]

Four days later, Hitler passed the Nuremberg Laws, which defined

German citizenship, preparing the way for characterizing Jewish status in terms of parenthood and marriage. Again, not a word of protest from Pacelli.

In order to keep dangling the prospect of reconciliation, and to manage the potential indignation of the Churches, Hitler on July 16 had created a Ministry of Church Affairs under Hans Kerrl. Kerrl met Cardinal Bertram early in September and invited the Catholic hierarchy once again to draw up a new list of Catholic organizations for official protection. The list was submitted to Kerrl's ministry by October 2, but the ensuing negotiations came to nothing. The Catholic bishops wanted to maintain the structure of Catholic associations, and Hitler's Reich was determined to thwart and destroy organizations that had potential for political Catholicism. In the meantime, the impression of negotiations and the prospect of future reconciliation kept the decision for a Vatican protest on hold.

Typical of the Nazi regime's carrot-and-stick tactic, however, was the first wave of "morality" trials conducted by the Reich throughout 1935–36, accusing Catholic religious of sexual abuse of minors and currency misdemeanors. The former allegations were leveled particularly against nuns and clergy responsible for children in orphanages and schools. The latter involved religious congregations financially responsible for missions and communities abroad. The Depression of the 1930s had culminated in complex laws relating to foreign exchange, creating difficulties for religious who had financial obligations outside the country.

Thrown onto the defensive within Germany, constrained by Vatican centrist control, the Catholic Church continued into 1936 in a state of wary inertia, cheered only by the dubious comfort that things might have been worse. By the summer, news of atrocities against nuns and priests in the Spanish civil war indicated—as the Pope himself was quick to point out—how much worse things were under "Bolshevism." And this was the theme of a three-hour private conversation between Cardinal Faulhaber of Munich and Adolf Hitler at the Führer's mountain retreat at Obersalzburg in November. Hitler harped continually on the dangers of communism, imploring the cardinal to persevere with efforts toward conciliation with the Reich. In a memorandum of the meeting, Faulhaber observed:

The Führer commands the diplomatic and social forms better than a born sovereign. . . . Without doubt the chancellor
lives in faith in God. He recognizes Christianity as the foundation of Western culture. . . . Not as clear is his conception
of the Catholic Church as a God-established institution.[2]

As a result of the meeting, Faulhaber issued an episcopal letter to be
read in churches in Bavaria in January 1937. It encouraged cooperation
between Church and State in combating communism, but called for respect for the Church's rights as laid down in the concordat.

The year 1937, however, was to see a deepening of tensions between
the Nazis and the Catholic Church. In the second week of January, the
German bishops met at Fulda and drew up a list of seventeen violations of the concordat. Armed with their familiar grievances, no fewer
than three cardinals (Bertram, Faulhaber, and Schulte), along with
two influential bishops (Clemens August von Galen and Konrad von
Preysing), set off in a determined mood for the Vatican to see Pacelli,
who met them on the evening of January 16. With this powerful representation insisting on action from the Pope, Pacelli had no choice but
to involve the Holy Father. Pius XI was ill with diabetes, heart disease, and ulceration of the legs, but he received Pacelli and the German
delegation in his bedroom. He lay on the bed "almost unrecognizable,
pale, emaciated, his face deeply lined and his eyes swollen and half-
closed."[3] He listened to them for a long time and talked to them at
length. He had learned much during his illness, he told them, of the
mystery of Christ's crucifixion and salvation through suffering. He decided that he would issue an encyclical on the plight of the Church in
Germany.

Faulhaber wrote the first draft at great speed and delivered it into
Pacelli's hands on the morning of January 21. Pacelli then edited the
draft and added material on the history of the concordat.[4] This is significant, for the published encyclical, Mit brennender Sorge (With Deep
Anxiety), a forthright condemnation of the Reich's treatment of the
church, remains for many Catholics and non-Catholics alike a symbol of
courageous papal outspokenness, cited in contrast to Pacelli's silence
during the war. While Pacelli can take much credit for the final document and the complex arrangements for its publication in Germany, the

encyclical arrived late in the day and failed to condemn National Socialism and Hitler by name.

The logistics of publication nevertheless revealed the capacity of the
parish networks throughout Catholic Germany and the scope of their un-
exploited potential for protest and resistance. The document was smug-
gled into the country, where it was secretly printed at twelve different
plants. During the weekend of Passion Sunday, March 14, 1937, it was
delivered by couriers, mostly boys on foot and on bicycle, many of them
traveling to their destinations across fields and through woods in order to
avoid public roads. The document was not entrusted at any point to the
official postal service. In some cases it was delivered to the parish priest in
the confessional. Many priests kept the document locked in the tabernacle by the side of the Eucharist until the moment when it was due to be
read.[5] It was written in German and addressed not only to the German
bishops but also to the Catholic episcopate throughout the world.[6]

The encyclical begins: "With deep anxiety and increasing dismay, We
have for some time past beheld the sufferings of the Church in Germany." The Pope then outlined the story of the negotiation of the concordat and his misgivings about concluding the treaty at the time. The
experience of the past years, he went on, had revealed that the Church's
partner in the concordat had "sown the tares of suspicion, discord, hatred, calumny, of secret and open fundamental hostility to Christ and
His Church, fed from a thousand different sources and making use of
every available means." In place of true belief in God, he declared, there
was a deification of race, people, and state. He warned the bishops to be
on their guard for pernicious practices that must follow from such
tenets, and he called for a recognition of natural law. "The believer has
an inalienable right to profess his faith and to practice it in the manner
suited to him. Laws which suppress or render difficult the profession
and practice of this faith are contrary to natural law."[7]

He asked Catholic youth to purge their country of hostility to Christianity. He called on priests and religious to pray for an increase of
charity. He implored the laity, and parents especially, to redouble their
efforts in raising children as Catholics. "When the attempt is made," he
wrote, "to desecrate the tabernacle of a child's soul . . . then the time of
spiritual profanation of the temple is at hand, and it is the duty of every
professing Christian to separate clearly his reponsibility from that of the

other side, to keep his conscience clear of any culpable cooperation in such dreadful work and corruption."

There were words here, especially in reference to natural law, that might be applied to the Jews, but there was no explicit condemnation of anti-Semitism, even in relation to Catholic Jews. Worse still, the subtext against Nazism was blunted by the publication five days later of an even more vehement condemnation of communism in the encyclical *Divini redemptoris*. But for all its papal circumlocution, *Mit brennender Sorge* contained strong words. The Nazis regarded the encyclical as a subversive act. The firms that had collaborated in printing the document were shut down and many of their personnel imprisoned; when Cardinal Bertram and Archbishop Orsenigo protested, they received a sharp riposte from the German Foreign Office and Kerrl's Ministry of Religious Affairs.

Heydrich ordered all copies of the document to be confiscated. Kerrl sent a letter to the German bishops claiming that the encyclical was "in flat contradiction to the spirit of the concordat ... [containing] serious attacks against the welfare and the interest of the German nation."[8] Hitler was sufficiently angered by the encyclical to raise it during his May Day address. Calling on the obedience of every single German, he warned that, "bend or break," the state would not tolerate any challenge to its authority. That held also for the churches. "When they attempt by any other means—writings, encyclicals, etc.—to assume rights which belong only to the state, we will push them back into their proper spiritual activity."[9]

That the Church had it in its power to shake the regime was evident from the official reaction to a speech by Cardinal George Mundelein of Chicago to five hundred of his diocesan priests on May 18, 1937. In frank American parlance, devoid of the papal lardings, Mundelein said: "Perhaps you will ask how it is that a nation of sixty million intelligent people will submit in fear and servitude to an alien, an Austrian paperhanger, and a poor one at that, and a few associates like Goebbels and Göring, who dictate every move of the people's lives?" The cardinal went on to suggest that the brains of sixty million Germans had been removed without their even noticing it.[10]

Göring responded with a two-hour harangue the following week, announcing the resumption of the morality trials that had been suspended in mid-1936. But the regime had little to fear from German Catholicism

while Pacelli pulled the strings, even to the extent of neutralizing the vehement public sentiments of the Pope. Greeting a group of pilgrims
from Chicago on July 17, 1937, Pius XI praised the city and its cardinal
"who is so solicitous and zealous in defense of the rights of God and of
the Church and in the salvation of souls."[11]

The previous day, however, Reich ambassador von Bergen had called
on Pacelli, and on July 23 filed the following report to his masters in
Berlin:

> In striking contradiction to the behavior of the Pope, how-
> ever, are the statements of the Cardinal Secretary of State
> during the call that I made on him on the sixteenth, the day
> before the Pope's discourse. . . . The conversation was of a pri-
> vate nature. Pacelli received me with decided friendliness and
> emphatically assured me during the conversation that normal
> and friendly relations with us would be restored as soon as
> possible; this applied particularly to him, who had spent thir-
> teen years in Germany and had always shown the greatest
> sympathy for the German people. He would also be prepared
> at any time for a discussion with outstanding personages such
> as the foreign minister and Minister President Göring.[12]

The note reveals the stark contrast between the Pope's sentiments and
Pacelli's appeasement policy. The fact was, the encyclical's circumlocutory
style was open to two distinct interpretations. It could be taken as a final
attempt on the part of the Church to insist on its rights within the
framework of the concordat. Equally, it could be understood as a call to
noncompliance and mass Catholic protest. These contrasting viewpoints
were separately espoused by Cardinal Bertram for the appeasers and
Bishop von Preysing for the rebels. As Scholder has noted, "It says much
for the skill of Pacelli that both parties felt that he was on their side."[13]
There can be no doubt, however, that Pacelli's policy, taken as a whole,
was emphatically on the side of conciliation. As crisis between the
Church and the Reich regime deepened through the next twelve months,
Pacelli offered in March 1938 to "come to Berlin for negotiations if that
is desirable" in order to save the concordat.[14]

Pacelli in Eastern Europe

In May 1938, Pacelli demonstrated, more dramatically and publicly than he had ever done before, his willingness to appease. Once again he was on his travels, this time to Budapest, where he was due to open the thirty-fourth International Eucharistic Congress on May 25. Days before his arrival, Béla Imrédy was appointed prime minister. Imrédy was a violent anti-Semite who insisted that anyone who could not prove that his ancestors were born in Hungary must be a Jew. Even as the congress progressed, the Hungarian parliament was discussing proposed anti-Jewish legislation. The regent of Hungary was Admiral Miklós Horthy, who was committed to making the country a satellite of Germany.

The congress occurred in the wake of the Anschluss, the German annexation of Austria on March 12–13, 1938. Himmler had forbidden Germans to travel into Hungary to attend the congress, and had banned all reporting of it in the Catholic press. The bans may have reflected Nazi anger following the Pope's departure to Castel Gandolfo from Rome earlier in the month, when Hitler came on a visit to the Eternal City.

Not only did Pacelli make no reference to the burgeoning anti-Semitism in Hungary, but he had no word of criticism, at this most public Catholic forum of that year, against the regime across the border. In fact, in a principal passage of his sermon before tens of thousands of the faithful, he called for an appeasement that would be matched that same year in secular political terms by France and Britain.

> In the concrete working out of its destiny and its potentialities, each people follows, within the framework of Creation and Redemption, its own particular way, promoting its unwritten laws and contingencies according as its forces, its inclinations, its characteristics, its general position, recommend and indeed, often compel.[15]

In another passage on the "message of love in action" he made an implied criticism of the Jews: "As opposed to the foes of Jesus who cried out to his face, 'Crucify him!' we sing him hymns of our loyalty and our love. We act in this fashion, not out of bitterness, not out of a sense of superiority, not out of arrogance toward those whose lips curse him and whose hearts reject him even today." Moshe Y. Herczl, who quotes this passage in his *Christianity and the Holocaust of Hungarian Jewry* (1993), argues that Pacelli relied on his audience to identify those foes of Jesus who had cried out to his face, "Crucify him!" "Pacelli," writes Herczl, "was sure that his audience understood him well."[16] Pacelli, representative of the Pope at the Eucharistic congress, was making it clear that the "comprehensive love" he preached at the meeting did not include the Jews.

Catholic Demoralization

As Hitler led the German people toward the abyss in the late 1930s, he continued to keep the Catholic Church in a state of nervous compliance, playing the local hierarchy off against the Vatican, routinely breaking the articles of the concordat, and yet encouraging the maintenance of the treaty insofar as it dissuaded Catholics from political action. The oppression was carried out at the grass roots rather than on orders from above. The overall impression, however, was of waves of persecution punctuated by brief periods of pacification from the top. The travails of the Church never amounted to a Kulturkampf in the manner of Bismarck's era. The process was widespread attrition through countless local restrictions, but various national agencies were also involved. Although Kerrl was officially responsible for Church relations in the cabinet, Catholicism was under pressure from a variety of authorities within the Reich: Baldur von Schirach, head of the Hitler Youth, was undermining Catholic youth organizations; the Labor Ministry was bent on attracting Catholic workers into the Nazi Party; the Finance Ministry was investigating Catholic missionary societies for offenses against currency laws; the military was attempting to suborn Catholic servicemen. Throughout Germany, there were piecemeal attempts to break the hold of Catholicism in schools— from the banning of crucifixes and religious pictures on the walls to the proscription of dual membership in Nazi and Catholic work organizations to the firing of Catholic instructors and religious.

In mid-July of 1937, directives were issued for information-gathering on the activities of the Churches, their organizations and leaders, including the rapid expansion of a network of SS and Gestapo informers and infiltrators. The directives laid down instructions for reporting the content of sermons and the reaction of congregations.

Yet the Nazis were careful not to push their restrictions to the limit. They did not shut down parish churches, and there were no attempts to hamper regular attendance at Mass and the sacraments. Hence the general Catholic response, encouraged from the Vatican pinnacle, was that things might have been worse, that compliance was the price of survival. Catholics did not submit uniformly. The laity refused in certain instances to accept the confiscation of religious objects from schools, and continued to gather for processions even when the police put obstacles in their way. There were many isolated examples of courageous initiative, moreover, especially on the part of the Jesuits, who organized frequent parish missions and retreats and were at times outspoken. But these were isolated exceptions that proved the rule of general inertia.

One striking dissenter was Monsignor Bernhard Lichtenberg, a parish priest in the diocese of Berlin. Lichtenberg protested openly against anti-Semitism and human-rights abuses from 1933 onward. He was to die on his way to Dachau in 1943. Another outstanding example was Father Rupert Mayer of Munich, a Jesuit who was active among workers' groups and was jailed for six months in 1937 for preaching against Nazi anti-Semitism. Mayer had served in the First World War, had lost a leg, and was the first Catholic chaplain to be awarded the Iron Cross. Cardinal Faulhaber originally defended Mayer, indicating yet again the potential within the Church for noncompliance. But a few months later, exemplifying the appeasement encouraged year after year by Pacelli in Rome, Faulhaber congratulated the Nazis in his New Year's Eve sermon in 1938 for their anti-smoking and anti-drinking campaign: "One advantage of our time: at the highest levels of the government we have the example of an austere alcohol- and nicotine-free life-style."

As a result of this sermon, Father Mayer declared that he was ceasing any further form of protest. "Since that moment, something struck my heart," he said, "and prevented me from ever putting in my appearance again."[17] All the same, Mayer was sent for a time to the Sachsenhausen concentration camp and spent the war under house arrest in a Benedictine monastery in Bavaria.

The shocking inappropriateness of Faulhaber's sentiments was revealed later in the year.

On November 7, 1938, a secretary in the German embassy in Paris, Ernst vom Rath, was assassinated by a Polish student protesting anti-Semitism. On November 9, the anniversary of the Beer Hall Putsch, Hitler sanctioned demonstrations against Jews throughout the country. The SA were unleashed to destroy and vandalize synagogues and Jewish businesses. About eight hundred Jews were murdered and some 26,000 rounded up and sent to concentration camps. In the aftermath, Jews were banned from theaters, cinemas, concerts, and exhibitions. Jewish children were prevented from attending state schools.

As Saul Friedländer comments, "abysmal hatred appears as the be-all and end-all of the onslaught. The only immediate aim was to hurt the Jews as badly as the circumstances allowed, by all possible means: to hurt them and to humiliate them. The pogrom and the initiatives that immediately followed have quite rightly been called 'a degradation ritual.' "[18]

The violence was highly visible, sustained, and repeated throughout German cities and the smallest towns. Friedländer cites a telling eyewitness account by the American consul in Leipzig: "The insatiably sadistic perpetrators threw many of the trembling inmates into a small stream that flows through the Zoological Park, commanding the horrified spectators to spit at them, defile them with mud. . . . The slightest manifestation of sympathy evoked a positive fury on the part of the perpetrators."

No clear word issued from either the Vatican or the German hierarchy following Kristallnacht. And yet, Pacelli had claimed for himself and the Holy See a position on the moral high ground of courage earlier in the year when he told the multitudes of worshipers at the Budapest Eucharistic Congress, as well as the world at large, "We love our times, despite their danger and their anguish; we love them precisely because of that danger, and because of the difficult tasks that the age imposes on us; we are ready to dedicate ourselves wholly and unconditionally, regardless of ourselves; otherwise nothing great and decisive can result."[19]

Pacelli's policy, as we have seen, however, had been one of public silence and private indifference on the Jewish issue. As correspondence between the German hierarchy and Pacelli's office had repeatedly revealed, the attitude was: the Jews must look after themselves. Yet indications are that Pius XI himself began to take a more sympathetic, if qualified, view of the plight of the Jews as events unfolded.

The "Lost" Encyclical

As anti-Semitism became more widespread, especially in Eastern Europe in the latter half of the 1930s, Pius XI became increasingly concerned. Eventually he commissioned an encyclical on Nazi racism and anti-Semitism in the early summer of 1938. But it was never issued, and a draft text in French has come to light only recently as a result of the work of Belgian scholars.

Drafts of encyclicals are no guarantee of a Pope's true sentiments, or of those of his Cardinal Secretary of State, but the discovered text confirms up to a point what is known of the Vatican's attitude toward the Jews. There is no firm evidence that Pacelli contributed to the draft, but as he was Pius XI's trusted adviser on German affairs and his favored successor it is unlikely that Pacelli was not intimately involved with its commissioning, or that it did not reflect his views. The exclusive input of the Jesuits, to whom Pacelli turned throughout his career for intellectual support, completes the impression of Pacelli's identification with the document.

The project was entrusted to the head of the Society of Jesus, the Polish Jesuit Wladimir Ledochowski, who in turn called on three Jesuit scholars—Gustav Gundlach (German), Gustave Desbuquois (French), and John LaFarge (American)—who brought the document to a draft stage. (This has recently become available in French, but not in the original German.)[20]

LaFarge had campaigned against racism in the United States and had written a book on the issue, *Inter-racial Justice*, which Pius XI had read. LaFarge had argued that the Catholic Church should see the achievement of racial equality as a crucial goal in the twentieth century. Gundlach, on the other hand, had written an article on anti-Semitism in the 1930 edition of the *Lexikon für Theologie und Kirche* in which he condemned ethnic and racist anti-Semitism as unchristian, while condoning state "anti-Jewishness" as a moral and legal means of combating "dangerous influences of Jewish ethnicity in the ambit of economics, politics, press, theater, cinema, science, and the arts." The historian and journalist Roland Hill, who knew Gundlach in the 1950s, has commented that "he was no anti-Semite, but he shared the dislike of his generation for the religiously uprooted Jewish immigrants from the East who were widely thought to have taken German jobs during the depression of the Thirties."[21] Be that as it may, the important question is the extent to which Pius XI and Pacelli shared such qualifying sentiments. Pius XI spoke to LaFarge at the papal summer residence at Castel Gandolfo on June 22, 1938, and told him: "Simply say what you would say if you were Pope!" But a more precise clue to Pius XI's mind can be gleaned from a remark the Pontiff made on September 6, 1938.

A group of Belgian pilgrims had presented him with an ancient missal. Turning to the second prayer after the elevation of the Host in the Mass, the Pope read out the passage in which God is besought to accept the offerings with the same graciousness with which He once received Abraham's sacrifice. "Whenever I read the words: *The sacrifice of our Father Abraham*," Pius said, "I cannot help being deeply moved. Mark well, we call Abraham our Patriarch, our ancestor. Anti-Semitism is irreconcilable with this lofty thought, the noble reality which this prayer expresses."[22] With tears in his eyes, he dwelled on the plight of the Jews in Europe: "It is impossible for Christians," he said, to participate in anti-Semitism. "We recognize that everyone has the right to self-defense and may take the necessary means for protecting legitimate interests. But anti-Semitism is inadmissible. Spiritually, we are all Semites."

The reflection on "self-defense" and "legitimate interests," before the crucial "but," strikes an ominous note, betraying that familiar strain of anti-Jewishness in early-twentieth-century Catholicism shared by Gundlach, and indeed clearly expressed by Pacelli in his correspondence to Gasparri from Munich in 1917. All the same, it appears that a chasm had opened up between Pius XI and Pacelli on the Jewish question. The words of the Pontiff were not published in *L'Osservatore Romano*, which Pacelli controlled, or in *Civiltà Cattolica*, once notorious for its anti-Semitic sentiments, and over which Pacelli had considerable influence. The papal comment survives only because the exiled Catholic politician Don Luigi Sturzo, head of the banned Partito Popolare, Fascism's keenest opponent, published them in the Belgian newspaper *Cité Nouvelle* a week later.[23]

It is open to doubt whether Pius XI ever saw the text of the first draft of the lost encyclical on anti-Semitism, entitled *Humani generis unitas* (*The Unity of the Human Race*), for by this time he was seriously ill and had only weeks to live. No record of his reaction to the text has survived; there is no evidence of any instruction to publish, although there is firm evidence that, between the death of Pius XI and the conclave, Pacelli quashed it. In 1950 Pacelli was to use the title, shortened to *Humani generis*, for an encyclical of a rather different sort.

The section of the unpublished encyclical which deals with racism is unexceptionable, but the reflections on Judaism and anti-Semitism, for all their good intentions, are replete with traditional Catholic anti-Jewishness. The Jews, the encyclical claims, were responsible for their own fate. God had chosen them to make way for Christ's redemption but they denied him and killed him. And now, "Blinded by their dream of worldly gain and material success," they had deserved the "worldly and spiritual ruin" that they had brought down upon themselves.

In another section, the text gives vent to the "spiritual dangers" that attend "exposure to the Jews, so long as their unbelief and enmity to Christianity continue." Hence the Catholic Church, according to the draft, is obliged "to warn and help those threatened by revolutionary movements which these unfortunate and misguided Jews have joined with a view to overthrowing the social order."

Both these sentiments find connections with Pacelli's personal past. First, there was the "obduracy," the "hard-heartedness" of the Jews, so much a part of the Roman anti-Jewish prejudice of the era of Pius IX.[24] Second, there is the identification of the Jews with the "Bolshevist plot" to destroy Christian Europe, which Pacelli believed he had witnessed firsthand in Munich.

The draft encyclical goes on to defend the Catholic Church against charges of anti-Semitism, as Pacelli himself would do after the war. But in a crucial reflection that anticipates Pacelli's unspoken wartime stance, the document points out the risks of the Church's "being compromised in defense of Christian principles and humanity by being drawn into purely man-made politics." The tortured thought being expressed here is expanded in the final claim of the text: that "the Church is only interested in upholding her legacy of Truth. . . . The purely worldly problems, in which the Jewish people may see themselves involved, are of no interest to her." This is saying that the Jews have brought their problems down upon their own heads, not because of their religion, not because of their race, but because of their purely secular man-centered political and commercial goals, for which they are now paying the price. Thus to defend the Jews, as "Christian principles and humanity" might demand, could involve unacceptable compromises—not least an association with, and furtherance of, Bolshevism, by hampering those nation-states that were willing to combat it.

The encyclical was delivered in the autumn of 1938 to Ledochowski, who sat on it. Eventually he passed it to the editor in chief of *Civiltà Cattolica*, who also appears to have sat on it. Why was the encyclical not completed in good time and delivered to the Pontiff? We do not know. For all its drawbacks as a thoroughgoing condemnation of anti-Semitism, it appears likely that the Jesuits and perhaps Pacelli, whose influence would have been paramount during Pius XI's illness, were reluctant to inflame the Nazis by its publication. The document reached Pius XI days before his death on February 9, 1939. For all its prejudices, the encyclical might have made clear to the world that the Pope condemned anti-Semitism. Pacelli, however, soon to be Pope, was to bury the document deep in the secret archives.

11

Darkness over Europe

From the mid-1920s until the late 1930s, Hitler had shown concern about the capacity of the Catholic Church to hinder his plans by protest, noncompliance, and active resistance. His anxiety harked back to the historical precedent of Catholic reaction to Bismarck's Kulturkampf in the 1870s and his fear of political Catholicism. How real were his fears of a Catholic reaction to the regime? How real had been the prospect of Catholic resistance before the outbreak of war?

The origins of the Kulturkampf, or struggle between cultures, are many and complex.[1] After the publication of Pius IX's *Syllabus of Errors* and the definition of papal infallibility at the First Vatican Council, Catholics were viewed as an "enemy within," a potential source of divisiveness in Bismarck's new Reich. Bismarck was suspicious, moreover, of the Polish Catholic populace in the new Reich, and deplored the formation of the parliamentary Catholic Center Party. Another element of the struggle, in the view of historian David Blackbourn, was Bismarck's calculation that he "could deflect the political aspirations of liberal majorities in the German and Prussian parliaments by drawing them behind a struggle against the Catholic Church."

The Kulturkampf started with a series of parliamentary anti-Catholic laws that curbed the "abuse" of the pulpit for political ends, suppressed the Jesuits, controlled Catholic religious education and the appointment of parish priests. Measures included confiscation of Church property, the dismissal of pastors, and the withdrawal of state subsidies from priests who refused to cooperate with the Kulturkampf. Many churches and seminaries were closed. Hundreds of priests were jailed, and more went into hiding or fled abroad. It is estimated that before the end of the crisis some eighteen hundred priests had been imprisoned or expelled. Catholic associations were spied upon, infiltrated, and hampered, especially where it was perceived that workers' organizations were linked with the Church; the press and publishing were curbed and harassed.

Overall, the persecution during the Kulturkampf outstripped the persecution of the Catholic Church by the Nazis between 1933 and 1938. But Catholics in the 1870s used their clubs, societies, sodalities, and guilds to plan communal action with their pastors and bishops. The Catholic reaction in communities, the workplace, and parishes astonished the government and local officials across Germany. When Bishop Eberhard was arrested for noncompliance with the laws in March 1874, Catholic crowds gathered and "threw themselves to the ground, tore their hair, and [made] lamentations that pierced the soul." When the bishop gave a last blessing to the crowds before entering the prison, "the agitation of the masses at this final moment was so great, their wailing and moaning so heartrending, and the emotion that seized even sturdy men so powerful, so overwhelming, that the whole scene is indescribable."[2]

Recognition that this solidarity came directly from the people rather than the leadership of the Pope was consciously articulated at the time, even by the bishops. Bishop Wilhelm von Keteler of Mainz, a noted leader in political Catholicism, observed, "I disapprove of ... a certain bragging and boasting about the power of the Pope, as if he were in a position to cast down his enemies and muster the whole world against them with a single word."[3]

The readiness of Catholics, at the grass roots, to meet violence with violence in many parts of Germany was one of the more remarkable aspects of the entire era. When officials came to lock the churches, they risked angry crowds and threats of physical reprisal. A mayor who ordered the breakup of a Catholic demonstration in the Rhineland in 1875 was beaten up and stabbed. When two Catholics were arrested in Emsdetten in 1876, a crowd of protesters gathered before the jail and hurled rocks; at length they destroyed the building, then released the detainees. In Namborn in 1874, a thousand Catholics stormed the railway station to free an arrested priest.

For the most part, however, there was no attempt, for tactical reasons, to take on the military when it appeared in strength. As David Blackbourn writes, commenting on the pattern of resistance across Prussia, "Catholics refused to cooperate with the authorities, stonewalling when questioned and finding non-violent ways of expressing their contempt for gendarmes and other officials: laughter, for example. The attempts of state commissioners to acquire parish records were hampered, church funds at risk of seizure were secreted, church property that was forcibly auctioned found no bidders."[4]

For the rest, there was widespread passive resistance: Catholics helped priests on the run or in hiding and accompanied those who were arrested all the way to the jail; they celebrated the release of prisoners with garlands and gunfire. Those who spied or colluded with the authorities were ostracized. Where churches were closed, the faithful would gather in forest clearings or cellars for Mass. The phenomenon of *Resistenz*, which meant something less dramatic than physically heroic resistance— the solidarity of a community in its refusal to cooperate—was everywhere evident.

In the 1930s there were indeed isolated acts of Catholic resistance comparable to the Kulturkampf experience: for example, protests against the removal of holy objects from schools in 1936 and the determination of Catholics to gather for Corpus Christi processions and to journey to famous places of pilgrimage such as the Marpingen shrine to the Virgin. But the principal difference between the two periods was the overwhelming influence in the 1930s of the Vatican policy of compliance, from the top down, via the bishops and other clergy and thence to the laity. In the 1870s, by contrast, the papacy made no attempt to control events from the center, except for Pius IX's encyclical *Quod nunquam* (February 5, 1875) declaring Kulturkampf laws null as far as Catholic consciences were concerned.

There were of course crucial differences in circumstances between the two eras. Communications and travel enabled the Nazis to control events much more swiftly than would have been possible in the 1870s, and parliamentary influence and a free press—still in operation during Bismarck's era—came to an end in 1933. Hitler, moreover, learning from the Kulturkampf experience, was careful at every juncture to avoid a frontal attack on expressions of popular devotion. The churches remained open and the faithful were not prevented from their everyday religious practice.

The contrast between grassroots action in the 1870s and its absence in the 1930s, however, still begs the question. What might have been gained had there been no such centrist control of the situation by Pacelli in the 1930s? Would a resistance comparable to the Catholic reaction to Bismarck's Kulturkampf prospered had political Catholicism not been betrayed and abandoned?

The strongest argument for believing in the success of a Catholic resistance, had it been early, widespread and concerted, are those sporadic instances where the SS and the Gestapo backed down in face of popular German protest. An outstanding example was the Rosenstrasse protest in Berlin in February 1943, an episode explored by Nathan Stoltzfus in his book *Resistance of the Heart*.[5] What makes the incident especially significant is that it occurred after Stalingrad, when Nazi security forces had become radicalized and recklessly vicious. During that month the Gestapo rounded up the remaining ten thousand Jews living and working in Berlin, most of whom had survived in "essential" jobs. Of these, two thousand were jailed in a facility on Rosenstrasse in the center of the city. All of them (most of them were men) had German non-Jewish spouses. As soon as news of the roundup spread, hundreds of wives gathered outside the jail to demonstrate. They chanted, "Give back our husbands!" and their demonstration continued for a week, day and night. Repeatedly the police and the SS chased the women, theatening to gun them down. But they regathered and advanced in a phalanx, outfacing the armed SS. Eventually the Gestapo backed down and freed the two thousand Jews. It was the sole public demonstration of its kind by German Gentiles to free Jews, and it was wholly successful.

In his analysis of the Rosenstrasse protest, Nathan Stoltzfus compares the demonstrations with similar Catholic-inspired protests in order to show that concerted grassroots resistance on the part of the Catholic Church might have resulted in widespread challenges to the Nazi regime during 1933 and 1934. Stoltzfus's persuasive argument is based on the regime's need to maintain popular accommodation. "Protests against secret programs not only displayed dissent," he writes, "but also threatened to unveil what the regime needed to hide. Public protests, especially, threatened secrecy." Thus public protest was the most powerful form of resistance, since it could expose differences among the leadership. The Nazi regime projected an impression of the German people as seamlessly pro-Nazi. In consequence, individual Catholic dissidents found themselves in a state of despair, swimming against an inexorable tide.

What made Catholic public protest, at a local level, extremely difficult was, as this narrative has repeatedly demonstrated, the policy of centrist papal primacy, which undermined political Catholicism through two decades. During a critical period in the 1920s and 1930s, when the Catholic parties—the Partito Popolare in Italy and the Center Party in Germany—were the only genuinely *center* Christian democrat option for the electorate, the Vatican chose to repudiate them because it could not control them. Without a flourishing political base supported by the Church (such as occurred with Solidarity in Poland during the 1970s and 1980s), there could be no viable and effective resistance.

As it was, the immense tragedy of the abdication of political Catholicism can be glimpsed by considering two examples of Catholic protest, one before and one during the war: reactions to the removal of crucifixes in 1936 and to the "euthanasia" program in 1941. Had these protests been repeated and extended in a multiplicity of local instances across Germany, from 1933 onward, the history of the Nazi regime might have taken a different course. Had Catholics protested, specifically, Kristallnacht and the rise of anti-Semitism, the fate of the Jews in Nazi Germany and indeed throughout Europe might have been different. Such a conclusion has been drawn by at least three distinguished historians of the period: Nathan Stoltzfus, J. P. Stern, and Guenter Lewy.[6] "It seems beyond any doubt," writes Stern, "that if the churches had opposed the killing and the persecution of the Jews, as they opposed the killing of the congenitally insane and the sick, there would have been no Final Solution."

In the two instances of Catholic protest cited above, a single powerful and courageous bishop, Clemens von Galen, showed what could be achieved by ignoring the primacy of the Vatican and encouraging the people toward collective protest and resistance. Galen supported the protest against the order to remove crucifixes from schools in Oldenburg in northern Germany in November 1936. After the decree had been passed by a Nazi official, there was a groundswell of Catholic indignation in the town of Cloppenburg. There is evidence that the unrest spread even among members of the Nazi Party, including the Hitler Youth, who put their services at the disposal of the protesters. On November 25, 1936, the order was countermanded, an event widely accepted by Catholics to be the first victory of the Church over the Nazi state.

A second instance involving the banning of crucifixes and Christian prayers and hymns occurred in April 1941 in Bavaria on the orders of Adolf Wagner, the Bavarian minister of education. In the ensuing protests and unrest, women in large numbers took the lead. In what has been described as a "mothers' revolt," delegations descended on the schools and threatened to take away their children.[7] In the end, Wagner capitulated, ordering a "stop decree" on the crucifix removal.

During this same period, ordinary Catholic people, with the support of Bishop Clemens von Galen, successfully protested and resisted Hitler's "euthanasia" program. Some seventy thousand Germans deemed mentally infirm were put to death in the nineteen months from January 1940 to August 1941, many of them in the gas chambers that would be used later to kill Jews. The entire population of the village of Asberg in Bavaria, including Nazi Party members, turned out in February 1941 to protest the deportation of "euthanasia" victims who were being bussed to their deaths. As the unrest spread, SD (Sonderndienst) reports indicated the unnerving effect on the local secret police of rumors, sarcasm, and jokes about the regime. SD spies were ordered, with Teutonic solemnity, to investigate. "Anyone voicing a rumor was to be interrogated about its origins. If possible, the specific instigator of a joke or rumor should be named."[8] The SD reported that "numerous political jokes and rumors of a character particularly detrimental and hateful to the state, for example, vindictive jokes about the Führer, leading personalities, the party, the army, and so forth, were being spread."[9] That summer Galen preached three sermons against the "euthanasia" program and the Gestapo, arguing that "mercy killing" could in time be administered to wounded soldiers, crippled people, and the old and infirm. The sermons were printed and distributed, and thousands of the faithful gathered at Münster Cathedral for silent demonstrations of solidarity with the bishop.

Hitler's personal assistant Martin Bormann and other Nazi leaders demanded that Galen should be executed. But the decision was Hitler's alone to make. Goebbels, who rightly saw the case as a major issue of public morale and propaganda, reasoned that the people of the entire region of Westphalia would withdraw their support from the regime if Galen were harmed. Although the "euthanasia" program was not entirely halted, and there are reasons to suppose that Galen's intervention was not crucial to the reduction of deaths,[10] the program went underground and was curtailed, the victims being those who had no voice among the people. Galen survived unharmed.

Here was an instance when public opinion influenced the Nazi regime even when Hitler's power was at its zenith. Had German public opinion been mobilized against other crimes and in respect to other issues, the course of history might have been different. Catholics in large numbers in a specific locale, with the support of their clergy and bishops, had successfully resisted when their kith and kin had been transported to the gas chambers. Without the deadening hand of Vatican control, resistance might have been multiplied across the country from the outset. And had Catholic officialdom, from the outset, not turned a blind eye to the expanding anti-Semitic propaganda and persecution, the terrible disaster that befell the Jews might never have occurred.

In *The Catholic Church and Nazi Germany*, Guenter Lewy concludes: "That German public opinion and the Church were a force to be reckoned with in principle and could have played a role in the Jewish disaster as well—that is the lesson to be derived from the fate of Hitler's euthanasia program."[11]

Pacelli, Pope in Waiting

As the decade came to a close, Pacelli appeared by his demeanor to regard himself as already destined for the supreme office; the year 1938 had found him increasingly withdrawn and elevated, as if seeing all things sub specie aeternitatis. The journalist Nazareno Padellaro saw him at close quarters and has left a vivid impression.[12] The occasion was a dinner given by the head of the Salesian congregation in Rome, with various cardinals and prelates present. Pacelli, attended by a "speechless" secretary, arrived a full hour late. Pacelli said grace, "carefully enunciating every syllable." His face was a "picture of concentration ... a man deep in study and a man deep in prayer." While all those present ate and drank heartily, engaging in affable conversation, Pacelli, "as the food was placed before him . . . was like a man opening his mail. . . . Each dish was a letter, a note, a communication that he contemplated always with the same detachment and the same care to judge what advantage or disadvantage its contents might ultimately bring." Padellaro says that Pacelli drank very little and mixed water with his wine, and while all the guests laughed a great deal, Pacelli "though good-humored, did not laugh; amusing stories seemed always to catch him in an abstracted mood."

Someone asked after the health of the Pope and the table fell silent as Pacelli, for the first time, it appears, spoke: "We all had time in that festive atmosphere—suddenly become serious—to catch one word as it fell from Cardinal Pacelli's lips: the word 'Peace.' The Pope was working for peace. How many times were we not to hear that phrase during the war."

When Pacelli rose early to depart, his secretary "hurrying forward with his cloak," Padellaro remembers noticing his face: "How far away seemed the specter of hunger that was so soon to be seen throughout Europe in millions of emaciated children, in hungry women and old people! Only one emaciated face was here to remind us that the world's greatest need was penance."

By this time Pacelli's household, a sort of kitchen cabinet, was well established. There was Mother Pasqualina with her two sister helpers; there was his doctor, Ricardo Galeazzi-Lisi, an eye specialist whom Pacelli entrusted with the task of choosing appropriate specialists for other ailments; there was also the doctor's half brother, "Engineer" Count Enrico Galeazzi, who advised on building projects within the Vatican, and Pacelli's nephew, Carlo, the son of Francesco, who had succeeded his father as the civil manager of Vatican City. The two Jesuits, Father Leiber and Father Guglielmo Hentrich, and Pacelli's old intimate Monsignor Kaas were close to hand as permanent private secretaries.

Pacelli's younger sister, Elisabetta, told the beatification tribunal that Pasqualina's hold over her brother had become "a true cross, a cross that he received from the hands of God as a means of sanctification." Pasqualina now controlled all access to Pacelli, even screening visits from the family, a situation that would continue for the rest of his life. And although Professor Galeazzi-Lisi's medical expertise was dubious, the nun also insisted that nobody knew Pacelli's medical requirements better than he.

Elisabetta also reported to the tribunal a strange tale involving Pasqualina, with no reference to a date—although it probably occurred in the mid-1930s. The incident reveals the tensions, jealousies, and intrigues with which the kitchen cabinet was riven. Duchess Brady (who had held the Long Island reception for Pacelli) had appointed the engineer Count Galeazzi to administer her Italian villa outside Rome, which she wished to put at the disposal of Pacelli. "Sister Pasqualina," Elisabetta declared, "went there and received various persons to stay. On one occasion my nephew Carlo, without being noticed, managed to take a photograph in which Sister Pasqualina was caught in an intimate posture with Count Galeazzi [un atteggiamento troppo confidenziale verso Il Conte Galeazzi]. Carlo passed the photograph to his father, who passed it on to Don Eugenio."[13] Elisabetta reported that no one knew what had passed between Pacelli and the nun as a result of the episode, but the consequence was that Pacelli became more isolated from his family. The implication was that Pacelli had been caught in a conflict of loyalties; such was the nun's force of personality, he gave her the benefit of the doubt.

The Demise of Pius XI

What was to prove the last year of Pius XI's pontificate saw a dramatic increase in the Catholic population of the Greater Reich. The addition of the Sudeten region following the Austrian Anschluss made Catholics virtually a majority in the nation. Cardinal Bertram issued a pastoral letter greeting the new citizens, but far from German Catholicism's gaining momentum for noncompliance and protest, moral appeasement remained the settled order as 1938 wore on.

Ironically, the Austrian primate, Cardinal Theodor Innitzer, archbishop of Vienna, went far beyond the bounds set by Pacelli. Without reference to the Cardinal Secretary of State, this Prince of the Church made so bold as to receive Hitler warmly in Vienna after his triumphal march through the capital. Then he expressed public satisfaction with Hitler's regime ahead of the plebiscite. Pacelli was outraged by this act of local assurance. He summoned the cardinal to present himself at the Vatican without delay. Innitzer dallied, being in no hurry to face the music that certainly awaited him; so Pacelli placed an article in L'Osservatore

Romano on April 1 declaring that the welcome expressed for Hitler by the Austrian hierarchy was done without the endorsement of the Holy See. This brought Innitzer hastening to Rome, intent on a papal audience. The Pope at first refused to see him, but Pacelli ordered Innitzer to his own icy presence on April 6. The interview and its sequel were masterfully stage-managed. The Cardinal Secretary of State had a document prepared for the primate's signature, stating that the Austrian hierarchy was subordinate to the Holy See and that the Austrian faithful were not bound in conscience by the hierarchy's welcome of Hitler.[14]

While Pacelli, in this instance, was on the side of the angels, it was a remarkable exercise in centrist power. Innitzer signed, then he was promptly sent in to face the Pope. The private audience, we are told, was one of the "most tempestuous" of the whole pontificate.[15] Innitzer went scurrying back to Vienna a thoroughly chastened and thenceforth obedient prelate.

Meanwhile, Cardinal Bertram felt sufficiently complacent about Hitler, the "man of peace," to send an effusive telegram, published on October 2 in the Nazi newspaper *Völkischer Beobachter*: "The great deed of safeguarding peace among the nations moves the German episcopate acting in the name of the Catholics of all the German dioceses, respectfully to extend congratulations and thanks and to order a festive ringing of bells on Sunday."

At the end of the year, brimming with self-confidence, Hitler delivered a harangue to the Reichstag on Church-State relations, refuting the charge that he had persecuted Christians in Germany. Reeling off statistics, he declared that the Churches had received more money from the Nazis than under any previous administration, more tax advantages, and more freedom. He granted that there had been problems, but these were due, he said, to the tendency of a minority of clergymen to engage in political agitation. As for the Catholic morality trials, pedophiles and sexual deviants must be punished in Germany no matter who committed such offenses. For the rest, he said, he turned a blind eye to clergymen who violated their vows of chastity in other ways: The government of the new Reich was not constituted of puritans. And for those who continued to complain: let them contemplate the fate of thousands of priests and nuns who had been slaughtered in Russia and Spain. Let them consider the volunteer soldiers of the Fatherland who had laid down their lives to prevent the spread of bloodthirsty Bolshevism. After a peroration on the wonderful achievements of the new Reich, he ended with a pious flourish, curiously echoing the words of Pacelli in Budapest earlier in the year: "Let us thank God, the Almighty, that he has blessed our generation and us, and granted us to be a part of this time and this hour."[16]

Pius XI, who was dying of heart disease and complications from diabetes, seemed at last to see matters more clearly than Pacelli. To the very end, he continued to conduct audiences from his sickbed, but there were long hours of solitude when he lay meditating on the darkness gathering over Europe. He continued to ponder the phenomenon of anti-Semitism, which had now come closer to home with Mussolini's adoption of Nazi-style racist and anti-Semitic laws, passed in September 1938, giving foreign Jews six months to leave Italy. He talked of the coming war, which, he prophesied, Italy would lose.

In January 1939, when Britain's prime minister, Neville Chamberlain, and foreign secretary, Lord Halifax, came to Rome to assuage Mussolini, Pius XI received them in the Vatican. According to *The Times* of London the following day, the Pope lectured the two politicians without seeking their opinion. It seems that he spent his time attempting to strengthen their resolve to stand up to Hitler. After they had gone, he remarked that the two Englishmen were like a pair of "slugs" and would prove ineffectual in the coming conflicts.[17]

As he drew closer to death, Pius XI appeared to regret the Holy See's concordat policy pursued by Pacelli since 1913. When he summoned the Italian hierarchy to attend an audience with him the second week of February, it was rumored that the dying Pontiff had an apocalyptic announcement against anti-Semitism in preparation (were this true, it is unlikely that it would have exceeded the sentiments in the draft text of *Humani generis unitas*).

The meeting with his bishops was set for February 11, 1939, the tenth anniversary of the Lateran Treaty and the anniversary of his coronation. Twelve days earlier, Pius had started to draft two addresses. In the course of the week, he suffered two heart attacks. One day short of the appointed day, on February 10, Pius XI died, and his addresses to the bishops remained unread. His final words, however, denoted a retreat into that special egotistical sublime, the papal consciousness: "Instead of talking about peace and good will to men who are not disposed to listen," he remarked to a friend of Daniel-Rops, "I prefer now to talk about them to God alone."

Pacelli, appointed *Camerlengo* of the Holy Roman Church four years earlier, was in charge of the arrangements for the burial and funeral as well as the preparations for the conclave. He stood at the bed of the dead Pontiff and by time-honored tradition declared him dead. As one hagiographer remarks: "Those who saw Cardinal Pacelli bend over the body of the dead Pope, to kiss the forehead and hands, understood how much he had loved him. For once he betrayed emotion."

Twenty years later, a fragment of one of the papal speeches prepared for the Italian hierarchy was issued by John XXIII, but it contained no clue to the real nature of the addresses. Unsubstantiated rumors have abounded ever since: that the speeches had been stolen by the Fascists; that the Pope's physician, Dr. Francesco Petacci—father of Mussolini's mistress, the starlet Claretta Petacci—had injected the Pope with poison to prevent him from giving the addresses.[18]

On hearing news of the Pope's demise, Mussolini commented, "At last the obstinate old man is dead!" According to his foreign minister, Count Galeazzo Ciano, news of the death of Pius XI left the Duce "completely indifferent." All the same, on February 12 Ciano confided to his diary that in "some American circles it is rumored that Pacelli has a document written by the Pope. The Duce desires Pignatti to find out, and, if it is true, to try to get a copy of the document."[19] He was referring to Count Pignatti, Italian ambassador to the Holy See. Pignatti eventually went to see Pacelli, who was able to put his mind at rest. "It will remain a dead letter," Pacelli told him. "It will be put in the secret archives."[20] Before Pignatti left, Pacelli congratulated the ambassador on the way in which the Italian government had taken part in the mourning for the deceased Pontiff.

It is not known whether Mussolini ever got hold of Pius XI's speeches; what is certain is that the Duce had been far from indifferent on the score of the late Pontiff's scope to upset his plans, even after his death.

12

Triumph

The conclave of 1–2 March, 1939, following the death of Pius XI on February 10, was an event of crucial international significance in an era of looming conflict between the great powers. Pius XI had eventually come out against the regime in Germany with his encyclical *Mit brennender Sorge* in 1937, and his relationship with Fascist Italy was in shreds by the time of his death. The Lateran Treaty and the Reich Concordat nevertheless stood. A new Pope, if he was pro-Hitler and pro-Mussolini, could cement the Berlin-Rome Axis of the dictators and provide them with a boost of moral approval in the eyes of the world. He might, on the other hand, remain neutral, a "man of prayer," a pastoral Pope who refused to speak for either side; or he might come down on the side of the democracies and encourage American public opinion to support France and Britain in the approaching conflict.

The politics of the new Pope could prove critical for the goals of the great powers on either side of the European divide. In the three weeks that elapsed between the death of the Pope and the beginning of the conclave, which was to confine the cardinals in the apostolic palace and the Sistine Chapel, Rome's diplomatic circles hummed with gossip and intrigue. The French diplomats and Foreign Office officials, conscious of the voting strength of the nine francophone cardinals (in contrast to three from the United States and four from Germany), had accused the Italians of attempting to pull strings—an allegation that appears to have been unfounded.[1] Meanwhile, the French were themselves guilty of attempting to influence the conclave.

The French ambassador to the Holy See, François Charles-Roux, interviewed all the francophone Princes of the Church on their voting intentions, prompting Cardinal Henri Baudrillart to accost the bustling diplomat with the sarcastic opening: "I have come to learn how my government wants me to vote."[2] Meanwhile, Britain's single cardinal, Arthur Hinsley, agonized over whether he should have invited the British minister to the Holy See, Francis D'Arcy Osborne, to lunch in the refectory of the English College, the Roman seminary for English ordinands.

The electoral college in 1939 (those eligible to vote in the election of the new Pope) consisted of sixty-two cardinals, of whom a two-thirds majority was required. There were thirty-five Italian cardinals, and so a new pope needed to be acceptable to an Italian majority; on the other hand, no candidate had a chance without significant support from the non-Italians. Members of the French and British foreign offices discussed the idea of attempting to influence the conclave in favor of Pacelli, who, it was assumed, would continue the pro-democracies stand of Pius XI. Pacelli, however, who had his bags packed to leave the Vatican, according to Sister Pasqualina, was not a foregone conclusion, any more than it was a foregone conclusion that he was for the democracies. Some Roman diplomats were adamant that the electoral college traditionally rejected a former Secretary of State on the grounds that the cardinals would wish to compensate for what had been missing in the deceased Pope. Others wondered whether Pacelli might not prove too weak after serving under such a forceful Pope.[3] Meanwhile, German diplomats in Rome appeared to favor Pacelli because he was thought to be a conciliator, although the Nazi view of him in Berlin was mixed and tending to lukewarm. The four German cardinals certainly favored Pacelli, while Cardinal Innitzer of Vienna, no doubt still reeling from his interview with the late Pius XI, seemed "very disorientated and frightened," according to the German embassy's counselor.[4]

It appears that Pacelli had the majority of the electoral college in his favor from the outset, although not quite all of them. Charles-Roux, the French ambassador, found the French curial cardinal Eugène Tisserant, immovably opposed to Pacelli, since that famously bearded prelate believed that Pius XI's Secretary of State was by nature indecisive. Charles-Roux went to see Tisserant a second time, fearing that the cardinal could have significant influence. The French believed that the Italians might be split between a pastoral Pope, such as the ascetic "holy man" Elia dalla Costa of Florence, and a politician, which obviously meant Pacelli as a front-runner. There might also be an Italian pro-politician constituency for Cardinal Luigi Maglione, former nuncio in Paris. Charles-Roux thought that Tisserant could exploit these potential splits to sway a sizable group of foreign cardinals away from Pacelli. Charles-Roux wrote to his political masters in Paris that, despite his attempts to persuade him otherwise, Tisserant was still "irreducible in his opposition to the election of Cardinal Pacelli." The French cardinal told the diplomat that Pacelli was "indecisive, hesitant, a man more designed to obey orders than to give them."[5]

The cardinals, all sixty-two eligible to vote, gathered to enter the conclave at six o'clock on March 1, 1939. Three transatlantic cardinals— O'Connell from Boston, Leme from Rio de Janeiro, and Copello from Buenos Aires—arrived at the last minute, having disembarked at Naples from the *Neptunia* that very morning. The cardinals were, according to tradition, lodged in simple cubicles with a priest secretary in attendance to care for their needs. Pacelli, already resident in the apostolic palace, continued to live in his apartment, cared for by Mother Pasqualina.

The electoral procedure in a conclave is subject to strictest secrecy under pain of self-excommunication. Leaks nevertheless occur, and the conclave of 1939 was no exception. According to Giancarlo Zizola, who recorded them in his book *Quale Papa?*,[6] the following voting patterns have been suggested. In the first ballot, Pacelli led with twenty-eight votes, trailed by dalla Costa and Maglione. In the second, dalla Costa's supporters went over to Pacelli to give him thirty-five votes.

On the afternoon of March 2, as Pacelli was proceeding to the Sistine Chapel for the third ballot, he fell on the stairs while turning to speak to Cardinal O'Connell. Cardinal Vedier of Paris is said to have exclaimed: "The Vicar of Christ, on earth!" Pacelli rose immediately and continued on his way, clutching his left arm in evident pain.[7] He entered the chapel, and by 5:25 he had been elected on the third ballot, with forty-eight votes. It was the swiftest conclave in three hundred years. According to Charles-Roux, Tisserant voted against Pacelli to the very end, believing him to be a mistaken choice.[8]

As is customary, Pacelli received the burden of the papacy with pious reluctance. A cardinal in his vicinity recorded that, as the last vote was called, "the holy cardinal, pale and deeply moved, closed his eyes, and, as though afraid, lost himself in prayer. Some minutes passed in that solemn silence."[9] He chose the name Pius in deference to the tradition that ran from Pio Nono through his hero Pius X to his immediate predecessor.

Charles-Roux's successor as French ambassador to the Holy See, Count Wladimir d'Ormesson, was struck by the contrast between Pius XI and the new Pius: "The two were very different men. To a robust Milanese mountaineer succeeded a Roman bourgeois, more passive in temperament. A diplomat took the place of a scholar."[10]

Pius XII Affirms Hitler

Four days after his election, Pacelli went into conference with the German-speaking cardinals: Bertram, Schulte, Faulhaber, and Innitzer. He had made it clear that he would handle all German affairs personally. He wanted to show them a draft of a letter he was planning to send Adolf Hitler to mark his accession to the papacy. Where his predecessor had tardily been preparing harsh words against Nazism and anti-Semitism, and intending the recall of the papal nuncio from Berlin, Pacelli proposed the following affirmation of the Führer:

> To the Illustrious Herr Adolf Hitler, Führer and Chancellor of the German Reich! Here at the beginning of Our Pontificate We wish to assure you that We remain devoted to the spiritual welfare of the German people entrusted to your leadership.... During the many years we spent in Germany, We did all in Our power to establish harmonious relations between Church and State. Now that the responsibilities of Our pastoral function have increased Our opportunities, how much more ardently do We pray to reach that goal. May the prosperity of the German people and their progress in every domain come, with God's help, to fruition![11]

With a remarkable lack of historical accuracy, Pacelli now sought to persuade the German Church leaders that Leo XIII's flattering missive to Bismarck in 1878, following the death of the fiery Pius IX, had led to the end of the Kulturkampf.[12] Should they not send this pacific greeting in the hope of a comparable outcome? The cardinals received this unusual version of their own history without comment, and the rest of the discussion was confined to minutiae, such as whether Hitler should be addressed as "Illustrious" or "Most Illustrious."

After agreeing on the draft as it appears above, Pacelli offered the observation that his predecessor had once said that keeping a papal nuncio in Berlin "conflicts with our honor!" Pius XI had said that "the world would not understand how we could continue diplomatic relations with a regime which treated the Church in such a manner." Pacelli now went on to inform the cardinals that he, as Cardinal Secretary of State, had replied: "Your Holiness, what good would that do us? If we withdrew the nuncio, how could we maintain contact with the German bishops?" Pius XI, he went on, had understood "and become quieter."

To which Cardinal Bertram said obediently: "Yes, it must not appear that the Holy See breaks them off [relations with Germany]."

Pacelli concluded with this reflection on the need to maintain diplomatic ties with Hitler's Reich: "Certain cardinals have approached me and asked why I still grant audiences to the German ambassador after all this. How, they say, has he the face to ask for an audience? My reply is, 'What else can I do? I must treat him in a friendly manner. There is no other course. To break off negotiations is easy. But to build them up again—God alone knows what concessions we would have to make! But you can be sure the regime would not take them up again without concessions on our part.' "

From the outset of his reign, then, Pacelli's approach to Hitler exceeded the politesse of diplomacy, and his German bishops took up the cue. His unusually friendly letter to the "illustrious Hitler" crossed with the arrival of "the warmest congratulations of the Führer and the government."[13] The following month, on April 20, 1939, at Pacelli's express wish, Archbishop Orsenigo, the nuncio in Berlin, opened a gala reception for Hitler's fiftieth birthday. The birthday greetings thus initiated by Pacelli immediately became a tradition; each April 20 during the few fateful years left to Hitler and his Reich, Cardinal Bertram of Berlin was to send "warmest congratulations to the Führer in the name of the bishops and the dioceses in Germany," to which he added "fervent prayers which the Catholics of Germany are sending to heaven on their altars."[14]

Talking to the cardinals of the Secretariat of State for Extraordinary Affairs on June 20, 1939, Pacelli told them that to break off negotiations would free Hitler from the last vestiges of the Reich Concordat.[15]

Coronation

Pacelli was crowned on March 12, 1939. The first of the forty thousand ticket holders were assembling on the steps of St. Peter's Basilica at three in the morning. By six, as the pale spring light broke across Michelangelo's dome, the massive bronze doors were open and the guests were flooding into the building. They were still arriving and searching for a perch in the vast marble amphitheater at eight o'clock.

Outside, the citizens of Rome and pilgrims from every quarter of the globe massed in the piazza. They filled the length of the Via della Conciliazione, the ceremonial route from the Tiber to St. Peter's Square celebrating the Lateran Treaty, and spread across the bridge into the Corso Vittorio Emanuele. Witnesses spoke of the mounting exhilaration as the multitudes, more than a million people it was estimated, jostled for hours in the cold sunlight.

For Hilaire Belloc, the militantly Catholic French-born English writer on assignment for the Hearst newspaper syndicate in the United States, the effervescence of the crowds owed much, so he reflected, to the suspension that day of Fascist conformity.

> It was an astonishingly fine sight, the finest I have ever seen in my life. . . . By far the most were Romans. I think the reason for this special excitement was that it was an opportunity for a genuine expression of emotion. Under these modern despotisms such opportunities are rare and every advantage is taken of them.[16]

For others, the mood was symptomatic of war nerves prompted by newspaper and radio reports of Hitler's latest act of brinksmanship. Even as the crowds gathered before St. Peter's, forty German divisions were mobilizing and there were reports of Wehrmacht troop movements on the Czech border preparing for the drive into Prague.

(*Top left*) Pacelli's mother, Virginia, a "pious daughter of the church" (Camera Press London)

(*Top right*) Pacelli's father, Filippo, a lawyer in the service of the papacy (Camera Press London)

(*Left*) Pacelli after his ordination at the age of twenty-three, in 1899 (Camera Press London)

(*Left*) Archbishop Pacelli as papal nuncio in Germany, where he remained from 1917 to 1929 (Camera Press London)

(*Bottom*) During World War I, Pacelli, pictured here with Italian prisoners of war, was renowned for his aid work in Germany (Topham Picturepoint)

(*Left*) Sister Pasqualina Lehnert (*left*), Pacelli's "extremely cunning" housekeeper of forty years, pictured with her two assistants (Popperfoto)

(*Bottom*) Pacelli leaving Berlin in 1929 to take up his post as Cardinal Secretary of State (Ullstein)

Pacelli presides over the signing of the Reich Concordat at the Vatican on July 20, 1933. Franz von Papen and Ludwig Kaas, intimate collaborator, are sitting on his right (Ullstein)

Hitler with Archbishop Cesare Orsenigo, the papal nuncio in Berlin during the Nazi era (AKG London)

(*Top*) Vice-Chancellor von Papen
(*left*) heads the Berlin Corpus
Christi procession, June 1933 (AKG
London)

(*Left*) Pacelli on his coronation day,
March 12, 1939, on the eve of
World War II (AKG London)

(*Left*) Pacelli gives his blessing after the most triumphalist papal coronation in more than a hundred years (Hulton Getty)

(*Bottom*) Hitler in July 1933. That month he declared that his negotiations with Pacelli had created "an area of trust . . . in the developing struggle against international Jewry" (AKG London)

Pacelli broadcasts to the world with Giovanni Montini, the future Paul VI, at his left shoulder. His 1942 Christmas Eve broadcast trivialized and denied the Nazi Final Solution (AKG London)

Pacelli comforts the Italian crowds after the bombing of Rome, August 13, 1943 (Camera Press London)

(*Top*) Pacelli blesses the Easter crowds in 1956. During the Cold War he threatened to excommunicate those who supported communism (Hulton Getty)

(*Left*) In old age Pacelli acquired a reputation for gentleness and saintliness as he continued his absolute control of a monolithic Church (Camera Press London)

There was a widespread feeling between the election and coronation day, evident in Catholic newspaper editorials, that Pacelli's accession must signal an end to the long period of cultic papal exaltation. Was not the new Pope an admirer of Marconi, who had designed the powerful radio transmitter in the Vatican garden? Did he not have an enthusiasm for modern media and broadcasting in particular? It was noted that he had visited England and Paris; he had served as papal nuncio in Munich and Berlin; and as Secretary of State he had crossed the Atlantic twice— to the United States and to South America—and had traveled into Eastern Europe. No Secretary of State in the history of the Church, no *papabile*, had journeyed so far and so wide.

Sensing the mood of the Church, and believing that he had Pacelli's measure, Douglas Woodruff, editor of the international Catholic weekly *The Tablet*, declared in his report on the coronation: "The Pope who had been driven into his cathedral during the heyday of progressive secularism was again among men."[17] Eugenio Pacelli, Woodruff declared, would combat the evils of progressive secularism not by triumphalist isolation but by going forth into the world to amplify the Christian message, for and on behalf of all people of good will, across the airwaves and on the flickering screens of the cinemas of the world. Eugenio Pacelli, Pius XII, he was telling *The Tablet*'s influential readership, was the Pontiff to bring down the wall of divide between the Church and the world. Here was the Pope who would desacralize, decentralize, and demystify the papacy, boldly taking the Christian message out to the peoples of the earth to combat the new paganism.

The prospects for such an outcome, however, were not altogether propitious that bright, chilly morning. To be sure, this was a coronation of unprecedented public visibility in this or any other age. But did the splendid service in preparation signal a dawn of new papal populism? Or the apotheosis of triumphalism?

Pacelli had decreed that no expense should be spared. In 1878 Leo XIII was crowned in the privacy of the Sistine Chapel, as was Benedict XV, austerely in the first dark days of the Great War. In 1922 Pius XI had been crowned on a dais before the shrine of St. Peter. Today, however, was to be a coronation like no other: the first papal coronation broadcast by radio to the whole world, the first to be filmed in its entirety, the first to be performed in the open air before the multitudes in St. Peter's Square since Pius IX's accession in 1846. The intention, however, seemed not so much to bring the Pope among the people as to distance him and elevate him, to amaze the world.

At 8:30 A.M. punctually, to a burst of applause, Pacelli arrived in the atrium, the great vestibule of the basilica, to bless assembled foreign dignitaries and royalty. Two by two, the princes, ambassadors, and distinguished representatives of the nations then processed down the south nave in glittering regalia to take up their positions on the left of the high altar. Among them the Prince and Princess of Piedmont; the Count of Flanders; the Duke of Norfolk, representing the United Kingdom; two ex-kings, Ferdinand of Bulgaria and Alfonso of Spain; Joseph Kennedy, American ambassador in London and foremost Boston Catholic, representing the United States; Paul Claudel, the poet and dramatist, representing France; and, "rather oddly," as Woodruff noted, Eamon De Valera, the prime minister of Ireland, walking in step with Count Galeazzo Ciano, Mussolini's son-in-law and foreign minister, who later caused a rumpus at having been placed below the Duke of Norfolk in the procession. "There was considerable disorder," Ciano noted wryly in his diary entry for that day, "in the organization of the pontifical protocol." Only Nazi Germany among the great powers failed to send a national figure of distinction, contenting itself with the presence of the local Vatican ambassador, Diego von Bergen.

Then up the grand central nave came the principal procession, the file of prelates in shimmering white chasubles and miters—Italian curial cardinals first, then the metropolitan Princes of the Church, followed by archbishops, bishops, and abbots of the great Benedictine houses. Finally, Pacelli himself came into view, wearing a golden miter and a cope stiff with gold filigree. *"Tu es Petrus,"* sang the Sistine Chapel choir, *"et super hanc petram aedificabo ecclesiam meam."* Thou art Peter, and upon this rock I will build my Church.

Pacelli, his ascetic face bloodless as parchment, his huge deep-set eyes gazing lugubriously out upon the faithful, looked for all the world like a demagogue, fanned by the ceremonial feathers known as *flabelli* and borne aloft by a bevy of white-gloved Black Nobility on the *sedia gestatoria,* the traditional papal sedan. Leaning forward, his neck nevertheless stiffly unbending, Pacelli deftly bestowed benedictions left and right, making deep and elegant gestures with his long, tapering fingers, as the congregation sank to its knees in waves on either side. Ahead of him went the master of ceremonies, who at intervals halted the procession. Facing the new Pope three times, he set fire to a piece of flax in a portable silver burner. The flame flared for a moment, then collapsed into ashes. *"Sancte Pater, sic transit gloria mundi,"* intoned the cleric: Remember, O Holy Father, that thus passes the glory of the world.

In the meantime, glory was to be given its fullest expression. Despite the gathering darkness of war, the world's newspaper correspondents were mesmerized that morning by the antique show of rubrics: the gorgeous vestments, pillars of incense smoke, forests of candle flames, the litanies, sung lessons and gospels in both Greek and Latin, the sedate choreography of the ministers robed in cloth of gold and beskirted in taffeta and Belgian lace. For those who had witnessed or seen newsreels of the great Fascist and Nazi gatherings, these liturgies, performed to the sound of Gregorian chants and bursts of baroque polyphony, were a grand challenge to the uncouth neopagan rallies of the dictators.

The knowing eye of London journalist Tom Driberg, always alert for high camp, was bewitched. It was, he ventured, "one of the most magnificent ceremonies I have ever attended."[18] Driberg, who arrived in St. Peter's resplendent in white-tie evening dress and gloves, noted with fascination that "cardinals kissed the Pope's foot and hand; archbishops and bishops kissed his foot and knee; mitred abbots his foot only."

Many witnesses, Catholics and non-Catholics alike, made special mention of Pacelli's rapt recollection, his striking sense of devotion. This was no "popular Pope"; here was no man come among men, but one who seemed already divinely transfigured.

Pacelli had been engaged in the Mass since 9:30, and it was one o'clock as the moment approached for the coronation itself. But he seemed to thrive on the drawn-out proceedings, as if to delay their consummation. "There was not the least sign of tiredness," wrote Douglas Woodruff, "as he blessed to right and left and his voice ... continued clear and strong like a silver trumpet." One observer enthused that "with his ascetic frame, his tall stature, and the first sign of gray above his temples, his dark eyes and gold-rimmed spectacles on his aquiline nose, he seemed ethereal, poised between heaven and earth: indeed a true Pontiff, suspended like a bridge between the divine and the human."[19] Another reflected that to "see him pontificating at St. Peter's was an unforgettably edifying experience," that he "seems to live on a supernatural plane."[20] Ciano noted in his diary that the new Pope "seemed truly touched by the divine spirit."

According to the bogus prophecies of Malachy, this, the 262nd Pope since St. Peter, would be known as "Pastor Angelicus," the Angelic Shepherd. Pacelli, it was said, had personally endorsed this appellation; by the day of his coronation, "Pastor Angelicus" was on everybody's lips.

The crowning was performed on the great loggia overlooking the square and the crowds. The choir sang "A golden Crown upon His Head," as the cardinal deacon, His Eminence Caccia-Dominioni, lowered the heavy triple tiara, an item of headgear dating back to the end of the first millennium of Christianity. "Receive this Tiara," he intoned, "adorned with three crowns, that thou mayest know thou art the father of princes and of kings, the ruler of the world, the Vicar on earth of our Savior Jesus Christ, to Whom is honor and Glory for ever and ever, Amen."

Finally, the moment had come for the papal blessing *urbi et orbi*, to the city of Rome and to the world. *The Tablet's* editor, still optimistic on the score of a new papal populism, later commented:

> It was a fitting sign of the new age that it should be broadcast by radio.... Might we hope for better things for religion from the great inventions of our own age? On that coronation morning we knew that it must be wholly good that the voice of the Sovereign Pontiff and his gestures would be heard and seen throughout the world. His city had made its peace with him, and half Rome was gathered for his blessing.[21]

Meanwhile, down in the piazza below, the papacy was not exactly making its peace with the city of Rome. The scene was witnessed by the English writer Hugh Walpole, who was in the thick of it.

Policemen had been pushing back the crowds that were pressing forward toward the steps of St. Peter's, at the top of which were barriers to contain the guests who had emerged from the basilica to witness the moment of coronation on the loggia above. The surging mass of people "became rhythmical as though following music." Then the good spirits deserted the crowd. People were punching and kicking. Walpole sensed his feet leaving the ground and had a premonition that he was about to be crushed to death. He fancied he saw Hilaire Belloc, now in his seventieth year, being lifted up into the air, waving a sandwich, and Tom Driberg in his evening dress and white gloves, "still smiling and courteous although he seemed to bend sideways." Next Walpole felt as if he had been hit in the back by a huge wave. "I rushed as though I were eagerly greeting a friend, to the outer wall." He was breathless, his waistcoat was torn and his shoes trampled to pieces. "I looked to the balcony, but the ceremony was over. I never saw Pope Pius crowned."[22]

Eugenio Pacelli, Pius XII, was already being transported back to the hallowed precincts of the apostolic palace to begin his long and eventful reign.

Who Is Pacelli?

How well informed were the diplomats and the press of the man who had inherited the *palium* of the bishopric of Rome and the tiara of the Supreme Pontiff, as the world approached the brink of war? What influence, what kind of leadership, did they expect him to exert upon the Catholic Church and upon secular statesmen?

As he looked out upon the powerful forces assembling for war, Pacelli could call on the loyalty and devotion of a half-billion souls—indeed, half the populations of Hitler's new Greater Reich were Catholics, including a quarter of the SS—and this at a time when the bishops, clergy, religious, and faithful were bound together in unprecedented unity of discipline. Pacelli had no armies to call upon, but half a century of burgeoning centrist papal authority gave him extraordinary sway over the hearts and minds of the Catholic faithful. The Pope, by his own self-estimation, was the supreme arbiter of moral values on earth and, in consequence, his responsibilities were all the more remarkable. How would the institution of the papacy, how would Pacelli, the man who embodied that institution, live up to the challenges ahead, the most extraordinary challenges in the Church's long history?

On the day of his election Pacelli had celebrated his sixty-third birthday. Now at an age when most people in public life are contemplating retirement, he had been a senior prelate for more than thirty years, and the highlights of his career were well known.

His years as a diplomat and as a high executive in the Vatican meant that he could count among his acquaintance most of the senior Catholic churchmen of the world. And yet his mode of life and personality, his talents and personal preoccupations, were, save for some well-known facts and generalizations, a mystery. He was said to be highly intelligent, to have a gift for languages, to have a prodigious memory, to be evidently pious. But who could really say what he was like, or of what he was capable?

Pacelli, it appeared, had no inner circle of friends who counted as equals. Since his elder brother, Francesco, died in 1935, he had not been close to any of his siblings. For twenty years his physical wants had been cared for by three German nuns; his private administrative assistant was a discreet and self-effacing German Jesuit, more enigmatic even than Pacelli himself. After leaving his mother's care when he was ordained bishop and went to Germany in 1917, Pacelli ate alone, save for ceremonial dinners.

He had traveled the world, meeting many statesmen, but in recent years his trips overseas had been the arrivals and departures of a head of state, with all the panoply of brass bands and red carpets. His lodgings abroad had been palaces, presidential suites, first-class staterooms that replicated his baronial Vatican apartments and offices; his mode of travel had been plush limousines, private railway carriages, specially chartered airplanes; not since his early forties, on a trip to a mining community in Bavaria, had he been seen in public out of his soutane, his magenta cummerbund, and his enveloping silk cloak. As papal nuncio in Berlin, he was known to have exercised a horse in great secrecy on the estate of a wealthy family. But, unlike his predecessor, he was not one for healthful walks in the hills. For more than twenty years he took his vacations in the cosseted sanctuary of a Swiss sanatorium run by enclosed nuns. If he came in contact with ordinary mortals, it was with chauffeurs and guards of honor. He was not given to fraternizing with people in lowly occupations.

On the day of his coronation, this much, and indeed probably much less, was known of Pacelli by those who professed to inform newspaper readerships and governments. The generally flattering and superficial verdicts of editorialists, diplomats, and civil servants were symptomatic not so much of poor judgment as of sheer scarcity of information about his character, psychology, and true history.

In Italy the press was universally delighted. "He seemed to be specially made for the service of the Holy See," declared *Avenire d'Italia*, "not only because of his inclinations and scholarship, but because he is a Roman.

He feels, like a Roman, in the highest degree, the universal mission of Apostolic Rome." Count Ciano publicly welcomed Pacelli's election as "a great success for Italy," although there were doubts in diplomatic circles as to Ciano's ingenuousness.

Opinion in Britain was generally favorable and uniformly bland. "His unique experience in the direction of the affairs of the Church as Nuncio, and with the execution of Vatican policy," wrote the leader writer of *The Times*, "is his first title to become the head of the Church." *The Sunday Times* commended his "well-tried character," the *Manchester Guardian* his "brilliant diplomacy," *The Observer* his love of "peace, his charity," and his "Christian ideals." Meanwhile, D'Arcy Osborne, the British minister at the Holy See, informed the Foreign Office in London of Pacelli's "saintly character," his "great political experience," and his "great personal charm." Pacelli, enthused Osborne, was "the sort of paragon that the Pastor Angelicus should be." He conceded just one scruple: that he was "not quite sure how strong a character he is, working as he did under an autocrat like Pius XI."23

The French likewise expressed their enthusiasm in orotund phrases. "The successor to Pius XI," claimed *Le Temps*, "has the necessary qualities to take his place in history." His election, opined *L'Oeuvre*, "may open an era of international peace." France's minister in the Vatican, Charles-Roux, had on March 2 informed the French foreign minister in Paris by telegram, "This is the election that could best maintain the papacy on the high moral level to which Pius XI has raised it."24

The Portuguese press were on the whole unhappy with Pacelli, having fancied the chances of their own Archbishop Cerejeira, the Patriarch of Lisbon and youngest cardinal. The Francoists of Spain were also glum, since they blamed Pacelli for Pius XI's perceived neutrality during the civil war—hardly an accurate verdict on the true stance of Pacelli, who was, and proved to be, a staunch defender of the Caudillo. But these isolated notes of acrimony were more than compensated by plaudits from the United States, from Central and South America, and even from the Protestant realms of Scandinavia.

That his election and coronation would find a mixed reception in Germany was only to be expected. On March 3 the *Berliner Morgenpost* wrote, "The election of Pacelli is not favorably accepted in Germany, since he has always been hostile to National Socialism." The *Frankfurter*

Zeitung of the same day wrote: "Many of his speeches have made it clear that he does not fully grasp the political and ideological motives which have begun their victorious march in Germany." The *Danziger Vorposten*, a Nazi mouthpiece, carped that: "Pius XII is not a *Pastor Angelicus....* Pacelli has never been a pastor of souls, a priest in the pulpit. For nearly forty years he has been a diplomat, a politician of the Vatican's worldly politics." Meanwhile in Austria the Nazi newspaper *Graz* declared that the new Pope was "a servile perpetuator of Pius XI's doomed policy ... but for the German people it is of no importance whether a Pius XI or a Pius XII sits in the Vatican."

Amid the torrent of newspaper dispatches and the telegrams from local diplomats to government foreign departments, however, none struck the peculiar note of skepticism articulated by Heinrich Brüning. Brüning, the former Reich chancellor and leading member of the once-powerful Catholic Center Party, whose last words with Pacelli had been in anger, knew the political Pacelli better than most.

After the election of Pacelli on March 2, Sir Robert Vansittart of the British Foreign Office asked Brüning, now in exile and staying in London, to lunch. What, Sir Robert asked Brüning, did he think of Pacelli as Pope? "Brüning," Vansittart could write to Lord Halifax, the foreign secretary, "does *not* share the general optimism in regard to Cardinal Pacelli." Brüning told Vansittart that "Pacelli may still have in his mind the possibility of proceeding by way of treating with the present regime in Germany and Italy."[25]

In fact, Brüning had for several years now been telling anyone willing to listen that Pacelli had forced the disbanding of Germany's Center Party in exchange for that concordat, thus demoralizing potential Catholic protest and resistance. Brüning's view of Pacelli was not simply that the new Pope would attempt to curry favor with Italy and Germany to secure peace, but that he had already silenced and surrendered German Catholics to the power and designs of Adolf Hitler.

13

Pacelli, Pope of Peace

The English writer Bernard Wall provides a rare and vivid impression of Pacelli's demeanor early in his papacy, the office where he conducted private audiences, the routine protocol.[1]

First there was an antechamber, small and "chock-full of cornices and frescoes, softly carpeted, gilded and ugly" with "atrocious" medallions of recent popes on the walls. Here the visitor was obliged to wait until a "purple-clad figure" approached so softly on thick carpets "that one would have imagined his invisible feet were shoeless." This prelate secretary indicated that the visitor should imitate his actions, then, genuflecting on the carpet just inside the door of the Pope's study, Wall following suit, the prelate made a low bow to the white figure of the Pontiff sitting at a desk, "his hands clasped before him, motionless." The Pope now held out his hand for his ring to be kissed, then indicated that Wall should sit on a chair at the side of the desk. Looking about the study, Wall was aware of "thick curtains and marble, an impression I can only describe as of an Empire background." Others have described this office as pervasively "red and gold." The desk was piled high with documents and newspapers. "The newspapers looked as though they had marked passages.... I couldn't see any books, only heaps and heaps of printed documents."

Pacelli insisted on speaking English. He had, Wall noted, a "thin, reedy" voice that almost piped the little prepared speech of welcome. "I

like England very much. I have been to England. I 'ave seen the fleet at
Spit'ead." This was a reference to the ceremony of the gathering of the
principal ships of the Royal Navy at Portsmouth for review by the
monarch, which Pacelli had witnessed in 1907, and which he used as a
stock item of conversation with the English after he became Pope. Wall
gathered that Pacelli, for all his reputation as a linguist, did not understand English very well. But, like many others, he was struck by the Pontiff's charm:

> The expressions on his mobile, highly civilized face varied
> from a gentle smile and a look of deep interest in one per-
> sonally as he made his way through his set piece. His gestures
> were poised like those of an actor. . . . A narrow forehead, a
> long head, subtle, clever, not very deep, I thought. . . . He ra-
> diated friendly concern for me in a way that made me almost
> sorry; it seemed so touching and pathetic that I shouldn't be
> more concerned about the concern.

Pacelli rose at about 6:30 and said a short prayer in front of an open
window overlooking St. Peter's Square. After a cold shower, he went to
celebrate Mass in the private chapel next to his bedroom. His butler,
Giovanni Stefanori, or his chauffeur-valet, Mario Stoppa, served the
Mass, which was always attended by Mother Pasqualina and the German
nuns who assisted her. He ate breakfast, just warm milk and a little
bread, and all his other frugal meals, alone. In addition to her household
duties, Mother Pasqualina, with the full collaboration and interest of
Pacelli, had a warehouse within the Vatican from which she dispensed
blankets, clothes, and food to the needy of Rome. The papal motorcar
was pressed into service for these visits.

The first half of the morning was taken up with work in his private
office, where he met Vatican officials, and which, according to Father
Leiber, was painted an "everyday gray." Then came formal audiences in
the more elaborate rooms below his apartment, where he met diplomats
and important people passing through Rome. After midday he began to
grant special general audiences of small and large groups, conducted in
an auditorium known as the Hall of Benedictions.

Every afternoon, after lunch and a brief siesta, he was driven to the

Vatican gardens by Mario Stoppa, in a huge old-fashioned Cadillac with gold handles and a throne in the back. There he would walk up and down for an hour while reading documents. Stoppa dogged his footsteps with a document case lest the Pontiff should wish to retrieve more information. His evenings were taken up with work and prayer, including the Rosary he said with the nuns in his private chapel. After supper he would work on, often until 2 A.M., but would never go to his small iron-framed bed until he had cleared his desk and filed all the documents.

One of his first acts as Pope was to appoint Cardinal Luigi Maglione to the key post of Cardinal Secretary of State. Maglione, a year younger than Pacelli, had, as we have seen, been considered *papabile* by a tiny minority of cardinals. He was born and raised in a village near Naples and educated by the Jesuits. After a period as a parish priest in Rome, he became nuncio in Switzerland in 1909, then nuncio in Paris in 1926. Maglione was decisive, highly intelligent, seasoned in diplomacy and the ways of the world; his experience in France, on the face of it, complemented Pacelli's knowledge of Germany. Maglione was fascinated by military history and kept maps of the Napoleonic campaigns on the walls of his office. Throughout the Second World War, he kept track of the battles with little flags on a map of the world. He could keep a secret, and had an unnerving habit of remaining silent in the company of others. Just as easily, however, and as the whim took him, he would become voluble. There is evidence that Maglione, from the outset, thought of his relationship with the new Supreme Pontiff as a partnership between virtual equals. It was not Pacelli's style to act the bully like Pius XI, but Pacelli was no less an autocrat and had no intention of accepting his Cardinal Secretary of State as a "colleague." Pacelli, whatever Maglione's personal obstinacies, was in charge.

Monsignor Domenico Tardini was deputy for Extraordinary Affairs, or foreign relations. Squat, with a wide mouth and ready grin, he came from the working-class district of the Trastevere in Rome. He gave any money that came his way to an orphanage. He had no love for Fascists or the Nazis, and dubbed Hitler "a motorized Attila." Tardini spoke bluntly and was to emerge as a popular and refreshing figure among the intriguing diplomats of the wartime Vatican.

His corresponding deputy, responsible for Ordinary Affairs—which was more or less everything not covered by Extraordinary Affairs—was

Giovanni Montini, the future Paul VI. The son of a newspaper owner and politician, he acted as chaplain to the students of Rome University when he was not hard at work for the Vatican as a career bureaucrat and diplomat. He had served in Warsaw and for many years in the Secretariat of State under Pacelli. Montini was a man of sweet and yielding disposition, assailed by scruples, contemplating each problem from all points of view, weighed down by the burdens of history—a disposition that was to affect his decision on birth control a quarter of a century later. He was thin, with deep-set eyes below thick, dark eyebrows, and his squeaky shoes could be heard coming from afar, according to the British minister to the Holy See. Pacelli loved him and was to favor him until, in the postwar years, he showed signs of sailing close to socialism.

Peace Plans

After systematically encouraging disruption in Czechoslovakia, and humiliating in person its aged and infirm president, Emil Hácha, Hitler on March 15, 1939, ordered the Wehrmacht into Prague and set about dismembering the country. Following the appeasement of Munich in the autumn of 1938, Hitler was bent on fresh triumphs and appeared to believe that his ambitions would have the acquiescence of the Western Powers. At the same time, an equivalence was emerging between his mounting campaign against the Jews and his expansionist goals in the East. He had railed against the Czech government, threatening heavy consequences because "the Jews in Czechoslovakia were still poisoning the nation."[2]

Within days of marching into Prague, the Führer was demanding a corridor to Danzig, the Baltic port he was claiming as Reich territory. In a move calculated to warn Hitler off, British prime minister Neville Chamberlain guaranteed Poland's independence and promised aid on March 31. As the crisis deepened in Europe, Pacelli devoted himself to initiatives that might lead to a peace conference in which the papacy would take a leading role. Much now depended on the diplomatic team that he had assembled around him.

Pacelli's goal was clear from the outset. There would be no more attempts to call the Nazis and Fascists to order. The policy of appeasement, which he characterized in a phrase that would echo through the war years—"the Pope is working for peace"—was to dominate the public face of the Vatican's initiatives. To set the tone of his pontificate, he chose as his coat of arms a dove carrying an olive branch.[3] In his first official homily as Pope, given on Easter Sunday, April 9, at a solemn papal Mass in St. Peter's, he had spoken to the text "Glory be to God on high and peace on earth to men of good will." Citing the Old Testament prophets, the Gospels, Paul, and Augustine, he spoke eloquently in Latin on the theology of peace. He spoke of law as the necessary basis of peace, and called on bishops and clergy everywhere to remind the people of their duty to preserve justice. "Is it not the case," he said, "that when violent weapons replace the scepter of justice, the shining prospect of peace gives way to the horrid and cruel fires of war?"[4]

Rarefied, pontifical, the sermon did not venture beyond abstractions and platitudes. Two days earlier, on Good Friday, Mussolini had invaded Albania in a move aimed at strengthening Italian power and forestalling potential German threats to the Balkans. Pacelli uttered neither a word of protest nor of support. Was this a token of strict neutrality?

Just a week later, in a Vatican Radio broadcast to the Spanish faithful, Pacelli revealed how partisan he could be, by praising Franco. Addressing the Spanish bishops, he called on them to combine in "a policy of peacemaking" according to "the principles taught by the Church and proclaimed with such nobility by the Generalissimo: namely, justice for crime and benevolent generosity for those who have been misled." He told them, speaking as "a Father," that he had pity for "those who had been led astray by lying and perverse propaganda."[5] A fortnight earlier, he had sent a telegram of congratulation to Franco for Spain's "Catholic victory." It was a victory that had cost half a million lives and was to cost a great many more.

Pacelli's ambition to become a judge of judges, a world mediator, *in* the world but not *of* the world, was not so much underpinned by neutrality as by his estimate of the supreme status of the Vicar of Christ the King on earth. The objective harked back to the "perfect sovereignty" of Leo XIII and those dreams of influence filling the vacuum of the papacy's loss of temporal power. How could Pacelli exercise such influence in the case of Poland, a Catholic country emerging as the ultimate test for peace or war?

Despite Britain's guarantee to Poland, there was a constituency of French and British politicians and diplomats still inclined to give Hitler a little more. If an agreed rail or road corridor to the city of Danzig stood between peace and world conflagration, perhaps it would be better for the Poles to relent. Favoring Germany, in the light of the "injustices" of the Versailles Treaty, Pacelli suggested that Poland might yield under pressure from a Vatican-sponsored international peace conference.

Pacelli sounded out Mussolini, who was enthusiastic. Then he asked his nuncios in Paris, Warsaw, Berlin, and London to approach the governments in their respective capitals about the feasibility of such a meeting. The response of Britain's Foreign Office was testy. Lord Halifax asked Britain's apostolic delegate, Archbishop William Godfrey, why Russia was not invited. (Bolshevism being beyond the pale for Pacelli, the answer should have been altogether obvious.) And who, Halifax demanded, was going to chair such a conference? Would Pius himself do it under Vatican auspices in Rome? Godfrey replied that His Holiness would not put himself forward in such a role, "but might no doubt be willing to consider it if suggested by the parties to the conference."[6]

Pacelli's tendency to extreme discretion had discouraged him from instructing his nuncios that Mussolini had already been sounded out. So when it went before the British Foreign Policy Committee on May 5, 1939, Chamberlain and Halifax balked because they were not aware that Mussolini had been consulted; some officials, however, were equally reluctant precisely *because* they thought it had been suggested by Mussolini in the first place. Finally, Chamberlain asked whether it might not be better for Pacelli to see individually all five leaders of the interested countries—France, Britain, Germany, Italy, and Poland.[7]

As it happened, Archbishop Cesare Orsenigo, papal nuncio in Berlin, had already sought an interview with Hitler. The meeting, in view of the fact that the Führer had ordered his generals to prepare for war against Poland, revealed the depths of his cynicism and the futility of Pacelli's initiative. The German nuncio was flown to Salzburg and thence to lunch at the Grand Hotel in Berchtesgaden before being conducted to Hitler's residence. They spoke for an hour, then lingered over tea in the presence of Ribbentrop and his aide V. Hewel, who was to leave his own account of the meeting.[8] In a letter to the Vatican that coincides with Hewel's account,[9] Orsenigo described how Hitler listened "with deference" to the papal peace conference plan. Hitler told Pacelli's representative that he did not see the danger of war—neither between France and Italy nor indeed between Germany and France, against whom he had "impregnable fortifications." He had no claim, he said, on Great Britain, except relating to the colonies, and that could hardly lead to war.

Then Hitler came to the Polish question. "As far as Danzig is concerned," he said, "this is a free town under the League of Nations; we can discuss and negotiate regarding the Danzig State, but it is not inevitable that we should reach a state of war. Regarding my other claims, they will come to maturity in time, in 1942, 1943, or maybe in 1945; I can wait. I do not see any reason for a war, unless the Polish people lose their heads and their claims are forced, such as the one that the Polish border should reach the Elbe. Everything depends on the calm and serenity of judgment of Poland."

Referring to the beautiful surrounding scenery of the mountains and the beneficence of their tranquillity, he recommended to the archbishop that participants in the proposed peace conference should prepare themselves spiritually. But after a short interval, he started to rant against Britain for pushing nations toward war—Italy, Spain, China, Czechoslovakia. Even now, he fumed, Britain was trying to encourage Poland to go to war.

At this point Orsenigo raised Pacelli's crucial question: the corridor to Danzig. Would an agreement from the Poles reduce the tension? But Hitler hit a new note. He was not afraid of Poland, he said, and he did not want to attack it, "unless forced by ill-advised Polish provocations," and he was very well protected, moreover, and was increasing the German defenses all the time.

Hitler now became a trifle maudlin, talking of Rome and the artistic beauty of Italy. Thence he moved to his relationship with Mussolini and how he would stand by him militarily, whatever happened. "Speaking of Rome," the archbishop reported, "he was pleased to hear that the Holy Father speaks German and expressed his sorrow for not having seen, during his stay in Rome last year, the basilica of St. Peter." Hitler was referring obliquely to Pius XI's departure to Castel Gandolfo during Hitler's visit; the Pontiff had not wished to remain in Rome while the distorted crosses of Hitler's swastika were displayed in its streets.

Later, Orsenigo had a private discussion with Ribbentrop in which

Pacelli's policy of appeasement and Hitler's capacity for flattery with menaces stood revealed in all their scope for mutual manipulation. Ribbentrop read to the nuncio a report dated April 25, 1939, written by the German ambassador in the Vatican "in which were related a few flattering—and he remarked also 'new'—words of the Holy Father addressed to Germany and to its revival." Ribbentrop went on to say that he had noted how, on Hitler's birthday, prayers were said in Catholic churches in Germany, and "all these respectful manifestations toward the head of the State did not go unobserved and certainly they will make a good impression also on the Führer himself." As a result of all this, the minister said, the time was approaching, although not quite yet, when they could have detailed conversations on the "slight disagreement existing between State and Church." In a separate enciphered dispatch to Cardinal Maglione, Orsenigo wrote that Ribbentrop had asked that "no mention [be] made in the press, including the Vatican newspaper, of my conversation with the Chancellor."[10]

Orsenigo's advice, then, as the diplomat on the spot, coincided exactly with Pacelli's appeasement policy: "I think . . ." wrote the nuncio, "that if Poland would calm down and be silent, without, for the time being, giving in on any point, the motive for a war, at least for the moment, would be set aside; by gaining time in this way it would be possible to start dispassionate negotiations, especially regarding an extraterritorial motorway through the 'Polish corridor to allow direct communications between the two German territories.' "

Three days later, Orsenigo talked to a British embassy staff member in Berlin. The nuncio declined to discuss what had passed between himself and Hitler, but he went out of his way to express the hope that "His Majesty's Government would note that the present Pope since his accession had not in public uttered a single word of criticism of German policy toward the Church. His Holiness had moreover intervened specially to see that *L'Osservatore Romano* did likewise."[11]

Vatican Information

As the likelihood of war increased, the Vatican was seen as an important purveyor of international information and a focus of manipulation for propaganda purposes. *L'Osservatore Romano*, which contained much routine information about curial appointments, acts of the Holy See, and speeches and writings of the Pope, also commented on international events and relations, and was at times misquoted to bolster the diplomatic interests of the European powers.

Vatican Radio, run by the Jesuits, was also exploited by news agencies that distorted its news and commentary for morale and propaganda purposes. The station had its own twenty-five-kilowatt German transmitter with omnidirectional antennae broadcasting on four short-wave bands from the highest point of the Vatican gardens. It carried news and analysis as well as homilies and religious addresses in many languages.

Vatican Radio was monitored by Germany's Sonderdienst Seehaus (Lake House Special Service), situated on the shore of the Wannsee; the German embassy in Rome also intercepted broadcasts. The Vatican thus attracted a flow of protest implying that the Holy See was continuously breaking the terms of the Reich Concordat, which eventually led to Pacelli's instructing the Jesuits to reduce the number of German broadcasts and to avoid political comment critical of the Nazis.[12] But such self-censorship still lay in the future.

As administrators of a universal Church strongly controlled from the center, the Curia (the senior departmental officials in the Vatican) communicated with the dioceses around the world on matters of routine management and clerical discipline, liturgy, and education. Since Church affairs constantly overlapped with state interests, the Holy See's diplomatic communications were of considerable political interest; interception of its messages became a priority for many intelligence services.

The Secretariat of State in the Vatican maintained communication with its nunciatures and legations throughout the world by means of cable and diplomatic bags. Before the war, the Secretariat routinely shared Italy's diplomatic pouches, but the practice was discontinued when it became evident that their enclosures were being tampered with. Later, the Vatican was to use Swiss, Spanish, British, and American couriers, much of the initial traffic accumulating in Switzerland before passing on to Madrid and Lisbon.

Highly secret communications were normally enciphered and dispatched on the airwaves from the Vatican transmitter. By the end of the First World War, the Secretariat had employed a two-part code of

228   Hitler's Pope

several thousand four-digit numerical groups, superenciphered for security by short cipher tables which replaced each pair of numbers in the
encoded version of the message with a pair from the table.[13] Italy and
Germany had cracked this code by 1918. Then, until 1939, the Secretariat employed a code known as RED: a one-part code of about twelve
thousand groups printed twenty-five lines to a page in the codebook. For
greater security, the groups were enciphered from numbers to letters by
replacing the page number with a digraph from a pair of tables that were
used on odd and even days. Top-secret Vatican messages during wartime
employed two new systems known as YELLOW and GREEN. YELLOW was a
one-part code of about thirteen thousand groups enciphered by di-
graphic tables for page numbers and random mixed alphabets for line
numbers. Tables and alphabets were varied on different circuits and every
day of the month. The GREEN code is to this day a closely guarded secret; but there is evidence that it was a numerical code of five-digit
groups enciphered by short additive tables, each of which contained one
hundred five-digit additive groups.[14] Neither YELLOW nor GREEN was mechanical. Later in the war it appeared that information to the Allies was
sent by special couriers and enciphered in specialized codes.

Italy's intelligence services spied on the Vatican's traffic from a listening
post at Fort Boccea, close to Vatican City, and recorded some eight thousand messages throughout the war. Of some six thousand radiograms, it
is estimated that the Servizio Informazione Militare (SIM) successfully
decoded about three thousand. The decoders were greatly helped by another intelligence division known as the Sezione Prelevamento (Special
Collection Service), which specialized in breaking and entering foreign
embassies and bribing janitors. Early in the war, the papal gendarmes and
even the cipher section of the Secretariat of State had been penetrated by
Italy's secret agents. In years to come, this intelligence gathering was to
cast doubt on allegations that the Vatican withheld secret information
from the wartime documents it later published on the orders of Paul VI.

Pacelli Pressures the Poles

Britain and France pondered Pacelli's suggestion of a peace conference,
this way and that, through the first week of May 1939, and despite the
secrecy of the project, details began to leak in the press in Paris,

London, and as far afield as New Zealand. Then, abruptly, on May 10, Pacelli withdrew and the plan was dropped. The Secretariat of State explained the Pope's withdrawal to the nuncios by claiming that there was no longer any danger of war. According to the historian Owen Chadwick, it was Mussolini who scuppered the peace conference idea because he did not relish having to face France—with whom the Duke had been at loggerheads over territorial disputes in North Africa—in the presence of Britain, Germany, and Poland.[15] Instead, Mussolini joined Ribbentrop in declaring that international tensions had been reduced. In the meantime, by May 7, Mussolini and Ribbentrop had discussed the preliminaries for the "Pact of Steel," committing Italy and Germany to joint belligerence, and it was signed in Berlin on May 22.

Still Pacelli had not done with appeasement. Badly shaken by the Mussolini-Hitler pact, on June 4 he informed Osborne, Britain's minister to the Vatican, that he was prepared to act alone as mediator between Germany and Poland over their differences.

The Western diplomats were astonished. Was it possible that Pacelli was acting clandestinely on behalf of Mussolini? That was the implausible question being expressed in the Foreign Office in London. At the same time, Pacelli intimated that Britain was making mediation more difficult in view of its guarantee to defend Poland.[16] Pacelli's eagerness to persuade Poland to make sacrifices to appease Germany thus led the British Foreign Office to speculate that the papacy had abdicated its moral authority. Sir Andrew Noble, for example, wished "that the Pope would see his way to make clear to the world the incompatibility between the worship of God and the worship of the State." Noble believed that Pacelli was attempting to "exorcise the devil with soft words."[17]

Sir Orme Sargent, also of the Foreign Office, wrote a memorandum that charged Pacelli with moral impotence. The Pope intended, Sargent reflected, to maintain a middle course between the democracies and the Fascist and Nazi dictatorships. Pacelli's motive, he recorded, was to secure a role as mediator at the appropriate moment. In other words, there was an element of self-seeking hubris in Pacelli's neutrality. "Personally," wrote Sargent, "I feel that he would be able to influence events far more effectively as champion of certain moral principles in the world of today than he is likely to be able to as a possible but improbable candidate for the post of mediator between the Axis and the Democracies."

Pacelli was not emerging creditably from his initiatives, especially in Poland. The American ambassador in Warsaw, A. J. Drexel Biddle, told Roosevelt that the Poles throught Pacelli was acting like an Italian; that he was pro-German and had no understanding of Poland and the Polish people.[18] By the summer, rumors that Pacelli would pressure the Poles to make concessions to Germany were so rife in European diplomatic circles that Maglione felt compelled to issue a denial. On July 15, 1939, he wrote to Lord Halifax via Osborne, asserting that the Pope had never attempted to take "the initiative in proposing to the two governments a concrete solution of the problem," but merely to urge them to treat it "calmly and with moderation."[19] Maglione added that he had assurances that Germany was not going to attack Poland; yet his only basis for saying this was of course Hitler and Mussolini's foreign minister, Count Ciano.[20]

By August 22, it became common knowledge that Germany was to sign its pact with Russia: war seemed inevitable. Could the Pope, at the last minute, use his influence to appeal for reason? No doubt with the propaganda value in mind, Halifax badgered the Pope, via Osborne, to make a radio appeal condemning violence and recommending peace. So it was that Osborne sat with Domenico Tardini on the eve of the Hitler-Stalin pact, polishing phrases that would excoriate the prospective aggressors, Nazis and Communists alike. Later, Tardini and Montini presented Pacelli with four different drafts of increasing condemnation. Pacelli chose the least vehement. All the same, his appeal was memorable, and Halifax quoted a phrase in his own broadcast to the British nation that night: "Nothing is lost by peace. Everything is lost by war. . . . Let men start to negotiate again. . . . I have with me the soul of this historic Europe, the child of Faith and Christian genius. All humanity wants bread, freedom, justice; not weapons. Christ made love the heart of his religion."[21]

Resolute at the end of March, when an alliance with Poland and Russia seemed guaranteed to stop Hitler in his tracks, the British government was now less than intrepid. The question arose in the Foreign Office: might not the Pope pull off that concession over Danzig after all and keep Germany happy? Perhaps, as one "standing above all public disputes and passions," as Pacelli told the world in a broadcast on August 22, he could play a major role in preventing war. On August 29, Maglione dispatched Father Pietro Tacchi Venturi, a Jesuit with legendary diplomatic skills, to Mussolini. He was asked to praise Mussolini's peace efforts effusively, then press him to do what he could with Hitler to prevent war.

Mussolini, who was no more eager to go to war than the French and the British (he told Tacchi Venturi that a new war could spell the "end of civilization"), composed a note for Pacelli to pass on to the Polish leadership. "Poland does not oppose the return of Danzig to Germany," it began, adding that the Poles should seek negotiations with Germany for reciprocal rights for minorities. Mussolini further recommended that Pacelli, "having addressed himself to all the heads of state in his speech by radio in the shadow of a danger growing graver every moment, and prompted by his great love toward Poland," should then address the president of the Polish republic personally on the lines suggested in the note.[22]

The message counseling Poland's acquiescence on Danzig, sanctioned by Pacelli and signed by Maglione, was sent to Monsignor Filippo Cortesi, Poland's papal nuncio, on August 30, 1939, using the precise words suggested by Mussolini. Cortesi cabled back, questioning the wisdom of such a capitulation so late in the day, but Maglione replied at once, instructing him to act (a copy of the plea to Poland's president was passed on to London). The following day, Pacelli issued a "last appeal in favor of peace," begging that the "governments of Germany and Poland do their utmost to avoid every incident and abstain from taking any step capable of worsening the present tension."

Germany Invades Poland

On September 1, 1939, Hitler invaded Poland with overwhelming superiority in up-to-date tanks, aircraft, and weaponry, employing the Wehrmacht's new military doctrine of blitzkrieg. On September 3, France and Britain declared war on Germany.

The Polish campaign was to last until October 5 and was greatly accelerated by the invasion of eastern Poland by the Red Army on September 17. Polish losses during the campaign have been estimated at 70,000 officers and men killed and about 130,000 wounded; German losses at 8,082 killed and 27,278 wounded.[23]

On September 1 Hitler cabled Pacelli via the German ambassador to the Holy See, thanking the Pope for his message and declaring that he "had waited two days for the arrival of a Polish emissary for the peaceful settlement of the German-Polish conflict.... As a reply to his efforts, Poland ordered general mobilization. Furthermore, the Poles had yesterday committed a number of still further unheard-of frontier violations, which this time involved regular troops entering German territory."[24]

Poland's agony was just beginning. By the end of the war, in addition to widespread uprooting of entire populations, starvation, and repression, some six million people were to suffer death or physical injury. Throughout September, as Pacelli pondered the appalling news from Poland, with its population of 35 million mainly Catholic souls, he remained silent. Was Pacelli maintaining a neutral stance in the hope that he could exercise future influence as supernegotiator? Was he frightened by the retaliatory impact a protest might provoke against the Catholic populations of both Germany and Poland? As far as the Poles were concerned, there was nothing worse that Hitler could inflict upon them. In the view of the British and the French, the lack of a resounding denunciation was baffling. So frustrated was the Polish ambassador at the Vatican, and so determined was he that Poland should use the Holy See's services to announce to the world what was happening in his country, that he prevailed on the Polish government to send the Polish primate, Cardinal August Hlond, to Rome. Hlond arrived on September 21 and was warmly received by Pacelli. Yet still the Pontiff refused to speak on Poland's behalf.

The cardinal, however, was given access to Vatican Radio, which was run by the Polish head of the Jesuits, Father Wladimir Ledochowski, and he used the opportunity to good effect. On September 28 he broadcast to the world: "Martyred Poland, you have fallen to violence while you fought for the sacred cause of freedom.... Your tragedy rouses the conscience of the world.... On these radio waves, which run across the world, carrying truth from the hill of the Vatican, I cry to you. Poland, you are not beaten! By the will of God you will rise with glory, my beloved, my martyred Poland!"[25] Two days later Pacelli addressed a group of Polish pilgrims led by Cardinal Hlond. He spoke to them with emotion, telling them that he foresaw the resurrection of their country, which would rise like Lazarus from the dead.

It was not enough. The Polish pilgrim group had expected a forceful denunciation of both Germany and Russia. They were bitter, and their disappointment echoed loudly around Rome. Hlond did the round of the curial cardinals, attempting to drum up support; their Eminences mostly listened sympathetically, but nothing happened. Then Édouard Daladier, the French premier, added his voice to the discontent. He had cabled his ambassador to the Holy See, saying that he was surprised that the Pope had failed to condemn. He stressed that the Pope needed to open the eyes of the Italian people; to remain silent, he declared, was virtually a token of approval. Describing the Polish anger in Rome, Osborne reported that it was being said that "papal pronouncements since the outbreak of war have pusillanimously evaded the moral issues involved."[26]

"Darkness over the Earth"

When Pacelli finally spoke, it was in the form of an encyclical entitled *Summi pontificatus* (Of the Supreme Pontificate), known in English as "Darkness over the Earth."[27] It was the most important act of his early pontificate, but it was a tardy production, in preparation from July 1939. Issued on October 20, it was published in *L'Osservatore Romano* on October 28.

He started by characterizing himself as the Vicar of Christ who speaks from a dimension separated from the world. Referring to Leo XIII's encyclical *Annum sacrum* as a message "from another world," he recollected the year in which that Pope had dedicated the human race "to the divine heart of Jesus." As he warmed to his theme, he condemned the growth of secularism and what he called "laicism," and called for a new world order in which all nations recognized the kingdom of Christ, the "King of Kings and Lord of Lords," and asked his readers to consider recent "external" events in "the light of eternity." There was an inherent and hopeless irony in a world picture that sought to deepen the divide between the sacred and the profane; for it was surely unrealistic, as the world plunged toward war, to call upon nations to abandon their secular concerns and contemplate matters of the spirit. At the same time, in order to denounce worship of the state, Pacelli set the nation-state in opposition to the individual and the nuclear family, as if there were no scope for complex social networks in between.

The writing was replete with early papal rhetoric that could only soften the tough things he had need of saying: "Our heart sickens, as a father's heart must, at the prospect of the harvest that will grow up from the dark seeds of violence and animosity, for which war is now tracing furrows in blood." There were powerful words, however, on the theme of the "unity of the human race" and its common Creator; an apt citing of Paul's "neither Greek nor Jew, circumcision nor uncircumcision, Barbarian, Scythian, bond nor free: but Christ is all and in all." Nor did he neglect to mention Poland by name: "The blood of so many who have been cruelly slaughtered, though they bore no military rank, cries to heaven especially from the well-loved country of Poland. . . . She puts her trust in that Virgin Mother of God who is the help of Christians, and waits for the day when she will be allowed at last to emerge, unharmed, from the waves that have engulfed her."

A token of his failure to clearly denounce Nazi Germany, however, can be seen in his personal editing, his cuts and nuances and changes of mind. "An authority," he wrote in an early draft, "that recognized no limits to its power, and abandoned itself seemingly [he added the enfeebling qualifier seemingly, *quasi*, as an afterthought] to an unrestrained expansionism, would tend to conceive the relations between peoples as a struggle, in which might would prevail; and the rule of force would take the place of the noble kingdom of law." Despite the "seemingly," he decided to cut the entire passage prior to publication, deeming it too strong.[28]

For all the encyclical's equivocations, Cardinal Hlond was grateful, London's Foreign Office approved, and the president of France praised it. Mussolini's Italy allowed the text to be published. The French air force scattered tens of thousands of copies over Germany. In Poland, the Nazi military had the encyclical reprinted, substituting "Germany" for "Poland,"[29] and in Berlin, von Bergen, the German ambassador to the Holy See, was told that Pius XII had ceased to be neutral.

Pacelli and the Anti-Hitler Plot

Then something extraordinary, and in deepest secrecy, occurred, revealing that whatever motivated Pacelli in his equivocal approach to the Nazi onslaught in Poland, it betokened neither cowardice nor a liking for Hitler. In November 1939 Pacelli became centrally and dangerously involved in what was probably the most feasible plot to depose Hitler during the war.[30] The plot centered on Hans Oster, a man of great principle and astuteness, who worked in the Military Intelligence Office in Berlin. Oster was in contact with a circle of officials and soldiers in the Abwehr, the intelligence branch of the armed services, whose leading figure was General Ludwig Beck, former army chief of staff, who was planning a military coup to depose Hitler. The plotters were committed to returning Germany to democracy, and envisaged a federation that would include Austria but not Poland or non-German Czechoslovakia, which would become independent again. They understood that the coup might erupt into a period of civil war. Before making their move, they wanted the assurance of the British government that the Western democracies would not take advantage of Germany's vulnerability. They wanted assurances that the Munich settlement would be honored. A key feature of their plan involved the services of Pius XII, who was judged by Oster, who had known Pacelli when he served as nuncio in Germany, as the ideal go-between.

Oster chose as his German contact with the Vatican a Bavarian lawyer and Catholic, Josef Müller, who had been drafted into the Abwehr when Poland was invaded. In the autumn of 1939, Oster sent Müller to Rome, ostensibly to report on Italian defeatism but in fact to establish links with the Vatican and ultimately the Pope. One of Pacelli's closest confidants in the apostolic palace was the former chairman of the Center Party, the German prelate Ludwig Kaas, now in permanent exile and employed as administrator of St. Peter's Basilica. Kaas put Müller in touch with the Jesuit Robert Leiber, who saw Pacelli two or three times a day.[31]

The plan envisaged that Pacelli would approach Neville Chamberlain (via Britain's Vatican minister, Osborne, communicating with Lord Halifax in London) to seek guarantees for an honorable peace between the democracies and Germany following the coup. This would then be passed back via Leiber and Müller to Oster.

The hazardous nature of such a plot for the Pope, the Curia, and all those associated with the Vatican can hardly be exaggerated. Historian Harold Deutsch has judged it "among the most astounding events in the modern history of the papacy." To the end of his life, Leiber could not get over the shock of it and continued to maintain that Pacelli "went much too far." The risks were extreme. Had Hitler learned of it, it is likely that he would have wreaked harsh revenge on the Catholic Church in Germany. At the same time, Mussolini could have seen it as a breach of neutrality and the Lateran Treaty, justifying radical, even violent, measures against the Vatican. The Vatican, after all, depended even for its water and electricity supply on Fascist Italy, and could be entered at any moment by Italian troops.

Pacelli was sufficiently aware of the dangers and complex ethical principles involved to ask for pause to consider. Kaas and Leiber both left on record their unhappiness about the scheme. Astonishingly, however, Pacelli said nothing to Cardinal Maglione, his Secretary of State, who remained completely in the dark from start to finish. Pacelli spent just one day in quiet reflection before surprising Father Leiber with his resolution. On November 6, 1939, Müller was informed that the Pope was prepared to do "all he can." The way in which Pacelli reached this crucial decision reveals the weakness and vulnerability of the modern papal autocracy. Believing that as Pope he was empowered to act, without consultation, even with others whose duty it was to advise, like Maglione, he was literally alone in such historic moral decisions.

Osborne's first encounter with the conspiracy occurred on December I, 1939, when he lunched with Kaas, who outlined in the most general terms what was afoot and received equally vague encouragement from the British minister. They met again on January 8, 1940, and Kaas informed Osborne that the plot was still in the air: the German prelate appeared rather testy and had still not named Müller.

Four days later, Pacelli summoned Osborne to a private audience. He told Osborne in strictest confidence that he had been visited by a representative of certain German army chiefs and had reliable information that a violent offensive was planned by Germany in the west in February. But the offensive might not occur if these army chiefs overthrew Hitler, which they could do only on the understanding that Britain would guarantee an honorable peace for Germany. Communicating the exchange to Halifax in a secret memorandum, Osborne conveyed an impression of Pacelli's strangely vacillating frame of mind:

He wished to pass the communication on to me purely for information. He did not wish in the slightest degree to endorse or recommend it. After he had listened to my comments on the communication he had received and passed on to me, he said that perhaps, after all, it was not worth proceeding with the matter and he would therefore ask me to regard his communication to me as not having been made. This, however, I promptly declined as I said I refused to have the responsibilities of his Holiness' conscience unloaded onto my own.[32]

Osborne expressed skepticism as to the plan and told the Pontiff that the French would have to be secretly informed. Pacelli then replied that, "having thus salved his conscience, he would not even expect any answer."

Osborne wrote to Halifax by diplomatic pouch from the Rome embassy that he found the whole thing "hopelessly vague" and "reminiscent of the Venloo affair," a false plot into which British agents in Holland had been lured by German agents. He ended by commenting that Pacelli's "spontaneous offer, after my expressions of scepticism, to cancel his communication to me shows that he does not relish being used as a channel and that he has little expectation of any result. But he certainly cannot be reproached for acting as he has."[33]

The secret letter from Osborne was read on January 17, 1940, by Halifax to the war cabinet, whose members agreed "that the Secretary of State for Foreign Affairs should take suitable steps to inform the French Government of the communication which had been made by His Holiness the Pope to Mr. Osborne."[34]

On February 6 Pacelli summoned Osborne once more to an audience, sending his *maestro di camera* in dead of night to inform the minister that the meeting would take place the following day at noon and that he was not to dress formally or even let it be known that he was seeing the Pope. Writing to Halifax on February 7,[35] Osborne reported that Pacelli had been approached again by the plotters, but that the Pontiff had declined to give any names except to say that a well-known German general was involved. The start of Hitler's planned offensive in the west in February had been postponed because of inclement weather; meanwhile, the organizers of the coup were still seeking confirmation that Germany would not be dismembered in the event of a British and French invasion and armistice. Osborne went on to inform Halifax: "The significant thing seems to be that this time we are offered a 'democratic, conservative, moderate,' and more important still, a decentralized and federalized Germany within the Munich frontiers."[36]

Halifax replied on February 17 in a three-page letter, the main substance of which was to put Pacelli definitively on the spot. The British had to broach the matter with the French, but they could not do this "on the basis of ideas emanating from undisclosed sources.... If any progress is to be made, a definite programme must be submitted and authoritatively vouched for."[37]

Halifax's letter crossed with another from Osborne, who on the sixteenth had taken Halifax's wife and son to see the Pope. "[Pacelli] drew me aside at the end of the audience to tell me that the German military circles mentioned in my previous letters had confirmed their intention, or their desire, to effect a change of government." Osborne's reaction to what Pacelli told him was curt. "I only observed," he informed Halifax, "that if they wanted a change of government, why didn't they get on with it. I added that even if the government was changed I didn't see how we could make peace so long as the German military machine remained intact."[38]

The parties to this curious conspiracy now fell silent. There were implausible rumors in London that Kaas was not to be trusted, that he was a Nazi spy. Halifax then learned that King George VI was already apprised of a plot "to bump off Hitler." Müller came and went between Rome and Berlin. The conspirators continued to wait for a British guarantee, and the British continued to wait for the identities of the conspirators.

On March 11, paying a visit to Mussolini in the hope of drawing Italy into the war, Ribbentrop, the German foreign minister, sought an audience with Pacelli, who made himself available without hesitation. Ribbentrop saw the visit as a propaganda opportunity (after all, the previous Pope had absented himself from Rome on Hitler's visit), but his principal motive was to dissuade Pacelli from criticizing the Nazi regime.[39] During the meeting, Ribbentrop forestalled all discussion of peace initiatives by his categorical insistence that Germany was going to win the war. When Pacelli raised the matter of attacks on Catholics and Church property, Ribbentrop replied that the German people were solidly behind the Führer, it was a "revolutionary" situation. "Even to-day the clergy has not yet understood that it is not their business to meddle in politics," he went on. "What is needed is time and patience to arrive at a perfect understanding and at a religious settlement which is desired by Hitler."[40]

When Pacelli asked Ribbentrop to sanction a Vatican envoy to Poland, Ribbentrop deflected the request. At one point Pacelli asked the minister whether he believed in God. The minister replied, *"Ich glaube an Gott, aber ich bin unkirchlich."* [I believe in God but I am not addicted to any church.] Pacelli repeated the phrase in German sarcastically two or three times, and told Ribbentrop that he could not help wondering about its truth.[41]

Dino Alfieri, the Italian ambassador to the Holy See, reported to Mussolini after the meeting. "It became clear (and the Pope is so convinced) that Ribbentrop wanted to be received in the Vatican only for the purpose of domestic politics—especially to impress the vast Catholic masses in Germany and to exploit in a manner favorable to Germany the repercussions which the conversation had in the world."[42]

On March 30 Pacelli spoke to Osborne again about the plot to topple Hitler. He had discovered that London had received peace feelers by other avenues. He was upset. Osborne did not enlarge on Pacelli's annoyance, but the Pontiff was probably vexed at the leakiness of the conspiracy and indignant that he had placed the Holy See in fruitless jeopardy.

Somehow, with a lack of trust and foresight on the part of the British and the Germans plotters, the conspiracy had run out of steam. As for Pacelli, in the judgment of historian Owen Chadwick, "The Pope risked the fate of the Church in Germany and Austria and Poland and perhaps he risked more. He probably risked the destruction of the German Jesuits. . . . He took this big risk solely because his political experience saw that, however unsuccessful this plan was likely to turn out, it was probably the one remaining chance of halting the coming invasion of Holland and France and Belgium, of saving untold bloodshed, and bringing peace back to Europe."[43]

London's Foreign Office, meanwhile, had formed the opinion that

Pacelli was "more open to influences than his predecessor." Osborne responded with a perceptive qualification: it was probably true, he wrote to London officials in late February 1940, "at any rate in the best sense; that is to say, he is more ready to listen and to weigh opinions, and less rigid and uncompromising in his own views and actions. But it does not at all follow that he is unstable and easily swayed."

As Pacelli faced the extreme moral choices and crises in the coming conflagration, two things seem clear in the light of his central part in the conspiracy to topple Hitler during the twilight war: whatever his decisions, good or bad, they were his own; and he was unafraid on account of his personal safety. His hatred of Hitler was sufficient to allow him to take grave risks with his own life—and, as Robert Leiber indicated, the lives of a great many others. When the risk seemed right, he was capable of acting promptly. His exterior personality seemed delicate, oversensitive, even weak to some. Pusillanimity and indecisiveness—shortcomings that would be cited to extenuate his subsequent silence and inaction in other matters—were hardly in his nature.

14

Friend of Croatia

In the spring of 1940, as the threat of Hitler's westward invasion loomed imminent, so the likelihood of Italy's joining Germany in arms became inevitable. Pacelli became an important focus for influencing Mussolini, and all Italians, to think again.

The papacy's scope for information-gathering and dissemination was put in peril, however, even before the outbreak of hostilities. Pacelli had no need of prompting to rebuke Italian warmongering, and his chief means of appealing for peace was *L'Osservatore Romano*, which by April 1940 had risen in circulation to 150,000 from its regular circulation of 80,000 in the 1930s—a small figure for a national daily but, as it was read by the clergy, its message was amplified from the pulpit. Although *L'Osservatore* kept to the strictures of noninterference in Italian politics as laid down in the Lateran Treaty, the newspaper promoted Pacelli's calls for peace on the basis of Christian principles. Responding to Vatican influence, pastors throughout the country had been inviting the faithful to church services to pray for peace. As German pressure on Italy to join the war increased, Pacelli attempted to restrain Mussolini by congratulating the Duce at every opportunity, in public and in private, for his "peace initiatives." Small wonder the Duce became irritated. In the last week of April 1940, Mussolini pronounced the Vatican a "chronic appendicitis of Italy," and attacks on the Pope's newspaper increased. For some leading Fascists, like Roberto Farinacci, the mere fact of an independent media voice in Italy was a continuing provocation. Farinacci, who had a newspaper of his own called *Regime Fascista*, accused *L'Osservatore* of siding with France and Britain against Italy. He declared that the majority of *L'Osservatore's* readers were Jews and Masons. In the first week of May, news vendors of *L'Osservatore* were beaten up on the streets; copies were seized and destroyed.

During that same week, however, and for quite different reasons, Pacelli became a wide target for Fascist fury. On May 3 he had received information from Josef Müller—the German agent who had been Oster's courier in the plot to topple Hitler—that Germany was about to invade Holland and Belgium. The Secretariat of State immediately warned the nuncios in The Hague and Brussels by ciphered cable, and the information was also passed to Paris and London via Charles-Roux and Osborne. In a private audience on May 6, moreover, Pacelli told Umberto, the Italian crown prince, of Hitler's imminent plan. Italian code-breakers operating from Fort Boccea had intercepted and deciphered the messages to the Dutch and Belgian nuncios. Umberto went straight to Mussolini and told him what Pacelli had imparted.

The Vatican's privileged position as a receiver of information, and its capacity for diplomatic outreach, thus put Pacelli in jeopardy on the very eve of Hitler's western offensive. In Berlin passing the advisory information to the nuncios was seen as an act of espionage; in Rome, Mussolini was placed in an extraordinary dilemma, for it looked for a moment as if he might be in league with Pacelli to stay out of the war. The circumstance, and the outcome, has led Owen Chadwick to assert that Pacelli's "imprudence" helped make it "inevitable that Mussolini would enter the war." After the information had been passed, "Mussolini could not do other," writes Chadwick, "than prove to the Germans that he totally rejected the Pope."[1] Whatever the case, Pacelli's role as neutral peacemaker, and above all his influence on Mussolini, was at an end.

When Hitler invaded Holland, Belgium, and Luxemburg on May 10, 1940, Pacelli was under immediate pressure from London and Paris to issue a condemnation of this violent breach of international law, and by all the means in his power to prevent the entry of Italy into the war. Tardini drafted a papal letter deploring the invasion of "three hardworking little peoples ... without provocation or reason.... We have to raise our voice to lament wickedness and injustice once again." But Pacelli thought the draft likely to aggravate the Germans and quashed it.[2] Instead he sent cables to the three sovereigns of Holland, Belgium, and Luxemburg, expressing his sympathy and affection. The telegrams were greeted warmly by their recipients, but displeased the powers on both sides of the European divide. London and Paris deplored the absence of an outright condemnation of aggression; Rome and Berlin accused him of political interference in a period of grave crisis.

When the texts of the telegrams were published in *L'Osservatore* on May 12, the Fascists tried to prevent distribution. Newspaper vendors were beaten. Anyone seen with a copy was attacked. Two people who had bought copies near the Trevi Fountain were thrown into the water. That same day, Italy's ambassador to the Holy See, Dino Alfieri, destined to represent Italy in Berlin, complained about the telegrams to Pacelli in an audience. Alfieri told him that the Fascist bands were furious and something serious could happen at any moment.

Pacelli replied that he was not afraid of being put in a concentration camp. He said that he had been reading the letters of St. Catherine of Siena, who had reminded the Pope of her day that God would judge him harshly if he failed in his duty.[3]

At about this time (the exact date is uncertain), Pacelli was waylaid in Rome as he went to celebrate Mass at one of the basilicas. Gangs of Fascists rocked his car at a crossroads and yelled "Death to the Pope! Down with the Pope!"[4] He closed the summer palace at Castel Gandolfo for the duration of the war and did not venture onto the streets again until after the fall of Mussolini. Unable to visit within his own diocese of Rome without fear of violence, Pacelli was a voluntary prisoner inside the Vatican. Hence it became all the more important to him to maintain publication of *L'Osservatore*, his chief means of communication with the faithful of Italy, and Vatican Radio, which was also under threat.

On May 15, 1940, as the Wehrmacht penetrated the French defenses near Sedan and raced for the Channel ports, Mussolini declared his intention to take up arms at the side of Hitler, although he gave no precise date. It was not until June 2, after the British had evacuated their armies from Dunkirk, that Mussolini eventually announced that he would declare war on France on June 10.

Into late May, the Foreign Office in London was still pressing Osborne to persuade Pacelli to make vociferous condemnation of the German offensive—even though, by May 20, *L'Osservatore* was on the brink of being banned beyond the walls of the Vatican. By May 28, in order to prevent a prohibition on sales in Italy, the Vatican agreed with the Italian government to publish only official war communiqués of the belligerents without comment.[5]

The Holy See was now besieged, surrounded by a country at war with the Church's eldest daughter, France, and with Great Britain, a country for which Pacelli had respect if little direct knowledge, save for coronations and naval reviews. Pacelli had only limited scope for action. His cables and messages to nuncios around the world could be intercepted. His newspaper could be stopped at the gates of the Vatican. His radio station could be jammed. An encyclical aimed at Germany could be destroyed, or altered before publication. Pacelli's first priority was to maintain his limited independence. These limitations were of less significance two years later, when he could have exploited the communications outreach of the Allies for a major statement, or statements.

Discussions within the Vatican about how the tiny city-state would fare in the eventuality of Italy's entering the conflict had been conducted throughout the twilight war. The fate of the Pope was the subject of imaginative speculation in diplomatic circles: suggestions that he might depart for the United States, Portugal, or South America spread and evaporated. Pacelli was determined to stay put in the Vatican, come what may.

According to the Lateran Treaty, the Vatican was a sovereign state. Would its sovereignty and its diplomatic personnel and apparatus be honored? Mussolini had been consulted in the summer of 1939 on the fate of the ambassadors and legates to the Holy See, resident in the city of Rome rather than within the walls of the Vatican. In the autumn he had made it plain that diplomats of unfriendly nations would be required either to move into the Vatican itself or leave the country. By May 30, 1940, after Wladimir d'Ormesson (replacing Charles-Roux as French ambassador to the Vatican) opted to move into quarters in Vatican City, Osborne followed suit, joining a village of representatives of nations occupied by Germany or considered unfriendly, including the Belgians and the Poles.

And what should the Vatican do for money? After the Lateran Treaty financial settlement, the Vatican had lost money along with everyone else following the Wall Street crash, despite a sensible policy of diversification. By 1935, however, things had begun to improve, and the Vatican had switched in any case to a policy of blue-chip investment in the United States that was to create the foundations of sound fiscal strength into the postwar era.[6] For the period of the war, however, the Vatican needed cash reserves. In the last week of May, the Vatican transacted an intriguing deal that became a well-kept wartime secret: it transferred to the United States a quantity of gold bars valued at $7,665,000, a portion of them immediately being sold for cash dollars.[7]

Defending Rome

It is a commonplace observation by historians of the Italian theater in the Second World War that throughout the period of hostilities affecting Rome, Pius XII was doggedly obsessed with one issue above all others—the preservation of the Eternal City from aerial bombardment. He appeared to his critics, in other words, to put the preservation of Rome above all the other cities in Europe facing the horrors of blitz-krieg, deportation, torture, and the Final Solution itself. The question of the bombing of Rome, therefore, has lent credibility to the allegations of Pacelli's culpable silence and inertia on other issues during the war.

At the same time, he declined to condemn the bombing of cities such as Coventry, in England, or to plead for the preservation of other places of religious and artistic importance. The inference drawn by critics of his policy was that he was guilty of double standards, that his priorities were scandalously unbalanced, that he was perhaps afraid of being bombed in the Vatican. The realities of the case, however, were more complex.

On June 10, 1940, the very day that Italy declared war on France and Britain, Cardinal Secretary of State Maglione requested Osborne to seek an undertaking from London that the RAF would not bomb Rome. Maglione was apparently clutching a copy of the London *Daily Telegraph* which carried an article predicting the aerial bombing of Italian cities, including the capital. Osborne dismissed the article as nonsense. But just three days later, Allied aircraft swooped over Rome and dropped propaganda leaflets, some of which landed on Vatican territory. It was an ominous signal to the Italians. For Pacelli it was ample evidence that the RAF had the range and the probable intention of leveling Rome and the Vatican. He could hardly issue a formal protest on behalf of Italy, but he asked Maglione to complain to London about the infringement on Vatican territory and promptly continued his pressure on Osborne to persuade his London masters not to bomb Rome.[8] The exchange of notes became voluminous as the months wore on.

London agreed that every effort should be made to avoid bombing the Vatican itself: St. Peter's and the apostolic palace, after all, were not part of enemy territory. But they saw no reason why Rome, the capital of a power at war with Britain and rumored to be sending Italian aircraft on bombing runs over England alongside the Luftwaffe, should be subject to special protection. In fact, there was every reason—whatever the British intentions—to refrain from declaring Rome an open city, demilitarized and thus immune from attack under international law. Surely it was best to keep Mussolini and the citizens of Rome guessing; would this not make them think again about bombing London and Birmingham and Liverpool? Above all, London thought it inappropriate for the Pope, the head of a neutral state, which the Vatican claimed to be, to plead on behalf of Rome, which was part of Italy. Did this not indicate that he was being used as a propaganda instrument by the Fascists?

For his part, Pacelli was moved by a fierce love of Rome as the Eternal City—the sacred center of Christendom, the site of St. Peter's tomb and the catacombs, a place of pilgrimage filled with ancient basilicas and churches and oratories and all the Christian artistic heritage of the ages. As he was bishop of Rome, it would have been strange had he not been anxious for the state of the Eternal City and had he failed to use all the influence in his power to secure its safety. While it was true that Rome had been the capital of the new nation-state since 1870, there were visible reminders on every street and square of its ancient status as the heart of the universal Catholic Church. Equally important, Pacelli's advocacy for Rome was a reason, in the eyes of the Fascist government, to sustain the sovereign status of the Vatican.[9] After Italy entered the war, the Vatican, with its warren of foreign diplomats of belligerent and occupied countries, began to look like a hive of espionage. There were calls from leading Fascists to take over the city-state and send these foreign "spies" packing. By employing its influence to stave off the bombing of the Eternal City, however, the Holy See was deemed to be providing a useful service to the Fascist government, giving Mussolini grounds to ensure the Vatican's immunity from interference or incursion. In time the Italian government would express its gratitude.[10] Thus Pacelli's efforts to have Rome declared an open city were evidence of a pressing priority: the very survival of the Vatican and the papacy. But this was hardly a case he could ask Osborne to argue with London. All the same, what made Pacelli's stance annoying to the British was his refusal to condemn the bombing of civilians in England, a policy Pacelli had apparently adopted in pursuit of strict impartiality.

Matters came to a head in mid-November 1940 when the English city of Coventry and its ancient cathedral were severely damaged by bombing. Osborne pleaded with Pacelli to issue a denunciation, but the result of his pains was a visit from the Portuguese ambassador to London's Foreign Office to plead with the British not to bomb Rome in retaliation. The groveling nature of the appeal irritated London officials and gave them pause for thought about renewing their pleas for papal denunciations of the Luftwaffe bombing raids. "I would urge," wrote Vansittart from the Foreign Office, "that [Osborne] should put it merely as a retort, and not offer any opening by which the Pope might say 'Very well, I will condemn the bombing of English churches, and now you will spare Rome.' That would be the rottenest interchange imaginable."[11] Vansittart need not have concerned himself, for no quid pro quo was forthcoming. All that Pacelli was prepared to do, after the Coventry raids, was make a cryptic reference in a prayer for nameless "cities destroyed and civilians killed."

Part in mischief, but ultimately in diplomatic earnest, London now asked Osborne to request that the Vatican should be well lit at night in order to avoid impending RAF bombing raids from Malta (the inference being that an illuminated St. Peter's would guide the bombers in to hit Rome). Archbishop Tardini retorted that the suggestion was "puerile," prompting Osborne to reply: "Impracticable, yes; puerile, no!" Then Tardini reminded him of something that both Osborne and London seemed to have forgotten: that the Vatican's electricity supply came from Italy. Tardini added that Mussolini and Hitler would be delighted should the RAF bomb Rome, for it would provide an instant propaganda coup for the Axis. Osborne appears to have been impressed by this reflection, for he began to remind London of it; his reminders became more frequent as the RAF received orders to plan raids on Italian cities in reprisal for the anticipated bombing of Athens in Mussolini's military campaign in Greece.

As the war lengthened, Pacelli's pleas on behalf of the sanctity of Rome were unrelenting, as were his attempts to have the city declared officially open. Such a move would have involved Mussolini removing his government from the capital, along with all military objectives. By 1942 there was much talk about such a plan and even support from the king of Italy, but it was to come to nothing until the weeks that preceded the Allied liberation of Rome. Pacelli's ceaseless attempts to persuade the Allies to honor the sacred nature of Rome paid off for much of the war, although the city was not to remain entirely unscathed.

His efforts were to cost him dearly in the eyes of history.

Catholic Croatia's Atrocious Regime

Pacelli and the officials in the Secretariat of State were convinced, as were governments throughout Europe, that a war between Germany and the Soviet Union was only a matter of time. Given the possibility of Europe under the heel of Stalin, and abundant evidence of the Soviet intention to suppress the Christian churches, Mussolini's Balkan campaign in October 1940 was viewed among some members of the Curia with a measure of optimism, for in this context Yugoslavia was seen as a last-ditch bulwark for Italy and the Mediterranean. Mussolini's failure to defeat the Greeks, however, meant that Hitler was obliged to come to his aid. In order for him to gain access to Greece, Yugoslavia had to be persuaded to join the Axis. The pact between Germany, Italy, and Yugoslavia was signed in Vienna on March 25, 1941. Two days later, a group of Serbian nationalists seized power in Belgrade, abolished the regency, and announced that Yugoslavia was siding with the Western democracies. Churchill declared from London that the Yugoslavs had recovered their "soul."

In reprisal, Hitler invaded Yugoslavia on April 6 in conjunction with his assault on Greece, bombing the open city of Belgrade and killing five thousand civilians. As the Wehrmacht entered Zagreb on April 10, the Croat Fascists were allowed to declare an independent Croatia. The following day, Italy and Hungary (another Fascist state) joined forces with Hitler for their share of the Yugoslav cake. By April 12 Hitler had issued his plan for a partitioned Yugoslavia, granting "Aryan" status to an independent Croatia under Ante Pavelic, who had been awaiting developments under the auspices of Mussolini in Italy. Pavelic's group, the Ustashe (from the verb *ustati*, meaning "to rise up"), had opposed the formation of the South Slav kingdom of Yugoslavia after the First World War and had planned disruption and sabotage from the safe haven of Italy: it was Pavelic who had plotted the assassination of King Alexander in 1934. Mussolini had granted Pavelic use of training camps on a remote Aeolian island and access to Radio Bari for propaganda broadcasts across the Adriatic.

This was the background to the campaign of terror and extermination conducted by the Ustashe of Croatia against two million Serb Orthodox Christians and a smaller number of Jews, Gypsies, and Communists between 1941 and 1945. An act of "ethnic cleansing" before that hideous term came into vogue, it was an attempt to create a "pure" Catholic Croatia by enforced conversions, deportations, and mass extermination. So dreadful were the acts of torture and murder that even hardened German troops registered their horror. Even by comparison with the recent bloodshed in Yugoslavia at the time of this writing, Pavelic's onslaught against the Orthodox Serbs remains one of the most appalling civilian massacres known to history.

The importance of these events for this narrative depends on three considerations: the Vatican's knowledge of the atrocities, Pacelli's failure to use his good offices to intervene, and the complicity it represented in the Final Solution being planned in northern Europe.

The historical legacy that underpinned the formation of the NDH (Nezavisna Drzava Hrvatska), or Independent State of Croatia, was a combination of ancient loyalties to the papacy going back thirteen hundred years, and a sense of burning resentment against the Serbs for past and present injustices. Croat nationalists nourished a powerful grudge against the Serbian ascendancy that had excluded them from the professions and from equality of opportunity in education. The Serbs were guilty, so the Croats perceived it, of favoring the Orthodox faith, encouraging schism among Catholics, and systematically colonizing Catholic areas with Orthodox Serbs. Both Serbs and Croats drew an equivalence between ethnic and religious identity—Orthodox Serb versus Catholic Croat. At the same time, Jews in the region were condemned on the grounds of race, as well as their links with communism, freemasonry, and alleged encouragement of abortion.

Pacelli had warmly endorsed Croat nationalism and confirmed the Ustashe perception of history in November 1939 when a national pilgrimage came to Rome to promote the cause of the canonization of a Croat Franciscan martyr, Nicola Tavelic. The Croat primate, Archbishop Alojzije Stepinac, represented the pilgrims and gave a speech in the Pope's presence. In his response, Pacelli used an epithet that had been applied to the Croats by Pope Leo X: "the outpost of Christianity"—as if the Serbs, Orthodox religionists in ancient schism from Rome, had no title to call themselves Christian. "The hope of a better future seems to be smiling on you," Pacelli told them in an address of terrible irony, "a future in which the relations between Church and State in your country will be regulated in harmonious action to the advantage of both."[12]

The boundaries of the new state encompassed Croatia, Slovenia, Bosnia, Herzegovina, and a large part of Dalmatia. Out of a population of some 6,700,000, 3,300,000 were Croats (and hence Catholics), 2,200,000 Orthodox Serbs, 750,000 Moslems, 70,000 Protestants, and some 45,000 Jews. The existence of the Protestant Germanic minority presented no problem to the Ustashe leadership, nor, strangely, did the large enclave of Muslims. But the Orthodox Serbs faced "radical solutions," as did the Jews, who were immediately marked down for elimination.

On April 25, 1941, Pavelic decreed that all publication, private and public, of the Cyrillic script (used by the Orthodox Serbs) was banned. In May, anti-Semitic legislation was passed, defining Jews in racist terms, prohibiting Jews from marrying Aryans, and setting in motion the "Aryanization" of bureaucracies, the professions, and Jewish capital. In the same month, the first Jews were deported from Zagreb to a concentration camp at Danica.[13] By June, Serb Orthodox primary and preschools were closed.

In this perilous new situation for Serbs, the question was raised: if life was to become unbearable on account of being Orthodox, why not seek conversion to Catholicism? Within weeks of the founding of the Croat state, Catholic pastors were beckoning Orthodox Serbs into the Catholic Church. On July 14, 1941, however, anticipating its selective-conversion policy and eventual goal of genocide, the Croatian Ministry of Justice instructed the nation's bishops that "the Croatian government does not intend to accept within the Catholic Church either priests or schoolmasters or, in a word, any of the intelligentsia—including rich Orthodox tradesmen and artisans—because specific ordinances in their regard will be promulgated later, and also so that they shall not impair the prestige of Catholicism."[14] The unspoken fate of those Orthodox Serbs, rejected in advance from the coming program of enforced conversion, was deportation and extermination. But in the crazed bloodletting that ensued, even Catholic baptism failed to secure immunity.

From the outset, the public acts and statements concerning ethnic cleansing and the anti-Semitic programs were well known to the Catholic episcopate and Catholic Action, the lay associations so vigorously promoted by Pacelli as papal nuncio in Germany and as Cardinal Secretary of State. These racist and anti-Semitic measures were therefore also known by the Holy See, and thus by Pacelli, at the point when he greeted Pavelic at the Vatican. These acts were known, moreover, at the very point when clandestine diplomatic links were being forged between Croatia and the Holy See. A central feature of this essentially religious war was the appropriation by Catholic Croats of churches vacated or requisitioned by the Orthodox: the issue was discussed by the Curia and rules of conduct drawn up.

But from the very beginning there were other atrocities, news of which spread rapidly by word of mouth.[15] Pavelic, it soon came to light, was not exactly a counterpart of Himmler and Heydrich, for he shared none of their coldhearted aptitude for the bureaucracy of systematic mass killing; but the Ustashe leadership embarked on their massacres with a cruel and haphazard barbarism that has few parallels in history.

The Italian writer Carlo Falconi was commissioned in the early 1960s to write the story of the Croat massacre of the Serbs, the Jews, and others. His researches in the appropriate Yugoslav archives, and among what was available in Vatican sources at that time, were painstaking.[16] He uncovered the following examples of widespread atrocities committed in Croatia starting in the spring of 1941.

On April 28 an Ustashe band raided six villages in the Bjelovar district and took out 250 men, including a schoolteacher and an Orthodox priest. The victims were forced to dig a ditch, then were bound with wire and buried alive. A few days later, at a place called Otocac, Ustashe rounded up 331 Serbs, including the local Orthodox priest and his son. Again the victims were forced to dig their own graves before being hacked to death with axes. The perpetrators saved the priest and his boy until last. The priest was forced to recite the prayers for the dying while the son was chopped to pieces. Then the priest was tortured, his hair and beard torn off, his eyes gouged out. Finally he was skinned alive.

On May 14, at a place called Glina, hundreds of Serbs were brought to a church to attend an obligatory service of thanksgiving for the constitution of the NDH. Once the Serbs were inside the building, a gang of Ustashe entered with axes and knives. They asked all present to produce their certificates of conversion to Catholicism. Only two had the required documents, and they were released. The doors were locked and the rest butchered.

Four days after the Glina massacre, Pavelic, the so-called Poglavnik or Führer, was in Rome to sign (under pressure from Hitler) a state treaty with Mussolini granting Italy a clutch of Croatian districts and cities on the Dalmatian coast. On this same visit, Pavelic had a "devotional" audience with Pius XII in the Vatican, and the Independent State of Croatia was granted de facto recognition by the Holy See. Abbot Ramiro Marcone, of the Benedictine monastery of Montevergine, was forthwith appointed apostolic legate to Zagreb. There is no evidence that Pacelli or the Secretariat of State knew of the atrocities that had already begun in Croatia in the spring of 1941, and it seems clear that rapid de facto recognition (new recognition of states by the Vatican was avoided in wartime) owed more to Croatia's status as a bastion against Communism than to any affirmation of its murderous policies. All the same, it was known from the very beginning that Pavelic was a totalitarian dictator, a puppet of Hitler and Mussolini, that he had passed a series of viciously racist and anti-Semitic laws, and that he was bent on enforced conversions from Orthodox to Catholic Christianity. Above all, Pacelli was aware that the new state was, as Jonathan Steinberg has put it, "not the result of a heroic rising by the people of God but of outside intervention." The Independent State of Croatia, as all the world knew, was the outcome of the violent and illegitimate invasion and annexation of the kingdom of Yugoslavia (which had official diplomatic ties with the Vatican) by Hitler and Mussolini; and here was Pacelli holding Pavelic's hand and bestowing his papal blessing.

It would take time for the Holy See to learn of the atrocities. But details of the massacre of the Serbs and the virtual elimination of the Jews and Gypsies were known from the outset to the Croatian Catholic clergy and to the episcopate as they unfolded. Indeed, the clergy often took a leading part.[17]

The tally almost defies belief. By the most recent reliable reckoning, 487,000 Orthodox Serbs and 27,000 Gypsies were massacred between 1941 and 1945 in the Independent State of Croatia. In addition, approximately 30,000 out of a population of 45,000 Jews were killed: 20,000 to 25,000 in the Ustashe death camps and another 7,000 deported to the gas chambers.[18] How was it that despite the strictly authoritarian power relationship between the papacy and the local Church—a power relationship that Pacelli had done so much to establish—no attempt was made from the Vatican center to halt the killings, the forced conversions, the appropriation of Orthodox property? How was it that when the atrocities became common knowledge inside the Vatican, as will be shown, Pacelli did not immediately and forthrightly dissociate the Holy See from the Ustashe actions and condemn the perpetrators?

Croatia and Vatican Knowledge

From the outset, the archbishop of Zagreb, Alojzije Stepinac (currently being considered for beatification in Rome), was wholly in accord with the general goals of the new Croatian state, and bent on having it recognized by the Pope. He called personally on Pavelic on April 16, 1941, and listened as the new leader declared that he would "not show tolerance," as Stepinac recorded in his diary, "toward the Orthodox Serbian Church because, as he saw things, it was not a Church but a political organization." This gave Stepinac the impression that "the Poglavnik was a sincere Catholic."[19] That same evening, Stepinac gave a dinner party for Pavelic and his leading Ustashe to celebrate their return from exile. On April 28, on the very day that 250 Serbs were massacred at Bjelovar, a pastoral letter by Stepinac was read from all Catholic pulpits calling on the clergy and faithful to collaborate in the work of the leader.

By what stretch of naiveté did Stepinac fail to understand what that collaboration might involve? By early June of 1941, the German general plenipotentiary accredited to Croatia, Edmund Glaise von Horstenau, declared that, according to reliable reports of German military and civil observers, the "Ustasha have gone raging mad."[20] The following month, Glaise reported the embarrassment of the Germans, who "with six battalions of foot soldiers" watched helplessly "the blind, bloody fury of the Ustasha."

Priests, invariably Franciscans, took a leading part in the massacres.[21] Many went around routinely armed and performed their murderous acts with zeal. A Father Bozidar Bralow, known for the machine gun that was his constant companion, was accused of performing a dance around the bodies of 180 massacred Serbs at Alipasin-Most. Individual Franciscans killed, set fire to homes, sacked villages, and laid waste the Bosnian countryside at the head of Ustashe bands. In September of 1941, an Italian reporter wrote of a Franciscan he had witnessed south of Banja Luka urging on a band of Ustashe with his crucifix.

In the Foreign Ministry archive in Rome there is a photographic record of atrocities: of women with breasts cut off, gouged eyes, genitals mutilated; and the instruments of butchery: knives, axes, meat hooks.[22]

And what was the attitude and the reaction of the Italian forces in the region? In some respects similar to the reaction of United Nations troops in Yugoslavia in more recent history (although with obvious differences), it was one of helplessness and dismay. Constrained by its alliance with Nazi Germany and the circumstances of world war, the Italian army had limited scope for action. All the same, it is estimated that by July 1, 1943, the Italians had given protection to as many as 33,464 civilians in their Yugoslav sphere of influence, of whom 2,118 were Jews.[23] Falconi has speculated that the humanity of the Italians in this regard may have been due in part to pressure from the Vatican, although he grants that the evidence is "sketchy and vague."[24] Jonathan Steinberg's extensive research and evaluation of Italian reluctance to engage in deportation and extermination would discount such a proposition. In a moving summary of the complex Italian phenomenon of humanitarianism in Yugoslavia between 1941 and 1943, Steinberg asserts: "A long process which began with the spontaneous reaction of individual young officers in the spring of 1941 who could not stand by and watch Croatian butchers hack down Serbian and Jewish men, women and children ended in July 1943 with a kind of national conspiracy to frustrate the much greater and more systematic brutality of the Nazi state. . . . It rested on certain assumptions about what being Italian meant."25

Much has been made in the postwar years of the personal holiness of Archbishop Stepinac, Croatia's Roman Catholic primate, and his eventual protests against the persecution and the massacres. Yet even if one believes him innocent of condoning murderous race hatred, it is plain that he and the episcopate endorsed a contempt for religious freedom tantamount to complicity with the violence. Stepinac wrote a long letter to Pavelic on the question of conversions and massacres, which the writer Hubert Butler translated from a typescript in Zagreb in 1946. It quotes the views of a number of his brother bishops, all with favor, including a letter by the Catholic bishop of Mostar, a Dr. Miscic, expressing the historic yearnings that the Croatian episcopate entertained for mass conversions to Catholicism.

The bishop starts by declaring that there "was never such a good occasion as now for us to help Croatia to save the countless souls." He writes enthusiastically of mass conversion. But then he says that he deplores the "narrow views" of the authorities who seize even the converts and "hunt them like slaves." He lists known massacres of mothers, girls, and children under eight, brought into the hills "and thrown alive . . . into deep ravines." Then he makes this astonishing statement: "In the parish of Klepca seven hundred schismatics from the neighboring villages were slaughtered. The Sub-Prefect of Mostar, Mr. Bajic, a Muslim, publicly declared (as a state employee he should have held his tongue) that in Ljubina alone seven hundred schismatics have been thrown into one pit."26

The letter reveals the moral dislocation implicit in the behavior of the bishops, who took advantage of Yugoslavia's defeat at the hands of the Nazis to increase the power and outreach of Catholicism in the Balkans. One bishop after another endorses the promotion of conversions, while conceding that it does not make sense to throw wagonloads of schismatics into ravines. The bishops' failure to dissociate themselves from the regime, to denounce it, to excommunicate Pavelic and his cronies, was due to their reluctance to lose the opportunities afforded by the "good occasion" to build a Catholic power base in the Balkans. The same reluctance to neglect opportunities for a Catholic ascendancy in the East went right up to the Vatican, and ultimately to Pacelli himself. Indeed, it was the same reluctance to lose a unique "evangelizing" opportunity that had led Pacelli in 1913–14 to press for the Serbian Concordat in the hope of creating a Latin-rite foothold in Eastern Christendom, whatever the attendant repercussions and dangers.

Pacelli was better informed of the situation in Croatia than he was about any other area in Europe, outside of Italy, during the Second World War. His apostolic delegate, Marcone, came and went between Zagreb and Rome at will, and military planes were put at his disposal to travel the new Croatia. The bishops, in the meantime, some of whom sat in the Croatian parliament, communicated freely with the Vatican, and were able to make their regular *ad limina* visits to the Pope in Rome.[27] It was during such visits that the Pontiff and appropriate members of the Curia were free to ask searching questions regarding the conditions in Croatia, and they certainly did.

Pacelli had alternative personal means of information, not least the daily broadcasts of the BBC that were faithfully monitored and translated for him throughout the war by Osborne, London's minister in the Vatican. There were frequent BBC broadcasts on the situation in Croatia, of which this on February 16, 1942, was typical: "The worst atrocities are being committed in the environs of the archbishop of Zagreb [Stepinac]. The blood of brothers is flowing in streams. The Orthodox are being forcibly converted to Catholicism and we do not hear the archbishop's voice preaching revolt. Instead it is reported that he is taking part in Nazi and Fascist parades."[28]

A flow of directives to the Croatian bishops from the Holy See's Congregation for the Eastern Churches, which had special care of the Eastern-rite Catholics in the region, indicates that the Vatican knew about the enforced conversions from July 1941. The documents focus on the Vatican's insistence that potential converts to Catholicism should be turned away when they are patently seeking baptism for the wrong reasons—these *wrong reasons* being (the documents implied without spelling it out) terror and avoidance of death.

On August 14 the president of the Union for the Israelite Community of Alatri wrote to Secretary of State Maglione pleading on behalf of many thousands of Croat Jews, "residents of Zagreb and other centers of Croatia who have been arrested without reason, deprived of their possessions and deported." He went on to describe how six thousand

Jews had been dumped on a barren and mountainous island, without means of protection from the weather, and with neither food nor water. All attempts to come to their assistance had been "forbidden by the Croat authorities."[29] The letter pleads for an intervention of the Holy See with the Italian and Croatian governments. There is no record of a response or action on the part of the Holy See.

On August 30, 1941, the papal nuncio to Italy, Monsignor Francesco Borgongini Duca, wrote to Maglione about a curious conversation he had with the Croat cultural attaché to the Quirinal and two Croat Franciscans. They got to talking about the 100,000 Orthodox converts to Catholicism, and the nuncio asked them about the protests he had heard of the "persecutions inflicted on the Orthodox by Catholics." The attaché, "with much nodding from the priests," attempted to disabuse the nuncio of such stories, emphasizing that "as the Pope continues to tell the clergy and the faithful, Catholics should follow the teaching of Our Lord and propagate the faith by means of persuasion and not violence."[30]

The following month, Pavelic's special ambassador, Father Cherubino Seguic, came to Rome to find out what was being said about the regime, so as to scotch unfavorable "rumors." In his defensive memoirs, he complains about the "hint of calumny" that one hears about Croatia in Rome, and declares that "everything is either distorted or invented. We are made out to be a crowd of barbarians and cannibals." He spoke with Giovanni Montini (the future Paul VI), who "asked for full information on the events in Croatia. I was not short of words. He listened with great interest and attention. The calumnies have reached the Vatican and must be convincingly exposed."[31] Thus the atrocities, or "calumnies," were common knowledge in Rome by the summer of 1941, and the Holy See had channels through which Pacelli could check and influence events.

The apostolic delegate, Ramiro Marcone, chosen by Pacelli to be his personal representative in Croatia, was an amateur who appeared to sleepwalk through the entire bloodthirsty era. A sixty-year-old Benedictine monk, he had no experience in diplomacy and had spent much of his adult life lecturing in philosophy at the college of San Anselmo in Rome. His ambit was the cloister and the classroom. His time in Croatia was largely spent in attending ceremonies, dinners, public parades, and

being photographed alongside Pavelic. He had clearly been selected to
soothe and encourage.

Marcone's diplomatic counterparts on the Croatian side were Nicola
Rusinovic, a medical doctor practicing in a Roman hospital, and his
planned replacement, a papal chamberlain in the Vatican, Prince Erwin
Lobkowicz (of Bohemian origin). These arrangements were semi-secret
since the Holy See still officially maintained diplomatic links with the
Royal Yugoslav government in exile. By March 1942, despite the abun-
dance of evidence pointing to mass killings, the Holy See was nevertheless drawing the Croatian representatives toward official relations.
Montini told Rusinovic: "Recommend gentleness to your government
and government circles, and our relations will work themselves out. As
long as you behave correctly, the form of the relations will come of their
own accord."[32] On October 22, 1942, Pacelli met Prince Lobkowicz in
audience. According to the prince, Pacelli, "in his usual extremely benevolent manner," said that "he hoped he would soon be receiving me in
a different capacity."[33]

Meanwhile, a cry for help on behalf of the persecuted Jews in Croatia
had been sent to the Holy See from the World Jewish Congress and the
Swiss Israelite community, via Monsignor Filippe Bernadini, the apostolic nuncio in Berne. In a substantial aide-mémoire dated March 17,
1942, less than two months after the Wannsee Conference outlining the
Final Solution, the representatives of the above agencies had docu-
mented persecutions of the Jews in Germany, France, Romania, Slovakia,
Hungary, and Croatia. The organizations were particularly concerned
that the Pope should use his influence in the latter three countries, which
were bound by strong diplomatic and ecclesiastical links to the Holy
See—in Slovakia, for example, a Catholic priest was at that time installed as president. The section on Croatia read as follows: "Several
thousand families were either deported to desert islands on the Dalmatian coast or incarcerated in concentration camps . . . all the *male* Jews
were sent to labor camps where they were assigned to drainage or sanita-
tion work and where they perished in great numbers. . . . At the same
time, their wives and children were sent to another camp where they, too,
are enduring dire privations."[34]

The aide-mémoire, the manuscript of which resides in the Zionist
Archives in Jerusalem, has been published by Saul Friedländer in his

collection of documents on Pacelli and the Third Reich. In October of 1998, Gerhard Riegner, a surviving signatory of the memorandum, revealed in his published memoirs, *Ne jamais désespérer*,[35] that the Vatican had excluded it from the eleven volumes of released wartime documents—indicating that, more than half a century after the war, the Vatican has still failed to make a clean breast of what it knew about the Croatian atrocities and the early stages of the Final Solution, and when it knew it.

The three heads of the Secretariat of State in the Vatican—Maglione, Montini, and Tardini—indicated repeatedly that they were aware of protests and pleas for help, but their interviews with Rusinovic and Lobkowicz followed, as Falconi has observed from the available documentation, an unvarying pattern of "simulated attack, patient listening, generous surrender." By the same token, the secret Croatian diplomats to the Vatican were more than satisfied with the way in which the cross-examinations were conducted: "I settled everything," wrote Rusinovic after one such session with Montini, "revealing the enemy propaganda in its true light and, as for the concentration camps, I said that he would do better to obtain his information from the Apostolic Delegation at Zagreb. . . . Foreign journalists were invited to visit the concentration camps and . . . when they left they declared that the camps were perfectly suited to regular habitation and satisfied the requirements of hygiene." At the end of the interview, when Rusinovic commented that there were now five million Catholics in the country, Montini said, "The Holy Father will help you, rest assured of that."[36]

The Vatican's knowledge of the true state of Croatian affairs by early 1942, moreover, can be gleaned from a conversation Rusinovic had with the French cardinal Eugène Tisserant, a Slavonic expert and now a close confidant of Pacelli, despite his earlier reservations in conclave. "I know for a fact," Tisserant told the Croat representative on March 6, 1942, "that it is the Franciscans themselves, as for example Father Simic of Knin, who have taken part in attacks against the Orthodox populations so as to destroy the Orthodox Church. In the same way you destroyed the Orthodox Church in Banja Luka. I know for sure that the Franciscans in Bosnia and Herzegovina have acted abominably, and this pains me. Such acts should not be committed by educated, cultured, civilized people, let alone by priests."[37] During a subsequent meeting on May 27, Tisserant told Rusinovic that, according to German figures, "350,000

Serbs had disappeared" and in "one single concentration camp there are 20,000 Serbs."[38]

For his part, however, Pacelli was never anything but benevolent to the leaders and representatives of the Pavelic regime. A roll call of his audiences, apart from those already mentioned, is significant. In July 1941 he greeted a hundred members of the Croatian police force headed by the Zagreb chief of police. On February 6, 1942, he gave an audience for an Ustashe youth group visiting in Rome. He greeted another representation of Ustashe youth in December of the same year.

And so it was, in 1943, when Pacelli, talking to Lobkowicz, "expressed his pleasure at the personal letter he had received from our Poglavnik [Pavelic]." Later in the conversation, Pacelli said he was "disappointed that, in spite of everything, no one wants to acknowledge the one, real and principal enemy of Europe; no true, communal military crusade against Bolshevism has been initiated."[39]

But had not Hitler launched just such a crusade in the summer of 1941? In Pacelli's tortuous ratiocinations on the theme of Communism, Nazism, Croatia, and the Catholic evangelization of the East, we begin to understand—though not condone—his reticence on the Croatian massacres.

Eastern Christianity and the Communist Threat, 1941–1945

When Hitler launched Operation Barbarossa, code name for the invasion of the USSR on June 22, 1941, Pacelli was confronted with a complex array of hopes and fears. For although his "one, real and principal enemy of Europe" seemed destined for imminent defeat through the summer of that year, there was no saying where this extension of the war might eventually lead. With the likelihood that the Soviet Union might become an ally of Britain, and in time of the United States, the Pontiff found himself faced with the prospect of giving tacit support to Communism in arms. And what if Hitler faltered and failed? Then the Red Army would come westward, heralding a new dark age of persecution and destruction for Christianity.

But what if Hitler prevailed and became master of Europe? Was Pacelli entirely convinced that the Nazis were the better of the two totalitarian evils? Certainly some members of the Curia, such as Tisserant, had always believed Nazism the greater menace, and Pacelli is credited with having come around to that view as early as 1942. "Yes," he remarked to a Jesuit visitor, "the Communist danger does exist, but at this time the Nazi danger is more serious. They want to destroy the Church and crush it like a toad."[40]

There were other alternatives, however, in the complex mix of possibilities, including an opportunity for Catholic evangelization in the wake of the Wehrmacht juggernaut as it headed for Moscow—and the prospect of ending the ancient rift between Roman Catholicism and the Orthodox East. What power of the spirit might not arise from such a new, unified Christendom as the totalitarian giants exhausted themselves in war?

To begin with, it looked as though the Wehrmacht was aiding the process of evangelization. As Ukraine was "liberated" in June 1941, German newsreel and print propaganda focused on the restoration of freedom of religion in the East. Churches used as atheistic museums, warehouses, and club rooms were being restored to their religious purpose and there was evidence of widespread religious renewal in the wake of the Soviet defeat.

Franz von Papen, the Catholic ex–vice-chancellor, had been pondering the opportunities for Catholicism in Hitler's newly conquered territories. He had sent the Führer a memorandum to this effect not long after the invasion. Hitler's response, by the middle of July, left no room for doubt about the inadmissibility of such a scheme. "The idea of the 'Old Jockey' [on] missionary activity was entirely out of the question," Hitler was quoted as saying. "If one did it at all, one should permit all the Christian denominations to enter Russia in order that they club each other to death with their crucifixes."[41]

Hitler had other plans. It was about this time, mid-July 1941, that Hitler declared: "Christianity is the hardest blow that ever hit humanity. Bolshevism is the bastard son of Christianity; both are the monstrous issue of the Jews."[42] Already he was plotting the destruction of the various Churches. "The war will come to an end," he remarked in December, "and I shall see my last task as clearing up the Church problem. Only then will the German nation be completely safe.... In my youth I had the view: dynamite! Today I see that one cannot break it over one's knee. It has to be cut off like a gangrenous limb."[43]

Hence the propaganda of the religion-friendly German invaders evaporated, and the idea of Catholic proselytism eastward was emphatically rejected by the Führer himself. In November 1941, Hitler issued an order through Martin Bormann that "until further notice nothing should be published about the religious situation in the Soviet Union."[44]

Papen would live to deny that his original enthusiasm for the re-evangelization of the Soviet Union had been inspired by the Vatican. Yet a department for missionary work in the East—the Congregation for the Eastern Churches, under Cardinal Eugène Tisserant—did exist in the Vatican. Tisserant hailed from Lorraine in France and was something of an oddity within the Curia for his independence and outspokenness. Carlo Falconi describes him as "a Prince of the Church, but with profane and worldly judgments, for whom politics are almost everything and the world is divided exclusively into allies and enemies. The priest rarely emerges, but when he does his words burn like red-hot steel."[45] It was Tisserant who, writing privately in May 1940 to Cardinal Emmanuel Suhard in Paris, declared: "I fear that history will reproach the Holy See for having practiced a policy of selfish convenience and little else."[46]

Tisserant's activities in the sphere of Eastern evangelization began to figure in Nazi discussions in July 1940. Alfred Rosenberg, the anti-Catholic head of the new Ostministerium, or Ministry of the East, promptly forbade the entry of missionaries into the "liberated" areas of the East. But it was Reinhard Heydrich, head of the Reich Main Security Office, or Reichssicherheitshauptamt (RSHA), who turned his attention specifically to thwarting Vatican intentions and scope for action. In a memorandum entitled "New Tactics in Vatican Russia Work," dated July 2, 1941, Heydrich told the Foreign Ministry that the Vatican had developed a new scheme, which he called the "Tisserant Plan." With Germany at war with the Soviet Union, he went on, the Holy See had decided to concentrate its entire Vatican-Russia policy in Slovakia and Croatia. The idea, according to Heydrich, was to recruit supernumerary chaplains, supplemented by Spanish and Italian priests, to accompany units fighting on the eastern front. These undercover clergy would be engaged in intelligence-gathering, looking for opportunities to establish Catholicism in the wake of the German advance. Heydrich concluded: "It is necessary to prevent Catholicism from becoming the real beneficiary of the war in the new situation that is developing in the Russian area conquered by German blood."[47]

Hitler was sufficiently concerned about the spread of political religious Catholicism in the Reich's new *Lebensraum* (living space) to issue two orders, on August 6 and again on October 6, forbidding all Church activity in the interests of the indigenous people. An order on September 4 instructed commanders to report to the high command of the army any "signs of the activating of Vatican Russian work."[48]

Heydrich's information was correct up to a point, but Pacelli's Eastern policy was more complex than the Nazi understanding of the so-called Tisserant Plan allowed. There had indeed been a long-term scheme for bringing Catholicism to the Soviet Union—not Cardinal Tisserant's but Pius XI's, with essential contributions from Pacelli. The lesson of the early 1920s, following a show trial of Catholic leaders in Moscow in 1923, was the impossibility of striking deals with Bolshevism. Pacelli attempted negotiations with Soviet diplomats when he was nuncio in Berlin, but got nowhere. (As we have seen earlier, he had formed deeply antagonistic attitudes toward Soviet Communism, or Bolshevism, when he witnessed and confronted the "Red Terror" at the Munich nunciature in 1919. His attitudes became more bitter and intransigent in subsequent years as he surveyed Catholic persecution in the "Red Triangle" of Russia, Mexico, and Spain.)

By 1925 most of the bishops of the Latin rite in Soviet Russia had been thrown out, imprisoned, or executed. That year, Pius XI sent a French Jesuit, Michel d'Herbigny, on a secret mission to Russia to ordain as bishop half a dozen clandestine priests. On his way to Moscow, Herbigny stayed in Berlin with Pacelli, who advised him and secretly ordained him bishop. Herbigny's mission was successful insofar as he managed to ordain his six secret Russian bishops, but they were all discovered and eliminated.

In 1929, the year Pacelli was appointed Cardinal Secretary of State, Pius XI founded a Vatican "Commission for Russia." Later that year he opened on Vatican territory the "Pontifical Russian College," better known as the Russicum, and the "Pontifical Ruthenian College" where students were to be trained for service in the Soviet Union. Other institutions were also secretly enlisted to educate men for the Russian mission, including the abbey of Grotta Ferrata outside Rome, the abbey of Chevetogne in Belgium, and the abbey of Velehrad in Moravia. Some of the most powerful orders in the Church—the Redemptorists, the Assumptionists, the Jesuits, and clergy of many backgrounds in Poland—

developed their own programs within the scheme of a clandestine evangelization in Russia. Typical of the zeal of ordinary parish clergy who volunteered from even farther afield for the Russian mission was the example of John Carmel Heenan, a parish priest in a district of East London, later to become cardinal archbishop of Westminster. Heenan got leave of absence from his local bishop and, unknown to that bishop (although with the blessing of the primate of Westminster, Cardinal Hinsley), set out for Russia in 1932 disguised as a commercial traveler, carrying in his baggage a collapsible crucifix inside a bogus fountain pen. In the midst of many adventures, he fell in love with his interpreter and was eventually arrested; at length he managed to talk himself out of trouble and hurried back to the safety of his parish in England.[49]

After Hitler's invasion of the Soviet Union in 1941, priests from the Russicum and the Ruthenian College in the Vatican, as well as volunteers from Poland, Hungary, Slovakia, and Croatia, set off for the East. They traveled as military chaplains; some claimed to be civilians enrolled in the German army; some got jobs as grooms, taking care of horses in the German Transport Command. Once they found themselves in an appropriate area for pastoral or missionary work, anywhere from the Baltic to the Black Sea, they then went solo. Those who arrived in former Catholic areas (of either Latin or Eastern rite) could find themselves in instant and dangerous demand, attracting hundreds of the people who had been without the sacraments for years. Most were eventually caught and shot as deserters and spies, or were sent to concentration camps. Those overtaken by the Russians ended up in the gulags. To this day, there is no published tally of the missing, the imprisoned, and the executed.[50]

Heydrich's understanding of the "Tisserant Plan" thus failed to appreciate the complexities of Pacelli's policy toward the evangelization of the East. An essential feature of that policy was the distinction between Catholics of the Latin rite and Catholics of the Eastern rite, sometimes also known as the Byzantine or Oriental rite. These Eastern-rite Catholics bore much in common with the "schismatic" Orthodox Christians, and in some areas, such as Ukraine, Eastern-rite Catholic priests had been allowed to marry according to the practice in the Orthodox Church. Cardinal Tisserant's Congregation for the Eastern Churches was principally concerned with Catholics who followed these Eastern liturgies but who were in communion with the Pope. In some areas, the Latin and Eastern rites existed side-by-side, as in Ukraine and, notably, in the new Croatia. The "Tisserant Plan" involved the encouragement of the Catholic Eastern rite by supplying these areas with priests and catechetical and liturgical books.

For Pacelli, however, the new situation of the Catholic Eastern rite in the Independent State of Croatia gave new impulse to the ambitious dream that had lured him and the Curia in 1913 into negotiating the Serbian Concordat: the prospect of evangelization under the auspices of both rites—Latin and Eastern, both loyal to the Pontiff—eastward through Romania, into Ukraine, and so into Russia, and southward into Greece. The potential for enticing mass conversions of the "schismatic" Orthodox, through their close proximity to the Catholic Eastern rite, explains Pacelli's indulgent policy toward Pavelic and his murderous regime. Had he combated Pavelic's forced conversions, deportations, and massacres with denunciations and excommunications, the existence of the Croatian bridgehead to the East might have been put in peril. Patience, acquiescence, connivance, were the options evidently Pacelli chose.

For Pacelli ecumenism had only one meaning: that the separated Christian brethren would see the error of their ways and return to full union with the Pope and Rome. In 1940 Archbishop Stepinac had told the Regent Prince Paul of Yugoslavia: "The most ideal thing would be for the Serbs to return to the faith of their fathers, that is, to bow the head before Christ's representative, the Holy Father. Then we could at last breathe in this part of Europe, for Byzantinism has played a frightful role in the history of this part of the world."[51] Expressing precisely this goal in his encyclical "Rome and the Eastern Churches" (*Orientalis ecclesiae decus*, April 23, 1944), Pacelli prayed for the removal of "the age-old obstacles" between the Eastern and the Roman Churches, as the "day dawns at last when there shall be one flock in one fold, all obedient with one mind to Jesus Christ and to his Vicar on earth." That unity, he argued, was all the more pressing so that "Christ's faithful ones should labor together in the one Church of Jesus Christ, so that they may present a common, serried, united, and unyielding front to the daily growing attacks of the enemies of religion."[52]

Pacelli's ambition for evangelization eastward, however, does not explain his silence on the extermination of the Jewish population of

Croatia, a silence parallel with his failure to speak out on behalf of the Jews of the rest of Europe. But before turning to Pacelli's record in relation to the Holocaust, a final reflection is necessary on the links between the fate of the wartime Ustashe treasury and the actions of the Vatican, which have reverberations to this day.

Croatian Gold and ODESSA

Investigations conducted after the war by the Allies revealed that the looted treasury of the fleeing Ustashe amounted to some $80 million, much of which was composed of gold coins.[53] Evidence of the Vatican's collusion in Rome with the Ustashe regime includes the hospitality of a pontifical religious institution, and the provision of storage facilities and safe-deposit services for the Ustashe treasury, part of which was stolen from the victims of extermination—Serbs and Jews.

During the war, the College of San Girolamo degli Illirici in Rome became home for Croatian priests receiving Vatican-sponsored theological education. Later it became headquarters for the postwar Ustashe underground, providing Croatian war criminals with escape routes. Here the Ustashe were given false passports and identities in order to evade arrest by the Allies.[54] The leading figure at San Girolamo was the Croatian seminary professor Father Krunoslav Dragonovic, described by U.S. intelligence officers as Pavelic's "alter ego." Dragonovic arrived in Rome in 1943 on the pretext of working for the Red Cross, but according to American intelligence sources his true role was to coordinate Italian-Ustashe activities. After the war he was a central figure in the provision of escape routes for former Ustashe to South America, principally to Argentina. It is also alleged by contemporaneous CIA sources that he was allowed to store the archives of the Ustashe legation inside the Vatican, as well as the valuables brought out of Croatia by the fleeing Ustashe.[55] Father Dragonovic worked with the U.S. Army's Counter Intelligence Corps (CIC) in order to organize the escape of the anti-Communist informant and Nazi war criminal Klaus Barbie to South America.[56] Barbie, as head of the Gestapo in Lyons (1942–44), had tortured and murdered Jews and members of the French Resistance. During the Cold War, the CIC protected Barbie and helped him reach Bolivia, this after he had lived under the protection of Dragonovic at San Girolamo from early 1946 to late 1947. Not until a few days after Pacelli's death, in mid-October 1958, was Dragonovic himself expelled from the College of San Girolamo by orders from the Vatican Secretariat of State, suggesting that the priest had the personal protection of the Pontiff until the very last.[57]

If Pacelli is to take credit for the use of Vatican extraterritorial religious buildings as safe houses for Jews during Germany's occupation of Rome, then he should equally take blame for the use of the same buildings as safe houses for Nazi and Ustashe criminals.

There is no evidence, however, that Pacelli and the Vatican were implicated in an organization widely known as ODESSA, which is said to have funded and planned the escape to South America of a number of notorious Nazi criminals. It is certainly the case that figures such as Franz Stangl, the commandant of Treblinka, were assisted with false papers and hiding places in Rome by the Nazi sympathizer Bishop Alois Hudal. But efforts by reputable journalists to establish an ODESSA organization with links into the Vatican and Nazi gold funding have proved fruitless.

Gitta Sereny declares in her book *Into That Darkness* that the existence of ODESSA "has never yet been proved."[58] But she emphasizes that it is important to examine the motives of individuals, such as Hudal, who proved as effective as any organization. Three British journalists—Magnus Linklater, Isabel Hilton, and Neal Ascherson—also investigated the ODESSA allegations in their book on Klaus Barbie and failed to come up with sufficient evidence to make a case. "American and British investigations led again and again to disappointing results." Something like ODESSA may well have existed, the authors conclude, but "no evidence was ever found that ODESSA was anything like a single coherent network."[59]

15

The Holiness of Pius XII

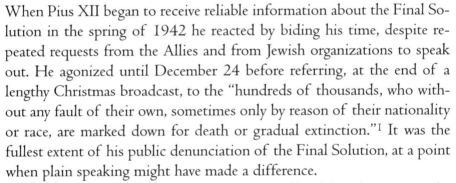

When Pius XII began to receive reliable information about the Final Solution in the spring of 1942 he reacted by biding his time, despite repeated requests from the Allies and from Jewish organizations to speak out. He agonized until December 24 before referring, at the end of a lengthy Christmas broadcast, to the "hundreds of thousands, who without any fault of their own, sometimes only by reason of their nationality or race, are marked down for death or gradual extinction."[1] It was the fullest extent of his public denunciation of the Final Solution, at a point when plain speaking might have made a difference.

A variety of reasons or motives were proffered by observers at the time, and have been mooted down the years. Timidity; indecisiveness; bias toward the Nazis; anti-Semitism; justifiable prudence for fear of consequences; a desire to remain impartial in order to qualify as future peace broker; uncertainty about the information; fear of the spread of Communism at the expense of the lesser evil of National Socialism. But how do we penetrate at this distance the conscience of such an intensely private Pope? One alternative, at the outset, is to examine—without sentimentality, prejudice, or misplaced reverence—the kind of Pope he proved for the Church of his era. For his personality was wholly subsumed in his consciousness of what it meant for him to be Vicar of Christ on earth. If he had a papal program, a scheme, how did it measure up to the crisis of world war and Hitler's regime? How did it measure up to the Final Solution? These are the questions that ultimately matter as we set about reaching a verdict on his reaction to the Holocaust.

Steeped from his very childhood in the culture and history of the papacy, conscious that he was eminently *papabile* throughout the 1930s, Pacelli was not content to be a reactive Pope responding to the pressures of world war. We know that by 1942 he was striving to be a great Pope according to a program. Many years later, Cardinal Giuseppe Siri, who knew Pacelli as Cardinal Secretary of State, declared that Pius XII had a grand plan that he had pondered long before he became Pope.[2]

First, Pacelli nourished a spiritual ambition: to strive for saintliness. Second, he sought to deepen and broaden the range and power of his office in relation to the Church and the world. Third, he attempted to make a historic contribution to Scriptural scholarship and the reform of the liturgy—the formal, communal worship of Catholics the world over. And fourth, he was determined, as all great Popes had done in the past, to leave his physical mark on the place; his ambition was to excavate the crypt of St. Peter's in the hope of finding the bones of the first bishop of Rome, a task he put in the hands of his intimate, Ludwig Kaas. He had a final aim, besides, which was to do something special, something spectacular, for the Virgin Mary.

The first and last ambitions involved his personal vision of an appropriate papal spirituality; the second and third drew him into profound theological issues with far-reaching consequences for papal authority. Thus, during the darkest days of 1941–1943, Pacelli's energies and concentration were divided between these mainly spiritual and theological aspirations in addition to his daily responsibilities in response to the events of the war.

Pacelli's spirituality was founded on a lifetime of individualistic piety that proclaimed itself in constant opposition to the profane, the worldly. Pacelli was brought up, as we have seen, on the *Imitation of Christ* by Thomas à Kempis. Recollection, humility, interiority, acquiescence, purity, simplicity, self-denial, detachment: these were the qualities that Pacelli himself had evidently cultivated from his childhood. They were enhanced by his ascetic appearance—naturally thin, parchment-pale, seeming at all times as if he were participating in a Church rite. The poses he struck in prayer put one in mind of a saint in a stained-glass window.

Against the background of the baroque decorum of the Vatican, his diffidence and simplicity looked all the more humble, his eager interest in his visitors all the more saintly. According to the beatification accounts, he slept no more than four hours a night during his pontificate.[3] He denied himself creature comforts such as coffee, rejected heating during the depths of winter, spent many hours of the day and night communing with the Lord—as if on the mountaintop or perhaps in a catacomb. Giovanni Montini, the future Paul VI, remembered witnessing Pacelli praying in the dead of night in the tombs of the Popes beneath St. Peter's. He recorded, marveling: "Never had the communion of saints and the spiritual genealogy of the successors of Christ been given, it seemed to me, a more moving expression. . . . The Church, this living reality, spiritual and visible, is more present than ever."[4] *Successors of Christ*, as opposed to *Saint Peter*, was a revealing slip of the pen.

And whereas other Popes, before and since, have found the solitude of the papacy agonizing, Pacelli appeared to relish the circumstance. Not for Pacelli the least intimation of a desire or need for peer-group discussion, consultation, or criticism in matters of secular international relations, let alone everyday Church policy. From his lofty pinnacle he viewed everything sub specie aeternitatis. The realms of spirit in which he proclaimed to have his being were the true reality, whereas the "vale of tears" of the world seemed shadowy and ephemeral, as he frequently reminded the faithful, looking down upon the warring parties as from a great height and assigning a moral equivalence between the belligerents on both sides—Allies and Axis, democracies and totalitarian states.

The solitude of the modern papacy was seen, at the time, as a mystical feature of the papal role, never a drawback or a weakness. Cardinal Agostino Bea, Pacelli's confessor for ten years, spoke of Pacelli's loneliness in glowing terms. He was, said Bea (like Leiber a German Jesuit), "fundamentally a lonely man in his greatness and in his keen sense of responsibility, and in this way, too, he was lonely in his personal austerity and life."[5]

Pacelli's own vision of this solitude was expressed in emblematic form in a film he commissioned about himself in the summer of 1942. Even as news of the Final Solution was coming into the Vatican, he was collaborating with Luigi Gedda, president of Catholic Action in Italy, to make an hourlong movie intended for world distribution entitled *Pastor Angelicus*, depicting the "daily life of the Pope and how he exemplifies the prophecy of the Irish monk Malachy that the 262nd successor to St. Peter was to be indicated by the name Angelic Shepherd."[6]

The film starts and ends with a statue of the good shepherd—Pacelli and/or Christ—carrying a lamb upon his shoulders, and progresses through a historical account of the Pontiff's edifying life, from birth to coronation, followed by a narrative of his daily routine.[7] Two brief sequences of guns firing and a ship sinking acknowledge the fact of war. There are clips of Vatican officials administrating the office for missing persons; Sisters of Mercy caring for the wounded. But the film lingers in the gardens and the loggias, the marble halls of Vatican City, the magnificence of St. Peter's Basilica. Against the background of massed choirs, all is tranquil; the monsignori and cardinals, resplendent in robes, genuflect and bow before the Supreme Pontiff. In one sequence, he glides beneath a grove of ancient olives, a pure white wraith, alone, reading a document; without raising his eyes he steps into his limousine, which has a single throne for a backseat, while the chauffeur falls to his knees and makes the sign of the cross. He greets the royal family of Italy, the king and princesses making obeisance to the superior of all earthly kings. In yet another segment, he greets First Communion girls clutching lilies. The brilliant white soutane amid the white communion dresses proclaims its message: the Pontiff is the fount of purity. He extends his arms in what Tardini called a gesture of "immolation," blesses the adoring multitude. In the early hours, his office light burns on, the vigilant Pope striving at every moment to serve all humankind, while the world sleeps.

It was this sense of detachment and timelessness within an earthly heaven set adrift from the mainland of life that beguiled so many. For a few, however, less romantic or perhaps less impressionable, the striking charisma smacked of autosuggestion in the visitor. The writer John Guest, who met Pacelli during the war, found himself baffled by a "pervading *scent*" that emanated from the Pontiff. "Not a scent in the worldly sense," Guest went on, "not sweet or exciting in any way, but a cool, very clean, smell.... A sort of delicious early-morning dewy smell that could almost be described as the sudden absence of all other smells.... Possibly it is imagination; possibly sympathetic nervous affection of the nose when one's other senses are highly stimulated; possibly, even, it is the genuine and original 'odour of sanctity.' "[8] As it happened, Mother

Pasqualina routinely doused Pacelli's hands and handkerchief in antiseptic lotion to combat the risk of his catching germs from human contact.

Such were the externals of Pacelli's papal piety. The strange thing is that so few at the time noted the lingering poses before lens's eye, the suspect origins of Pacelli's sobriquet Pastor Angelicus.[9] Casual visitors to the Vatican, moreover, would have been unaware of Pacelli's insistence that no human presence should mar his daily walk in the gardens (workers finding themselves in his presence had to hide in the bushes).

But what was the moral and spiritual content beneath the surface?

Central to Pacelli's personal everyday spirituality was his devotion to the Virgin Mary. With the advent of war, he turned in particular to the cult of Our Lady of Fátima, the credence given to a series of Marian apparitions to three children in Portugal during the First World War, along with associated Marian messages and secrets. A central feature of the messages focused on the requirement that the faithful should pray to Mary in order to avoid world conflict, the spread of Communism, and ultimately the destruction of the world in a holocaust of divine punishment. Pius XI had endorsed the visions of Fátima, and the dictators of Portugal and Spain, Salazar and Franco, had celebrated the cult as a rally-rousing emblem of Fascistic solidarity. Pacelli not only gave it credence (as would John Paul II) but also saw a personal, a mystical link in the circumstance that he had been raised to the episcopate on May 13, 1917, the date of the first apparition, and subsequently the cult's feast day. In 1940 the surviving seer, now a nun who had taken the name Sister Lucia, wrote to Pacelli requesting him, as the Virgin had commanded, to consecrate Russia to the Immaculate Heart of Mary.

Pacelli left it until October 31, 1942, to make a tentative allusion to Russia and the Virgin (avoiding mention of Russia by name) in a broadcast message to Portugal in which he prayed: "To those . . . among whom there was not a house where Thy venerable icon was not seen . . . give them peace and bring them again to the one fold."[10]

Finally, on December 8, 1942, he responded to Sister Lucia's Marian request, although not strictly to the letter. Gathering forty cardinals around him in St. Peter's, he consecrated not Russia but the whole world to the Immaculate Heart of Mary (the fact that he had not carried out the Virgin's instruction to the letter was later deemed to have resulted in the expanding power of the Soviet Union during the Cold War). Later, in 1944, Sister Lucia entrusted to Pacelli the famous Third Secret of Fátima, rumored to contain the date of the Third World War, to be opened by the reigning Pope in 1960. Pacelli stored the sealed secret in a cabinet on his desk, where it remained until his death. When John XXIII retrieved the message in 1960, he read it, then buried it without comment deeply in the Vatican archive, unpublished.

The significance of the Fátima cult in Pacelli's thinking is its flavor of gnosticism—the notion of dual realms of darkness and light beyond the mere "veil of appearances," where reside the Godhead, the Virgin Mary, Michael, and all the angels and the saints, opposed by the powers of the Prince of Darkness and his fallen angels, "who wander through the world for the ruin of souls," as Pope Leo XIII had put it in a prayer to be said at the end of every Mass. What happens in this world of ours, according to such a perspective, depends on Mary's intercession with her Son to so curb the power of Satan that war and discord will be vanquished. The conditions of this virtual appeasement operate on the basis of Marian revelations sanctioned as authentic by the Pope, whose power is thus parallel to Mary's. Ever since Pius IX defined, without mention of episcopal approbation, the dogma of the Immaculate Conception of the Blessed Virgin Mary in 1854, there had been a close link in the minds of modern Popes between Mary and papal authority. In short, the unfolding of human history depends not on communitarian and societal action and responsibility but upon miraculous interventions mediated by Mary and endorsed by the papacy.

Such a worldview coincided, in certain respects, with another Catholic cult espoused by the Popes of the first half of the century: the Kingship of Christ, a devotion particularly popular with Pius XI and aired in Pacelli's first encyclical, "Darkness over the Earth." The Second World War, according to some interpreters of the cult, had seen Christ's Kingship challenged by the powers of Satan, and Christ's victorious supremacy temporarily suspended.[11] Consonant with this view, according to one of Pacelli's nephews in the beatification testimonies, the Pope was in the habit during the war of conducting a form of exorcism to cast out the devil that he assumed inhabited the soul of Hitler—which he did in the dead of night in his private chapel in the papal apartments.

Pacelli, the Mystical Body, and the Holocaust

While nurturing his personal spirituality and his attachment to the cult of Mary, Pacelli, in common with his modern predecessors, regarded himself as the sole protector of the *magisterium*—the Church's official teaching handed down through the centuries. Pacelli, knowledgeable as he was in every aspect of the nature and history of his Church, had spent his formative years not as a theologian but as a canon lawyer. Between 1941 and 1943, however, as war raged on every continent, he ruminated long and deeply, with the assistance of the Belgian Jesuit theologian Sebastian Tromp of the Gregorian University, on a series of interrelated and crucial questions. How is the Catholic Church most truly itself? And how does Christ remain a living reality within that Church? Who is in communion with the Church? And how?

Such questions had been raised since the very origins of Christianity and had invoked powerful corresponding metaphors—the "Mystical Body of Christ" and the "Real Body of Christ"—metaphors, and indeed living symbols, which culminated in the "realism" of the Sacrifice of the Mass and the "real presence" of the sacrament of the Eucharist: the offering of bread and wine, its consecration as the body and blood of Christ, and its reception in Holy Communion. Pacelli's decision to immerse himself in the history, the Scripture, and the huge circuit of commentary on these doctrines in the midst of world conflict might seem an extraordinary evasion. Yet since it dwelt on notions of sacrifice—the outflowing of blood shed for humankind—it was, perhaps, a subconscious response to the destruction of the entire "body" of a people of God in progress at that very time in Europe. Was this not the moment to find solidarity with the parent religion of Christianity? Certainly, there had been powerful tendencies toward just such solidarity within Catholicism.

As the world plunged toward war in the final years of the 1930s, a group of French Catholic scholars, and notably the Jesuit Henri de Lubac (1896–1991), had begun a work of theological renewal.[12] They were striving to end a long period of Catholic antimodern and anti-Protestant bias in France while combating Nazi neopaganism and anti-Semitism. In the process they were returning to the roots of Christian belief. De Lubac believed that Catholicism had abandoned the conviction that the Church is truly itself in the celebration of the Eucharist, the offering and sharing of the Communion bread and wine. He believed, moreover, that Catholicism was in danger of losing a sense of the communion of humankind, its solidarity through God's incarnation in Jesus Christ.

De Lubac sought in his prewar writings to convince Catholics that Christianity was a social religion. Catholicism[13] meant salvation not only for individuals but also for communities. Yet the individual could never be sacrificed in the interests of the community, as totalitarian ideologies insisted, because each person is created in the image of God. But neither did it mean that one sought the presence of God, or that God gave His presence to humankind, solely through private, individual worship or exclusively in the milieu of institutionalized "official" religion.

In de Lubac's second book, *Corpus Mysticum (The Mystical Body)*,[14] completed in 1938 but achieving wide currency in the early years of the war (although not officially published until 1944), these ideas were given deeper expression in a commentary on the Eucharist and the Mystical Body of the Church. De Lubac argued that in the eleventh century a sense of the "real presence" of Christ in the community had weakened. The consecrated bread became the "real presence" by virtue of a miracle, and the presence of Christ in the actual communities of the Church had become symbolic and hence less real. The consequence, according to de Lubac, was a weakening of social Catholicism and an increase in the power and control ritual, evident, for example, in Corpus Christi processions.[15]

De Lubac's ideas challenged the power structure of the twentieth-century Catholic Church, with its emphasis on the "miraculous," on individual, privatized popular piety, and especially on the privileged power of priesthood, with the Pope as supreme priest primate. Above all, he challenged the notion of the Church as an organizational and juridical power structure. De Lubac's work, moreover, was an encouragement to Christian unity between Catholics and Christian non-Catholics, and between Christians and other religions, including Judaism.[16] Such ideas may seem, at this distance, abstruse and hardly relevant in the context of a world war, but they form a crucial background to Pacelli's attitude toward the Jews and the Holocaust.

On July 20, 1943, Pacelli published his *Mystici corporis* (Of the Mystical Body), echoing the title of de Lubac's thesis.[17] While appearing to grant credence to some of the ideas circulating as a result of the work of de Lubac and his circle, the document comprises, in fact, a soaring new claim for papal power and papal moral righteousness, associated with a definition of Christian unity that excludes all not in communion with the Pope. Was not the Church most truly itself, Pacelli was claiming, by reason of its allegiance to the Pope, who was none other than the Vicar of Christ upon earth and thus the living, physical head of the Mystical Body?

The war, he argued, with its "hates, animosities, and seeds of discord," will turn human hearts from "the transitory things of earth to those which are heavenly and eternal." Thus, throughout the world, the children of Christ will "look up to the Vicar of Jesus Christ as the loving Father of all, who with complete impartiality and unbiased judgment, unruffled by the tempestuous winds of human passion, devotes his energies to promoting and defending the cause of truth, justice, and charity."

While seeming to endorse common humanity as "called to the one salvation," he insists that there can be only one faith: the faith that is in communion with Rome. "Schism, heresy, or apostasy," he proclaims, "are such of their very nature that they sever a man from the Body of the Church."[18] Nevertheless, he goes on, in a further reflection astonishing for the times, "Not every sin, even the most grievous, is of such a kind, nor does all life depart from those who, though by sin they have lost charity and divine grace, and are consequently no longer capable of a supernatural reward, nevertheless retain Christian faith and hope." In other words, Catholics, no matter how grievous their sins, could rest assured that they were part of the people of God, while those who refused to pay allegiance to the Pope, however good and decent, were to be regarded as excluded. "It is therefore a dangerous error," he concludes, "to hold that one can adhere to Christ as head of the Church without loyal allegiance to his Vicar on earth."

How did these theological ideas relate to the most devastating war in history? How does he link the powerful symbolism of the Mystical Body to the evil of Nazism and its victims? Conscious of the "heavy responsibility which rests upon Us," he concludes, he is obliged to make a "weighty pronouncement." "We see to Our profound grief that death is sometimes inflicted upon the deformed, the mentally defective, and those suffering from hereditary disease, on the plea that they are an intolerable burden upon society; and, moreover, that this expedient is hailed by some as a discovery made by human progress and as greatly conducive to the common good." The blood of these "unhappy creatures, especially near to our Redeemer because especially to be pitied, cries to God from the earth."[19]

There was nothing particularly remarkable or courageous in this "weighty" pronouncement, which, incidentally, carried no mention of the Nazi perpetrators, since Germany's Bishop Clemens von Galen had already preached on August 5, 1941 a most damning denunciation of the Nazi "euthanasia" program, copies of which had been leafleted over Germany by the RAF. The peculiar irony of the situation is, as Michael Burleigh points out in his *Death and Deliverance* (1994), that the program had been scaled down not just because of Galen but because the killing resources had by late 1941 been redirected to the Final Solution. Quite apart from this fact, however, Pacelli's concern eloquently exposes, amplifies, and draws attention to, his total silence in the document on the vast atrocity of the Shoah in progress.

Pacelli's own piety was marked, then, by an intensely private interiority that paralleled his gnostic-style Marian devotion in its rejection of social responsibility in the working-out of Christian redemption. In his doctrinal speculations, moreover, he distanced himself from contemporary attempts to reclaim a theological basis for social Christianity and for the solidarity of the human race. In fact, his version of the doctrine of the Mystical Body deepened his convictions about the papal ideology of power and confirmed his prejudice that non-Catholics were alien to the people of God.

Above all, in the very depths of the war, Pacelli's papal program—his aspirations to holiness and his attempts to identify the people of God with papal allegiance—was inimical to a sense of responsibility for, and common identity with, the Jews of Europe.

16

Pacelli and the Holocaust

The Final Solution evolved during the first three years of the war, coinciding with the first three years of Pacelli's papacy. Much was planned and executed in secrecy, for the Nazi regime was sensitive, fearful even, of uncontrolled public opinion. But anything so widespread as a plan to destroy an entire people could not be hidden for long, and Adolf Hitler had made clear his intentions toward the Jews on January 3, 1939. "If international Jewry," he declared, "should succeed, in Europe or elsewhere, in precipitating nations into a world war, the result will not be the bolshevization of Europe and a victory of Judaism, but the extermination of the Jewish race."[1] At the end of July 1941, a month after the attack on Russia on June 22, 1941, Reinhard Heydrich was ordered to make all the necessary preparations for "a complete solution" of the Jewish question in the German sphere of influence in Europe. By the autumn of 1941 preparations were in hand for something unprecedentedly massive and wholly unique in history: the systematic enslavement, deportation, and extermination of an entire people.

In September 1941, Hitler had decreed that all German Jews must wear the Yellow Star, already obligatory in Poland. The Yellow Star naturally had a devastating, stigmatizing, and demoralizing effect on those forced to wear it, which included Jews who had become Christians. The German Catholic bishops lodged a plea with the regime: they asked for the stars to be removed, not from all Jews but only from Catholic

Jews. The Gestapo refused. October saw the first mass deportations of German Jews to the East, prompting the bishops again to discuss whether they could not ask for preferential treatment of Jewish converts to Catholicism; they decided not to incite the regime, even for the sake of their own faithful.[2] That same month, officials in the Ministry for the Eastern Territories decided on the use of poison gas for extermination. In November Goebbels declared that "no compassion and certainly no sorrow is called for over the fate of the Jews. . . . Every Jew is our enemy."[3]

On January 20, 1942, a meeting took place at number 58 am Grossen Wannsee, a villa overlooking the Grosser Wannsee, a lake outside Berlin. There were fifteen high-ranking officials present, and Reinhard Heydrich took the chair. Heydrich asked all present to cooperate in the implementation of "the solution." Reading from a draft prepared by Eichmann, Heydrich ordered that, "in the course of the Final Solution, the Jews should be brought under appropriate direction in a suitable manner to the East for labor utilization. Separated by sex, the Jews capable of work will be led into these areas in large labor columns to build roads, whereby doubtless a large part will fall away through natural reduction."[4]

According to statistics prepared by Eichmann for the conference, eleven million Jews would "fall away," including Jews in countries as yet unconquered. Croatia, the Catholic state that had enjoyed Pacelli's special approval, was declared a place where there was no longer a problem, as "the essential key questions have already been resolved." Eichmann was to head the operation of the "Final Solution" from his headquarters in Berlin, and his representatives were to travel to all the occupied capitals, reporting back as each deportation was planned and executed.

The deportations began in March 1942 and continued until 1944. Death camps were designed and staffed in remote areas of former Poland—Auschwitz-Birkenau, Treblinka, Belzec, Sobibor, Chelmno, and Majdanek. Transportation became a priority, involving a complex bureaucracy of timetables, rented railway cars, shunting arrangements, and provision of guards. Eichmann's representatives were dispatched for these purposes to France, Belgium, Holland, Luxemburg, Norway, Romania, Greece, Bulgaria, Hungary, Poland, and Czechoslovakia.

By the end of the war, some six million Jews had perished.

The "Final Solution" constituted an unprecedented test of the Christian faith, a religion based on the concept of *agape*, the love that accords each individual, irrespective of difference, equal respect as a child of God—the love that, as Pacelli had declared in his first encyclical of 1941, quoting St. Paul's utterance of Christian universality, does not discriminate between "Greek nor Jew, circumcision nor uncircumcision, Barbarian, Scythian, bond nor free: but Christ is all and in all." Christians were thus faced with a historic moral challenge. Was it not a clear Christian duty to protest and resist the extermination of the Jews, whatever the consequences?

Christianity, and Catholicism in particular, had a long history of anti-Judaism on religious grounds that had by no means abated in the twentieth century. It was not part of Catholic culture to persecute Jews on the basis of Hitlerian racial ideology, let alone condone the extermination of the race. And yet Catholicism appeared, on the face of it, to have links with the very right-wing nationalism, corporatism, and Fascism that sustained anti-Semitism or complicity in anti-Semitism on racial grounds. Practically every right-wing dictator of the period had been born and brought up a Catholic—notably Hitler, Horthy, Franco, Pétain, Mussolini, Pavelic, and Tiso (who was a Catholic priest). There were isolated but significant examples of Catholic bishops expressing anti-Semitic views even as the persecution of Jews gathered pace in Germany in the mid-1930s. In 1936, for example, Cardial Hlond, primate of Poland, opined: "There will be the Jewish problem as long as the Jews remain."[5] Pius XI had tardily repudiated racism in his famous encyclical *Mit brennender Sorge* in 1937, but there was residual anti-Judaism within the treatise, as we have seen. Despite a clear lead from the Pontiff, the Slovak bishops, for example, issued a pastoral letter that repeated the traditional accusations that the Jews were deicides.[6] There was evidence of anti-Judaism, even anti-Semitism, in the heart of the wartime Vatican. The leading Dominican theologian and neo-Thomist Garrigou-Lagrange was a theological adviser to Pacelli and at the same time a keen supporter of Pétain. He was a close friend of the Vichy ambassador to the Holy See. In an infamous dispatch, the diplomat told his government that the Holy See did not object to the Vichy anti-Jewish legislation and he even supplied source notes from Thomas Aquinas which had been assembled by Rome-based neo-Thomists.[7]

But where did Eugenio Pacelli, now acclaimed and self-proclaimed as Vicar of Christ upon earth, stand on the issue of the persecution, deportation, and destruction of the Jews?

Pacelli's Journey into Silence

Throughout 1942, Pacelli received a flow of reliable information on the details of the Final Solution. It came not all at once but gradually. At the same time, he was obliged to listen to mounting pleas from all over the world for a clear denunciation.

On February 9, 1942, just twenty days after the Wannsee Conference, Hitler made a hysterical broadcast declaring that "the Jews will be liquidated for at least a thousand years!" The speech was reprinted in Rome's *Messaggero* newspaper and it caught the attention of both Osborne, the British minister to the Holy See, and Cardinal Secretary of State Maglione, who commented to Osborne on "Hitler's new outburst against the Jews."[8] The story of Osborne's attempts from inside the Vatican to get Pacelli to speak provides an ideal perspective from which to track the course of Pacelli's knowledge and reactions.

On March 18, 1942, the Vatican received the memorandum by Richard Lichtheim and Gerhard Riegner sent via the nuncio in Berne, outlining violent anti-Semitic measures in Slovakia, Croatia, Hungary, and Unoccupied France. The plea focused attention on those Catholic countries where the Pope had influence. Apart from an intervention in the case of Slovakia, where the president was Monsignor Josef Tiso, no papal reactions or interventions resulted, as far as we can see from the Vatican's own documents, save for mild local initiatives of the nuncio in France.[9]

During the same month, a flow of dispatches came into the Vatican from various sources in Eastern Europe describing the fate of some ninety thousand Jews, among whom there were significant numbers of "baptized," who had been sent to camps in Poland.[10] The nuncio in Bratislava commented that the deportation was the equivalent of sending a large number to certain death.

Throughout the spring of 1942, the world was increasingly apprised of the Nazi policy of slaying hostages in occupied territories in reprisal for partisan attacks. These were well known in the Vatican because the Germans were happy to advertise the fact to discourage further attacks. Osborne had been keeping a tally to pass on to the Pope, and he wrote on April 21 to his friend and frequent wartime correspondent Mrs. Bridget McEwan: "Yesterday being Hitler's birthday, I wore a black tie in mourning of the millions he has massacred and tortured." He mentioned that day to Cardinal Maglione a private theory of his—that "Hitler and all his diabolic works may be the process of the casting out of the devil in the subconscious of the German race" and that "they may, when the painful process is completed, turn into decent members of the society of nations." Maglione, however, "seemed to wave it indulgently aside as a childish folly."[11]

The hostage atrocities came to a crisis after Reinhard Heydrich, the Final Solution chief, was assassinated in Prague by two Czech resistance fighters flown in from Britain by British intelligence. Ten thousand people were arrested and thirteen hundred of them murdered. On June 9–10, the village of Lidice, held responsible for sheltering the assassins, was destroyed and all of its men and boys were executed.

The next day, Osborne wrote to Mrs. McEwan: "It has been made clear to me that H.H. [His Holiness] is in rather bad odour with the F.O. [British Foreign Office], and, I daresay, the British public too. It's a good deal his own fault, but on the other it isn't, he being as he is. I'm sorry about it, but I think there is much to be said on his side."[12]

The remark aptly reveals the collapse of Pacelli's reputation in Britain as a result of his silence, and yet the ambivalence evoked in those who were close to him within the Vatican. Two days later, Osborne felt less ambivalent when he saw below the papal apartments a multitude of First Communion children awaiting the Pope. It was "an appealing sight," Osborne conceded in his diary entry for June 13, "but unfortunately the moral leadership of the world is not retained by mass reception of Italian first communicants." Adolf Hitler, Osborne reflected, "needed more than the benevolence of the Pastor Angelicus, and moral leadership is not assured by the unapplied recital of the Commandments."[13]

When the United States entered the war in December of 1941 following the Japanese bombing of Pearl Harbor, Washington asked its counselor at the Rome embassy, Harold Tittmann, to take up residence within the Vatican on the same basis as Osborne. The Vatican was at first reluctant, but after much diplomatic wrangling Tittmann got the appropriate accreditation on May 2, 1942, and there began an unprecedented diplomatic relationship between the Holy See and Washington.

From this point on, Osborne and Tittmann had conversations, records of which appear in their official papers, about the stance of Pacelli. Osborne, according to Tittmann, declared that the Pope was unpopular in Britain and that his government was convinced that the Pontiff was hedging his bets on an Axis victory. On June 16, 1942, Tittmann filed a report to Washington expressing the view that Pacelli was diverting himself, ostrichlike, into purely religious concerns and that the moral authority won for the papacy by Pius XI was being eroded. He had pleaded with Cardinal Maglione to issue a denunciation of the reprisals taken for Heydrich's death, but the Secretary of State had merely shaken his head, remarking that it would only make things worse.[14] Tittmann ended by rehearsing his usual theory about Pacelli's inertia and silence: that Pacelli thought it better to anger his friends rather than his enemies, since the friends were more likely to forgive the sins of omission. The impression is that the diplomatic corps within the Vatican was baffled by Pacelli's behavior and casting around for explanations.

In the last week of that month, June 1942, the plight of the Jews within Nazi Europe—a million of whom had died by this stage—became a matter of world knowledge through the press and radio. The first newspaper to report that the Jews were being not only persecuted but exterminated was the London *Daily Telegraph*, which ran a prominent series. The first article on June 25 stated: "More than 700,000 Polish Jews have been slaughtered by the Germans in the greatest massacres in the world's history." The report, based on a dispatch sent secretly to Shmuel Zygilebojm, the Jewish representative on the Polish National Council, claimed that the killings were being carried out with the use of poison gas. Zygilebojm later committed suicide as a result of what he felt to be the indifference of the West. A second article, which appeared on June 30, carried the headline: "MORE THAN 1,000,000 JEWS KILLED IN EUROPE," and claimed that it was the aim of the Nazis "to wipe the race from the European continent." Both articles were reported on the BBC, and thus came via Osborne to the Pope's attention. *The New York Times* carried the stories on June 30 and July 2, and this led to a protest rally in New York's Madison Square Garden on July 21. At about this time, detailed information about Polish death camps was leaked to the West by three Jewish escapees; their stories also appeared in American newspapers.

During the last week of July, Osborne, Tittmann, and the Brazilian ambassador Pinto Accioly met to agree on a plan to make Pacelli speak out against the Nazi atrocities. Two days later, Osborne confided in his diary, "I have no doubt that, if it were possible, he would expend his sympathies on other peoples. Only why, then, does he not denounce the German atrocities against the populations of the Occupied Countries?"

The historian Owen Chadwick casts doubt on whether, despite this flow of information, Pacelli was yet fully in the picture about the true plight of the Jews, and suggests that even Osborne himself had his doubts about the reports.[15] Osborne's recently discovered letters, written from inside the Vatican, tell a different story. On July 31, 1942, he wrote to Mrs. McEwan as follows:

> You remember your last letter, at least the last I have received, with its diatribe against the silence of the Vatican in the face of the German atrocities in the Occupied Countries? It is so exactly what I feel, and have been saying, and what others have been saying, and it is so admirably expressed, that I am sending a very slightly edited copy of it to the Pope. I do hope you won't think this an abuse of confidence. I say that it comes from a Catholic friend of mine and that I think it is of interest as an indication of British opinion, Protestant *and* Catholic. Personally I agree with every word of it and have said much the same at the Vatican. It is very sad. The fact is that the moral authority of the Holy See, which Pius XI and his predecessors had built up into a world power, is now sadly reduced. I suspect that H.H. [His Holiness] hopes to play a great role as peace-maker and that it is partly at least for this reason that he tries to preserve a position of neutrality as between the belligerents. But, as you say, the German crimes have nothing to do with neutrality . . . and the fact is that the Pope's silence is defeating its own purpose because it is destroying his prospects of contributing to peace. Meanwhile

he canalizes his frustration by being the Pastor Angelicus, thereby exhausting himself and sapping his own morale. It is most unfortunate that that Irish monk, Malachi, wasn't it, selected "Pastor Angelicus" for the 262nd Pope. If he had said "Leo Furibundus" [Ferocious Lion] things might have been very different. A film is being made here, for world distribution, to be called "Pastor Angelicus." I cannot say how I deplore this. It is like Hollywood publicity.[16]

The historian Chadwick knew about the McEwan letter because he quotes Osborne's diary making mention of it. But in his systematic attempts to exonerate Pacelli, Chadwick then casts doubt on whether the Pope ever saw the letter. "We have no evidence," Chadwick tells us, "that he did show the letter to the Pope." On August 25, however, Osborne wrote again to Mrs. McEwan that he had indeed passed the letter to the Pope, or what he termed "a bowdlerized extract from it," adding that he felt faintly guilty about it, "but really you expressed so admirably what so many of us feel and what it is so desirable that he should hear from as many quarters as possible."[17] In the same letter, he wrote that in his weekly public audience the Pope had "delivered three long, eloquent, but to my mind very tedious, lectures on the relations between master and servants. One might have thought that the relations between the German occupiers and the populations of the occupied countries offered a more suitable and more urgent subject of discussion and advice."

The following month, Osborne confirmed again that he had passed the letter to the Pope, but had received no response. "I had an audience last week. . . . I thought the Pope looked older and thinner and more tired than when I had last seen him. . . . He was as simple and friendly as ever and we passed lightly over delicate questions and he made no reference to the extract from your letter which I had sent him. I hope we have him headed off any peace talk this autumn."[18] In fact, it would take Pacelli another year to admit that he had read the McEwan extract: "He referred to your letter, which I had sent him and in which you advocated a little plain speaking."[19]

Meanwhile, the deportations had begun in France and Holland. On July 16–17, 1942, the Vélodrome d'Hiver, an indoor sports arena in

Paris, was turned into an internment center for Jewish families that had been rounded up. These were victims destined for Drancy, a northeast suburb of Paris, which served as an antechamber to Auschwitz. The ultimate objective was to seize the 28,000 Jews in the greater Paris area, a task to be carried out by nine thousand French police. Only half the objective was achieved on this roundup—12,884 Jews, a disappointment from the German point of view. The victims, it appears, remained stunned and incredulous to the very end. But according to one source, there were more than a hundred suicides during the roundup and in subsequent days.[20]

Through the summer of 1942, some fifteen thousand Dutch Jews were deported to the death camps. Certain accounts of the exterminations were made known in Holland despite the Nazi grip on the media. Nevertheless, as in France, a tragic optimism persisted among the Jews themselves as to their eventual fate at the destination of the deportation routes, emphasizing a new urgency for a major initiative from an authoritative moral voice with substantial outreach. The failure of Pacelli to take a lead in issuing a warning to the Jews of Europe, once the enormities were known, cannot be underestimated. The point has been summarized by Guenter Lewy:

> A public denunciation of the mass murders by Pius XII, broadcast widely over the Vatican radio and read from the pulpits by the bishops, would have revealed to Jews and Christians alike what deportation to the East entailed. The Pope would have been believed, whereas the broadcasts of the Allies were often shrugged off as war propaganda.[21]

In Holland, the Catholic bishops combined with the Protestant Churches to send a telegram of protest against the Jewish deportations. They sent it to the German *Reichskommissar*, threatening widespread Christian protest. In response, the Nazis offered to exempt Christian Jews (but only those converted before 1941), provided that the Churches remained silent. The Dutch Reformed Church acquiesced, but the Catholic archbishop of Utrecht rejected the bargain and issued a pastoral letter of clear denunciation to be read in all the churches. As a result, the Germans rounded up and deported all the Catholic Jews they could find, including Edith Stein, the Jewish Carmelite philosopher who had pleaded with Pius XI to make an urgent statement against anti-Semitism back in the spring of 1933. Stein later died in Auschwitz.

There are exculpatory statements in the testimonies for the beatification of Pius XII pleading that the Dutch episode prompted Pacelli to make an irrevocable decision not to speak out against the Nazi deportations. Mother Pasqualina told the beatification tribunal that the Pope had written a document "condemning the work of Hitler" when the news came in of "forty thousand" Dutch Jews killed on the orders of Hitler after the archbishop's pastoral letter. "I remember," she said, "the Holy Father came into the kitchen at lunchtime carrying two sheets of paper with minute handwriting. 'They contain,' he said, 'my protest against the cruel persecution of the Jews and I was to have published it in *L'Osservatore* this evening. But I now think that if the letter of the bishops has cost the lives of 40,000 persons, my own protest, that carries an even stronger tone, could cost the lives of perhaps 200,000 Jews. I cannot take such a great responsibility. It is better to remain silent before the public and to do in private all that is possible.' "[22] Mother Pasqualina claimed that Montini had said that since an invasion of the Vatican was expected at any time, it was best not to leave any important documents lying around. "I remember," she said, "that he stayed in the kitchen until the entire document had been destroyed."

There is no evidence, however, that forty thousand Jewish Catholics were rounded up as a result of the Dutch bishops' protest. The most recent and painstaking research on this question, conducted in Holland by researchers for the BBC producer Jonathan Lewis, concluded that the number arrested and deported was no more than ninety-two Catholic converts from Judaism in all.[23] In fact, up to September 14, 1942, the total number of deportations from Holland of all Jews was 20,588 according to figures published by Martin Gilbert.[24] The important thing about the faintly ludicrous episode in the kitchen, and the declamatory speech Pacelli allegedly made to his housekeeper, is that it has become an alibi ever since for his defenders on the silence issue. If one credits the story, it is interesting that he should have so wildly exaggerated, for Mother Pasqualina's benefit, the number of victims in order to defend his silence, and yet underestimated them on other occasions for precisely the same reason—as would happen at Christmas.

The following month, a major roundup began in the Unoccupied Zone of France; once arrested, the prisoners were transported to Drancy like those in the North. Passengers witnessed the deportation cars as they passed through the stations en route and were horrified by the hideous stench from inside, where the unsanitary conditions were exacerbated by the summer heat. By the end of the year some 42,000 Jews had been sent from France to Auschwitz. As the Vatican's published documents show, the nuncio in France fully apprised the Vatican of every stage of the deportation; he also went through the motions of confronting Pétain with the distress of the Catholic Church at the measures, but Pétain turned a deaf ear. More important, Pacelli remained silent both in public and in private. In the New Year of 1943, Cardinal Emmanuel Suhard of Paris visited Pacelli to discuss important matters relating to France and the Vatican. An eyewitness to these talks reported that Pacelli "warmly praised the work of the Marshal [Pétain] and took a keen interest in government actions that are a sign of the fortunate renewal of religious life in France."[25]

In the meantime, the Vatican diplomats representing France, Poland, Brazil, the United States, and Britain decided in mid-September to act both jointly and separately in requesting that the Pope denounce Nazi atrocities, the British specifically mentioning the mass killing of Jews. In his contribution, Osborne wrote: "A policy of silence in regard to such offenses against the conscience of the world must necessarily involve a renunciation of moral leadership and a consequent atrophy of the influence and authority of the Vatican; and it is upon the maintenance and assertion of such authority that must depend any prospect of a Papal contribution to the reestablishment of world peace."[26]

The American Envoy

While the initiative of the ambassadors was in progress, President Roosevelt sent a personal representative to plead with Pacelli to say something clear about the extermination of the Jews. It was a hazardous mission, involving travel into enemy territory. Myron Taylor came to visit the Vatican on September 17, 1942, being driven from Littario Airport in a car in which the windows had been covered with brown pa-

per. It was remarkable that Mussolini allowed into Rome the representative of the leader of a country with which he was at war, and the Germans made known their displeasure. Osborne was full of admiration:
"Myron Taylor arrived here yesterday evening, via clipper from New
York and plane from Lisbon to Rome. He is an amazing man, he takes a
journey like that in his stride in spite of being well over sixty. He will be
very good for the Pope."[27]

Taylor had his first audience with Pacelli on Saturday, September 19,
and aimed to convince the Pontiff that the Americans could not lose the
war and that their determination was fired by a moral crusade against a
gangster regime; he brought fresh information about Germany's war
crimes in occupied Europe, especially in France. One of his objectives
was to forestall any moves Pacelli might be making to encourage a compromise peace: "There is reason to believe," Taylor told the Pope, "that
our Axis enemies will attempt, through devious channels, to urge the
Holy See to endorse in the near future proposals of peace without victory."[28] But his principal mission was to plead with Pacelli to speak out,
and to this end he assured him that America was on the side of right.
"Because we know we are in the right, and because we have supreme confidence in our strength, we are determined to carry through until we shall
have won complete victory."[29]

In subsequent meetings with Tardini and Maglione, Taylor continued
to hammer away at the need for a papal statement. Tardini's notes record
that "Mr. Taylor talked of the opportunity and the necessity of a word
from the Pope against such huge atrocities by the Germans. He said that
from all sides people are calling for such a word. I assented with a sigh,
as one who knows the truth of this all too well! I said in reply that the
Pope has already spoken several times to condemn crimes by whomso-
ever they are committed. . . . Taylor said, 'He can repeat.' "[30] It is significant that at this stage of the war neither Pacelli nor Maglione cited
communication with the outside world as a problem. Clearly the Allies
would have seen to it that an important papal message got through.

During his last interview with Maglione, Taylor again raised the
importance of Pius XII's making a clear statement. The American monsignor who recorded the meeting wrote: "Mr. Taylor said that there was a
general impression both in America and Europe—and he said that he
could not be wrong in reporting this impression—that it was necessary

now for the Pope again to denounce the inhuman treatment of refugees, hostages, and above all the Jews in the occupied countries. Not only Catholics want the Pope to speak but also Protestants. Cardinal Maglione replied that the Holy See is continually at work trying to help the sufferers."[31] Maglione's last word on the matter was that at the first opportunity the Pope "would not fail to express anew his thought with clarity."

At the end of Taylor's visit, however, Pacelli delivered himself of a formulaic response that illustrated the depths of his intransigence. In the first place, he was determined to put on record that he *had* spoken clearly and with great moral force, and that he deserved credit for having done so. Second, he was not inclined to make a distinction between the moral claims of the belligerents. "The Holy See has always been, and still is, greatly preoccupied, out of a heart filled with constant solicitude, with the fate of civil populations defenseless against the aggressions of war. Since the outbreak of the present conflict, no year has passed that We have not appealed in Our public utterances to all the belligerents—men who also have human hearts molded by a mother's love—to show some feeling of pity and charity for the sufferings of civilians, for helpless women and children, for the sick and the aged, on whom a rain of terror, fire, destruction, and havoc pours down out of a guiltless sky. Our appeal was little heeded."[32] Not a word in all this about the Jews; not a word about Nazi Germany.

While Myron Taylor was still in the Vatican, the news was coming in of the destruction of the Warsaw Ghetto and the extermination of its inmates. The information came via two eyewitnesses to the Jewish agency in Palestine, thence to Geneva, and from Geneva to Washington, which forwarded the information to Myron Taylor, who laid it before the Pope. Then silence.

Meanwhile the Allies were enjoying military success in several major theaters of war: the German humiliation at Stalingrad, the news of El Alamein, the American landings in North Africa—but still Pacelli remained noncommittal. "The Pope is still considering," Osborne wrote to Britain's foreign secretary, Anthony Eden, in the first week of November. "I doubt myself if he is going to say anything."[33]

The close of 1942 found Pacelli hard at work attempting to prevent the bombing of Rome—so much so that Osborne confided to his diary on December 13: "The more I think of it, the more I am revolted by

Hitler's massacre of the Jewish race on the one hand, and, on the other, the Vatican's apparently exclusive preoccupation with the . . . possibilities of the bombardments of Rome." He concluded that the "whole outfit had become Italian."[34] A few days later, he wrote to the Cardinal Secretary of State that the Vatican "instead of thinking of nothing but the bombing of Rome should consider their duties in respect of the unprecedented crime against humanity of Hitler's campaign of extermination of the Jews."[35] Throughout October, pleas had been coming in from Jewish communities and organizations the world over. Among them were the detailed eyewitness reports of Jan Karski, who had been inside the Warsaw Ghetto and the Belzec death camp.[36] Pacelli had told Montini to reply to these requests by saying that the Holy See was doing all that it could.

On December 18 Osborne handed Tardini a dossier replete with information on the Jewish deportations and mass killings in the hope that Pacelli could be influenced to make a clear denunciation in his Christmas Eve broadcast to the world. As Tardini took the dossier from Osborne's hands, he commented that "the Pope could not take sides." Osborne's outrage seared into the pages of his diary. "His Holiness is clinging at all costs to what he considers to be a policy of neutrality, even in the face of the worst outrages against God and man, because he hopes to be able to play a part in restoring peace. He does not see this silence is highly damaging to the Holy See and is entirely destructive of any prospects of his being listened to."[37]

Osborne did not give up. In London, Washington, and Moscow the Allies published a joint declaration on the persecution of the Jews, and Osborne took it to the Pope, pleading within him to simply endorse it. The response, through Maglione, was a definite no. The Pope could not condemn "particular" atrocities, neither could he verify the Allies' reports on the number of Jews murdered.[38]

The Christmas Eve Broadcast

On December 24, 1942, having made draft after draft,[39] Pius XII broadcast his Christmas homily to the world.[40] His theme was the Rights of Man and the problems of the individual in relation to the state. He began by asserting that an imbalance between the state and the individual had been brought about by the "damaging economic policies" of recent decades in which everything had become "subordinated to the profit motive." This had led to the reduction of the individual to the "utility of the state, to the exclusion of all ethical and religious considerations." No discrimination, no insight, is to be found in the sermon on the contrast between totalitarianism and democracy, social democracy and communism, capitalism and welfare capitalism. From his papal overview, he declared that what the world lacked was the peaceful ordering of society offered by allegiance to Holy Mother Church. Pacelli's concept of an ideal society, however, beyond appeals to individual and family piety, was a hybrid of corporatist nostrums and appeals to "responsible Christian" spirit.[41] Underpinning all, however, was the premise of papal primacy.

Following this lengthy and dry sermonizing on Catholic social doctrine, he came at last to the atrocities of war, the moment the world beyond Nazi Europe had been waiting for. The war, he said, was the result of a social order that "concealed a fatal weakness and an unbridled lust for profit and power." (Such a vagary could have been applied, of course, to both sides, Axis and Allies.) The initiative the Holy Father had to offer the world at this juncture was to plead for a vow to be made by men of good will to bring society back to its immovable center of gravity in divine law, and for all men to dedicate themselves to the service of the human person and the service of a divinely ennobled human society.

"Humanity owes this vow," he now said, "to those innumerable exiles whom the hurricane of war has torn away from their native soil and dispersed in a foreign land, who might make their own and the Prophet's lament: 'Our inheritance is turned to aliens, our houses to strangers.'"

Then came the famous statement intended, as he later claimed, to be understood as a clear denunciation of the Nazi extermination of the Jewish people: *"Humanity owes this vow to those hundreds of thousands who, without any fault of their own, sometimes only by reason of their nationality or race, are marked down for death or gradual extinction."*

Here was the fullest extent of his protest and denunciation, after a year of encouragement, pleading, argument, proof upon proof of what had been happening in Poland and all over Europe. It was to remain the fullest extent of his protest and denunciation for the rest of the war.

It is not merely a paltry statement. The chasm between the enormity of the liquidation of the Jewish people and this form of evasive words is shocking. He might have been referring to many categories of victims of the many belligerents in the conflict. Clearly the exhibition of ambiguous language was intended to placate those who urged him to protest, while avoiding offense to the Nazi regime. But these considerations are overshadowed by the implicit denial and trivialization. He had scaled down the doomed millions to "hundreds of thousands" and expunged the word *Jews*, making the pointed qualification "sometimes only." Nowhere was the term *Nazi* or *Nazi Germany* mentioned. Hitler himself could not have wished for a more convoluted and innocuous reaction from the Vicar of Christ to the greatest crime in human history.

Perhaps the most fitting commentary on the address was the contemptuous dismissal of it by Mussolini. Count Ciano came upon the Duce listening to the broadcast on Christmas Eve. "The Vicar of God, who is representative on earth of the Ruler of the Universe," Mussolini scoffed, "should never speak; he should remain in the clouds. This is a speech of platitudes which might better be made by the parish priest of Predappio." Predappio was Mussolini's backwater native village.[42]

Harold Tittmann told Washington on December 28 that the "message does not satisfy those circles which had hoped that the Pope would this time call a spade a spade and discard his usual practice of speaking in generalities." The Pope affected to be surprised when Tittmann expressed his disappointment to him in person. The French ambassador asked the Pope why he had not mentioned the word *Nazi* in his condemnation, and the Pope told him that he would have had to mention the Communists too.[43] It might have been more to the point to ask why he had not mentioned the word *Jews*. Osborne told London that the Vatican diplomats were disappointed, but that Pacelli was convinced that he had been "clear and comprehensive." Pacelli told Osborne in person that he had condemned the Jewish persecution.[44] Osborne knew that Pacelli would never exceed this form of words. Kasimir Papée, Polish ambassador to the Holy See, conceded that it might just be possible to discern a vague denunciation of totalitarian doctrines in general when the speech was "stripped of verbiage and rhetoric"; but where was the word *Nazi*?[45]

Indifference

Pacelli, in common with many other religious figures, found it difficult to comprehend and to respond to the Jewish mass death. The difference between him and other religious leaders was, of course, that hundreds of millions believed him to be the Vicar of Christ on earth; he carried unique obligations upon his individual shoulders. But the sheer magnitude of the horror put his values and beliefs, his world picture, to a test no pope had ever faced in the long history of that institution. Hence we are obliged to scrutinize not just Pacelli the man but also the modern papacy—the institution that he represented and did so much to shape anew through the century. We are obliged, in fact, to ask not only whether the institution of the papacy was inadequate to the challenge of the Final Solution, but also whether in some shocking way it was hospitable to Hitler's plans from as early as 1933. Was there something in the modern ideology of papal power that encouraged the Holy See to acquiesce in the face of Hitler's evil rather than oppose it?

As we have seen, Pacelli encouraged, as had popes since Pius IX, a spirituality that emphasized the soul over the body, and the supreme importance of eternal life whither that soul was inevitably destined. His sermons and discourses betrayed a poor sense of history and of social Christianity, a neglect of the presence of God in community, a rejection of openness and respect to other cultures and faiths. And all this indicated a narrow view of the meaning of life and death itself. If the death of an individual is a mere passage of the soul through the veil of appearances to eternity, what price the death of six million individuals that are "other," that do not belong, that form no part of the Mystical Body? The traditionalist Roman Catholic view, espoused by Pacelli, and indeed by his father Filippo—so attached to the little book *Massime eterne* and those pilgrimages to the cemetery—appears utterly uncomprehending in the face of what was happening to the Jewish people. Uncomprehending it was, too, in its failure to find in the isolation of the Jews a parallel with Christ alone in Gethsemane, Christ alone on Golgotha. "Alone. That is the key word, the haunting theme," writes Elie Wiesel. "Alone with no allies, no friends, totally, desperately alone.... The world knew and kept silent.... Mankind let them suffer and agonize and perish alone. And yet, and yet they did not die alone, for something in all of us died with them."[46]

The immensity of the Holocaust struck speechless many devout Christian and even Jewish leaders after the war. The Jewish scholar Arthur A. Cohen has written that he could not speak about Auschwitz for many years, "for I had no language that tolerated the immensity of the wound."[47] Pacelli's failure to respond to the enormity of the Holocaust was more than a personal failure, it was a failure of the papal office itself and the prevailing culture of Catholicism. That failure was implicit in the rifts Catholicism created and sustained—between the sacred and the profane, the spiritual and the secular, the body and the soul, clergy and laity, the exclusive truth of Catholicism over all other confessions and faiths. It was an essential feature of Pacelli's ideology of papal power, moreover, that Catholics should abdicate, as Catholics, their social and political responsibility for what happened in the world and turn their gaze upward to the Holy Father and, beyond, to eternity.

And there is a darker issue yet: the question put by Guenter Lewy in his essay in *Commentary* (February 1964). Having surveyed the documents and the arguments, Lewy writes: "Finally, one is inclined to conclude that the Pope and his advisers—influenced by the long tradition of moderate anti-Semitism so widely accepted in Vatican circles—did not view the plight of the Jews with a real sense of urgency and moral outrage." He adds, advisedly, "For this assertion no documentation is possible, but it is a conclusion difficult to avoid."

Pacelli and Anti-Semitism

Until now, it has not been possible to relate the full history of Pacelli's career as diplomat and as Cardinal Secretary of State. The new material made available in this narrative, however, reveals Pacelli's long-standing anti-Jewishness.

This is what we know with certainty about Pacelli's attitudes, policies, and decisions relating to the Jews, spanning a quarter of a century.

Pacelli displayed a secret antipathy toward the Jews, evident from the age of forty-three in Munich, both religious and racist, a circumstance contradicting later claims that he respected the Jews and that his wartime actions and omissions had been performed with the best of intentions.

From 1917 through to the recovered "lost encyclical" of 1939, *Humani generis unitas*, Pacelli and the office for which he was responsible betrayed an antagonistic policy toward the Jews, based on the conviction that there was a link between Judaism and the Bolshevik plot to destroy Christendom.

Pacelli's concordat policy, as he well knew, thwarted potential Catholic protest in defense of Jews, whether they were converts to Christianity or not, as a matter of "outside" interference. The potential in the Reich Concordat for sanctioning the destruction of the Jews was acknowledged by Hitler himself in his cabinet meeting on July 14, 1933.

While publicly repudiating racist theories through the mid- to late 1930s, Pacelli failed to sanction protest by the German Catholic episcopate against anti-Semitism. Nor did he attempt to intervene in the process by which Catholic clergy collaborated in racial certification to identify Jews, providing the essential information that aided Nazi persecution.

After Pius XI's *Mit brennender Sorge*, Pacelli secretly attempted to mitigate the strength of that encyclical by private diplomatic reassurances to the Germans.

From a variety of evidence, it is clear that Pacelli believed that the Jews had brought misfortune on their own heads; intervention on their behalf could draw the Church into alliances with forces—principally the Soviet Union—whose ultimate aim was the destruction of the institutional Church. For this reason, as war began, he was determined to distance himself from any appeal on behalf of the Jews at the level of international politics. This did not prevent him from issuing instructions to alleviate their plight at the level of basic charity.

Given this background, we are obliged to conclude that his silence had more to do with a habitual fear and distrust of the Jews than a strategy of diplomacy or a commitment to impartiality. He was perfectly capable of partiality when Holland, Belgium, and Luxemburg were invaded in May 1940. And when German Catholics complained, he wrote to the German bishops pointing out that neutrality was not the same as "indifference and apathy where moral and human considerations demanded a candid word."[18] So, did not moral and human considerations involved in the murder of millions merit a "candid word"?

That failure to utter a candid word about the Final Solution in progress proclaimed to the world that the Vicar of Christ was not moved to pity and anger. From this point of view he was the ideal Pope for Hitler's unspeakable plan. He was Hitler's pawn. He was Hitler's Pope.

As we have seen, Pacelli's single breach of his self-imposed silence on the liquidation of the Jews was that ambiguous sentence during his Christmas 1942 broadcast, which failed to use the words *Jew, non-Aryan, German,* and *Nazi.*

Deliberate ambiguity—diplomatic language—is understandable in cases where an individual's conscience is subjected to irreconcilable pressures and especially in time of war when there is constant need to choose between the lesser of two evils. Even if Pacelli's Christmas broadcast is defended along these lines, the setting aside of a presumptive obligation does not entitle one to abandon an inherent obligation indefinitely. The original duty to denounce the Final Solution remained until such time as Pacelli's conscience was "liberated" from these pressures. As it was, he not only failed to explain and apologize for his reticence, but he claimed retrospective moral superiority for having spoken candidly.

Speaking to delegates of the Supreme Council of the Arab People of Palestine, on August 3, 1946, he said: "It is superfluous for me to tell you that we disapprove of all recourse to force and violence, from wheresoever it comes, just as we condemned on various occasions in the past the persecutions that a fanatical anti-Semitism inflicted on the Hebrew people."[49] His complicity in the Final Solution through failure to register appropriate condemnation was compounded by a retrospective attempt to portray himself as an outspoken defender of the Jewish people. His grandiloquent self-exculpation in 1946 revealed him to be not only an ideal Pope for the Nazis' Final Solution, but a hypocrite.

But there was a much more immediate test of Pacelli's papacy that occurred before the liberation of Rome when he was the sole Italian authority in the city. On October 16, 1943, German troops entered the Roman ghetto area, rounded up all the Jews they could find, and imprisoned them in the Collegio Militare on the Via della Lungara, in the very shadow of the Vatican. How did Pacelli acquit himself?

17

The Jews of Rome

In July 1943 the Allies invaded Sicily. Despite Pacelli's ceaseless diplomatic efforts to make Rome an open city, five hundred American bombers attacked the capital on July 19, aiming for the rail yards near Stazione Termini. A number of bombs went astray; five hundred citizens of Rome were killed and many injured. The Church of San Lorenzo, the great basilica where Pio Nono had been buried, was damaged. Pacelli, accompanied by Montini, hurried to the site and spent two hours among the people, distributing money and sympathy. Kneeling amid the rubble, he prayed the *De profundis* (Out of the Depths, O Lord). As he came away, his long white coat, it was noticed, was covered in blood. Mussolini was conspicuous by his absence. The Pope, it seemed, was once again patriarch of Rome.

After the bombing of Rome, the Duce was indeed finished. A week later, on July 24, 1943, tired and senile, although only sixty years of age, Mussolini was called before the Fascist Grand Council and voted out of office by 19 votes to 8. The council demanded the restoration of constitutional monarchy, a democratic parliament, and that the armed forces be placed under the command of King Vittorio Emanuele III. The Fascist Party was officially disbanded and Marshal Pietro Badoglio, who had been governor-general of Libya and viceroy of Ethiopia and had never been close to Mussolini, formed a temporary government of generals and civil servants.

Mussolini was hauled off to jail in an ambulance and thence to detention. But on September 12 he was rescued by a German commando unit from an isolated ski resort high in the Apennine mountains; eventually Hitler was to set him up as the leader of the puppet republic of Salò in the occupied north of Italy.

Badoglio ordered that the war should continue, while privately negotiating a separate peace with the Allies; the delay in coming to terms, however, was to cost Italy dear in human suffering. It was not until October 13, 1943, that Italy joined the Allies as a "co-belligerent" and declared war on Germany. In the meantime, German armies had poured into Italy, and on September 11 Rome came under German occupation. Field Marshal Albert Kesselring issued a proclamation to be posted on billboards around the city instituting martial law. Strikers, saboteurs, or snipers were to be shot immediately. Private correspondence was forbidden and telephone calls monitored. Pacelli found himself shouldering responsibility both for the universal Church and (in a direct and immediate sense) the citizens of Rome, including its ancient community of Jews.

Rome's Jewish community was the longest-surviving Diaspora in Western Europe, reaching back 2,082 years. Antedating the Christians in Rome, the Jews had been residents when Julius Caesar was assassinated; they had seen the decay of the Roman Empire, the sackings of the Visigoths, the pogroms of the Tridentine Church. They had been persecuted from generation to generation, but there had been great and saintly Popes who had loved and protected them as special members of an extended family.[1] In the seventh century, Gregory the Great thwarted attempts to ban the Jewish liturgy. In the twelfth century, Innocent III stopped enforced conversions and violation of Jewish burial grounds. In the eighteenth century, Benedict XIV denounced the Jewish blood libel. But no periodic kindness to this ancient community could eradicate the stains on Christian consciences down the centuries, including the legislation of the medieval Lateran Councils that had confiscated the Talmud and enforced yellow badges centuries before the Nazis had imposed the Yellow Star. Alexander VI had given the Jews of Spain hospitality in the city, but Paul IV in the sixteenth century had established the Roman ghetto. For more than two centuries thereafter, the Jews in Rome were ritually humiliated and degraded at the annual Carnival, until they escaped the ignominy by footing the entire bill for each year's festivities. Also in the sixteenth century, Gregory XIII instituted the enforced Christian sermons insulting Judaism. The practice was abolished by Pio Nono, along with the ghetto; but, as we have seen, he reestablished the ghetto after the collapse of the Roman Republic in 1849 when he made Jews underwrite the financial cost of his return to Rome. Through all these vicissitudes of two millennia, the Jews of Rome had never surrendered their faith or the practice of their liturgies and scriptures.

The number of Jews in central Rome at the time of the German occupation in 1943 was about seven thousand. The former ghetto, on the banks of the Tiber, was a pleasant enough place by the late 1930s, its disease-ridden tenements demolished or renovated, but the district was mainly inhabited by poor members of the Jewish community.

In the weeks between the German occupation and the roundup on October 16, there had been a clash of policy and sentiment between the president of the Jewish community, Ugo Foa, and the chief rabbi, Israel Zolli. The unflappable president, responsible for social and political decisions of the Roman Jews, counseled business as usual. Zolli was convinced that there was about to be a bloodbath, and urged that the community emigrate or disappear into hiding. Foa overruled him.

One man who happened to share, quite independently, the same concern as Zolli was Baron Ernst von Weizsäcker, formerly Ribbentrop's number two in the Foreign Ministry in Berlin, now recently appointed German ambassador to the Holy See (which indicated the importance Hitler attached to papal diplomacy). Weizsäcker's task, as the war entered this critical phase in Italy, was to encourage Pacelli to maintain the strict impartiality of the Holy See, which the Pontiff had performed admirably despite the many atrocities committed by the Nazi regime. Pacelli had already denied in the pages of *L'Osservatore* that the Vatican had had anything to do with the politicking surrounding the Italian armistice.[2]

Could the Vatican be persuaded to remain compliant? Weizsäcker informed the Pontiff that his government would honor the extra-territoriality of the Vatican and its 150 properties around the city.[3] In exchange, it was understood, the Holy See would cooperate with the occupying power. The linkage clearly involved an understanding that Pacelli would remain silent on Nazi misdeeds in its occupied territories, of which Rome was now one.

Weizsäcker, however, was convinced that the SS might soon inflict its worst on the Jews of Rome in the wake of occupation. He, in common with the Nazi occupying authorities, feared the deportation of Rome's Jews, since they were convinced that Pacelli's impartiality would come under unendurable strain and that any consequent move by the SS against the Vatican could prompt a popular uprising.

The Vatican had also anticipated trouble for the Jews and had increased its charitable activities, especially assistance with emigration. One of the more notable Jews who took advantage of help offered by Church agencies was Israel Zolli, along with his wife and daughter. They found sanctuary in the home of a Catholic family before eventually moving inside the Vatican, to the fury of Jewish community leaders who were to accuse Zolli of abandoning his people.

The Gold Ransom

The order to proceed with the deportation of the Jews of Rome had been received by SS Major Herbert Kappler from Himmler's office in Berlin in the second week of the occupation.[4] Kappler, however, had delayed, because he did not believe that a "Jewish question existed in Italy." That view was shared by Field Marshal Kesselring, commander in the Italian theater, who was reluctant to deploy troops for such a purpose. Kappler, meanwhile, had formulated his own policy—to hold on to the Jews of Rome so as to exploit them for espionage purposes, for example, penetration of "the international Jewish financial conspiracy"; and to use the threat of deportation to raise a ransom from the community. "It is your gold we want," he told Foa, "in order to provide new arms for our country. Within thirty-six hours you will have to pay fifty kilograms of gold."[5]

The gold collection began on September 27 at 11 A.M. in Rome's synagogue on the banks of the Tiber. The reception of the precious metal was being supervised by an accountant and three Jewish goldsmiths. By the afternoon, very few donors had come forward, although news of the crisis had spread throughout Rome with extraordinary rapidity.

The idea then arose that the Pope should be approached for help. An emissary was dispatched to speak with a religious superior at the

Convent of the Sacred Heart who had links with the Curia. Meanwhile, to speed things up, the Jewish leaders decided to take cash contributions in order to buy the necessary gold, which was now being enthusiastically offered for sale within the Christian community. Gradually, all manner of Romans came forward, both Christians and Jews, bringing their rings, jewelry, medals—not for sale, not as loans, but as gifts.[6]

At four o'clock that afternoon, word came from the Vatican. The Pope had authorized a loan. The priest at the Sacred Heart made it clear that the Vatican contribution was a loan and not a gift: "It is obvious," he said, "we want it back." There was no time limit on the repayment, however, nor was interest required. Did the Jews want ingots or coins? The Jewish leaders said that they thought they were going to reach their target without Vatican help.[7] The rumor nevertheless made the rounds, and persists to this day, that Pius XII had made a generous gesture, offering to make good the bulk of the ransom from sacred vessels hastily melted down. In the end, not an ounce of Vatican gold was donated or loaned.[8]

The gold ransom was paid in full and on time. It had to be weighed twice, because the Germans accused the Jews of cheating. No receipt was given for this prodigious fortune. Kappler sent a message, saying, "To the enemy who is being relieved of his arms, one does not give receipts."[9] The gold was dispatched to Berlin, where it was to stand untouched on the floor of a ministry office in cardboard boxes until after the war.

The Deportation

The man ultimately responsible for executing the deportation of Rome's Jews, despite the payment of the gold ransom, was Adolf Eichmann, chief of the Gestapo Section IVB4. At the Wannsee Conference in January 1942, an objective was proposed of 58,000 Italian Jews to be included in the eleven million Jews to be "handled." As of September 1943 not a single Jew had been deported from the Italian sphere of occupation in Yugoslavia, southeastern France, and Greece. As Jonathan Steinberg has shown in his study of the Holocaust and Fascist Italy, *All or Nothing*, it was not in the nature of Italians to countenance, or to collude in, the liquidation of the Jews; in fact, the overwhelming evidence is that they did all in their power to hamper and thwart the process.[10]

In the last week of September, Kappler informed Eichmann that there were not sufficient numbers of SS in Rome to achieve a roundup and that a violent reaction could be expected from the non-Jewish population. Eichmann, however, was determined to go ahead now that Rome was under German occupation. Leadership was needed, and this he provided in the person of SS Hauptsturmführer Theodor Dannecker, a "troubleshooter" in the matter of killing Jews.

Armed with a document providing him with the necessary authority, and accompanied by a group of fourteen officers and NCOs and thirty troops from a Waffen SS Death's Head formation, Dannecker took a train for Rome at the beginning of October. In the following week, the SS prepared to round up Rome's Jews, despite continued initiatives among German authorities in Rome to impede the plan. (One suggestion was that the Jewish community should be used for forced labor.)

At 5:30 A.M. on Saturday, October 16, Dannecker and 365 SS police and Waffen SS armed with submachine guns entered Rome's old ghetto area in open army trucks. It was dark and raining hard. The plan was to round up the first thousand and transport them to the Collegio Militare, situated between the Tiber and the Janiculum hill, not half a mile from St. Peter's Square. The idea, as in Paris, was to bring the Jews to a gathering point so that the task of entraining them would proceed smoothly after the arrests and checks had been made. Armed with names and addresses, which had been researched in the previous week, the officers and NCOs handed each head of household a document. It contained a list of what could be brought, including "food for eight days . . . money and jewelry . . . clothing, blankets, etc." Where Dannecker's crew found them, they pulled out the telephone wires.

Pacelli was one of the first to learn of the roundup. A young aristocrat well known to the Pontiff, Principessa Enza Pignatelli-Aragona, took a phone call from a friend who had seen the trucks parked along the Lungotevere. The princess hastened to the Vatican and was admitted by the *maestro di camera*. She says that she was immediately conducted to the Pope's private chapel, where she found him at prayer. When she informed him of the roundup, he made an agitated phone call to Cardinal Maglione to contact ambassador Weizsäcker.[11]

Meanwhile, the trucks filled with men, women, and children were finding their way through the heavy downpour, many with difficulty, to the bleak barracks of the Collegio Militare. Some trucks passed the boundary of St. Peter's Square, driven deliberately by that route, it has been said, so that the SS soldiers who had been drafted into Rome for the roundup could catch a glimpse of the famous church. The Jews, it has also been said, called out for the Pope to help them as they passed along the perimeter of the square. Eyewitness accounts are full of pathos. An Italian journalist reported: "The eyes of the children were dilated and unseeing. It seemed as if they were asking for an explanation for such terror and suffering."[12] In one street, three trucks with an exceptionally large number of children had come to a halt. The Marquise Fulvia Ripa di Meana passed through the street: "I saw in their terror-stricken eyes, in the faces grown pale as if with pain, and in their little quivering hands that clung to the sides of the truck, the maddening fear that had overtaken them."[13]

The scenes enacted that morning had been repeated countless times and in countless places throughout Europe in the previous two years. The difference was that in this city there was a man with a powerful voice, who commanded the allegiance of half a billion human beings and whose capacity to protest could give even Hitler serious pause for thought.

According to Weizsäcker, on that morning "pressure from all sides was building, calling for a demonstrative [papal] censure of the deportation of the Jews of Rome."[14] Much of that pressure was coming from the German authorities, notably the German consul in Rome, Albrecht von Kessel. Kessel urged Pacelli that day to make "an official protest."[15] The fear of the German leadership in Rome was that a deportation would spell a violent reaction from the Italian populace. In Kessel's view, if Pacelli were to protest immediately and achieve a successful outcome, the people would be pacified.

According to an autograph note made by Maglione on October 16, and published in the Vatican wartime documents, Weizsäcker presented himself at the Secretariat of State at an unspecified time, presumably in the morning. Maglione writes that he asked the ambassador to intervene on behalf of these unfortunate people for the sake of "humanity and Christian charity."[16]

Maglione's report is strangely ambiguous, generally casting himself in a favorable light, as one reluctant to make a formal protest, while omitting the details of Weizsäcker's conversation. As will be seen later, Weizsäcker evidently used this meeting to attempt to persuade the Cardinal Secretary of State to ask Pacelli to protest vigorously against the deportations. Maglione makes no reference to this. Weizsäcker, for obvious reasons, kept no record of the meeting, and he was at pains to impress on Maglione that their conversation was confidential and off the record, which Maglione acknowledges three times in his note.

Maglione quotes the ambassador as saying, after a long pause, "What will the Holy See do if these things continue?" Evidently the envoy was referring to the roundup.

Maglione's answer is equivocal: "I replied: The Holy See would not wish to be put in a situation where it was necessary to utter a word of disapproval."[17]

According to the cardinal, Weiszäcker now embarked on a series of vaguely flattering remarks, praising the Holy See for not having rocked the boat throughout the previous four years of the war. He ended by saying, although Maglione does not quote him directly, that the Holy See should consider whether it is worth "putting everything in danger just as the ship is reaching port." Then, once again, he begged the cardinal to treat what he had to say in greatest confidence.

Having reassured the ambassador, Maglione then made a second statement of historic significance: "I wanted to remind him that the Holy See had shown, as he himself had acknowledged, the greatest prudence in not giving the German people the least impression of having done, or wished to do, the least thing against the interest of Germany during this terrible war."[18]

Yet again, Maglione told the diplomat that he "had no wish to be put in a position where it was necessary to protest,"[19] but that if the Holy See were obliged to do it, he trusted the consequences to Divine Providence. Then, once more, he assured the ambassador that he would make no mention of their conversation, according to his express wishes.

Maglione thus leaves for posterity the claim that he had protested verbally against the roundup of Rome's Jews; but while he makes no mention of Weizsäcker's request for an official protest, the repeated references to confidentiality and his ambiguous references to not wishing to be pressed to protest, lend credence to the German version of events.

As it happened, neither Pacelli nor his Cardinal Secretary of State took initiatives to protest, in their own name or under the auspices of the Holy See, that day or subsequently. Their failure to speak or act astonished the German leadership in the city. Eventually, on the advice of the senior German authority, General Rainer Stahel, Pacelli sought the offices of Father Pankratius Pfeiffer, a German priest known for charitable works in Rome and one of Pacelli's personal liaisons with the Germans. The Pope gave Pfeiffer permission to speak in his name, but since Pfeiffer was of low rank in the clergy it was thought by the German leadership that a letter signed by a senior German prelate, a bishop, would be preferable. And so Bishop Alois Hudal, rector of the German Catholic church in Rome, Santa Maria dell'Anima, was called upon. Hudal was later to achieve fame as a key figure in assisting Nazi criminals to escape justice via Roman religious houses.[20]

Kessel and the German legation secretary, Gerhard Gumpert, sat down and dictated a letter addressed to General Stahel and simultaneously to Weizsäcker, as if it had been Bishop Hudal speaking in the name of Pius XII. Here was the first of two historic letters of protest on the morning of the roundup of the Jews of Rome:

> I must speak to you of a matter of great urgency. An authoritative Vatican dignitary, who is close to the Holy Father, has just told me that this morning a series of arrests of Jews of Italian nationality has been initiated. In the interests of the good relations that have existed until now between the Vatican and the high command of the German Armed Forces—and above all thanks to the political wisdom and magnanimity of Your Excellency, which will one day go down in the history of Rome—I earnestly request that you order the immediate suspension of these arrests both in Rome and its environs. Otherwise, I fear that the Pope will take a position in public as being against this action [*ich fürchte dass der Papst sonst öffentlich dagegen Stellung nehmen wird*], one which would undoubtedly be used by the anti-German propagandists as a weapon against us Germans.[21]

After many bureaucratic delays, the text of the letter was sent to Berlin, where it was received in the Foreign Office at 11:30 P.M. on Saturday evening. It was followed by a second letter, from Ambassador Weizsäcker:

> With regard to Bishop Hudal's letter (cf. the telegraphed report of October 16 from Rahn's office) I can confirm that this represents the Vatican's reaction to the deportation of the Jews of Rome. The Curia is especially upset considering that the action took place, in a manner of speaking, under the Pope's own windows. The reaction could be dampened somewhat if the Jews were to be employed in labor service here in Italy.
>
> Hostile circles in Rome are using this event as a means of pressuring the Vatican to drop its reserve. It is being said that when analogous incidents took place in French cities, the bishops there took a clear stand. Thus the Pope, as the supreme leader of the Church and as bishop of Rome, cannot but do the same. The Pope is also being compared with his predecessor, Pius XI, a man of more spontaneous temperament. Enemy propaganda abroad will certainly view this event in the same way, in order to disturb the friendly relations between the Curia and ourselves.[22]

The memorandum was not sent off until late on Sunday, and then as a night letter. Meanwhile, time was running out for the families incarcerated in the Collegio Militare.

Pacelli's Intransigence

As darkness fell on Saturday night, people began to arrive at the barracks gates on the Via della Lungara to leave food, clothing, letters, or simply to keep watch. There were family members and friends among the visitors, most of them pretending to be Christian friends or servants. They could not gain entrance and were eventually chased away. Conditions in the barracks were appalling, with no food, drink, or proper sanitary arrangements. A pregnant woman went into labor and was dragged out into the courtyard to give birth. The baby, like its mother, came under immediate arrest, and was to share her fate. When night fell, a platoon of SS men returned to some of the Jews' apartments armed with keys appropriated from their prisoners. On the pretext of fetching food and clothing, they plundered the homes of the prisoners for valuables.

Under pressure from the prisoners, Dannecker now scrutinized the documents of those who pleaded that they were not Jewish or who had non-Jewish spouses. The captain interviewed them individually. Thus 252 persons came to be released, a fact that gave rise to tales about the good offices of the Vatican. There is a story that a cardinal materialized at the Collegio Militare and pleaded with Dannecker on behalf of the Pope, and won reprieve for the 252. While the Vatican has never disowned the story, Robert Katz's research has conclusively discredited it. More than 1,060 remained within the barracks, listed for departure to Auschwitz.

On Sunday, October 17, news of the roundup was appearing in newspapers around the world, along with myths that would be perpetuated to this day. *The New York Times*, for example, carried a UPI dispatch datelined London reporting that the Pope had paid the ransom the Germans had demanded for the release of one hundred hostages. "The Germans, after receiving the gold, refused to release the hostages, however, and instead began a general round-up of Jews during which Italians helped hunted families to hide and escape."

Before dawn on Monday, October 18, 1943, the Jewish prisoners were ordered to get ready. The trucks drove them in relays to the rail yards close to the Tiburtina station, where a line of cattle cars waited on the siding. They were boarded sixty to a car. Inside, all was dark. Those arriving earliest were obliged to wait eight hours before the departure.

The deportation train set off at five minutes past two, crossing the Tiber and heading north. Not far from the city, the train was attacked by Allied aircraft. By nightfall, as the train climbed into the Apennines, the temperature dropped to below freezing. Cold, hunger, thirst, and a lack of toilet facilities combined the deportees' acute suffering with fear and humiliation. The cattle cars passed through Padua, and the diocesan bishop there told the Vatican that the Jews were in a pitiable condition. He pleaded with the Pope to take urgent action. Later, when the train reached Vienna, the Vatican was informed that the prisoners were begging for water.[23] At each step of the way, the Vatican was informed of the train's progress and its condition.

As the train continued northward on October 19, Pacelli's thoughts, however, were preoccupied not with the fate of the deportees, but with the impact of the Jewish roundup on the Communist partisans (the same fear, of course, was shared by the German masters in Rome and had been imparted to their colleagues in Berlin). Pacelli's fear of the "Communists"—this is how he habitually characterized the Italian partisans—far exceeded his empathy for the Jews on that day. Pacelli was anxious that the Nazi occupiers should increase their policing presence in the capital to thwart the eventuality of a "Communist" takeover. We know this because on October 18, the very day the Jews were entrained for the death camps, Pacelli had shared his anxieties with Harold Tittmann, the U.S. representative. Tittmann consequently cabled Washington, informing the State Department that the Pope was worried that "in the absence of sufficient police protection, irresponsible elements (he said it is known that little Communist bands are stationed in the environs of Rome at the present time) might commit violence in the city." According to Tittmann, Pacelli went on to say that the "Germans had respected the Vatican City and the Holy See's property in Rome and that the German General Officer Commanding in Rome (Stahel) seemed well disposed towards the Vatican." Tittmann informed Washington that Pacelli had added that "he was feeling restriction due to the 'abnormal situation.'"[24] The "abnormal situation" was the deportation of Rome's Jews.

Osborne also saw Pacelli that day and was assured that the Vatican had no complaints against the German army commander in the city, or against the police, who had respected the neutrality of the Vatican. Writing to London, Osborne reported that it was the opinion of "a number of people that [Pacelli] underestimated his own moral authority and the reluctant respect in which he was held by the Nazis because of the Catholic population of Germany." Osborne went on to say that he had urged Pacelli to bear that moral authority in mind, in case "in the course of coming events an occasion might arise for taking a strong line."[25]

Osborne wrote again to London on the deportation episode at the end of October. He had learned, he informed the Foreign Office, that, on hearing of the arrests, Cardinal Secretary of State Maglione sent for the German ambassador and formulated a protest. Weizsäcker, according to what Osborne was told by Maglione, took immediate action "with the result that large numbers were released." Osborne added that "Vatican intervention thus seems to have been effective in saving a larger number of these unfortunate people." Osborne then inquired of the Secretary of State whether he might report this act of Vatican courage and generosity, but he was asked to keep quiet about it. "[I] was told that I might do but strictly for your information," he told London, "and on no account for publicity since any publication of information would probably lead to renewed persecution."[26]

It was certainly the case that Maglione summoned Weizsäcker and protested verbally, making a note, as we saw earlier, of their conversation.[27] But he could take no credit for the release of the Jews as a result of that feeble protest. His assertion that this initiative had led to the release of many Jews was untruthful.

Five days after the train had set off from the Tiburtina station, the estimated 1,060 deportees had been gassed at Auschwitz and Birkenau; 149 men and 47 women were detained for slave labor. Only fifteen survived the war, all men except for one young woman, Settimia Spizzichino, who served as a human guinea pig in Dr. Mengele's experiments. When Bergen-Belsen, the camp to which she had been transferred, was liberated, she was found among a heap of corpses where she had been sleeping for two days.

The initiatives of Weizsäcker and others on behalf of Pacelli appeared to have halted the further persecution of Rome's Jews, but only temporarily. The remaining Fascists in Rome, working under the auspices of the Germans, rounded up a further 1,084 Jews, by individual arrests after October 16. The later victims were sent to Italian concentration camps and thence to Auschwitz, where few survived. To these numbers must be added the seventy Jews taken from Rome's prisons on March 24, 1944, who were executed along with 265 non-Jews by the Gestapo in the Ardeatine Caves massacre in reprisal for a partisan bombing of German troops in the Via Rasella in Rome.

An unspecified number of Rome's remaining Jews escaped arrest because they had gone into hiding in the Vatican-protected "extraterritorial" religious institutions in Rome, including Vatican City itself. Much of the work of protection was conducted by ordinary Italian religious and laity and was consistent with Italian hospitality and protection of the Jews throughout the Italian sphere of military occupation in the previous two years. But what of the 1,060 deported from beneath the shadow of the Vatican?

When the fate of the arrested Jews was sealed, and they were beyond the reach of help or rescue, an article appeared in *L'Osservatore Romano* for October 25–26, 1943. It is hard to imagine how the writer could have improved on this self-incensing exercise:

> The August Pontiff, as is well known ... has not desisted for one moment in employing all the means in his power to alleviate the suffering, which, whatever form it may take, is the consequence of this cruel conflagration.
>
> With the augment of so much evil, the universal and paternal charity of the Pontiff has become, it could be said, ever more active; it knows neither boundaries nor nationality, neither religion nor race.
>
> This manifold and ceaseless activity on the part of Pius XII has intensified even more in recent times in regard for the increased suffering of so many unfortunate people.

Weizsäcker read it and dispatched a translation to Berlin with a covering letter:

> The Pope, although under pressure from all sides, has not permitted himself to be pushed into a demonstrative censure of the deportation of the Jews of Rome. Although he must know that such an attitude will be used against him by our adversaries and will be exploited by Protestant circles in the Anglo-Saxon countries for the purpose of anti-Catholic propaganda, he has nonetheless done everything possible even in this delicate matter in order not to strain relations with the German government and the German authorities in Rome. As there apparently will be no further German action taken on the Jewish question here, it may be said that this matter, so unpleasant as it regards German-Vatican relations, has been liquidated.
>
> In any event, there is one definite sign of this from the

Vatican. *L'Osservatore Romano* of October 25–26 gives prominence to a semi-official communiqué on the loving-kindness
of the Pope, which is written in the typical roundabout and
muddled style of this Vatican newspaper, declaring that the
Pope bestows his fatherly care on all people without regard
to nationality, religion, and race. The manifold and growing
activities of Pius XII have in recent times further increased
because of the greater sufferings of so many unfortunate
people.

No objections need be raised against this statement, insofar as its text, a translation of which is enclosed, will be
understood by only a very few as alluding in any particular
way to the Jewish questions.[28]

The letter indicates the subtle double game that Weizsäcker had
played throughout the deportation episode. It was Weizsäcker who
helped stop further arrests of Jews by raising the threat of papal protests
that Pacelli had no intention of making. Now that no further arrests
were to come, he could speak complacently of the Pope's willingness to
remain silent. But what of the thousand who had died? Pacelli's decision
not to make a "demonstrative censure" on their behalf on October 16
had condemned them, and it was a decision that had less to do with fear
of greater reprisals than fear of the "Communists."

In Berlin a nameless official had underlined the significant phrases:

> Pope ... not ... *pushed into a demonstrative censure of the deportation of*
> *the Jews of Rome.... Done everything possible even in this delicate*
> *matter.... It may be said that this matter, so unpleasant as it regards*
> *German-Vatican relations, has been liquidated.*[29]

But how real had been the risk of an SS reprisal in response to a papal
"demonstrative" protest over the deportations of October 16? How feasible would it have been for the SS to enter the Vatican and to arrest the
Pope?

Hitler's Plan to Kidnap Pacelli

The occupying authorities in Rome were not the only Germans considering the consequences of a violent reprisal against the Vatican in the autumn of 1943. Hitler himself had been obliged to consider the issue as a result of his plan to capture Pacelli and bring him to Germany.

On July 26, 1943, Hitler notoriously remarked (in a rant at his headquarters): "I'd go straight into the Vatican. Do you think the Vatican impresses me? I couldn't care less.... We'll clear out that gang of swine.... Then we'll apologize for it afterward.... I couldn't care less." Firm evidence for the plan to kidnap Pacelli is in the keeping of the Jesuits responsible for the cause of Pacelli's beatification. It exists in the form of an affidavit made by the German officer assigned to the plan, General Karl Wolff. Wolff made his story available to Father Paul Molinari, S.I., with appropriate documentation, accompanied by a letter dated March 24, 1972, unpublished until now.[30]

In 1943 Karl Friedrich Otto Wolff, forty-three, was supreme commander of the SS and the German police in Italy. A few days after the occupation of Italy on September 9, Wolff was flown to the "Wolf's Lair," Hitler's headquarters in East Prussia, in order to discuss with the Führer the "occupation of the Vatican and the transfer of Pope Pius XII to Liechtenstein."[31] Wolff recalled that the Führer flew into a rage over what he referred to as "the treason of Badoglio" and uttered "dark threats" against Italy and the Vatican. Wolff recorded in writing the following conversation he had with Hitler:[32]

> HITLER: Now, Wolff, I have a special mission for you, with significance for the whole world, and it is a personal matter between you and me. You are never to speak of it with anyone without my permission, with the exception of the Supreme Commandant of the SS [Himmler], who is aware of everything. Do you understand.
>
> WOLFF: Understood, Führer!
>
> HITLER: I want you and your troops, while there is still a strong reaction in Germany to the Badoglio treachery, to occupy as soon as possible the Vatican and Vatican City, secure the archives and the art treasures, which have a unique value,

and transfer the Pope, together with the Curia, for their protection, so that they cannot fall into the hands of the Allies and exert a political influence. According to military and political developments it will be determined whether to bring him to Germany or place him in neutral Liechtenstein. How quickly could you prepare this operation?[33]

Wolff replied that he could not give an immediate answer because "SS units and police are already at full stretch." Hitler, according to Wolff, pulled a face of disappointment. He told the general that he would be patient, since he had need of every soldier on the southern front, and in any case, he wanted to use SS units for the task. Then he asked Wolff again, "How long before you could give me an assessment of the plan?" Wolff replied that, given the requirement to assess and secure the Vatican treasures, he did not see how he could come up with a plan in less than four to six weeks. To which Hitler said: "That's far too long. It's crucial that you let me know every two weeks how you are getting on. I should prefer to take over the Vatican immediately."

Wolff wrote that he sent in about six to eight personal reports in subsequent weeks, and spent the time making a detailed investigation of the state of security in Italy. At the beginning of December 1943, he went on, Hitler was again pressing him to produce his plan. At about this time, Wolff informed the tribunal, he asked Weizsäcker to put him in touch with somebody within the Vatican. The person chosen was the rector of the German College, the Jesuit Ivo Zeiger. "The purpose of my talks was to impede the deportation of the Pope and to assure the Holy Father that no harm would come to him."[34]

Early in December, anxious to know the state of preparations, Hitler summoned Wolff once more.

Wolff wrote that he told the Führer: "I've completed my preparations for the execution of your secret plan against the Vatican. May I make a brief observation about the situation on the ground in Italy before you issue your final order?"

Hitler told him to proceed.

Wolff gave an assessment of the state of allegiance and morale in the Italian population: the collapse of Fascist sympathy, war-weariness, hatred of the Duce, hostility toward the Germans, the destruction of the fabric of Italy, the mounting anger at the continuation of the war. Then he came to his most compelling argument:

"The only uncontested authority that remains in Italy is that of the Catholic Church, which remains firmly unassailed ["saldamente strutturata" in the Italian text of the Jesuit manuscript], and to which the women of Italy are deeply devoted, exerting, however indirectly, a huge influence that must not be underestimated despite the fact that many of their husbands, brothers and sons may not on the face of it seem particularly well disposed toward the clergy."

Wolff went on to tell the Führer that the Italian people would defend their Church at all costs. "In the past three months of my work in Italy, we have been careful not to treat the Italians harshly, and in consequence we have had the discreet support [appoggio discreto] of the clergy. Without the support of the Church, which has kept the masses quiet, I could not have done my job with such success." The tranquillity of the populace, he said, had aided the southern front and precluded the need to withdraw troops from the fighting.

Hitler thanked him, then asked him what his honest opinion was of the situation.

"Give up the Vatican project," Wolff told him, "which is born out of an understandable irritation with Badoglio's treachery. In my opinion an occupation of the Vatican and the deportation of the Pope would prompt an extreme negative reaction in Italy, and also on the part of German Catholics within the Fatherland and at the front, as well as among all Catholics in the rest of the world and in neutral states—reactions that outweigh any temporary advantage that will be gained by the political neutralization of the Vatican or the gain of Vatican booty."[35]

With this, Adolf Hitler acquiesced, and the kidnap plan was dropped.

All the facts indicate, therefore, that an attempt to invade the Vatican and its properties, or to seize the Pope in response to a papal protest, would have prompted a backlash throughout Italy that might have seriously hindered the Nazi war effort. And thus even Hitler came to acknowledge what Pacelli appeared to ignore: that the strongest social and political force in Italy in the autumn of 1943 was the Catholic Church, and that its scope for noncompliance and disruption was immense.

Pacelli's Liturgical Silence

In summary, the German occupiers had guaranteed the extraterritorial status of the Vatican and its religious houses around Rome, and the price of that advantage had been compliance and "noninterference"— silence about Nazi atrocities not only in Italy but everywhere else in occupied Europe. When the roundup began on October 16, the German occupation authorities were nevertheless convinced that Pacelli was bound to protest sooner or later. They believed that an immediate papal protest might work in their favor by forestalling the actual deportation and a spiral of post hoc papal protests and reprisals, culminating in an SS invasion of Vatican territory and a civilian backlash.

But Pacelli was not inclined to protest officially at any stage against the roundup and deportation of Rome's Jews. He was concerned, as he put it to Harold Tittmann, that a protest would prompt a clash with the SS that could benefit only the Communists. Pacelli's silence, in other words, was no act of pusillanimity or fear of the Germans. He wanted to maintain the Nazi-occupation status quo until such time as the city could be liberated by the Allies. Haunted by personal visions of Bolshevik atrocities from his past in Munich, perhaps, or by the appalling catalogue of violence perpetrated against the Church within the "Red Triangle" of Russia, Mexico, and Spain, he was prepared to countenance the deaths of a thousand Roman Jews to prevent the consequences of a Communist takeover in Rome.

There was, however, another, more profound failure in all this, that reveals a remarkable moral and spiritual dislocation in his papacy. Pacelli's reticence was not just a diplomatic silence in response to the political pressures of the moment; it was a stunning religious and liturgical silence. After the liberation of Rome, he is said to have hastened to the Jewish cemetery to pray there in private.[36] But there is no record of a single public prayer, no lighted votive candle, no psalm, no lamentation, no recital of the De profundis (as he had performed standing in the ruins of San Lorenzo), no Mass celebrated in solidarity with the Jews of Rome, either during their terrible ordeal or after their deaths. Nor has there been an adequate explanation, apology, or act of reparation to this day (despite John Paul II's initiatives in 1986 and 1998, discussed in the final chapter of this book). This spiritual and moral silence in the face of an atrocity committed at the heart of Christendom, in the shadow of the shrine of the first apostle, persists to this day, and implicates all Catholics. This liturgical silence proclaims that Pacelli had no genuine spiritual fellow feeling for the Jews of Rome who had been his neighbors from childhood. Believing, as Catholics do, that they are members of the Mystical Body of Christ, that the Eucharist makes the Church, they must know that what is done, and not done, in their name, especially by the successors to the apostles, affects them all.

How do Catholics come to terms with the fact that the bishop of Rome failed to make a single liturgical act for the deported Jews of the Eternal City? And yet, on learning of the death of Adolf Hitler, Adolf Bertram, by then cardinal archbishop of Berlin, in his own handwriting ordered all the parish priests of his archdiocese "to hold a solemn Requiem in memory of the Führer and all those members of the Wehrmacht who have fallen in the struggle for our German Fatherland, along with the sincerest prayers for Volk and Fatherland and for the future of the Catholic Church in Germany."[37]

Jewish Testimony

There were nevertheless Jews who gave Pacelli the benefit of the doubt, and who continue to do so. On Thursday, November 29, 1945, Pacelli met about eighty representatives of Jewish refugees from various concentration camps in Germany, who expressed "their great honor at being able to thank the Holy Father personally for his generosity toward those persecuted during the Nazi-Fascist period." One must respect a tribute made by people who had suffered persecution and survived. And we cannot belittle Pacelli's efforts on the level of charitable relief, or his encouragement of the work of countless Catholic religious and laypeople bringing comfort and safety to hundreds of thousands.

But by the same token, we must hear and respect the voice of Settimia Spizzichino, the sole Roman Jewish woman to have survived the deportation, who was found after having lain among a pile of dead bodies for two days and who then returned to Rome aged twenty-four, in 1945. Speaking in a BBC interview in 1995, she said: "I came back from Auschwitz on my own. I lost my mother, two sisters, a niece, and one brother.

Pius XII could have warned us about what was going to happen. We might have escaped from Rome and joined the partisans. He played right into the Germans' hands. It all happened right under his nose. But he was an anti-Semitic Pope, a pro-German Pope. He didn't take a single risk. And when they say the Pope is like Jesus Christ, it is not true. He did not save a single child. Nothing."[38]

We are obliged to accept that these contrasting views of Pacelli are not mutually exclusive.

It is a hard thing for a Catholic to accuse the Pope, the universal pastor, of acquiescing, for whatever reasons and in whatever state of conscience, in the plans of Hitler. But one of the greatest ironies of Pacelli's papacy centers specifically on his own pastoral self-image. At the beginning and end of his self-promoting film, *Pastor Angelicus* (Angelic Pastor), the camera focuses on the statue of the good shepherd in the Vatican gardens, the shepherd carrying the lost sheep upon his shoulders. The parable of the good shepherd in the Gospels tells of the pastor who so loves each of his sheep that he will do all, risk all, go to any pains, to save one member of his flock that is lost or in danger. To his everlasting shame, and to the shame of the Catholic Church, Pacelli disdained to recognize the Jews of Rome as members of his Roman flock.

18

Savior of Rome

While continuing their slow progress against the defending Germans in the south of Italy, the Allies established a beach landing south of Rome at Anzio on January 22, 1944, in the hope of opening a second front. Rumors were rife that the Germans would withdraw from Rome to fight the invaders in the hills to the north. Thus Pacelli again became anxious lest the Communist partisans, particularly strong around Rome, should stage a coup after the Germans left the city. The Allies, he insisted, must enter Rome as the Germans left. But he had another anxiety, which Francis d'Arcy Osborne imparted without comment to London on January 26:

> The Cardinal Secretary of State sent for me today to say that the Pope hoped that no Allied coloured troops would be among the small number that might be garrisoned at Rome after the occupation. He hastened to add that the Holy See did not draw the colour line but it was hoped that it would be found possible to meet the request.[1]

No further mention of the "colored troops" appears in Vatican documents or in British and American government archives. The *relator,* or biographer, of Pacelli's cause for beatification, Father Peter Gumpel, links Pacelli's request with the case of the "Black Shame" after the First

World War in Germany, when occupying black French troops were accused of rape and pillage by the German authorities. According to Gumpel, Pacelli was convinced that black troops were more prone to acts of rape than white troops; the Pontiff believed, moreover, that there had been evidence of just such atrocious behavior on the part of American blacks as the Allies proceeded northward through Italy.[2]

In the event, the Anzio beachhead faltered and failed to make progress; the Germans remained in the Eternal City while the Allies continued their slow grind forward from the south. The postponement of liberation gave rise to hardship and a sense of despair in Rome that winter. Gas, electricity, heating oil, and even drinkable water were in scarce supply. Above all, there were food shortages. Writing to Mrs. McEwan, Osborne described conditions in Rome as "a kind of dream bordering at times dangerously upon nightmare."[3] Food prices soared on the black market. Pacelli sanctioned the use of Vatican resources to alleviate the worst hit. Osborne told London that the Holy See was supplying 100,000 meals a day at one lira a head. Amid the hardships, there were deaths and injuries from Allied bombing. Then came a disaster that all Romans had dreaded, not least Pacelli.

On March 23 Communist partisans bombed a company of German soldiers as they marched down Via Rasella in Rome (many of the soldiers were middle-aged family men from the Alto Adige). Thirty-three men died. The next evening, on the orders of Hitler, 335 Italians, some seventy of them Jews, were rounded up, mainly from Rome's prisons, and murdered in reprisal by the Gestapo in the Ardeatine Caves south of the city. The entrances to the caves were sealed with dynamite.

Pacelli has been criticized for his failure to intervene to prevent the massacre; he was denounced by the partisans at the time, moreover, for failing to condemn the reprisal with a sufficient sense of outrage. His defenders reply, to this day, that he had no way of knowing about Hitler's order. At 10:15 on the morning after the bombing, however, an official from Rome's municipal government visited Cardinal Maglione. Maglione took notes of their conversation, recording the following item: "No reprisals are known about so far: but it is expected that for every German killed, there will be ten Italians executed."[4] That day L'Osservatore Romano, in its usual convoluted fashion, condemned acts of terrorism, referring to the Via Rasella bombing. In the afternoon a cardinal visiting

Regina Coeli prison was informed that prisoners had been taken away to be executed. He hastened to tell the Pope. Pacelli apparently covered his face with his hands and moaned: "It is not possible, I cannot believe it."[5]

It appears that Weizsäcker called Kesselring, the army commander-in-chief in Italy, to stop or to limit the expected reprisals. Defenders of Pacelli claim that the papal go-between with the Germans, Father Pankratius Pfeiffer, also attempted to plead with the German command.[6] On March 26 *L'Osservatore Romano* carried an article sympathizing with the German soldiers who had been killed, then expressed sorrow for "the 320 [*sic*] persons sacrificed for the guilty parties who escaped arrest." The Germans complained about this article, pointing out that the victims were in any case condemned to die (which was not true of all of them); but the partisans complained too, for the statement sympathized with the Nazi enemy occupiers while condemning those fighting for Italy's freedom.

Given Hitler's ferocious reaction to the Via Rasella bombing, and the speed with which the Führer demanded a reprisal, it is unlikely that any initiative taken by Pacelli would have achieved an effect. But the Pontiff had sent a signal to the partisans, if signal they needed, that he had no sympathy with their methods.

Liberation

Rome was liberated on June 4, 1944, and Pope Pius XII and St. Peter's Basilica and its square became a focus for jubilation for both Italians and the victorious Allied troops. In the final weeks before the German departure, Pacelli had at last succeeded in negotiating Rome's open city status, hence the Romans attributed to him the fact that the city had not been more extensively bombed and that there had been no destructive street-to-street fighting (such as Mussolini had urged over the radio from his puppet Salò Republic in the north). Pacelli was hailed on all sides as *defensor civitatis*, the savior of the city. He was acclaimed, as Carlo Falconi has put it, "as the most inspired moral prophet of victory." But the Communists had also emerged with much credit and a substantial following throughout Italy.

Liberation was not without its miseries. There were reprisals for collaboration; the chief of Regina Coeli prison was beaten to death with oars in the Tiber. Rabbi Israel Zolli, who had taken refuge in the Vatican and was to be Pacelli's greatest Jewish supporter in future years, was bitterly attacked by those who accused him of abandoning his duty. A street confrontation between Zolli and his Jewish antagonists was witnessed by the American correspondent Michael Stern:

> The lay head of the Jewish community came up to me. "This man deserted his people in the time of need," he said. "He is no longer our Rabbi." Rabbi Zolli looked pleadingly at me. "He knows that my name was on the top of the Gestapo list of Jews to be liquidated. Dead, what good would I have been to my people?" A new Rabbi was named for Rome's synagogue, but Zolli refused to leave. The fight did not end until Zolli, in one of Judaism's great scandals, converted to Catholicism.[7]

The cast of characters offered diplomatic protection by the Vatican was now reversed. The Slovakian minister, then the German and Japanese ambassadors, Weizsäcker and Harada, moved into the Vatican, taking the place of the British, the Americans, the Poles, and the rest. A number of British soldiers, mainly escaped prisoners of war who had been hiding in the Vatican or in pontifical buildings in the city, were replaced by German soldiers who had escaped from camps in southern Italy.

Pacelli granted many daily general audiences for troops and showed himself from the loggia of St. Peter's. Apart from the stance of the Communist partisans, there was no hint of criticism of him at this time, only congratulation and gratitude. Again, countless strangers came away with an impression of his remarkable charisma. The British novelist Evelyn Waugh, who was an army captain in Rome after the liberation, later wrote:

> All felt that they had been in personal contact with a man of the first importance, one of themselves yet quite unlike themselves. . . . I never heard anyone who had ever been in his presence speak cynically of Pius XII. That is the combination of human genius and Divine Grace.[8]

For a few weeks there was talk in Allied circles of returning the whole
of Rome to the papacy; of granting the Pope his own airport or at least
extending the territory of the Vatican. The Vatican aid organizations
were bringing food into Rome from various parts of Italy by motorboats
with the papal flag flying from their mastheads; there were murmurs
about the reappearance of a "papal fleet."[9] All such stories of a return of
papal temporal power were hollow.

As the war ground to an end, Pacelli was not consulted on the postwar settlement of Europe. But the great figures of the Western World
queued up to meet him, including Winston Churchill and Charles de
Gaulle. Harold Macmillan, a future prime minister of Britain, then the
Allies' chief political officer in Italy, has left a memorable account of his
audience. Pacelli, he wrote, seemed crestfallen, "with a bird-like mind
that flitted from one point to another." Macmillan "murmured encouraging little sentences as to a child," and found the Pope a "saintly man,
rather worried, obviously quite selfless and holy—at once a pathetic and
tremendous figure."[10]

Seemingly pathetic he may have seemed to one British visitor, but
Pacelli was at that very time in the process of assuming unprecedented
autocracy and exaltation. Not long after the liberation, Cardinal Secretary of State Maglione died and Pacelli took over his duties. There
was now no need to consult at any level. Pacelli told Tardini at this
time: "I don't want colleagues, but people who will obey!"[11] "Pius XII,"
wrote Tardini, "was the great Solitary.... Alone in his work, alone in his
struggle."[12]

This was the postwar routine. Pacelli entered his study at 8:50 A.M.
At one minute to nine precisely, he pressed the floor button with his
crimson-slippered foot to summon Tardini. At 9:14 A.M. Montini was
summoned, and he left fourteen minutes later. At 9:23 A.M. precisely, the
audiences of the day began. In the postwar years Pacelli was reluctant to
waste even a few seconds' time. Everything was done by the book and in
accordance with his rigid timetable.

At 6:30 P.M. the two deputies entered Pacelli's presence with documents and correspondence that required the papal signature. In the dia-
logues that took place, there must be no semblance of advice on the part
of the underlings; questions were not permitted.[13] Tardini testified that
if Pacelli did not like the way a document had been drafted he sent it

back without explanation. He declined to sign a document with even a minor error, including incorrect spacing at the beginning of a paragraph. The administration of the papal office was indicative of a remarkable absence of collegiality and consultation, although the Pontiff never lacked charm and striking humility. "One day Pacelli lost a book that he had need of instantly," a Vatican bureaucrat reported to the beatification tribunal. "He sent for his secretary, Father Hentrich, intimating that the underling had misplaced it. He shouted at him: 'I've looked everywhere and I've lost an enormous amount of time searching.'" Pacelli, according to the informant, was conscious, however, that Father Hentrich was mortified by these words, so he shortly went and found him in his office. Going down on his knees before the priest, Pacelli begged his underling's forgiveness for having offended him. Father Hentrich was so shocked that he burst into tears.[14] The incident did not mean that Pacelli had relented one iota in his scrupulosity over time-wasting, or that he discouraged groveling subservience toward his person on the part of Vatican bureaucrats. From this period onwards Vatican officials took telephone calls from Pacelli upon their knees.

Pacelli and the Hungarian Jews

In addition to immediate problems in Italy, a multitude of tasks relating to the war absorbed Pacelli's time. Following the Nazi occupation of Hungary in March 1944, Eichmann had taken personal charge of the "Final Solution" plan for the country's 750,000 Jews with the assistance of Hungary's three thousand police. Between March 23, when the new government under occupation was inaugurated, and May 15, when the mass deportations of Jews from the provinces began, the papal nuncio in Hungary, Angelo Rotta, had made frequent representations to cabinet ministers on behalf of the Jews. On May 15 Rotta submitted a note to the government condemning the treatment of the Jews: "The Office of the Apostolic Nuncio ... requests the Hungarian government once again not to continue its war against the Jews beyond the limits prescribed by the laws of nature and God's commandments, and to avoid any action against which the Holy See and the conscience of the entire Christian world would feel obliged to protest." According to a scholar of the Hungarian Jewish genocide, Randolph L. Braham, the note is of great importance in the annals of the Vatican because it was the first official protest against the deportation of the Jews lodged by a representative of the Pope.[15] The note was diplomatic in character, emphasizing, as another Holocaust scholar, Helen Fein, has pointed out, that "no representative of the Vatican ever publicly told Catholics that they must not cooperate because Germany was killing Jews systematically and totally, and killing Jews was a sin."[16]

Pacelli himself had been under pressure to denounce the deportation of Hungarian Jews ever since the Nazi occupation of that country. On March 24 the U.S. War Refugee Board pleaded with Pacelli via the apostolic delegate in Washington, D.C.; Harold Tittmann, the U.S. Vatican representative, begged Pacelli on May 26 to remind the Hungarian authorities of the moral implications of "mass murder of helpless men, women, and children"; there were pleas, too, from Jewish leaders in Palestine, via the apostolic delegate in Cairo, for the Pontiff to use "his great influence ... to prevent the diabolical plan to exterminate the Jews of Hungary."[17] Also in May 1944, two Slovak Jews escaped from Auschwitz and reported that the death camp was being prepared for Hungarian Jewry. The report eventually found its way into the hands of Monsignor Angelo Roncalli, papal nuncio in Istanbul, the future Pope John XXIII, and was thence passed to the Vatican and to President Roosevelt in Washington.

Late in June, the Swiss press began to report the horrors of the deportations of Jews from Hungary. On June 25 Pacelli at last cabled President Horthy of Hungary, asking him to "use all possible influence in order to stop the suffering and torments which countless people are undergoing simply because of their nationality or their race."[18] The next day President Roosevelt sent a message via Switzerland to the Hungarian government, demanding that it stop deportations of Jews immediately or suffer the consequences. On that same day, Horthy informed his crown council that "the cruelties of the deportations" were to be stopped immediately.[19] On July 1 Horthy cabled Pacelli confirming that he would do all in his power "to make prevail the demands of Christian humanitarian principles." The deportations, however, continued until July 9. By that date, however, most of the regions in Hungary had been made *judenrein*, free of Jews.[20] The hunting of Jews and deportations continued under the direction of Eichmann, but many thousands of Hungarian Jews remaining in Budapest were saved by special letters of accreditation supplied by the Holy See and the provision of hiding places in Catholic homes and religious houses. According to one testimony: "During the autumn and winter of 1944, there was practically no Catholic Church institution in Budapest where persecuted Jews did not find refuge."[21] All the same, Randolph L. Braham claims: "The success of Horthy's belated action is another piece of evidence demonstrating that the German demands of the Final Solution could have been refused or sabotaged even after the occupation. Had Horthy and the Hungarian authorities really been concerned with all their citizens of the Jewish faith, they could have refused to cooperate."[22] According to a study by Holocaust scholar David Cesarani, between May 15 and July 7, 437,000 Jews were rounded up and sent to the concentration and extermination camp complex at Auschwitz-Birkenau in Upper Silesia. Of the fraction selected for work, only a few thousand survived.[23]

Pacelli's initiatives in Hungary and elsewhere no doubt contributed to Catholic rescue efforts. But his protest was too late to prevent the nearly half-million Jews deported from the provinces. To the very end, moreover, he declined to name the Nazis or the Jews. Finally, it must be acknowledged that, along with Rotta the courageous nuncio, it was ordinary religious, clergy, and laypersons, acting alone or in small groups without Pacelli's encouragement, who were largely responsible for Catholic rescue efforts in the city of Budapest during the summer of 1944. An earlier protest from a higher authority, however, might have made a significant difference.

Pacelli Combats Italian Communism

The political situation in Italy overshadowed all of Pacelli's concerns in 1945. With the collapse of the Fascist movement, Italy found itself in search of a new social and political identity. Two leading, largely mythical models presented themselves to the Italian people. On the one hand there was the pro-Moscow Italian Communist Party, which hero-worshiped Stalin and saw itself as the true defender of social justice and the authentic victor over Fascism. On the other there was the allure of an

American-style free-enterprise democracy, extolling individualism, consumerism, and the American way of life. With the large number of U.S. troops in the country, Italy was flooded with American clothes, movies, popular music, beer, cigarettes, chewing gum, and Coca-Cola. *Reader's Digest* was distributed with U.S. government backing to half a million families in Italy.

Publicly disdaining these "foreign" models (the Communists above all), Pacelli was to urge a third option—the prospect of winning over Italians to Catholic renewal according to the Pontiff's vision of the Church. For Pacelli, the best of all possible worlds was the Spanish model of a seamless Catholic-corporatist state (that is, a leadership based on selection rather than election), a partnership between two sovereignties, the temporal and the spiritual, both Catholic and loyal to the Pontiff. Despite Franco's readiness to impose his will on the Church, Pacelli was to honor the Caudillo with the highest Vatican decoration, the Supreme Order of Christ.[24] Pilgrims sponsored by Franco would cry out in St. Peter's Square, "Spain for the Pope," and Pacelli would call back, "And the Pope for Spain."

But the complex situation in Italy following the demise of Fascism precluded any such dreams, despite the continued existence of the Lateran Treaty, which granted the Catholic Church a privileged position in the Italian constitution. Instead, Pacelli sought to manipulate the newly formed Christian Democrats, who, under the leadership of Alcide De Gasperi, became a rallying point against the Communists. The Christian Democrats were not a confessional Catholic party in the sense of the old Partito Popolare under Don Luigi Sturzo (disbanded at the urging of Pius XI in 1923) or the German Center Party (disbanded at the urging of Pacelli in 1933), but they were to thrive under Pacelli's auspices, the support of Catholic Action, the energies of the clergy and religious, and the formidable constituency of voters who feared the Communists.

In his Christmas broadcast in 1944, Pacelli grudgingly and guardedly gave democracy his blessing.[25] First he quoted his predecessor Leo XIII, conceding that the Catholic Church does not condemn "any of the various forms of government, provided they are in themselves adapted to secure the welfare of the citizens."[26] Then he pointed out the dangers of democracy as the mindless rule of the "masses," while declaring that democracy is unworkable without the auspices of the Catholic Church: "[The Church] communicates that supernatural strength of grace which is needed to implement the absolute order established by God, that order which is the ultimate foundation and guiding norm for every democracy." There were no Christian arguments here to underpin the ideal of cultural, religious, and political pluralism. No exploration of social Catholicism and the need for complex webs of communities to enrich the space between the state and the individual.

He ended his message with a word of special gratitude to the United States for "the vast work of assistance accomplished, despite extraordinary difficulties of transport."

Pacelli's lukewarm concession to democracy came not a moment too soon, for there were others like De Gasperi coming to the fore—Robert Schuman in France and Konrad Adenauer in Germany—who were to represent the ideals and aspirations of Christian democracy in the new Europe.

For Pacelli, democracy led either to the dubious values of the United States, which in many ways he deplored despite its useful wealth, or to the specter of socialism, which he deemed a precursor of Communism. The United States, he believed, stood for a dangerous relativism that entertained all manner of creeds, denominations, and affiliations, including Protestantism and freemasonry. America's unabashed materialism, in Pacelli's view, was a counterpart to the atheistic materialism of the Soviet Union. Pragmatically, however, the choice between the two great postwar blocs was between being for Communism or being against it. Separated from Yugoslavia by the short distance across the Adriatic Sea, Italy was in the front line of the East-West divide; the enemy was at the gate, and Pacelli feared an imminent Communist takeover of Italy followed by the martyrdom of the Catholic Church. He was therefore emphatically on the side of the West as the lesser of two evils, a fact that was to earn him the ironic title "Chaplain of the North Atlantic Alliance." He was not inclined to give the least concession to Italian Communists, despite the fact that Palmiro Togliatti, leader of the Italian Communist Party had renounced violence, publicly at least. The view in the Vatican, where events in Eastern Europe were being closely and anxiously monitored, was that the Communists said one thing when they were aspiring to power and did something quite different when they attained it. The same went for the socialists. Thus, after the formation of a postwar Italian Constituent Assembly, pending general elections (the monarchy had been dislodged by referendum, with Pacelli's wholehearted approval), a pragmatic alliance came into being between the United States, the Italian Christian Democrats, and Pope Pius XII—to prevent "the Cossacks and Stalin camping in St. Peter's Square," as the slogan went.

Convinced that the appeal of the Communists was a result of grassroots organizations, Pacelli enlisted the help of Luigi Gedda, who controlled the mass movement Catholic Action and was setting up Catholic electoral associations called *comitati civici* (civil committees) in emulation of Communist cells. Gedda had produced Pacelli's wartime propaganda film *Pastor Angelicus* and was thus an apt figure to work closely with the Pontiff and lead Catholic Action into counterpropaganda activities. The twenty thousand *comitati civici* became local recruiting agents for the Christian Democrats, and played a crucial role in the election campaign in 1948 after the Communists had been thrown out of the first coalition government.

The 1948 election, fought between the Christian Democrat coalition and the Popular Front of Communists and socialists, was characterized by Pacelli as a battle for "Christian Civilization." Pacelli provided 100 million lire from his personal bank, the Istituto per le Opere di Religione (established in 1942), a sum of money apparently raised from the sale of surplus U.S. war matériel and earmarked for the Vatican to spend on anti-Communist activities.[27] In the twelve months before the election on April 18, the United States poured $350 million into Italy for relief and political purposes. On the urging of Pacelli, Catholics were told that it was their "civic duty" to vote. Cardinal Tisserant declared that Communists and Socialists could not receive the sacraments; in fact, he said, they could not even receive Christian burial.[28]

Violence was anticipated in the run-up to the election, even civil war. Joseph Walshe, Irish ambassador to the Holy See, had an audience with Pacelli on February 26, 1948, seven weeks before the election, and found the Pontiff "looking very tired indeed and, for the first time, I saw him in a mood of deepest pessimism." Pacelli was "hunched up, almost physically overcome by the weight of his present burden ... the imminent danger to the Church in Italy and the whole of Western Europe."[29] He asked the diplomat, "If they have a majority, what can I do to govern the Church as Christ wants me to govern?"[30] Walshe suggested that if things went badly the Pontiff could always find a welcome in Ireland, whereupon Pacelli perked up: "My post is in Rome, and, if it be the will of the Divine Master, I am ready to be martyred for him in Rome."

The April 18 polling was conducted with maximum involvement of bishops, clergy, religious, and seminarians throughout Italy. The Christian Democrat slogan, which echoed Ignatius's *Spiritual Exercises*, was "Either for Christ or against Christ." Ildefonso Schuster, the austere cardinal archbishop of Milan, told the faithful that "the struggle between Satan and Christ and his Church has entered an acute phase of crisis."[31] On the eve of the election, the archbishop of Genoa, Giuseppe Siri, told his diocese that it was a "mortal sin" not to vote, that "voting Communist was not reconcilable with being a Catholic," and that confessors "should withdraw absolution from any who have failed to heed his instructions."[32] The United States forces made a show of strength, landing a consignment of tanks, destined for Greece, at Naples. Frank Sinatra, Bing Crosby, and Gary Cooper made special broadcasts to the Italian people, reminding movie fans that the outcome of the election spelled "the difference between freedom and slavery."

Pacelli's fears, as it turned out, were unfounded; the election result was a victory for the Christian Democrats, with 48.5 percent of the votes in a 90 percent turnout. The party would dominate Italian politics for the next thirty-five years. The Popular Front of Communists and socialists secured 31 percent of the poll. But the threat of violence remained in the air. After an unsuccessful assassination attempt on the Communist leader Togliatti in Sicily on July 14, the Communists called a general strike, prompting the U.S. embassy to pump funds, via Gedda, into the Catholic trade union organizations.[33]

Pacelli had won, but the Vatican was much out of pocket. There is evidence that in August 1948 Cardinal Francis Joseph Spellman went with a Vatican begging bowl to General George Marshall, initiator of the Marshall Plan to boost the economies and consolidate the anti-Soviet forces of Western Europe with a fund of $12 billion.[34] In the previous year, Pacelli had given the Marshall Plan his support by sanctioning a positive article in *L'Osservatore Romano*. A further supportive article appeared in *Quotidiano*, written by Montini, the Deputy Secretary of State.[35] According to Spellman's biographer, John Cooney, the American cardinal informed Pacelli in a secret memorandum that as a result of his meeting with Marshall the U.S. government had secretly "released large sums in 'black currency' in Italy to the Catholic Church.' "[36]

August 1948 was a period of mounting tension between the West and the Soviet bloc. The Berlin Airlift (counteracting the blocking of the overland route to the Western sectors) was under way, and a Third World War looked imminent against the background of America's burgeoning nuclear arsenal. Within a year the Soviet Union, too, would possess the atomic bomb, successfully achieving its first test in September of 1949. Pacelli had five years earlier uttered a warning against the destructive use of nuclear energy in an allocution to the Pontifical Academy of Science (a select group of international scientists honored and funded by the Holy See) two years before the atomic bomb was dropped on Hiroshima. On August 3, 1948, the House Committee on Un-American Activities called on Whittaker Chambers, a *Time* magazine editor, to testify on American officials who were known to be Communists: he named, among others, Alger Hiss, a former State Department official. This was the starting point of the witch-hunts for Communists led by Senator Joe McCarthy. The Knights of Columbus, an all-male Catholic association, collaborating with the "radio bishop" Fulton J. Sheen and Cardinal Spellman, supported McCarthy's anti-Communist crusade. The Knights raised "truth dollars" for Radio Free Europe and with Bishop Sheen sought funds for the Vatican. Through the 1950s an average of $12.5 million a year was raised in the United States for the Holy See.[37]

Meanwhile, a suggestion arose from an up-and-coming curial figure, Alfredo Ottaviani, backed by *Civiltà Cattolica*, that the Communist Party should be officially outlawed by the government in Italy. Pacelli's instincts were against it: "To take such action would encourage a revolution," he is credited with saying, "and would be inconceivable in the light of democratic procedures."[38] But he was prepared to do the next-best thing by issuing a decree on July 2, 1949, that it was not lawful for Catholics to subscribe as members of the Communist Party; it was not lawful to publish or write articles advocating Communism; and it was not lawful for priests to administer the sacraments to any who did either of the above.[39] The decree, pinned up in the confessionals of Italy, made it clear that one could not be a Catholic and a Communist, and the warning was directed toward not only Italians but the Catholics of Eastern Europe.

The decree did not prompt a collapse of the Communist Party in Italy, nor did it even affect the Communist vote in years to come, but it was arguably a sufficient moral deterrent to hold the line.

Catholicism in Eastern Europe

The unbearable weight of responsibility on Pacelli in the late 1940s, as described by Joseph Walshe, was in part due to the Pontiff's fear that Italy might suffer the devastation of a civil war similar to Spain's. At the same time, he was conscious of the fate of the Catholic Church in Eastern Europe under the heel of Stalin. The view from the apostolic palace of those countries with large Catholic populations—Poland, Slovakia, Lithuania, Hungary—was unrelievedly dark, exemplifying a likely future for the rest of Europe if Communism was not checked. By issuing the excommunication decree, Pacelli was declaring war on Communism wherever it flourished. That determination—later to be softened under Paul VI and his Cardinal Secretary of State, Agostino Casaroli—anticipated, and formed deep connections with, an equivalent intransigence, thirty years later, in the archbishop of Kraków, Karol Wojtyla, the future John Paul II.

Pacelli saw no possible accommodation with an ideology that systematically espoused and taught atheism, the dictatorship of the proletariat, class war, the abolition of private property (which for the modern Popes underpinned family values), an ideology that denied "the existence of the spiritual and immortal soul." The Communists' attitude toward Catholicism was no less hostile. In the eyes of the Eastern European Marxist governments, Catholicism was divisive; it encouraged idleness, bourgeois attitudes, and injustice. Catholics were accused of siding with the Nazis during the war. The vehemence with which Catholicism was attacked varied from country to country, ranging from low-level repression to show trials, imprisonment, torture, and murder. The overall policy, however, was to sweep the practice of religion out of sight, to ban religious education, to outlaw religious publishing and broadcasting, to hamper recruits to the priesthood. At the same time, education in schools positively expounded scientific materialism, ridiculed religious belief, and systematically taught atheism.

The Church was faced with an agonizing dilemma. Was it best to compromise with these regimes in order to maintain a structure with which to survive and hope for better days? Or was it best to resist, to speak out, to confront, risking annihilation? In Germany in the 1930s, Pacelli had made his choice when Hitler's party was still aspiring to power and might yet have been thwarted. Pacelli had led the Catholic Church in Germany into compromise from the very outset, assisting Hitler legally to dictatorship. In Eastern Europe in the late 1940s, the Marxist regimes were faits accomplis with the backing of the immense military and totalitarian might of the Soviet Union. Hope for better days seemed an impossible dream. This time, however, Pacelli supported unrelenting noncooperation in the face of Soviet Communism. There were no deals to be made.

The story of József Mindszenty of Hungary illustrates the difficult decisions that faced Pacelli as he contemplated Eastern Europe under Communism. It reveals, with the benefit of hindsight, the enduring moral power and reputation of those who chose to resist Communism on the score of its hostility to Christianity. In late 1945, Hungary went to the polls in a free election. A conservative democratic party won a majority and formed a government. Following a surge of inflation, however, the Communists staged a coup and instituted a reign of terror backed by the occupying Red Army. József Mindszenty had been made a bishop in March 1944 after the Nazis invaded Hungary. He openly condemned the Nazis who had thrown him in prison, then he condemned the Russian invaders because of their attacks on the Churches. Pacelli approved of the new bishop's outspoken stand. In October 1945 he appointed Mindszenty primate of all Hungary and asked him to come to Rome. The following month, Mindszenty traveled with difficulty to Bari and thence by bus to the Vatican. Pacelli, we are told, interrupted his Advent spiritual exercises to receive him.

Mindszenty wrote in his memoirs that he had "always esteemed Pius as a towering personality"; now he was able to see for himself "what a kindly Holy Father God had given us." Mindszenty told the Pontiff how glad he was that Rome had been spared the worst effects of the war, and Pacelli said, "You who have suffered so much still have the strength to rejoice at that?" At the end of the audience, Pacelli told Mindszenty that he was going to make him a cardinal.

The Hungarian primate, fifty-four years old, traveled to Rome once again in February of 1946 for the ceremony. As Pacelli placed the red hat on Mindszenty's head, he said: "Among the thirty-two [new cardinals] you will be the first to suffer the martyrdom whose symbol this red color is."[40] In contrast to his appeasement of the Nazis in Germany in the 1930s, Pacelli was now openly encouraging resistance unto death. With Pacelli's blessing, Mindszenty became a focus of opposition to the regime, making no distinction between religious and political Catholicism. Mindszenty condemned the Communist government as the worst in Hungary's history.

After a propaganda campaign against him in the government-controlled media, Mindszenty was arrested at Christmas 1948 on charges of collaboration with the Nazis, spying, treason, and currency fraud. None of the allegations was true. He was tortured mentally and physically, beaten daily with rubber truncheons until he signed a confession of sorts. On February 3, 1949, the show trial began. It was condemned by the United Nations and roundly and publicly condemned by Pacelli. The trumped-up proceedings, fully reported in the West, gripped and horrified Catholics the world over. Mindszenty, who had evidently been drugged (allegedly with "actedron," said to undermine "psychic resistance"), admitted all the charges and was sentenced to prison for life after a three-day court ordeal.

The week after the trial ended, Pacelli delivered an address to cardinals in the Vatican:

> We deem it especially our duty to brand as completely false the assertion made in the course of the trial that the whole question at issue was that this Apostolic See, in furtherance of a plan for political domination of the nations, gave instructions to oppose the Republic of Hungary and its rulers; thus, all responsibility would fall on the same Apostolic See. Everybody knows that the Catholic Church does not act through worldly motives, and that she accepts any and every form of civil government provided it be not inconsistent with divine and human rights. But when it does contradict these rights, the Bishops and the faithful themselves are bound by their own conscience to resist the unjust laws.[41]

These were fighting words, quite unlike anything he had addressed to the Catholic bishops and the faithful of Germany in the 1930s. But they had no effect on the Hungarian episcopate. Mindszenty's brother bishops, yielding on July 22, 1951, took an oath of loyalty to the regime in a blaze of media publicity. Hungarians who publicly professed their Catholicism faced dismissal; religious orders were disbanded and their members turned out of their monasteries and convents. The Catholic Church was given a subsidy from its own former funds. Catholic priests and laity known as "progressive Catholics" collaborated with the Communists. Neither Mindszenty in his prison nor Pacelli in Rome ceased to repudiate these accommodations. "At every juncture," wrote Mindszenty after his release, "[Pacelli] denounced the machinations of the communists and also those of the so-called 'progressive Catholics.'"[42]

Mindszenty was to languish in prison until October 1956, when he was released during the Hungarian anti-Communist revolution. He traveled to Budapest, where he was greeted as a hero, but he was obliged to escape into the American embassy when Russian tanks poured through the streets and surrounded the parliament building. Pacelli publicly condemned the crushing of the Hungarian uprising.

Mindszenty remained in the embassy in Budapest for the next fifteen years; the Hungarian government wanted him out of the country and offered deals for safe passage, but he rejected every opportunity to be brought back to Rome. In the end he became an embarrassment to the Holy See during those years when a new administration in the Vatican sought accommodation with the Communists in a policy known as *Ostpolitik*. Eventually, in 1971, Paul VI ordered Mindszenty to leave Budapest under an agreement with the Hungarian government. He took up his abode in a Hungarian seminary in Vienna, where he wrote his outspoken memoirs. Pope Paul VI advised him not to publish, fearing that the book would disturb the fine balance of relationships developing between the Vatican and the Eastern bloc countries. Mindszenty went ahead and published all the same. Agostino Casaroli, Paul VI's Cardinal Secretary of State, said that Mindszenty was "like granite, and he can be just as disagreeable as granite."[43]

19

Church Triumphant

Pacelli's hostility toward Communism did not indicate a softening toward diversity and decentralization in internal Church politics. On the contrary, the late 1940s and early 1950s saw a hardening of his ecclesial attitudes. He had a triumphant vision of the Church and papal authority; and the universal plaudits that he had attracted at the war's end seemed to confirm him in a sense of unerring certitude. His vision of the papacy, for all his personal humility and decency, was of unchallenged power, mystically bestowed by God, in what he deemed the interests of the survival and unity of the Catholic Church.

Robert Leiber, his assistant of forty years, strove to describe Pacelli's peculiar combination of instincts: "Because he was a realist, Pius XII had a clear sense of power. He thought little of plans, however idealistic, which lacked the backing of power.... His matter-of-factness did not mean, however, an absense of feeling. Pius XII was, on the contrary, extremely sensitive and understanding."[1]

Pacelli's triumphalism achieved remarkable physical and historical expression in 1950, when, following a tradition going back to 1300, he declared a Holy Year—a year in which many millions of pilgrims were encouraged to travel to the Eternal City from all over the world. The notion of holy years was borrowed from the Jews, who held such jubilees every half century; in the Catholic Church the frequency was increased to every twenty-five years. So many were the pilgrims that they were obliged to camp out on the hills around Rome. There was a *plenary indul-gence*, meaning a complete amnesty from time to be spent in Purgatory, for those who visited specified basilicas in the Eternal City; special trams were added to make these tours more convenient. Shops selling holy ob-jects included a mechanical plaster statue of Pacelli with an arm that automatically raised itself in a blessing. St. Peter's Square became an amphitheater for regular mass rallies and exhibitions of papal pomp and circumstance. Pacelli's liking for gymnastic and sports displays echoed demonstrations in Red Square in Moscow. The mammoth assemblies in St. Peter's Square of Catholic Action groups, moreover, had less to do with social and communitarian Catholicism than with exhibitions of loyalty to the cult of the papacy.

This external confirmation of monolithic, autocratic Catholicism was paralleled by a profound ideological reaction in the intellectual life of the Church. In 1943, in the depths of the war, Pacelli had published his encyclical *Divino afflante spiritu* (By the Inspiration of the Holy Spirit) on the study of Holy Scripture, to encourage modern methods in biblical scholarship and urging a return to biblical sources among theologians. Reputedly written by his confessor, the Jesuit Scripture scholar Agostino Bea, it appeared to signal a long-awaited rejection of the anti-Modernist campaign, a thawing of curial attitudes toward modern approaches to scriptural commentary. In 1947, moreover, Pacelli had published his en-cyclical *Mediator dei* (Mediator Between God and Men), heralding reforms in Roman Catholic liturgy, making it more relevant and accessible to the faithful. These two encyclicals seemed to indicate a much-needed en-couragement of creativity and openness in the Church, but they proved to be a false spring. In the light of Pacelli's subsequent hardening of atti-tudes, the writing of *Divino afflante* appears mysterious. In 1950, in the midst of the great Holy Year, Pacelli delivered an encyclical that froze creative scholarly endeavor and prompted an intellectual witch-hunt comparable to the anti-Modernist campaign in the first decade of the century. Aimed at combating new theological ideas, principally coming out of France and widely referred to as New Theology, Pacelli's ency-clical *Humani generis* (Of the Human Race) harked back to rigid prewar orthodoxies.

Issued on September 2, 1950,[2] the encyclical is carping and narrow. "Error and discord," he began, "is only to be expected outside the fold of Christ," for there we find the opinion propagated by Communists that the "world is in continual evolution." But there were, besides, according to the letter, a host of old philosophical errors masquerading under new guises, including "existentialism," which "concerns itself only with existence of individual things and neglects all consideration of their immutable essences." In addition, there was "a certain historicism" (a gibe at the emphasis given to history by the New Theology movement in France), which he placed alongside rationalism and pragmatism as the intellectual diseases of the times—modern intellectual attitudes that militated against the absolutes and immutable dogmas of the "magisterium" of Rome.

These errors, he insisted, could not be "properly treated unless they are rightly diagnosed." Even Catholic scholars, he went on, through an "imprudent zeal for souls," were being misled. There was a "reprehensible desire for novelty . . . and others more audacious were causing scandal to many, especially among the young clergy and to the detriment of ecclesiastical authority." There were scholars who questioned the literal truth of Holy Scripture, promoting a new "exegesis that they are pleased to call symbolic or spiritual"; others cast doubt on the original sin of Adam, suggesting that there were "many Adams" (a heresy known as "polygenism"). Worst of all, these Catholic scholars, thirsty for novelty, were espousing "dogmatic relativism," meaning that dogmas were good for their day, but in a constant state of decay.

Pacelli's remedy for these various diseases was a clarification of the Code of Canon Law, the manual of Church decrees that he himself had been responsible for drafting almost half a century earlier. "It is incumbent," he declared, quoting Canon 1324 (which conflates error and heresy), "to flee also those errors which more or less approach heresy, and accordingly 'to keep also the constitutions and decrees by which such evil opinions are proscribed and forbidden by the Holy See,' "[3] by which he meant documents such as papal encyclicals. Then came a dogmatic bombshell. The Pope's encyclicals, generally considered "ordinary teaching authority" and therefore not infallible, are in the future, he asserted, to be accepted without argument, even among competent theologians, when the Pope intends them to be definitive. Canon 1323 of the 1917 Code had prepared the way for such a view even though the First Vatican Council had made it abundantly clear that only "solemn definitions," dogmas made ex cathedra for the whole Church, were "irreformable." But any loopholes theologians might have thought available were now to be stitched up tightly:

> If the Supreme Pontiffs in their official documents purposely pass judgment on a matter up to that time under dispute, it is obvious that that matter, according to the mind and will of the same Pontiffs, cannot be any longer considered a question open to discussion among theologians.[4]

Pacelli was not bluntly stating that every encyclical or apostolic letter, or papal document, was in itself irreformable, but that it was a question of the language used within the encyclical. Hence, when the Pope deliberately stepped in, making it clear that he was settling an argument, there was to be no further discussion, even among those competent specialists who thought themselves qualified to enter into contention. In other words, he had introduced the notion of a kind of infallibility by the back door, or "creeping infallibility," as it was to be called later in the century.

The target of this extraordinary expansion of papal inerrancy was Pacelli's domineering response to new thinking, creating a reactionary circumstance reminiscent of the anti-Modernist campaign fifty years earlier. Just as scholars like Louis Duchesne and Alfred Loisy had prompted original and disturbing challenges to Rome's perception of Catholic orthodoxy in the first decade of the century, so French scholars in the postwar era had pressed for fresh directions in liturgy, Church history, Scripture, and theology, filling Pacelli and the Curia with dread.

The obligation for many thousands of French Catholic clergy to serve in the army during the First World War and to work in Nazi labor camps in the Second World War had prompted a widespread desire for a Church more relevant to the modern world. At the same time, a group of priests in France had started the worker-priest movement, an apostolate that penetrated the industrial realities of postwar France. Fearing that Rome was losing intellectual control of the New Theology and thus flirting with socialism and Communism, Pacelli disciplined the worker-priests and silenced the scholars by bringing pressure to bear, via the Holy Office (originally the Inquisition) under Cardinal Giuseppe Pizzardo, upon the bishops and the leaders of the religious orders.

Among the most distinguished victims of Pacelli's intellectual oppression of the 1950s was Pierre Teilhard de Chardin, the French Jesuit and paleontologist who had attempted to integrate biological and cosmological evolution and the theology of the Mystical Body. He was given the stark choice of being confined under strict surveillance in a rustic retreat house or being exiled to the United States. He chose to go to New York. All those who had been influenced by him were deprived of their teaching posts and relocated far from one another and their students.[5] Jesuits of liberal tendencies, including Henri de Lubac, whose work espoused social Catholicism, were removed in order to break up suspected cabals, and forbidden to teach or publish. Their books were proscribed. The American Jesuit Daniel Berrigan informed a journalist chronicling these events: "I saw at close hand intellectual excellence crushed in a wave of orthodoxy, like a big Stalinist purge. It hit me directly, it made me suffer deeply, it filled me with determination to carry on the work of the men who had been silenced."[6]

The other great intellectual order of the Church, the Dominicans, was similarly hit.[7] Father Emmanuel Suárez, master general of the Dominicans, had received a stream of complaints from Cardinal Pizzardo, including this: "You know well the new ideas and tendencies, not only exaggerated but even erroneous, that are developing in the realms of theology, canon law and society and that find a rather large resonance in certain orders. . . . This deplorable state of affairs cannot help but preoccupy the Holy See when it considers that the religious orders are forces upon which the Church can and must depend in a special way in this struggle against the enemies of truth."[8]

Eventually the very survival of the Dominican order in France was in doubt. Two of its famous "new theologians" were Fathers M.-D. Chenu and Yves Congar; they had considerable influence throughout the order and particularly among the younger religious. The priests were told that they must "give some satisfaction to the Holy See, signs of obedience and of discipline." Chenu had been singled out because he had written on the worker priest movement, encouraging priests to take employment in factories, join unions, and become political activists. Congar had encouraged ecumenism and Church reform. Rome blocked new editions of their works. Congar was ordered to stop publishing and was sent into exile in England.

The damage done by Pacelli to this generation of scholars, many of whom became advisers at the Second Vatican Council of the 1960s, was not just their loss of influence through teaching and publishing, but the frustration of their growth and development through peer-group interaction.

Equally tragic was Pacelli's oppression and eventual abolition of the worker-priests. The project had grown out of the conscription of clergy to work for German industry during the war, and a consequent report, known as *France, pays de Mission*, written by two young priests on the condition of the working classes in France. One of the movement's most stalwart supporters had been the cardinal archbishop of Paris, Emmanuel Suhard, who wrote in 1946 that "when I go out into the factory areas, my heart is torn apart with sorrow. . . . A wall separates the Church from the masses."[9] As a result, the Mission de Paris, a missionary program among the working classes of the capital, was established and various dioceses followed suit across France. Seminarians studied to become missionaries in the factories and workshops; young priests worked full shifts, living in the industrial districts and sharing the same conditions as their coworkers. Chenu had written background articles for them. He revealed how the mendicant religious orders in the Middle Ages had shown the way for the worker-priests. "Real evangelization develops into not just an institution or some people in an institution, but proper to the nature of the Church, a teaching, that is, a new way of thinking, of grounding theology, of explaining religion."[10]

The worker-priests became aware of Pacelli's displeasure as early as 1949, but they were still at that stage protected by many of the French bishops, who welcomed the movement's missionary enthusiasm and its identification with the needs and spiritual aspirations of working people. After 1950 pressure increased until, in 1953, a group of worker-priests operating from Paris was ordered to accept no further vocations. The same year, Cardinal Pizzardo told the hierarchy of France that seminarians should not work in mines or factories. Later that year, three French cardinals (Lienart, Gerlier, and Feltin) went humbly to Rome to seek a compromise. The result was surrender. They agreed that worker-priests should no longer live in the communities in which they worked but in priests' houses or religious communities; that they should do only part-time jobs, and that they should drop their union memberships.

The Dominicans were not so acquiescent, and it was their continuing defiance of Rome that led to the dismissal of three provincials (local heads of the order) in Paris, Toulouse, and Lyons. By January of 1954 the worker-priest movement had been banned. The bishops of France sent out a letter to all the working groups, ordering them under pain of excommunication to cease full-time work. They must abandon union membership, attach themselves to a religious community, and desist from forming groups.[11] Daniel Berrigan commented, "Our ice-box Pope, Pius XII, had the movement dissolved in one swift stroke, ordering every single worker-priest in France to report to his bishop."[12]

What was lost in this catastrophe was a yearning for a social, more pluralist Church that reached out to its separated brethren, that broke down the barriers between the sacred and profane, the clergy and laity, that recognized the importance of the apostolate to the workers. Above all, Pacelli's move against these stirrings within the Church was a stifling of love in the interests of conformity and power. The late Charles Davis, a distinguished Catholic theologian of this period in England, put it this way: "The constant frustration of dynamic movement towards truth prevents personal expansion and blocks the source of personal freedom. And all genuine love rests upon truth. Christian love is no exception."[13] The suppression of these pioneers was not without cost; many, like Davis, were to leave the priesthood and the Catholic Church, either then or later in the 1960s. For those who stayed, the influence of Pacelli's repression continued right into the sessions of the Second Vatican Council.

On June 3, 1951, Pacelli was carried in the gestatorial chair from the bronze doors to the steps of St. Peter's, where he read a homily preparatory to beatifying Pius X, the Pope of the anti-Modernist campaign, the Pope who had persecuted and silenced many hundreds of Catholic scholars in the first decade of the century. "If today the Church of God," Pacelli declared, "far from giving way before the forces which are the destroyers of its spiritual values, suffers, fights and advances for the divine truth, it is owing in great part to the far-seeing action and the sanctity of Pius X."

Pacelli's Mariology

For all his suppression of authentic creative theology, Pacelli did not lack an urgent sense of the Church's need for spiritual and liturgical renewal. He was to encourage, for example, practical alterations in the liturgy of Holy Week and the rules for fasting before Communion. His restoration of the Easter Vigil ceremony remains one of his most positive and enduring legacies. His institution of evening Mass made it easier for the working faithful to attend Mass on holidays of obligation, and arguably checked a greater exodus from the Church in the 1950s. But his attempts to revitalize Catholic spirituality focused on a hybrid of popular piety and the autocracy of the papal office. His devotion to the Virgin Mary, inculcated in his youth and maintained into adulthood with the daily recital of the Rosary and the twice-daily Angelus, now found grandiloquent amplification by means of papal dogma.

On November 1 of the Holy Year 1950, Pacelli came out on the loggia above St. Peter's Square and announced to the thunderous applause of a million-strong crowd that "the Immaculate Mother of God, Mary ever a Virgin, when the course of her life was run, was assumed in body and soul to heavenly glory." The formal definition of the dogma of the Assumption, entitled *Munificentissimus deus* (God the Most Generous),[14] was published three days later. It was the first (and remains to date the only) solemn and irreformable decree made by a pope according to the definition of infallibility at the First Vatican Council in 1870.

The dogma proclaimed that, befitting one born without stain of original sin, Mary's body did not corrupt and die to await the Resurrection but was taken, or *assumed,* in a state of glory straight into Heaven, where she sits enthroned as queen above all the angels and saints. This solemn statement drew on disputed early Christian tradition for which there is no Scriptural basis, but there can be no doubt that it was supported by the bishops, theologians, and faithful of the universal Catholic Church and that Pacelli kept well within the rules laid down at the First Vatican Council.

The dogma was fraught with significance. At the very heart of it was the triumph of an individual who had combined obedience and chastity to overcome time, corruption, and death. Thus the central metaphor emphasized an essential dualism: the corruptibility of time and sexual gratification; the incorruptibility of the realms of the spirit and chastity. In the text of the papal bull, Pacelli quoted an eighth-century Early Father of the Church, John Damascene: "There was need that the body of her who in childbirth had preserved her virginity intact, be preserved incorrupt after death." As with Pius IX, who had defined the dogma of the Immaculate Conception in 1854, the dogma of the Assumption lent exaltation to the Supreme Pontiff by association. It indicated, moreover, Pacelli's determination to invoke his infallibility more as a celebration of that power than as a reponse to a disputed issue of vital concern to the Church. There had, after all, been an approved cult of the Assumption since the early Christian Church, and Mary's feast day had been fixed on August 15 since time immemorial. But there was a sense of militancy and defiance about the timing of this dogmatic formulation. Ever since 1940, Generalissimo Franco had used the cult of the Assumption, associated in Spain with Mary's queenship of Heaven, as a rallying cry against Communism. The Assumption was central to Marian privileges extolled by various Spanish legionaries and armies of Mary. Holy pictures and medallions illustrating the Assumption mystery accompanied Francoist volunteers to the eastern front against the Red Army.

The dogma was doing something spectacular for Mary; it had the power to inspire and revitalize mass loyalty to her cult. At the same time, it inspired loyalty to the Pope and his unique power to bind or loose in Heaven and on earth. Unfortunately, it flew in the face of painful contemporaneous efforts toward Christian unity on behalf of Catholics, Protestants, and Orthodox. Protestants could not see that the tradition of the Assumption was on the same level as, for example, the doctrine of the Holy Trinity; and the Eastern Orthodox were unhappy with a development that appeared to deify Mary and separate her from the human race. According to one Protestant theologian, "Creation of a dogma of the Assumption [is] interpreted today in the midst of efforts at closer relationships between the churches as a fundamental veto on the part of the Roman Church."[15]

Pacelli's Marian fervor was confined and intensified at the time of the issuance of the dogma by a personal "mystical" experience. Walking in the Vatican gardens, he witnessed, he claimed, the phenomenon of the spinning sun associated with the "public miracle" of the visions of Our Lady of Fátima in 1917. This event, all the more strange in a Pope who eschewed the emotional and sentimental, was revealed by the papal legate Cardinal Federico Tedeschini (the official protector of the Spanish religious association Opus Dei) to an audience of a million pilgrims at Fátima the following year.[16]

The Assumption dogma, and the papal vision, anticipated the declaration of a Marian Year for 1954, prompting widespread "crusades" of Marian prayer, rallies, coronations of her statues, special Masses and dedications of her shrines, together with countless Marian apparitions and sightings. A Spanish Jesuit reported sourly that "gusts of apparitions are sweeping through the Eastern and Western peoples of Europe, and the marvellism has flown as far as America and Asia, where it has produced a no less splendid flowering of prodigies."[17] In the United States, Father Patrick Peyton's campaign aimed at encouraging the recital of the Rosary in the home was accompanied by the slogans "The family that prays together stays together" and "A world at prayer is a world at peace."

The vacuum created by the suppression of dynamic, creative theology in the postwar period was thus filled by Marianism, whose appeal was a popular combination of private devotion and exhibitions of mass loyalty and fervor. Its central ecclesiastical features were papal exaltation and triumphalism. The personal virtues it encouraged were discipline, obedience, humility, scrupulous chastity. Politically, Marian devotion was seen as a crucial weapon in the Cold War. At a "Rosary proclamation" in Cádiz in 1954, a Jesuit preacher declared that "the pacification of the Cold War" could be achieved only through "interviews of celestial diplomacy" conducted at Lourdes and Fátima.[18] The Fátima cult, with its dreaded Third Secret, continued to emphasize the threat of a Third World War "annihilating nations" if the faithful rejected the call to pray to the Mother of God. The first Soviet H-bomb was tested in 1953, making recourse to the Virgin Mary all the more urgent. In 1954 Franco talked to the Spanish nation about the threat of Soviet nuclear weapons: "With the hope that his hour does not come, we confide ourselves in full faith to the protection, which cannot fail us, of our holy patron and the intercession of the Immaculate Heart of Mary."[19]

Maria Goretti, Saint of Chastity

Pacelli's elevation of chastity to the highest throne of virtue had achieved remarkable expression during the Holy Year with the canonization of Maria Goretti on the evening of June 24, 1950, before the largest crowd ever assembled for such an event in St. Peter's Square. The ceremony was conducted on the steps outside the basilica and relayed by loudspeakers placed down the Via della Conciliazione all the way to the Castel Sant'Angelo. "Will you take her as an example?" Pacelli cried out. "Sì, sì," the multitude chanted.

Maria Goretti was the daughter of a peasant of the Roman Campagna. At the age of eleven, in 1902, she was the target of a sexual attack by Alessandro Serenelli, who lodged in the same house. He threatened her with death if she revealed the matter to her mother. Just five weeks after she made her First Communion, he ensnared her for a third time. As the story went, her refusal to give in to his sexual demands resulted in her murder. He stabbed her fourteen times in his rage. She lived just long enough to forgive him and to receive Holy Communion in her final moments. In his homily, Pacelli said that her canonization was earned by her readiness to shed her blood rather than besmirch her purity.[20] He inferred that to submit under threat was an imperfection. He was telling the youth of the world that they should be prepared to face martyrdom rather than acquiesce in order to save their lives in a sexual assault. The principle was enlarged upon by various pious commentators, including this from the *Concise Biographical Dictionary of the Saints*, published in 1958: "People like Maria Goretti . . . have an ever-present realization that lightly to surrender one's bodily integrity, even to the most compelling needs of the moment, upsets the whole rhythm of the universe." In the 1950s, Catholic classrooms throughout the world found a place of honor on the wall for a picture or statue of St. Maria Goretti.

In stark contrast with Pacelli's expectations for moral behavior in those guilty of participating in the mass killing of Jews during the war, he did not hesitate to counsel martyrdom for those whose sexual morality was being challenged.

20

Absolute Power

‿ᴡᴘ‿

By the mid-1950s, Pius XII ruled over a prodigious Church. Never in the history of the world had one man held sway over the compliant hearts and minds of so many. According to official Vatican figures, the number of practicing Catholics in 1958 stood at 509 million in a total global population of some two billion. Pius XII was at the center of a curial bureaucracy consisting of twenty departments. In the postwar era, the curial activities had proliferated rapidly, their outreach amplified by modern communications to a Church that was truly coextensive with the entire world: the annual "acts" of the Holy See, published in the *Acta Apostolicae Sedis*, had expanded from three hundred pages in 1945 to a thousand pages in 1953.

The role of the Pope was to teach and correct as the single voice of the Vicar of Christ on earth. His departments—the various congregations, tribunals, and offices—neither advised nor consulted with the Pontiff; they interpreted his mind and will and obeyed his explicit instructions.

The Holy Office kept watch on heresy and error, administering censorship. Its eyes and ears missed nothing, although its reactions were sometimes ludicrously delayed (the Catholic author Graham Greene was rebuked for "errors" in his novel *The Power and the Glory* noticed fourteen years after publication). The Congregation for the Propagation of the Faith managed the missionary activities of the Church to the ends of the earth; the Congregation of Rites imposed liturgical uniformity; the

Congregation for Seminaries and Universities supervised the curricula of
Catholic tertiary education and priestly formation. Congregations for
Clergy and Religious regulated the lives of some 400,000 diocesan
priests, a quarter-million ordained priests of religious orders, and a million nuns. Priests and nuns were obliged to live celibate and obedient
lives; during this era they generally kept to their vows, and absconding
clergy and nuns, or religious dispensed from their vows, were virtually
unheard of.

Nuns were still dressed, head to foot, in a hide-all habit; as well as
providing the Church with teachers and nurses, large numbers of them
performed menial tasks as cleaners and laundrywomen, frequently in the
service of priests. In the United States, one of the most rapidly expanding Catholic populations (26 million by 1950), there were 141,000
nuns working in 260 different orders.

At the very heart of the bureaucracy was the Congregation of the
Consistory, charged with vetting candidates for bishoprics. Only the
names of those who had shown strict obedience and reliability went forward to Rome. Every two years, nominations were sent via the apostolic
delegate or nuncio (the papal representative in each country) to the
Vatican, where they were further scrutinized by the congregation. Ultimately, only the Pope had the right to approve and appoint. And each
bishop in the world must then come to Rome to report to the Pontiff in
person every five years.

Pacelli nevertheless paid lip service to the idea of subsidiarity, expounded by Pius XI as the principle whereby higher institutions should
not take over what lower ones can perform by themselves. On December 20, 1946, Pacelli reiterated his predecessor's definition, adding:
"Such words are indeed enlightening: they apply not only to society, but
also to the life of the Church." Unfortunately his appeal to the principle
was exclusively in support of the importance of the individual against
the community.[1]

Meanwhile, Pacelli was arguably the most exalted autocrat in the world,
and yet his style of life remained simple, monklike, rigidly regulated. If he
showed signs of grandiosity it was in his tendency to expatiate on an ever-
expanding range of topics. So numerous and so beyond his competence
were these specialized talks, or "allocutions," that the practice seemed
symptomatic of ripening delusions of omniscience. He lectured visiting

groups on subjects such as dentistry, gymnastics, gynecology, aeronautics, cinematography, psychology, psychiatry, agriculture, plastic surgery, and the art of newscasting. Nor did he hesitate to make technical recommendations. A visitor to his study once remarked on the piles of fat manuals around his desk; Pacelli responded that he was preparing a talk on gas central heating. When T. S. Eliot, arguably the leading English-language poet and literary critic of his day, came to the Vatican for a private audience in 1948, Pacelli delivered him a lecture on literature.[2]

To source his huge circuit of seeming expertise, Pacelli kept an enormous library of technical works, encyclopedias, and compendia, numbering more than fifty thousand volumes. He was assisted in his researches by Father Hentrich and the ever-faithful Father Robert Leiber, as well as an impromptu band of willing Jesuits. A stickler for accuracy, he pressed these minions into service, checking and double-checking every reference and citation. He once told a monsignor: "The Pope has a duty to do everything better in every kind of fashion; for others it is possible to forgive their imperfections, but never the Pope. No!"[3] Leiber, who lived and worked at the Gregorian University, three miles from the Vatican, complained after Pacelli's death that he was expected to drop whatever he was doing to hasten to the Vatican when his Pontiff called. Although Leiber suffered from acute asthma, he was never offered the Pontiff's car but was obliged to struggle on and off trams through the busiest part of the city.

Pacelli wrote his talks in the small hours, drafting them in ink before typing them on a portable white typewriter. His obsession with tidiness was such that, according to his assistant secretary of the antechamber, he would stay up until two in the morning in order to return every document and book to its rightful place before he retired.[4] Tardini has left an acidulous impression of Pacelli's scrupulosity even when signing a document: "He carefully scrutinized the nib to make sure there was no tiny speck that might spoil the writing. If he saw anything of that nature, or just suspected it, he took a black pen wiper (always in the same place) and carefully polished the nib." So the ritual went on, the careful dipping of the nib in the inkpot, the great caution to prevent it from collecting too much ink and thus polluting the desk or the paper. "At last the Holy Father started writing his signature ... then he carefully wiped the nib with the same black cloth, and made sure that no trace of ink was left on it. ('Otherwise,' he used to observe, 'the nib will get rusty and cannot be used anymore.') Then he replaced the pen and the cloth in their proper places."[5]

Another indication of Pacelli's late panoptic tendencies was a desire to appear multilingual. In addition to Italian and Latin, he spoke French and English, and his German was reasonably fluent after thirteen years in that country. During his pontificate he reputedly added Spanish and Portuguese, then Danish, Dutch, Swedish, and Russian—but he liked to greet visitors from overseas in any and all languages. He had a large collection of grammars and dictionaries, which he constantly consulted. And yet Evelyn Waugh suspected, as had Bernard Wall, that Pacelli's English was poor. Waugh remarked in a letter to his wife: "The sad thing about the Pope is that he loves talking English and has learned several elegant little speeches by heart parrotwise and delivers them with practically no accent, but he does not understand a word of the language."[6] Pacelli was relieved when Waugh began to speak in French.

As the years passed, there was a growing atmosphere of staleness in the apostolic palace, and yet of underlying stress. Robert Leiber claimed in his memoir of Pacelli that the Pontiff's behavior was always marked by "sober matter-of-factness."[7] There is an impression of what spiritual writers once called *accidie*—aridity of spirit—which may have given rise to neurotic and sometimes even psychotic symptoms: multifarious phobias about his health and occasional visionary or hallucinatory episodes. Walking in the Vatican gardens, he had seen the sun spinning in a pyrotechnic display of different colors on October 30, 1950 (although his driver, Giovanni Stefanori, who was accompanying him, saw nothing);[8] on another occasion he believed that Jesus Christ had appeared to him in person in his bedroom. He spoke publicly of both these experiences, and they were reported in various newspapers around the world. But the "sober matter-of-factness" reasserted itself and before long he snappishly refused to discuss the subject of his visions when they were broached by pious visitors. There were signs, nevertheless, of his not being unduly troubled by the idea that he was destined for sainthood. The beatification testimonies speak of a miracle of healing being performed at his behest; as he was carried in his gestatorial chair he regularly swapped skullcaps with those bought by pilgrims from Gamarelli's, the clerical outfitters. Instant second-class relics!

After the war he regularly met with his nephew Carlo and with Count

Galeazzi, mainly about the running of the Vatican city-state. He liked talking with Monsignor Kaas, the blunt old chairman of the Center Party, who was probably the only person allowed to speak his mind in the papal presence, although never on religious matters.[9] After Kaas died in 1952 Pacelli's days were marked by gregarious solitude. Even his close and extended family saw him just once a year, on Christmas Day. It was a strictly managed affair. Promptly at four o'clock, three generations of Pacellis would troop into his study under the watchful eye of Mother Pasqualina. First he led the children to inspect the German crèche he had bought during his time in Munich; then he handed out presents and the nuns brought in cakes and hot chocolate. After entertaining the adults sitting in a circle in his study, he showed them the door and returned to his lonely, unvarying schedule.

It was said that Mother Pasqualina, the "cross he had to bear" (according to his younger sister), increasingly controlled his day and vetted access to his presence. She denied in her beatification testimony a rumor that she had once burst in on an audience with U.S. Secretary of State John Foster Dulles to inform the Pontiff that his soup was getting cold.[10] Such stories nevertheless were given credence down the years and have clearly worried the beatification tribunal.

As the 1950s wore on, there were indications of eccentricity. "Pope Pius XII had hands like lizards," the famous actor and film director Orson Welles told an informant. "They gave off almost a palpable vibration—he had such a strong papal personality! I had forty-five minutes alone with him. He held my hand and never let it go. There we sat alone, and he said, 'Is it true that Irene Dunne is contemplating divorce? What do you think of Ty Power's marriage coming up?' All the *hot stuff* from Hollywood is what we discussed."[11]

Pacelli seemed to trust the future generation less and less. As we have seen, he refused to appoint a new Cardinal Secretary of State, preferring to add the job to his other great burdens. Tardini revealed in his memoir of Pius that the Pontiff disliked making appointments and promotions. He held only two consistories for the creation of new cardinals, in 1946 and 1953. Under pressure from the Americans he made the postwar selection of cardinals, thirty-two in all, more international than ever before in the history of the Sacred College. In the second consistory, he restored the balance, appointing ten new Italian cardinals out of twenty-four, most of the Italians destined for the Curia, the Vatican bureaucracy.

He rarely held regular audiences for the department heads of the Curia. This accentuated his lofty isolation, but it also gave a freer hand to the strong members of the Curia. The victims were the dioscesan bishops, who were, as Falconi has put it, "ignored by the Pope and humiliated by the [curial] departments." This accentuation of a division of command at the apex of the Church led to the neglect of the ordinary clergy, their education, their welfare, their growing problems in the face of a rapidly changing world.

In October 1954 he expelled, in a promotion-demotion, his once-beloved Giovanni Montini, sending him up to the awkward, over-populated archdiocese of Milan with no hope of getting a cardinal's hat. It has been suggested that Montini, the future Pope Paul VI, had offended Pacelli by exposing irregularities at the Vatican Bank, now run by two of Pacelli's nephews; more to the point, enemies within the Curia thought that Montini was getting soft on socialism.[12]

The older Pacelli got, the narrower he became in outlook. In 1952 he had complained about the Miss Europe and Miss Italy beauty competitions.[13] He thought they were lewd and wanted such contests banned. As the years passed, he constantly inveighed against jazz and films with overt sexual content. According to beatification testimony he asked press correspondents to desist from writing that he had "caressed" the heads of children. He wanted them to write that he had "placed his hand" on a child: "It is an evil world," he explained. He refused to sanction the cause of a candidate for beatification because the "Servant of God" was a smoker; in another instance he rejected a candidate who had been known to utter an "obscene word."[14] He asked Monsignor Kaas, in charge of the fabric of St. Peter's, to cover up nude statues and pictures in the basilica. He made it known, moreover, that he did not approve of priests leading groups of single young women on pilgrimage to Rome: such pastoral activity constituted, in his view, an occasion of sin.[15] Then there was his campaign against cigarette-smoking Jesuits. Ever since the war, he had paid for the tobacco bills of the Jesuit fathers at the Gregorian University in recognition of the research services they rendered. But on checking the expenditure one year in the mid-1950s, he was appalled at the amount of tobacco they consumed and commanded all members of the society throughout the world to henceforth refrain from smoking: surely, he told them, it ill accorded with holy poverty. The Jesuits, who were enthusiastic smokers, lost no time in applying Jesuitical casuistry to the situation and continued to smoke as was their wont.[16]

Pacelli had yielded little or nothing to the liberation of women in the Church. The stipulation that "the female person may not approach the altar under any circumstances, and may only respond from afar"[17] still held, although he grudgingly allowed that female choristers could legitimately sing in church, although not within the altar precincts.[18]

As for contemporary issues of sexual morality, it fell to Pacelli's lot to ponder and pronounce on pharmacological developments that anticipated the birth control pill. His verdict was to constrain Paul VI, twenty years later, to a final condemnation of the pill in the encyclical *Humanae vitae*.

Pacelli's predecessor, Pius XI, had in the early 1930s guardedly sanctioned the use of the so-called rhythm method by which couples took advantage of infertile periods to have sex without the risk of pregnancy. From this point began the tyranny of charts and temperature-taking that marked the sexual lives of countless millions of Catholic couples attempting to avoid (often unsuccessfully) unwanted pregnancies, and mortal sin. In 1934, however, biologists had isolated the natural hormone progesterone (associated with the onset of ovulation) and a devout American Catholic pharmacologist, John Rock, began research on the therapeutic possibilities of regulating ovulation for women experiencing difficulty in becoming pregnant. By the 1950s, Rock became more interested in progesterone as a means of *preventing* pregnancy, arguing that the potential effect was the same as that of the body's endocrine system and therefore "natural." In 1955 Rock and colleagues mounted a clinical trial in Puerto Rico that proved successful.[19] Pacelli thus came under increasing pressure to pronounce.

On September 12, 1958, a month before his death, Pacelli issued a verdict on an extreme case so as to settle all further arguments. The question was whether it was permissible to use progesterone therapy to prevent ovulation (before the mass manufacture of the handy pill itself) if a woman knows that any pregnancy she is otherwise likely to have will not come to term. Pacelli asserted that "direct and impermissible sterilization is induced if ovulation is prevented in order to preserve the organism from the consequences of a pregnancy which it cannot consummate."[20]

Thus, as the feminist theologian Uta Ranke-Heinemann interprets the matter: "Nature's generative intention must on no account be thwarted even when nature cannot accomplish that intention and the woman dies in pregnancy."[21] Underpinning the pronouncement, however, was the traditionalist viewpoint, already confirmed by Pius XI in his encyclical *Casti connubii* (1930), which asserts that individuals may not enjoy the pleasures of sex without "cooperating" fully in its divine procreative purpose.

Hypochondria

In the mid- to late 1950s, despite a pervasive sense of puritanical oppression, the atmosphere in the Vatican proved less than morally bracing and psychologically healthy. There was a noisome scandal in 1954 when Prince Filippo Orsini, who enjoyed the prestige of being an "assistant to the papal throne," cut his wrists as a result of the breakup of his love affair with the English actress Belinda Lee. The Vatican conspired with the prince's wife to have him committed to a mental hospital and he was naturally deprived of his special "papal throne" status, but the impression of something rotten lingered in the apostolic palace.[22]

Ever more fastidious and hypochondriacal, Pacelli became convinced that he was seriously ill, although the pattern of his ailments suggests a psychosomatic disorder. His relations with his personal physician, the eye doctor Professor Ricardo Galeazzi-Lisi, half-brother to Count Galeazzi, became significant. Galeazzi-Lisi had been Pacelli's personal doctor since the late 1930s. As Cardinal Secretary of State, Pacelli had consulted him about new eyeglasses and had been sufficiently impressed with his medical knowledge to appoint him official papal doctor, or Archiatra. In the view of many, Galeazzi-Lisi was a quack, and there were frequent recommendations within the Curia that he be removed; but, as the beatification depositions show, and especially the testimony of Pacelli's younger sister, the eye doctor was protected by Mother Pasqualina, who thought him perfect for the Pontiff. Galeazzi-Lisi's combination of ignorance, neglect, and bizarre recommendations was to have repercussions for Pacelli's long-term health prospects.

According to his nephew, Prince Carlo Pacelli,[23] the Pontiff frequently had recourse to dental specialists, fearing that the loss of his teeth might result in even poorer digestion and degeneration of his diction, so crucial for all those allocutions in various languages. Pacelli was convinced that his gums were going soft and could not be reassured by the appropriate specialists. On Galeazzi-Lisi's recommendation he consulted an obscure Roman dentist who prescribed chromic acid, used in the tanning of hides. In time he was to swallow sufficient quantities of the substance to cause the esophageal complications that probably led to the extended bouts of hiccups that plagued him day and night and eventually became chronic. The Vatican received many hundreds of thousands of letters from children the world over offering their prayers and remedies for the hiccups.[24]

In October 1953, he fell ill from an unspecified combination of complaints. At a loss for diagnosis, Galeazzi-Lisi proposed a solution fashionable in those days among film stars and narcissistic world leaders. He called for the Swiss practitioner Paul Niehans, who had invented a so-called cellular therapy. The treatment, usually performed at his clinic above Lake Geneva but in this instance conducted at the Vatican, involved injecting under the skin of the patient the "living" cells of the fetuses of sheep and monkeys, favoring cells from the front part of the fetal brain. Niehans claimed that his therapy was a cure-all, citing benefits for cirrhosis, nephritis, cancer, and sexual deficiency.[25] Niehans also claimed that his treatment reversed the aging process. Fortunately for Niehans's reputation in the Vatican, there were no harmful effects, and Pacelli improved naturally and went back to work—only to have a relapse in November 1954; whereupon Niehans was called once more and administered another round of injections.[26]

In 1956 Galeazzi-Lisi was dismissed as Archiatra. There had been talk of gambling debts and a "change of personality";[27] he was replaced by a Dr. Antonio Gasbarrini. The eye doctor nevertheless continued to haunt the Vatican and would show up at public audiences.

In the autumn of 1958, Pacelli was again racked with hiccups. On October 5, 1958, the actor Alec Guinness attended an audience at the papal summer residence at Castel Gandolfo for a group of plastic surgeons. Pacelli gave his customary expert advice, punctuated by hiccups. "We sat on gilded chairs facing His Holiness, who looked pale and drawn."

When the Pope came down from his podium to bless them, Guinness recorded this exchange between the Pontiff and the couple next to him:

> The man burst into loud sobs. . . . "He's so moved, Your Holiness," [his wife] said. "And just think, Your Holiness— we've come all the way from Michigan!" The Pope mastered a hiccup . . . "I know Michigan," the Pope said, and managing to free himself from the plastic surgeon's grip he raised a hand in blessing: "A special blessing on Michigan!"[28]

Guinness speculates that these were probably the last words of English Pacelli spoke. The entourage sped him away from the audience chamber, the papal doctor following, glowering at each of the "plastic surgeons" in turn, but particularly at Alec Guinness.

Death and Burial of Pius XII

Two days after the plastic surgeons' audience, on October 6, 1958, Pacelli took to his bed, ill. At 12:30 that evening, Father Hentrich, the papal secretary, was called to the Pontiff's bedside. "He showed me a little Spanish volume of the *Spiritual Exercises* and said over and over again with tears: 'This week I have read all the time in this book and constantly recited the prayer "Anima Christi" [Soul of Christ].' "

The following day his condition worsened. There were at least three papal doctors on hand, and the dismissed Galeazzi-Lisi also managed to insinuate himself into the sickroom, carrying a camera. Paul Niehans rushed from Switzerland to the bedside, but did not administer cellular therapy.

Pacelli's three nuns hovered over the dying Pontiff. Monsignor Tardini said Mass and administered the last rites in the presence of Father Leiber. At one point in his death agony he seemed to rally. He called out: "To work! Files! Documents! To work!"

At ten minutes to four on the morning of Thursday, October 9, Dr. Gasbarrini declared the Pontiff dead of a "circulatory phenomenon." Soon after, he was confirmed dead by the *Camerlengo* of the Holy Roman Church, Cardinal Tisserant, who from this point had charge of the corpse and the arrangements for the funeral and burial. It was Tisserant who had voted to the last against Pacelli in the conclave in 1939, convinced that he was the wrong choice. As he gazed on the dead Pontiff, he may well have considered himself vindicated.

The next evening Pacelli's body was driven in a motorized hearse to the church of St. John Lateran in Rome, crowds of mourners lining the full extent of the route. The future John XXIII, Angelo Giuseppe Roncalli, watching the journey on Italian television in Venice, speculated in his diary whether any Roman emperor had enjoyed such a triumph. The people of Rome, he reflected, were honoring not the passing of a mere temporal ruler but the embodiment of "spiritual majesty and religious dignity."[29]

In the hours following Pacelli's death, there were abundant tributes from Western statesmen. Harold Macmillan, Britain's Conservative prime minister, said: "The world is poorer by the loss of a man who has played so great a role in the defence of spiritual values and in work for peace." President Eisenhower said: "His was a life full of devotion to God and service to his fellowmen. . . . [He] was an informed and articulate foe of tyranny." Both Macmillan and Eisenhower knew Pacelli personally as well as publicly. Golda Meir, Israel's foreign minister, wrote: "When fearful martyrdom came to our people in the decade of Nazi terror, the voice of the Pope was raised for the victims. The life of our times was enriched by a voice speaking out on the great moral truths above the tumult of daily conflict. We mourn a great servant of peace."[30]

At dusk, to the somber clash of bells in a hundred campaniles across the Eternal City, the body was again transported by motorized hearse, followed by processions of clerics and nuns reciting the Rosary, through the streets, past the Colosseum, over the Tiber, to St. Peter's Basilica. The pavements were lined with hundreds of thousands of silent Romans who blessed themselves as the coffin passed. During the lying-in-state in St. Peter's over the next three days and nights, it was estimated that more than five hundred people per minute passed rapidly in two files, five deep, past the exposed body. According to one account, his corpse was viewed by more than a million people before his requiem Mass on Monday the thirteenth.[31]

L'Osservatore Romano described his funeral as the "greatest in the long history of Rome, surpassing even that of Julius Caesar." The body lay on a catafalque beneath the great Bernini baldachino; to the right were the three coffins in which his body would be placed. Inferring that Pacelli was already enjoying the beatific vision, the Pope's secretary for briefs, Monsignor Antonio Bacci, said in his eulogy: "With his death a great light went out on earth, and a new star lit in heaven." The requiem Mass was televised and relayed live by the Eurovision link throughout the continent. The BBC's Richard Dimbleby, doyen of great-events broadcasters, somberly conducted the commentary in English. The cameras discreetly shifted their focus away as the body was laid within the first casket; the face was covered with white silk, then the entire corpse wrapped in a crimson shroud. The eulogy was placed in a brass tube alongside a purse containing gold, silver, and bronze coins minted during his pontificate, then this inner coffin was secured with silk ribbons attached with seals before being placed in the protective case of lead. The outer elm coffin was now secured with golden nails, and the huge weight of the triple coffin was finally wheeled before the high altar and lowered on pulleys from a scaffold into the grottoes below, where it came to rest just twenty feet from the tomb of St. Peter.

So passed one of the most remarkable pontiffs in the history of the papacy, his memory fragrant with esteem. Such was the reverential self-censorship surrounding his name and pontificate that it was to take several years for more candid accounts of the death and obsequies to reach a wider public. His death agony, for instance, had been photographed by his former doctor, Galeazzi-Lisi, and the pictures offered to various magazines. The good doctor, moreover, had taken charge of the embalming, experimenting with a new method and leaving the intestines in place; in consequence, the corpse began to rot immediately in the autumn heat. As the hearse paused outside St. John Lateran, a series of dreadful farts and eructations was heard to issue from the coffin, a result, apparently, of rapid fermentation. During the lying-in-state in St. Peter's, the dead Pope's face turned gray-green and then purple, and the stench was so overpowering that one of the attendant guards fainted. A final indignity, his nose went black and fell off before interment.[32]

In years to come, critics of his reign were to dwell on these insalubrious circumstances, as if to exemplify the corrupt finale of the most absolutist papacy in modern history. In time, however, there were other issues, of commission and omission, more shameful, more damaging to his memory and the institution of the papacy than anyone had thought credible during his lifetime.

The first words of his personal testament read:

> *Have pity on me, Lord, according to thy mercy; knowledge of the deficiencies, failures, sins committed during so long a pontificate and in so grave an epoch has made clearer to me my inadequacies and unworthiness. I humbly ask pardon of all I have offended, harmed and scandalized.*

21

Pius XII Redivivus

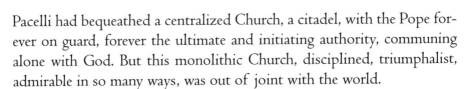

Pacelli had bequeathed a centralized Church, a citadel, with the Pope forever on guard, forever the ultimate and initiating authority, communing
alone with God. But this monolithic Church, disciplined, triumphalist,
admirable in so many ways, was out of joint with the world.

Pacelli had found it hard to dissociate social democracy from Bolshevism, pluralism from relativism. He only grudgingly acknowledged that
the Christian Churches owed their freedom and expansion to the pluralist environment of more or less democratic societies in the West. Spain
under Franco and Portugal under Salazar continued to characterize his
notion of ideal societies. He gave no indication that he had learned
lessons from his dealings with Nazi Germany during the 1930s.

As we have seen, there had been a constituency of worker-priests
and theologians, principally in France under the auspices of the New
Theology, who had urged Catholics to participate in a lay apostolate
with new ministries in the industrial heartlands, a pluralist Church open
to the possibilities of ecumenism and joint action against totalitarianism. Their social and political concerns were inseparable from new approaches to biblical scholarship, reform of the liturgy (including the use
of the vernacular), and interfaith dialogue. In short, they wanted a
Church that engaged with the world and moved with the times rather
than standing against them.

After his death, these exponents of the New Theology became a catalyst for profound change. There was an irresistible groundswell, moreover, for reform and renewal among the faithful. Catholics yearned for a different kind of Church; they wanted an end to the legalistic monolith that had been shaped and governed by Pacelli.

Angelo Roncalli, the man who was John XXIII, was the son of peasant farmers from Bergamo. He had spent much of his priestly life as a nuncio and knew the Eastern Churches well. He had tried to help the Jews during the war. One of his first acts as Pope was to seek forgiveness of the Jews for Christian anti-Judaism. Just three months after his election on January 25, 1959, he called a general Council with a view to pastoral renewal and the promotion of Christian unity.

There was considerable opposition from within the Vatican. When senior officials failed to stop the project, they attempted to put a stranglehold on its deliberations and decisions. The old guard wanted it to be a Council that condemned modern heresy. They did not succeed. Pope John intervened to ensure that there would be no anathemas or excommunications, that representatives of other Christian Churches would be present. His insistence on the principle of aggiornamento (that the Church should develop and change with society and history) signaled the potential for radical reform.

The decisions of the Second Vatican Council gave rise to many historic changes—in liturgy and biblical studies; dialogue with the Protestant and Orthodox Churches; a declaration on religious freedom. Many things would never be the same again: the Latin Mass went. But the single most important decision for change was the call for "collegiality"—a recognition of the need for a sharing of authority between the bishops and the Pope. The long-term spirit and success of the Council depended upon this. It involved a belief in the presence of the Holy Spirit in the wider community of the Church, locally and at large, not just at the center. The Council signaled, in other words, the end of the ideology of papal power set in motion by the First Vatican Council and pursued over seventy years to its apotheosis under Pius XII in the 1950s. An expression of collegiality was the Council Fathers' new metaphor for the Church, altogether different from the image of an impregnable, static citadel. They spoke of "the pilgrim Church," which emphasized the passage of history, human fallenness despite providential guidance, respect for the spiritual authenticity of other Churches.[1] Adopting the phrase from Hebrew Scriptures, they spoke of the Church as the "People of God." "Led by the Spirit of the Lord," the Council Fathers said, the faithful should seek to "discern in the events, the needs, and the longings which it shares with other men of our time, what may be genuine signs of the presence or of the purpose of God."[2]

Collegiality Fails

Collegiality, however, was challenged and resisted at the Vatican power center. Some of the blame attaches to the reactionary curial factions, especially in the Holy Office (the keepers of doctrinal orthodoxy), but there were also the continuing effects of the suppression of creative theology, the rigid intellectual and institutional conformism that went back to the days of Pius X. It had been unrealistic to imagine that the permafrost of sixty years could thaw in the span of a decade. The bishops and their advisers entered the Council inhibited by years of caution.

Pope John XXIII did much to prevent the Council's falling into the hands of the reactionaries, but he died on June 3, 1963, and was succeeded on June 21 by Paul VI, Pacelli's former undersecretary Giovanni Battista Montini. Paul VI presided over the third and fourth sessions of the Council and was Pope in the critical postconciliar era. During that period, the Church found itself polarizing between the progressives, who believed that a profound transfer of authority had been affirmed but not applied, and the traditionalists, who were insistent that no such thing should or would occur.

The Council Fathers did not dismantle the structures that underpinned the ideology of papal power. No reform of the Curia was sanctioned (if anything, the Vatican bureaucracy became more powerful); and there was no attempt to repeal the 1917 Code of Canon Law, or at least the provisions protecting centralized power. Total authority, therefore, remained exclusively with the papacy. There was a moral obligation on popes to apply collegiality, but no institutional mechanism. The popes that followed John were unwilling to let go.

The key issue was, and remains to this day, how bishops are chosen. Collegiality cannot prosper while the Pope assumes the right to appoint and control each of the world's bishops. Everything else flows from this, revealing how profound and far-reaching was the effect of the ruling on the nomination of bishops in the 1917 Code of Canon Law: the disenfranchising and demoralization of the diocesan clergy and the laity; the undermining of the synods (the bishops' special meetings instituted by Paul VI to continue the work of the Council), the blighting absence of pluralism and local discretion.

Paul, at heart a liberal, appeared to waver between the progressives and the traditionalists until he intervened in the deliberations on contraception. Appropriate consultative bodies had been assembled, which, with the majority of the world's bishops, wanted to sanction the contraceptive pill under certain conditions—a change of course that would have brought spiritual consolation to millions and healed the opening breach between doctrine and practice. Paul, however, resolved the issue personally by autocratic fiat with his encyclical *Humanae vitae* (1968). Vatican diehards had advised Paul not to budge, citing the declarations of previous popes. He decided alone, after communing with the Almighty, as if the Council and its revolution had not taken place. He never wrote another encyclical during the next ten years of his papacy. His intervention to forestall the outcome of the Collegial process on a question of utmost importance to lay Catholics proved disastrous. It was the beginning of the massive split between progressives and traditionalists inherited by John Paul II when he was elected Pope on October 16, 1978, after the three-week pontificate of John Paul I.

John Paul II

On the eve of Whitsunday, Saturday, June 2, 1979, Karol Wojtyla, John Paul II, Pope for less than a year, faced more than a million people in the very navel of Communist Poland: Victory Square, Warsaw. "Come, Holy Spirit," he intoned, "fill the hearts of the faithful and renew the face of the earth." Then he added, to the ecstatic roar of the multitude, "Of *this* earth," indicating with a sweep of his right hand the country and people of Poland.

If there was a defining moment in the pontificate of John Paul II, it was this declaration made in the heart of his oppressed homeland. History will give him unstinting credit for having inspired and sustained the people's movement that freed Poland from atheistic Communism and contributed to a process that led to the eventual collapse of the Soviet system. His vision of solidarity, the collaboration between the infrastructure of the Church and Poland's faithful to overthrow tyranny, connects with the Catholic opposition to the Kulturkampf, the grassroots response to Bismarck's persecution. At the same time, it represents a striking contrast with Pacelli's accommodation with Hitler and the suppression of political Catholicism in Germany in the 1930s. And yet there are deep contradictions in Wojtyla's papacy, taken in the round. Advocate and enabler of social and political activism in Poland in the 1970s and the 1980s, he has emerged a traditionalist autocrat as despotic in his management of the Church as Pacelli ever was.

Yet one could hardly think of a figure less like Eugenio Pacelli; broad-shouldered skier and mountain walker, actor and poet in his youth, Wojtyla is the antithesis of the ascetic "icebox" Pope. He brought a sense of panache, humor, and humanity to the apostolic palace. His Irish secretary's first encounter with him expresses vividly his human presence:

> He was sitting at *my* desk. His *zucchetto* [skullcap] was just thrown to one side, his cassock was all unbuttoned down his chest, no collar, and he was sitting sideways-on to the desk, writing, not as Pope Paul VI did, upright and elegant, but slouched, his hand on his head, like a man more used to physical action than to scholarship. I knocked, and as he turned it was the physical posture of a man of the world—it was un-Popish. This was a very human, down-to-earth man. He jumped up and came over. He wouldn't let me kiss his ring. He caught hold of me, put his arms around me.[3]

Wojtyla had been elected by his brother cardinals on the eighth ballot by a huge majority: 104 out of 111 votes. When he emerged on the loggia above St. Peter's Square, he described himself as a man "from a far country," and he declared that his papacy would be "the witness of universal love." The progressives believed that this was a Pope to implement the reforms of Vatican II. The traditionalists, however, trusted that a prelate reared in the Catholicism of Poland would restore the old disciplines and values. Few suspected the extent to which he would disappoint the progressive side of the growing Church divide.

The world's politicians lined up to seek his notice, advice, and approval. He reminded them—Reagan, Bush, and Clinton, Gorbachev and Yeltsin in their time—of their moral responsibilities to the poor, the disenfranchised, the underprivileged. He was the enemy of totalitarianism in all its forms. A number of leading postwar dictators—Marcos in the Philippines, Baby Doc in Haiti, Pinochet in Chile, Jaruzelski in Poland, Stroessner in Paraguay—lost power after Wojtyla had kissed the soil of their countries.

As for the internal politics of the Church, Wojtyla's papacy seemed at first a living rejection of the lonely exaltation of his predecessors. Here was a man who, until the onset of Parkinson's disease, relished congenial breakfasts with nuns and priests and laypeople, working lunches and dinners with theologians and bishops. And as he ate, he listened—or at least appeared to do so.

But his pontificate has seen the reemergence of the historic dilemma of the modern papacy, unresolved as the Catholic Church approached the third millennium. Is the Roman Catholic Church a pyramid ruled from the apex by the man in the white robe? Or is it a pilgrim Church, a people on the move, as characterized by the Fathers of Vatican II?

Wojtyla was born on May 18, 1920, in Wadowice, a market town some twenty miles southwest of Kraków, not far from the Czech border. When he was not yet twenty, Wojtyla witnessed the horrors of the Nazi occupation of Poland and soon gained firsthand knowledge of the genocide of the Jews. Auschwitz was just seventeen miles from his hometown.

Following his ordination in 1946, he began an intellectual quest that would shape his distinctive, apocalyptic vision of God's action in the world. He went to Rome to research a doctoral thesis on St. John of the Cross, the sixteenth-century Spanish mystic. St. John's notion of "The Dark Night of the Soul" argues that divine knowledge is infused into a mind purged by suffering, doubt, and prayer. John Paul II, wrote the late Cardinal John Krol of Philadelphia, commenting on Wojtyla's thesis, "studied theology on his knees."

Back in Poland, assigned to various posts as a parish priest and teacher of seminarians, Wojtyla spent the next seven years studying philosophy. His meditations on the "acting person" were influenced by the work of the German philosopher Max Scheler, whose impact was felt, as we have seen earlier in this narrative, in 1920s Germany. As his thinking matured, however, Wojtyla continued to fall back on a narrow reading of neo-Thomist philosophy, especially on questions of morality—an insistence on the intrinsic evil of "illicit" sexual acts. Isolated intellectually from the West, his thinking honed by the constant need to engage Marxism-Leninism in antagonistic debate, Wojtyla appears sympathetic to pluralism on the surface; underneath, there is an intransigently absolutist cast of mind.

Wojtyla's meditations focused on the riddle of his early life experience: how can human beings share an exalted destiny toward God and be capable of the horrors of Auschwitz? As he entered middle age, he was increasingly convinced that the world's wickedness was beyond human responsibility and understanding. "The evil which exists in the world," he said in a sermon, "seems to be *greater than ever*, much greater than the evil for which each of us feels personally responsible." During a period in which many theologians were turning to more rationalist, sociological solutions, Wojtyla was renewing his belief in the otherworldly conflict between the powers of darkness and the powers of light, and in the efficacy of the Virgin Mary in history—a devotion, like Pacelli's, to Our Lady of Fátima, who, he believes, saved him during the attempt on his life in 1981. "One finger pulled the trigger," he told a vast crowd at Fátima's shrine on the Feast of Our Lady of Fátima in 1982, "another guided the bullet." A year after the attack he placed the bullet in the crown above the Virgin's statue.

He was ordained bishop in September 1958, one of the last episcopal appointments made by Pacelli, and succeeded in 1964 to the archbishopric of Kraków. He was a wily opponent of Poland's repressive Communist regime, and was created a cardinal at the age of forty-six. He boldly reformulated the concept of solidarity as a practical inspiration for a popular, nonviolent uprising. His encouragement of the Solidarity trade union, the only free workers' organization in the Eastern bloc, gave heart to the challenge to Communism in Poland and beyond, contributing significantly to the forces that led to the drastic reformation of the political landscape of Eastern Europe. With typical modesty, he has said: "The tree was rotten; I merely gave it a good shake."

But there was another force driving him: the burden of history itself.

Looking out at the Church from the epicenter, pulled this way and that, shouldering the myriad burdens of a billion-strong Church, he has become increasingly inclined to act by himself; the longer his pontificate, the more closely he has followed his modern predecessors. A key to the apparent contradiction is his dualistic view of human nature. He believes, as papal biographer Michael Walsh puts it, that the human person "both needs society and transcends it." Thus social and political action is best left to the laity, whereas transcendent reality is the preserve of the Church, which means for him the initiating decisions and authority of Christ's Vicar on earth. He has reinstated the ideology of papal power. Pluralism, he believes, can only lead to centrifugal fragmentation; only a strong Pope, ruling from the apex, can save the Church.

Throughout the longest papal reign of the century, beginning in November 1978, John Paul II has confronted without respite a series of global crises threatening the integrity and survival of the Universal Church, as if everything depended upon him and him alone. In Latin America, he staunchly resists what he sees as "Marxist-inspired" liberation theology, the notion that sin is not so much a refusal to listen to the word of God as the outcome of unjust social and political structures. Only four years into his reign, he shook with indignation when he faced heckling Sandinistas in Managua, Nicaragua, at an open-air Mass. He resented the slur that he did not support the "option for the poor." Why did they not understand that Christ, not Karl Marx, was the liberator of the oppressed? At the end of the century, despite the collapse of Communism, Catholicism in Latin America is still beset by explosive conflict between Catholic Left and Right against the background of the missionary inroads of Protestant pentecostals.

In the United States, with its sixty million Catholics, single-issue interest groups—gays, lesbians, feminists, pro-choicers, New Agers—have sought individualistic expression of their faith. Traveling through North America in 1987, Wojtyla preached forgiveness while Catholic dissidents rejected his compassion with banners and slogans. If Latin America was seeking liberation from political and social oppression, North American Catholics appeared to be demanding liberation from papal authority no less than from original sin itself. In Denver in 1993, he appealed to a mass gathering of young people to "reject false prophets and false teachers leading [you] along the paths of an impossible liberation." His targets were abortion, contraception, hedonism, and un-bridled capitalism. Perhaps the next generation would heed his warnings, he seems to be saying, for the present generation appears beyond re-demption: he loves the mass demonstrations of the Catholic youth movements, reminiscent of Catholic Action in the 1930s and 1950s.

Meanwhile, in Africa and Asia, the tenacity of traditional indigenous religions, incorporating elements from animism to ancestor worship, challenges the Roman mold of belief and worship. There are pressures to relent on clerical celibacy in cultures where an absence of male sexual expression is deemed a perversion. There are the hardworking mission-aries who distribute condoms to halt the AIDS epidemic in Central Africa.

Then there are questions of doctrinal orthodoxy. The progressives have witnessed the spectacle of John Paul exploiting his awesome power to humiliate theologians. In the first year of his papacy, he revoked the teaching license of Father Hans Küng, the Swiss theologian who has challenged papal infallibility. The revered Flemish scholar Edward Schillebeeckx was summoned to the Vatican three times to be inter-rogated regarding his interpretation of Scripture. In the mid-1980s Charles Curran of the Catholic University in Washington, D.C., had his teaching license revoked because of his moderate views on sexuality. Archbishop Raymond Hunthausen of Seattle, a well-known opponent of nuclear arms, was required to accept a monitor to scrutinize his com-ments on marriage annulments and his dealings with the local homo-sexual community. In 1997 Wojtyla excommunicated the Sri Lankan writer-priest Tissa Balasuriya for diluting Roman doctrinal orthodoxy: Balasuriya's writing had cast doubts on the doctrines of original sin and the virginity of the Mother of God. He was eventually rehabilitated.

Embattled on all sides, Wojtyla appears to have held the myriad cen-trifugal forces in tension. His formidable physical and psychological stamina matched an extraordinary certitude in the mystical nature of his vocation, which gives confidence to his principal strategy for unity: rigid control over the selection of the world's bishops and their conduct.

At public gatherings for the laity, he enthralls huge crowds in the sta-diums of the world. Behind closed doors, he lambastes the local bishops over their failure to denounce contraception, abortion, homosexuality, and divorce. Repeatedly he has favored the most reactionary candidates for bishoprics; repeatedly he has deprived the local Church of its pre-ferred choice. His appointment of Wolfgang Haas, an unpopular archconservative, as bishop in Chur, Switzerland, resulted in parishioners forming a human carpet in front of the cathedral and forcing the celebrants to step over them in order to enter the building. A similar outcry was provoked when he appointed the ultraconservative Hans Groer as archbishop of Vienna; the Austrian Church faithful were obliged to accept three other reactionary choices against their will. Groer has since been accused of pedophilia and has been banished to a monastery, where he awaits ecclesiastical investigation.

In the United States, Archbishop Pio Laghi's appointment as apostolic pro-nuncio, the Pope's personal ambassador to the local Church, carried the express mandate of vetting new bishops in order to combat liberal tendencies in the Church in North America. Three quarters of the American and British bishops are now John Paul's appointees. Wojtyla characteristically remarks: "You must not allow any doubts to arise about the right of the Pope freely to appoint bishops."

Secular and non-Catholic observers and commentators have congratulated him on his defense of absolutist moral standards against a tide of relativism. In 1994 he was declared Man of the Year by *Time* magazine precisely because of his "stand-alone" authoritarianism. "In a year when so many people lamented the decline in moral values or made excuses for bad behavior," went the citation, "Pope John Paul II forcefully set forth his vision of the good life and urged the world to follow it." The traditionalists are delighted with so much unqualified approval from the non-Catholic world. Non-Catholic media supporters overlook the fact, however, that John Paul has proved a friend to Opus Dei, the right-wing modern religious order of Spanish origin, and that he promotes the interests of the sectlike mass movements, such as Communione e Liberazione, which specialize in a high degree of military-style control and which deprecate the pluralist media.

More than twenty years into Wojtyla's papacy, and thirty-five years since the beginning of the Second Vatican Council, "the great tide powered by Vatican II," as Adrian Hastings puts it, "has, at least institutionally, spent its force."[4] Pacelli's monolithic pyramidal model of the Church has once again reasserted itself, and the metaphors of the "pilgrim Church on the move" and the "People of God" are seldom employed. Pluralism and collegiality are characterized as antagonistic to central authority.

Many of the faithful, in large and perhaps increasing numbers, in fact wholly approve of John Paul II's reaffirmation of the ideology of papal power, believing that it offers the best hope of unity and survival. This can only mean a widening divide in the future, and an inevitable clash. Early signs of a titanic struggle can be seen in North America, where the episcopate remains silent and conformist while the theologians in most Catholic universities are, for the present, beyond Vatican control and increasingly, outspokenly "dissident."

On the one hand, there is the constituency that reaffirms the right of the man in the white robe to rule autocratically from the apex, with a domineering Curia imposing conformity, and the diocesan bishops abdicating their proper authority and freedom. This vision of the Church is increasingly inimical to Christian ecumenism, insistently male-dominated and celibate. Marian devotion prevails, with an emphasis on miraculous and gnostic-style revelation. Saint-making is a central preoccupation. John Paul II has canonized more saints during his pontificate than all the other Popes put together since the formal process was established. The significance of Pacelli's canonization of Pius X, the anti-Modernist Pope, connects with Wojtyla's beatification of Opus Dei founder Esrivá de Balaguer, and his enthusiasm for the canonization of Eugenio Pacelli. Making Pius XII a saint would be a decisive victory for the traditionalists over the progressives in the interpretation of Vatican II.

The progressives, also vast in number, continue to declare that the Pope and the Curia have failed to apply the crucial decision of the Council for collegiality. They are happy to forgo the certainties of a Pope who provides an infallible mechanism as the need arises. They deplore the machinery whereby the Pope intervenes to appoint bishops the world over, frequently against local wishes, for that is not the way in which colleges are formed or work. They want a Pope who will preside over the Church in charity as a final court of appeal. They argue that the modern ideology of papal power lacks tradition, that it rejects the historic wisdom and authority of the conciliar Church.

Those who long for the realization of collegiality in the Catholic Church may also come to accept, in the light of this narrative, that the reassertion of Pacelli's power model ignores the harsh lessons of recent world history; that papal autocracy, carried to the extreme, can only demoralize and weaken Christian communities.

In many parts of the world, the Catholic Church enjoys the benefits of a pluralism widely undervalued by its traditionalists. In an era largely hospitable to religious freedom it is difficult to assess the full extent of the moral and social enfeeblement of the local Churches. It has been the urgent thesis of this book, however, that when the papacy waxes strong at the expense of the people of God, the Catholic Church declines in moral and spiritual influence to the detriment of us all.

Sources, the "Silence" Debate, and Sainthood

Studying the recent history of the papacy is no easy task, since the Vatican archives maintain a seventy-five-year rule of secrecy. Eugenio Pacelli, moreover, was a solitary and secretive individual who kept, as far as we know, no diaries before he became Pope, and wrote few intimate letters. None that exists is available to scholars. Students of Vatican wartime history have been greatly assisted, nevertheless, by the eleven volumes of documents published under the instructions of Paul VI between 1965 and 1981, although there are questions about the integrity of this collection, as I have made clear in my narrative.

Invaluable, moreover, is the work of the late Ludwig Volk, S.J., and others on the documentation of the long process that led to the signing of the Reich Concordat between the Third Reich and the Holy See in July 1933. Voluminous documents pertaining to the relations between the Vatican, the Churches, and the Nazi regime have been made available in government archives in Paris, London, and Germany (and especially in the Catholic Archive in Munich).

That Pacelli's history could be told here, in the light of fresh evidence, is owed to unprecedented access to two sets of unpublished sources in closed archives in Rome. First, the collection of sworn depositions for the beatification of Pius XII in the keeping of the Society of Jesus. Given that modern processes for beatification and canonization are qualified by a strenuous search for evidence *against* the holiness of the "Servant of God," these documents, consisting of seventy-six interviews (amounting to a thousand pages of text) conducted under oath a quarter of a century ago, have proved crucial. They are cited here for the first time.

The second collection, comprising documents relating to Pacelli's activities as a Vatican bureaucrat from 1913 to 1917, and as papal nuncio in Germany from 1917 to 1922, was made accessible by kindness of the *sostituto* in the Secretariat of State in the Vatican, Archbishop Jean-Louis Touran, and the kind assistance of the secretariat's archivist, Marcel Chapin, S.J.

By the generosity of Christian Lady Hesketh, I have been able to quote from a series of private wartime letters from Francis d'Arcy Osborne, Britain's minister at the Vatican, to her mother, Mrs. Bridget McEwan. These letters complement the diaries of Osborne, cited in Owen Chadwick's *Britain and the Vatican during the Second World War* (Cambridge, 1986), providing a unique portrait of Pacelli during the war years and settling questions raised by Chadwick.

Given the importance of Pacelli's role in reshaping canon law, I have been fortunate to be guided by Professor Giorgio Felliciani of the Catholic University in Milan on the process that led to the publication of the 1917 *Codex Juris Canonici* and the extent of Pacelli's influence on that work. Professor Felliciani has been working on the historical origins of the code from microfilmed copies of the entire process.

My greatest debt, and indeed homage, is to the magisterial scholarship of the late Klaus Scholder, whose work on Pacelli's Reich Concordat with Hitler and its consequences for the Catholic Church in Germany has provided a new focus for the failure of a Catholic resistance to the rise of Hitler and the Nazis.

Anyone embarking on a study of Pius XII must follow in the footsteps of those who have attempted to solve the issue of his wartime silence. Arguments over Eugenio Pacelli's reaction to the Final Solution have raged now for more than thirty-five years in a voluminous series of scholarly and media contributions, every attempt at a final verdict evoking a challenge from the opposite extreme. The bases on which these judgments of papal knowledge and conduct have been made involve arguments about documents and dates; they also allege, sometimes, bad faith with respect to missing documents and form speculations about the conscience of the man who was Pius XII. As Jonathan Steinberg puts it, it is "a vexed and terrible question, which nobody should approach rashly." But the continuing interest indicates that new generations are still attempting to come to terms with outstanding debts of conscience on the part of the papacy and the Catholic Church more than half a century after the end of the Second World War. The Evangelical churches of Germany acknowledged, in the Stuttgart Declaration of October 1945, their guilt for the crimes of the regime,[1] as did the Catholic hierarchy; the Holy See by contrast has made no such specific affirmation.

There have been papal initiatives, however, to heal the breach between the two religions: John XXIII's general acknowledgment of religious anti-Judaism through the centuries, Paul VI's visit to Israel, John Paul II's two synagogue visits and his "Remembrance" statement in the spring of 1998 on the history of offenses against the Jews. But John Paul used this last occasion to exonerate Pius XII's wartime conduct, proclaiming that Pacelli had nothing for which to apologize and everything to be proud of. "The wisdom of Pope Pius XII's diplomacy was publicly acknowledged on a number of occasions by representative Jewish organizations and personalities," he wrote. "For example, on September 7, 1945, Dr. Joseph Nathan, who represented the Italian Hebrew Commission, stated: 'Above all, we acknowledge the Supreme Pontiff and the religious men and women who, executing the directives of the Holy Father, recognized the persecuted as their brothers and, with effort and abnegation, hastened to help us, disregarding the terrible dangers to which they were exposed.'"[2]

The earliest and most notorious attack on Pacelli's wartime conduct occurred in 1963 with the staging of Rolf Hochhuth's play *The Representative* in Berlin.[3] It also appeared that year in London, and the following year in New York as *The Deputy*, and was subsequently translated into more than twenty languages. Written in blank verse, with echoes of Schiller, it forms to this day the basis of a popular perception of Pacelli, even among people who have never seen or read the play.

The attitude of the Holy See is established in the first scene when a historical character, Kurt Gerstein, who has been an eyewitness to the gas chambers, reports what he has seen to the nuncio in Berlin, Archbishop Orsenigo. Orsenigo, however, declines to acknowledge anything he has heard, and refuses to pass on the information to the Pope.[4] Eventually an emissary of Gerstein reaches the Vatican and is granted an audience. But Pacelli, who first appears in the fourth act, proves indifferent.

Hochhuth's papal portrait is of a heartless, avaricious cynic, angry with the West and friendly toward Germany, preoccupied with his investments, which are suffering as a result of Allied bombing raids on Italian factories. Hochhuth's Pacelli speculates about the advantage of selling off some of his investments to influential Americans in the hope that this might deter further bombing of Rome. Informed about the death camps in Poland, he turns a deaf ear. The point is dramatically reinforced by the coincidence that the Jews of Rome are being rounded up even as Gerstein's messenger makes his plea for help.

The Deputy is historical fiction based on scant documentation.[5] Gerstein never met Orsenigo, and the long interview portrayed on stage never took place. More seriously, the characterization of Pacelli as a money-grubbing hypocrite is so wide of the mark as to be ludicrous. Importantly, however, Hochhuth's play offends the most basic criteria of documentary: that such stories and portrayals are valid only if they are demonstrably true. The Deputy was nevertheless given significant credence; and the eradication of such a powerful, simple view of the man was going to prove difficult if not impossible.

Hochhuth's play, however, had another far-reaching outcome for historians. The war of words, condemnations, and counter-condemnations that followed Hochhuth's production gave impetus to the pursuit of authentic documentation. Work already in hand before The Deputy had been staged was boosted by the controversy. The author Elie Wiesel, a survivor of Auschwitz and Buchenwald, relates how he had met a downhearted Saul Friedländer in Paris in 1962. Friedländer, born in 1932, was a historian of the Nazi period; his parents had died in Auschwitz, and he himself had survived the war hidden in a Catholic monastery in France. "As we sat at an outdoor café on the Boulevard Saint-Germain," writes Wiesel, "he took a Valium and told me his troubles." In the course of preparing a thesis on the diplomacy of the Third Reich, Friedländer had come upon sensational documents about Pope Pius XII's policy toward Nazi Germany. "I immediately understood what the problem was, for I had lived it," writes Wiesel. "Publishers were no longer interested in that period." The next day, Wiesel introduced Friedländer to the Paris publisher Paul Flamand at Editions Du Seuil, and it became the "beginning of a career" for Friedländer.[6]

Friedländer's *Pius XII and the Third Reich* was published in Paris in 1964 amid the fallout from the Hochhuth book, and appeared in New York and London in 1966. It is a rigorous attempt to let the available documents speak for themselves. Based mainly but not exclusively on reports passing through the German ambassadors at the Holy See during the war, it had a profound effect on the Vatican, for it revealed, as Friedländer cautiously states in the book's conclusion, that "the Sovereign Pontiff seems to have had a predilection for Germany which does not appear to have been diminished by the nature of the Nazi regime and which was *not* disavowed up to 1944." It was naturally Friedländer's hope that the Vatican would open its own archives, since "the truthfulness of the [documents] could be checked only if compared with the corresponding documents from the Vatican archives." And that is what happened.

In 1964 Paul VI had directed a group of Jesuit scholars to edit the Vatican's wartime documents for speedy publication. The work appeared in eleven volumes published between 1965 and 1981. Collected under the overall title of *Actes et Documents du Saint Siège relatifs à la Seconde Guerre Mondiale*, the documents were published in their original languages with accompanying apparatus in French; only one volume, the first, appeared in English. The scope of evidence thus made available was impressive and scholarly—but was it complete? Amid the battle of words over what Pius XII knew and when, was it not possible that incriminating documents were withheld by the Vatican? The last surviving editor of the four, Pierre Blet, S.J., a Church historian at the Gregorian University, informed me recently that the documents were stored in boxes in a dust-laden room in the Vatican and appeared to have been neglected since the war. He is convinced that there had been neither tampering nor weeding out before the material was made available to the editors. "In any case," he told me laconically, "the Italians had cracked our codes and they had practically everything we sent. Nobody has discovered anything we kept back."[7]

That confident assertion was challenged recently, as mentioned earlier, in the memoirs of Gerhard Riegner, *Ne jamais désespérer*.[8] Riegner, who coordinated information in Switzerland from all over Europe during the war, calls attention to the absence in the Holy See's documents of a crucial memorandum he had given to the papal nuncio in Berne, Monsignor Filippe Bernadini, for transmission to the Vatican on March 18, 1942. "Our memorandum," writes Riegner, "revealed the catastrophic situation of the Jews in a number of Catholic countries, or countries with large Catholic populations, such as France, Romania, Poland, Slovakia, Croatia.... The situations were exposed in detail country by country. We were able to show the measures taken by the Nazis to destroy the entire Jewish people."[9]

The Vatican-published documents—*Actes et Documents*—show that the memorandum from Riegner and his colleague, Richard Lichtheim, had been received in the Secretariat of State, and that the document has survived and is in their keeping, for there is a bland description of its contents *"des mesures antisemites"* in a footnote in Volume 8.[10] And yet the actual text of the document is omitted.

Riegner adds that the omission is all the more regrettable since he and his colleagues had stressed that "in some of these countries the political leaders were Catholics susceptible to a Vatican initiative." But he alleges that only in the case of Slovakia, where the Catholic priest Josef Tiso was president, did the Vatican intervene and bring about a "moderation of these anti-Semitic policies."[11] Riegner concludes with the hope that the Vatican will produce all the documents that it has in its keeping on Pius XII and the Shoah.

In any event, while the Vatican was thus proceeding in the 1960s with its eleven-volume project, various writers were proceeding to judgment. Notably there was Guenter Lewy's *The Catholic Church and Nazi Germany* (New York, 1964), an extract of which also appeared in *Commentary* in February 1964. Lewy makes a fair appraisal of Pacelli's agonizing dilemma, granting that protest might have made things worse for the Jews as well as for the Catholics. Lewy, however, questions eloquently although not in any depth the ethics of employing diplomatic language, or deliberate ambiguity, to combat such unprecedented evil. "Catholic theologians," he writes, "have long debated the dividing line between Christian prudence and un-Christian cowardice. This line is often hard to locate, and no amount of casuistry about silence in the face of a crime that is permissible in order to prevent worse will alleviate the arduous task of search for it. Situations exist when moral guilt is incurred by omission. Silence has its limits."[12]

The issue next received compelling treatment by journalist and former priest Carlo Falconi in *The Silence of Pius XII*, published first in Italian in 1965 and subsequently in English in 1970.[13] Falconi's special contribution to the debate was the abundant and damning Croatian material, which remains an essential source for anybody venturing into the polemic and which charges Pacelli with having known of the Ustashe atrocities, with having said and done nothing, and with having shown his approval of the regime. Falconi's overall conclusions on Pacelli and the Final Solution, however, are cautious: he was not prepared to go beyond the story the documents told—"the Vatican was very well informed and ... the Pope was continually being urged to speak out.... They certainly do not favor a justification of Pius XII's caution and silence." All the same, he warned that the field still "holds unpredictable secrets," and expressed the hope that "soon others will follow and profit by the threads I have discovered—and with even better results."[14]

Falconi's book was followed by an enthusiastic exoneration of Pacelli in Pinchas E. Lapide's *The Last Three Popes and the Jews* (London, 1967). Lapide, who was Israeli consul in Milan in the early 1960s. Lapide had ransacked the Yad Vashem Archive, the Zionist Central Archives, and the Jewish Historical General Archives in Jerusalem for details of Vatican assistance to Jews during the war. Armed with tributes from many Jewish quarters, he claimed that the Holy See had done more to help the Jews than any other Western organization, including the Red Cross. He calculated that Pius XII, directly and indirectly, saved the lives of some 860,000 Jews. He was eager in particular to acknowledge Pope John XXIII's efforts to apologize for the long tradition of Catholic anti-Judaism, and gave prominence to John's prayer for forgiveness by printing it on the book's title page: "Forgive us for the curse we falsely attached to their name as Jews. Forgive us for crucifying Thee a second time in their flesh. For we knew not what we did."[15]

Lapide, however, appeared not to have benefited from Falconi's research, even though Falconi's book had been published two years prior to his. Nor was there a mention of Croatia, which headed the list of Pacelli's silences and which became a focus of public interest in the early 1950s on account of the trial of Cardinal Stepinac in Tito's Yugoslavia. It is doubtful, however, whether Lapide would have been swayed by any amount of negative evidence about Pius XII, since his principal purpose was to welcome the "Jewish Schema" in the Second Vatican Council, "which," wrote Lapide, "has all the impact of an official Catholic recognition of the Jewish people, its equal rights, and the unseverable ties which link Christianity to the elder creed." This celebration of new beginnings was inseparable, in Lapide's mind, from the desire that Israel should be recognized by the Vatican. Hence the reference at the book's end to "Papa Roncalli ... Pontifex Maximus—the supreme bridge-builder, who had told Maurice Fisher, the Ambassador of Israel in Rome, 'I would recognize the State of Israel here and now.' "[16] Lapide's book was a formidable and scholarly riposte to those who would paint Pius XII and the Holy See as villains, but it carried the taint of diplomatic self-interest. Yet, reading between the lines, Lapide does not seem entirely convinced of his own case. Perhaps its saddest reflection was the passing disclaimer that Pius XII was merely less lacking in courage than others, that he was merely less infected by the "sickness that lay in the soul of the free world."[17]

Three years after Lapide's book, the writer Robert Katz undertook a reconstruction of the October 16 episode in his book *Black Sabbath*. (Earlier, Katz had published *Death in Rome*, about the murder of 335 Romans, including seventy Jews, in the Ardeatine Caves on March 24, 1944. Katz suggested Pacelli knew of the Nazi reprisal and failed to sympathize with its victims.) The more Katz studied Pacelli's reaction to Nazi atrocities in Rome during the German occupation, the more he was convinced that the papacy had a case to answer. His original, anthropological account of the deportation of the Roman Jews, which he subtitled *A Journey Through a Crime Against Humanity*, published in 1969, explored the relationship between victim and persecutor in a new light. He had started his researches for the book in 1964 against the background of the controversy surrounding Hannah Arendt's book *Eichmann in Jerusalem: A Report on the Banality of Evil*, in which she challenged the Nazi monster theory and explored levels of complicity among the ordinary citizens of the Reich and even within the Jewish community itself. In the case of the Jews of Rome, Katz believes that the deportation revealed far more about that ancient community than the accepted story of Nazi tyranny allowed, telling us "a great deal about the real worth of that which was valued in Rome, [and] clearly it also speaks of the mud flats and everything between. No one in Europe, Jew and non-Jew alike, lived outside the system of values created or transmitted by twentieth-century society." Katz's subtle exposition of Pacelli's reticence concludes that he had colluded with the Nazi system, which rewarded his silence with a semblance of honoring the extraterritorial status of the Vatican and key institutions around Rome. Katz argues that in order to protect the institutional Church, Pius was prepared to expend the lives of a handful of Jews. Katz was sued in Italy, where it is possible to bring libel actions on behalf of the dead, by Pacelli's sister and nephew after a film of his *Death in Rome* was made by Carlo Ponti. The Pacellis lost, but appealed, and the case was eventually judged inconclusive.

The next set of allegations against Pacelli's wartime conduct was published in 1980, in Walter Laqueur's *The Terrible Secret* (London, 1980), focusing on what was known about the Final Solution and when. Although Laqueur had available to him several of the volumes of the Vatican wartime documents, he does not appear to have availed himself of that material, although he cites, from Friedländer, the Riegner memorandum sent to Rome via the Swiss papal nuncio. Laqueur was convinced that the Vatican "was better informed than anyone else in Europe"[18] by reason of its "superior organization and more extensive international connections." Laqueur alleged that the Vatican systematically lied about its early ignorance of the Final Solution, a policy that is not far-sighted, he writes, "for sooner or later at least some of the facts will become known."[19] A calculated guess, albeit from a distinguished scholar and historian, Laqueur was banking on the emergence of damning evidence from Italian and German espionage archives that had stored intercepted Vatican information, incoming and outgoing. Eighteen years on, no such evidence is forthcoming, although the Riegner memorandum is proof sufficient that the Vatican held back important documents. Laqueur's judgment on Pacelli was similarly guesswork. Why did Pacelli not speak out? "Probably," wrote Laqueur, "it was a case of pusillanimity rather than anti-Semitism. If the Vatican did not dare to come to the help of hundreds of Polish priests who also died in Auschwitz, it was unrealistic to expect that it would show more courage and initiative on behalf of the Jews."[20]

Laqueur, however, seemed unaware of General Ludwig Beck's plot to topple Hitler, and Pacelli's almost foolhardy valor in the role as go-between. Clearly an authentic grasp of Pacelli's character was as much a key to understanding the mystery of his behavior as was the hunt for documents. Yet no writer had attempted to capture his complex character in the round.

The first and, up to this time of writing, the only serious and extended portrait of the wartime Pacelli by a nonpartisan scholar is that attempted by the British Church historian Owen Chadwick in his book *Britain and the Vatican during the Second World War* (Cambridge, 1986). Not only did Chadwick have the entire papal *Actes et Documents* at his disposal, but he benefited from Foreign Office and War Cabinet material at the public records office in Kew, and French diplomatic records at the Quai d'Orsay. Crucially, moreover, he had been given access to the diaries (owned by Elizabeth the Queen Mother) of Francis d'Arcy Osborne, the British minister to the Holy See trapped in the Vatican at close quarters to Pius XII during the war.

Chadwick's Pacelli is very much a Pontiff as seen by an upper-class English gentleman in the British diplomatic service. Osborne was charmed by Pacelli, beguiled by his "saintliness." Occasionally he complained bitterly about Pacelli's silence during the early years of the war, but his later verdict, following the Hochhuth affair, was this:

> So far from being a cool (which I suppose, implies cold-blooded and inhumane) diplomatist, Pius XII was the most warmly humane, kind, generous, sympathetic (and incidentally saintly) character that it has been my privilege to meet in the course of a long life. I know that his sensitive nature was acutely and incessantly alive to the tragic volume of human suffering caused by the war and, without the slightest doubt, he would have been ready and glad to give his life to redeem humanity from its consequences. And this quite irrespective of nationality or faith. But what could he effectively do?[21]

The general drift of Chadwick's benevolent account of Pacelli's response to the news of the Final Solution does not vary much from this assessment. Pacelli, for Chadwick, was a timid, sensitive, holy man trapped in an imponderable dilemma. Should he speak out and make things worse for both Jews and Christians? Chadwick's verdict is underpinned by an unquestioning conviction that Pacelli was incapable of guile, narcissism, ambition, interest in power, or cowardice. If Pacelli erred, and Chadwick is not at all sure that he did, then it must have been with the best of intentions.

Chadwick's identification with Osborne's view of Pacelli was called to account by Jonathan Steinberg in his review of the book in *The Journal of Ecclesiastical History* in October 1987: "There is no introduction in which [Chadwick] addresses his readers directly nor a conclusion in which he directs our attention to the main points of his argument. Except for the acknowledgments, he never uses the word 'I.' His characters do all the talking and the only direct comment on the Hochhuth charges comes from Osborne, not from Owen Chadwick." Steinberg concludes that "Like Pius XII, Professor Chadwick is silent."

While these "secular" studies of Pacelli were appearing over a span of more than twenty years, an investigation of a rather different kind was in progress in Rome at the headquarters of the Jesuits in Borgo Santo Spirito, and continues at the time of this writing. This is the research and writing of a *positio*, a special "sacred" biography, in support of the beatification and, ultimately, the canonization of Pacelli. Beatification and canonization are infallible declarations by the Pope that a dead individual has led a life of heroic virtue and resides in Heaven. Beatification indicates that the Pope has sanctioned a local cult of the individual's "sainthood," and that this person may be prayed to; canonization indicates the celebration of a worldwide cult. The *positio*, which can run to many thousands of pages, is a story of an individual's holiness; it must be accurate and must reflect the views of many people who knew the "servant of God."

The beatification process for Pacelli is fraught with political significance, both within and outside the Church. If it succeeds, Pacelli's policies will be dramatically confirmed—endorsing the modern ideology of papal power and justifying Pacelli's wartime record. The process began in the autumn of 1964 when progressive fathers of Vatican II wished to canonize John XXIII by an act of acclamation, bypassing the drawn-out process which can take centuries. The progressives saw the move as a means of endorsing the reformist spirit of the Council. Pope Paul VI forestalled the initiative by announcing that the Congregation for Saints was to begin formal processes for both Pius XII and John XXIII. "In yoking the causes of Pius and John," comments Kenneth L. Woodward, "Pope Paul had not solved a delicate issue of Church politics; he merely postponed it."[22]

The Franciscan order assumed responsibility for the process for Pope John, and the Jesuits were given Pope Pius. Two specialist "saint-makers," Father Paul Molinari and Father Peter Gumpel, were appointed to head the task in 1965 and, in their seventies, at this time of writing they are still at work on their subject.

Gumpel, a German of aristocratic origins whose family was persecuted by the Nazis, is the key figure. He is the *relator*, the independent, autonomous judge appointed by the Pope to examine the materials presented by the promoters of Pacelli's cause. Over a period of two years, as I worked in archives in Rome, I talked with Gumpel on many occasions, seeking information. He is a man of great intelligence, hugely knowledgeable on Pacelli and his times, and I found him both fascinating and puzzling. The *positio*, or biography, of Pacelli which Gumpel oversees is meant to bring together an enormous diversity of academic (or "scientific," as he likes to describe them) studies. Hundreds of people have been contacted to give evidence to the beatification tribunal, and detailed testimonies have been taken under oath in many countries of the world. A huge circuit of documents from many archives in Europe has been assembled and scrutinized. The material continues to accumulate, but nobody outside of the Congregation for Saints will have sight of the *positio* until the beatification has been successful.

There is certain to be a highly controversial interim period in the run-up to beatification, if and when the Pope makes Pacelli a "venerable"— meaning that he has sanctioned the penultimate stage of the process, when the tribunal will scrutinize claimed miracles in support of the imminent declaration of Pacelli's "sainthood." Molinari and Gumpel both knew Pacelli personally, and forty years after his death they are convinced of his sanctity. Gumpel, who of the two is probably the greater expert on the documents, is combatively defensive of his subject, and has published an abrasive attack on Pacelli's critics in the pages of the international weekly *The Tablet*.[23]

Throughout our many conversations over many months, he was not inclined to entertain the slightest criticism of Pacelli. This might indicate, of course, that his vast knowledge has brought him to an unassailably favorable conclusion. My impression, however, was that his information gathering was far from comprehensive and that his choice of "experts" was highly selective. He admitted, for example, that not only had he not read Klaus Scholder's extensive and crucial scholarship on the Reich Concordat, but that he was unaware of its existence.

Comparing the rival works in the debate over Pacelli's wartime record, he praises Father Michael O'Carroll's *Pius XII: Greatness Dishonoured*

(1981), and Pinchas Lapide's *The Last Three Popes and the Jews* (1967), while pouring scorn on the work of Robert Katz, Guenter Lewy, and Saul Friedländer, which he characterizes as "unjustifiable and calumnious attacks against this great and saintly man."[24]

There have been criticisms of the beatification process in recent years because of the disappearance of the role of the "Devil's Advocate," an independent scrutinizer whose task it was to take serious account of criticisms of the "servant of God." The new rules for the writing of the *positio*, dating from 1983, are meant to compensate for this adversarial loss by the incorporation of studies critical of the candidate. Gumpel, however, it seems to me, has become so apologetically prejudiced for Pacelli that he regards even the most scholarly expressions of criticism, of which Friedländer is an example, as "gratuitous attacks."[25]

Gumpel's last word on the matter, in his published *Tablet* essay, is that critics of Pacelli (such as Katz, Lewy, and Friedländer) "should realize that they are trampling on the sensibilities of Catholics and in doing so they hinder efforts to build better relations between the Catholic Church and Jews." This sort of special pleading (there are, after all, as he well knows, a great many Catholic critics of Pacelli) only distances the *relator* of Pacelli's cause from the role of academic historian, placing him squarely in the ambit of apologist.

If better relations are to be built between the Catholic Church and Jews it will result not from blind faith in the single oracular voice of Catholic apologetics, but from Catholics heeding unflinchingly the pluralist narratives of history. Having come to the end of my own journey through the life and times of Pacelli, I am convinced that the cumulative verdict of history shows him to be not a saintly exemplar for future generations, but a deeply flawed human being from whom Catholics, and our relations with other religions, can best profit by expressing our sincere regret.

Acknowledgments

A number of scholars and friends have generously provided me with information and advice. I must thank in particular Dr. Mary Heiman of Glasgow University; Christian Lady Hesketh; Professor Jonathan Reilly Smith of Cambridge University; Michael Walsh, librarian at Heythrop College, London; Dr. Adam Tooze of Cambridge University; Professor Owen Chadwick of Cambridge University; Peter Glazebrook of Jesus College, Cambridge; John Thompson of Cambridge University; Marjorie Weekes of the Vatican Commission for Social Communications; the late Philip Caraman, S.J.; Dan Grisewood; Robert Boas; Jonathan Cornwell; Gabrielle Cornwell; Dorothy Wade; Cathy Galvin; Peta Dunstan of the Divinity School Library, Cambridge; John Heilpern; Ian Harris of Leicester University; Dr. John Pollard of Anglia University; Pierre Blet, S.J., of the Gregorian University; the late Robert Graham, S.J.; Roland Hill; Dr. Gerard O'Collins, S.J., of the Gregorian University; Dr. Paul MacPartlan of Heythrop College, London; the late Peter Hebblethwaite; Monsignor Charles Scicluna; John Wilkins of *The Tablet*; Peter Gumpel, S.J.; Paul Molinari, S.J.; Marcel Chapin, S.J., archivist at the Vatican Secretariat of State; Felicity O'Brien; Professor John Milbank of the University of Virginia; Dr. Catherine Pickstock of Emmanuel College, Cambridge; Monsignor Charles Burns, formerly archivist in the Vatican Secret Archive; David Willey of the BBC in Rome; Simon Kidd; Henning Grunwald; Paul Mason; and Carole

McCurdy. The manuscript was generously read by Dr. Eamon Duffy, Professor Nicholas Lash, and Dr. Jonathan Steinberg, all of Cambridge University. Their painstaking recommendations denote neither agreement with my conclusions nor responsibility for remaining error.

I must also thank Peter Carson, Hannah Robson, and Robert Lescher, and my editors, Wendy Wolf and Juliet Annan. While researching this book in Rome, I enjoyed the hospitality of the rector, staff, and students of the Venerable English College. The writing was completed at Jesus College, Cambridge, whose master and fellows I must thank for creating the ideal auspices for research and writing. Above all, I am grateful to Crispin Rope, without whose unflagging encouragement this book would never have seen the light of day.

Notes

⌇⌇

ABBREVIATIONS, ARCHIVAL SOURCES

AAS   *Acta Apostolicae Sedis*
ADSS *Actes et Documents du Saint Siège relatifs à la Seconde Guerre Mondiale* (Records and Documents of the Holy See Relating to the Second World War), Vatican, 1965–1981.
CAB   Cabinet Office papers in Public Record Office, Kew
CIC   *Codex Juris Canonici* (Code of Canon Law), Rome, 1917
DBFP Documents of British Foreign Policy
DGFP Documents of German Foreign Policy
FO   Foreign Office papers, in Public Record Office, Kew
Osborne Letters in the keeping of Christian Lady Hesketh
SRS   *Sezione per i Rapporti con gli Stati*, Vatican Secretariat of State Archive
Teste Testimonies for beatification process of Pius XII, in the keeping of the Society of Jesus at the Borgo Santo Spirito, Rome

PROLOGUE

1. *Teste*, 229: Prince Carlo Pacelli, the Pope's nephew, told the beatification tribunal that for much of his life his uncle was just over five feet eleven inches tall and about 125 pounds in weight.
2. C. Pallenberg, *The Vatican from Within* (London, 1961), 27.
3. J. Lees-Milne, *Midway on the Waves: Diaries, 1945–1949* (London, 1985), 98.
4. Quoted in P. Hebblethwaite, *Paul VI* (London, 1993), 339.
5. C. Dessain, ed., *Letters and Diaries of John Henry Newman* (London, 1961), Vol. 22, 314–15.
6. Quoted in S. Friedländer, *Nazi Germany and the Jews, Vol. I: The Years of Persecution, 1933–39* (London, 1997), 49; Friedländer's German Source, *Der Nationalsozialismus: Dokumente 1933–1945.* (Frankfurt am Main, 1957), 130.

CHAPTER ONE: THE PACELLIS

1. Apart from the depositions for Pacelli's canonization, cited as *Teste*, the most reliable published source on Pacelli's childhood and family is *Articoli per il processo*, the chronological account researched by the Jesuits for the beatification cause, published privately at the Borgo Santo Spirito, Rome, 1967. Others include I. Giordani, *Pio XII: Un Grande Papa* (Turin, 1961); I. Konopatzki, *Eugenio Pacelli: Kindheit und Jugend in Dokumente* (Munich, 1978); N. Padellaro, *Portrait of Pius XII*, Eng. trans. (London, 1956); and J. Smit, *Pope Pius XII* (London, 1961).

2. Quoted in G. Trevelyan, *Garibaldi's Defence of the Roman Republic* (London, 1928), 228.

3. See passim D. Kertzer, *The Kidnapping of Edgardo Mortara* (London, 1997).

4. Quoted in C. Butler, *Vatican Council* (London, 1962), 355.

5. Denzinger-Schönmetzer, *Enchyridion symbolorum definitionum declarationum* (Rome, 1976), 508.

6. H. E. Manning, *True Story of the Vatican Council* (London, 1877), 145.

7. *Teste*, 30.

8. Quoted in J. D. Holmes, *The Triumph of the Holy See* (London, 1978), 160.

9. J. N. D. Kelly, *The Oxford Dictionary of Popes* (Oxford, 1987), 310.

10. N. Padellaro, *Portrait of Pius XII*, 10.

11. Ibid., 10–11.

12. Quoted in Konopatzki, *Eugenio Pacelli*, 34.

13. Quoted in Giordani, *Pio XII*, 14–15.

14. *Teste*, 109.

15. Quoted in P. Lehnert, *Ich durfte Ihm dienen: Erinnerungen an Papst Pius XII* (Würzburg, 1982), 9ff.

16. R. Leiber, S.J., "Pius XII As I Knew Him," *The Tablet*, December 13, 1958.

17. Ibid.

18. Quoted in B. O'Reilly, *Life of Leo XIII* (London, 1887), 483.

19. Encyclical, *Aeterni patris*, 1879.

20. *Teste*, Elisabetta Pacelli (Rosignani), 3.

21. Quoted in P. Lapide, *The Last Three Popes and the Jews* (London, 1967), 83.

22. See G. Kisch, *The Jews in Medieval Germany: A Study of Their Legal and Social Status* (Chicago, 1949).

23. There is an extensive literature on the blood libel and associated Host desecration. See especially R. Po-chia Hsia, *The Myth of Ritual Murder: Jews and Magic in Reformation Germany* (Yale, 1988).

24. "*Oremus et pro perfidis Judaeis: ut Deus et Dominus noster auferat velamen de cordibus eorum; ut et ipsi agnoscant Jesum Christum Dominun nostrum.*" At this bidding prayer in the Tridentine Rite, the celebrant and people omit the usual genuflection.

25. *Civiltà Cattolica*, August 20, 1881, 478; December 3, 1881, 606; January 21, 1882, 214.

CHAPTER TWO: HIDDEN LIFE

1. See *Articoli per il processo* (Rome, 1967), 16; I. Giordani, *Pio XII: Un Grande Papa* (Turin, 1961), 31–32.
2. See *Articoli per il processo*, 16.
3. Eugenio Pacelli, *La personalità e la territorialità delle leggi specialmente nel diritto canonico* (Vatican, 1912).
4. *Teste*, 255–56.
5. Ibid., 256.
6. Quoted in C. Falconi, *Popes in the Twentieth Century*, Eng. trans. (London, 1967), 2.
7. G. Daly, *Transcendence and Immanence: A Study in Catholic Modernism and Integralism* (Oxford, 1980), 165.
8. N. Lash, "Modernism, *Aggiornamento* and the Night Battle," in *Bishops and Writers*, ed. Garrett Sweeney (Cambridge, 1977), 55–56.
9. Quoted in G. Fogarty, *The Vatican and the American Hierarchy from 1870 to 1965* (Wilmington, Delaware, 1985), 178.
10. Quoted in O. Chadwick, *A History of the Popes: 1830–1914* (Oxford, 1998), 357.
11. Quoted in C. Falconi, *Popes in the Twentieth Century* (London, 1967), 54.
12. Quoted in Chadwick, *History of the Popes*, 55.
13. Quoted in Daly, *Transcendence*, 51.
14. AAS 40 (1907), 593–650.
15. Ibid., 631.
16. The *motu proprio*—*"Sacrorum antistium."*
17. P. Collins, *Papal Power* (London, 1997), 66.
18. See N. Padellaro, *Portrait of Pius XII*, Eng. trans. (London, 1956), 22–23, on Romolo Murri, founder of the Christian Democratic movement.
19. H. Dal-Gal, *Pius X* (Dublin, 1953), 234.

CHAPTER THREE: PAPAL POWER GAMES

1. For background history of the *Codex Juris Canonici* (Rome, 1917), hereafter CIC, see: C. van de Wiel, *History of Canon Law* (Louvain, 1989); J. Coriden, *An Introduction to Canon Law* (New York, 1990).
2. See G. Feliciani, "La Codificazione del Diritto Canonico e la Riforma della Curia Romana," in *La chiesa e la società industriale*, Part 2, ed. E. Guerriero and A. Zambarbieri, in *Storia della Chiesa*, vol. XXII/2 (Milan, 1990), 293–315.
3. U. Stutz, *Der Geist des Codex Juris Canonici* (Stuttgart, 1918), 50.
4. See CIC, Canon 246: "Singulis Congregationibus praeest Cardinalis Praefectus vel, si eisdem praesit ipsemet Romanus Pontifex, eas dirgit Cardinalis Secretarius; quibus adjunguntur Cardinales quos Pontifex eis adscribendos censuerit, cum actiis necessariis administris." ["Each congregation is presided over by a cardinal prefect, or, in case the Roman Pontiff himself presides over it, it is directed by a Cardinal Secretary; it consists of such

cardinals as the Roman Pontiff shall assign to each, along with essential assistants."]

5. CIC, Canon 1323: "Fide divina et Catholica ea omnia credenda sunt quae verbo Dei scripto vel tradito continentur et ab Ecclesia sive sollemni judicio sive ordinario et universali magisterio tanquam divinitus revelata credenda proponuntur." ["All those truths must be believed *fide divina et Catholica*, which are contained in the written word of God or in tradition and which the Church proposes for acceptance as revealed by God, either by solemn definition or through the ordinary and universal teaching."]

6. T. Lincoln Bouscarew, S.J., and Adam C. Ellis, S.J., *Canon Law: A Text and Commentary* (Milwaukee, 1951), 743.

7. CIC, Canon 1325: "Caveant Catholici ne disputationes vel collationes, publicas praesertim, cum acatholicis habeant, sine venia Sanctae Sedis aut, si casus urgeat, loci Ordinarii."

8. G. Sweeney, *Bishops and Writers* (Cambridge, 1977), 208.

9. See Canon 749.2, CIC (Rome, 1983).

10. See R. Astorri, "Diritto comune e normativa concordataria. Un scritto inedito di Mons Pacelli sulla decadenza degli accordi tra chiesa e stato," in *Storia contemporanea*, August 4, 1991, 685–701.

11. Quoted in A. Rhodes, *The Power of Rome in the Twentieth Century* (London, 1983), 122–23.

12. E. E. Y. Hales, *The Catholic Church in the Modern World* (London, 1958), 252.

13. Quoted in N. Padellaro, *Portrait of Pius XII*, Eng. trans. (London, 1956), 24.

14. Quoted in C. Falconi, *Popes in the Twentieth Century*, Eng. trans. (London, 1967), 76.

15. Ibid., 76.

16. Pacelli succeeded Benigni on March 7, 1911. See E. Poulat, *Integrisme et Catholicisme Integral* (Paris, 1969), 258.

17. Rhodes, *The Power of Rome*, 223.

18. Quoted in ibid., 224.

19. Cardon's story was reported in *L'Eclaireur de Nice*, June 26, 1914, evidently based on an interview with the priest. Other versions of Cardon's story appeared on June 27, 1914, in *Le Journal* (Paris) and *Echo de Paris*.

20. Vatican SS [Segreteria di Stato] SRS [Sezione per i rapporti con gli stati]: Austria-Ungheria (1913–14), Fasc. 448, folios 26–29.

21. Ibid., Fasc. 448, folios 32–34.

22. Ibid., Fasc. 449, folios 53–54.

23. Ibid., Fasc. 448, folios 34ff.

24. Ibid., folio 38.

25. Ibid., Serbia (Rapporti sessioni), 1914, Fasc. 1186.

26. Ibid., fasc. 1187.

CHAPTER FOUR: TO GERMANY

1. A. Hasler, *How the Pope Became Infallible* (New York, 1981), 253.
2. Quoted in H. Daniel-Rops, *A Fight for God* (London, 1963), 241.
3. A. Hatch and S. Walshe, *Crown of Glory: The Life of Pope Pius XII* (London, 1957), 62.
4. F. Johnston, *Fatima: The Great Sign* (Exeter, 1980), 28.
5. S. Antonio, *La conciliazione ufficiosa: Diario del Barone Carlo Monti, 1914–1922*, Vol. 2 (Vatican, 1997), 96.
6. Vatican SRS, Guerra Europa, 1914–18, I, viii, 17, Vol. III folios 50–51.
7. Ibid., folio 62.
8. Ibid., folio 64.
9. Theobald von Bethmann-Hollweg's account in *Betrachtungen zum Weltkriege*, Vol. 2, 211ff; quoted in Hatch and Walshe, *Crown of Glory*, 62.
10. *New York Times*, October 17, 1922.
11. See Hatch and Walshe, *Crown of Glory*, 74.
12. N. Padellaro, *Portrait of Pius XII*, Eng. trans. (London, 1956), 41.
13. Vatican SRS, Germania, 1917, Fasc. 852, folios 2–5.
14. Ibid., folio 4.
15. Vatican SRS, Germania, 1917, Fasc. 853, folios 6–7.
16. Vatican SRS, Baviera, Fasc. 40, folios 6, 9, 10.
17. Ibid., folio 11.
18. Ibid., folio 17.
19. Vatican SRS, Baviera, Fasc. 42, folio 57. The first letter extant in the files from Pacelli in Munich in 1919 is dated February 3.
20. Vatican SRS, Baviera, letter from Pacelli to Gasparri, April 18, 1919.
21. Ibid., folio 37.
22. See, for example, M. Martin, *Decline and Fall of the Roman Catholic Church* (London, 1981), 262.
23. P. Lehnert, *Ich durfte Ihm dienen: Erinnerungen an Papst Pius XII* (Würzburg, 1982), 15ff.
24. Vatican SRS, Baviera, folios 46–47 RV.

CHAPTER FIVE: PACELLI AND WEIMAR

1. S. Stehlin, *Weimar and the Vatican* (New Jersey, 1983), n. 275.
2. See encyclicals of Leo XIII, *Diuturnum Illud* (1881), *Immortale Dei* (1885).
3. See. H. Spiegelberg, *The Phenomenological Movement* (The Hague, 1969), 228–68; see also M. Scheler, *Il formalismo nell'etica e l'etica materiale dei valori* (Milan, 1996), especially the introduction by Giancarlo Caronello.
4. For the interconfessional tendencies in the Center Party and Catholic unions versus the Holy See's "integrale," see H. Hürten, *Deutsche Katholiken, 1918–1945* (Paderborn, Germany, 1992), 7–8.
5. Study by M. Scheler, dated 1915, entitled *Sociological Reorientation and the Task*

of German Catholics after the War, quoted in K. Scholder, *The Churches and the Third Reich*, Eng. trans., Vol. I (London, 1987), 15.

6. See Stehlin, *Weimar and the Vatican*, ix.

7. Quoted in E. R. Huber and W. Huber, *Staat und Kirche*, Vol. 2 (Berlin, 1976), 540.

8. The papal bull *De salute animarum* and accompanying apostolic letter *Quad de fidelium*, both 1821.

9. Vatican SRS, Germania, Fasc. 885, folio 3.

10. Vatican SRS, Germania, Fasc. 885, folio 5.

11. Quoted in N. Trippen, *Das Domkapitel und die Erzbischofwahlen in Köln, 1821–1929* (Cologne and Vienna, 1972), 504, quoted in Scholder, *The Churches and the Third Reich*, Vol. I, 59.

12. Vatican SRS, Germania, 1919, Fasc. 885, folio 10.

13. Ibid., folio 17.

14. Ibid., folio 11.

15. Ibid., folio 18.

16. Ibid., folios 11–12.

17. Quoted in Scholder, *The Churches and the Third Reich*, Vol. I, 61.

18. Quoted in ibid.

19. Erzberger to Aversa, March 2, 1917, quoted in Stehlin, *Weimar and the Vatican*, 12.

20. Scholder, *The Churches and the Third Reich*, Vol. I, 61.

21. See E. C. Helmreich, *The German Churches under Hitler* (Detroit, 1979), 98.

22. See Scholder, *The Churches and the Third Reich*, Vol. I, 62 and 249.

23. Ibid., 62.

24. Quoted in ibid., 62.

25. Stehlin, *Weimar and the Vatican*, 53.

26. *Teste*, 6ff.

27. Ibid., 6.

28. Ibid., 69.

29. Vatican SRS, Germania, 1921, Fasc. 902, folio 9 RV.

30. Ibid., folios 20ff.

31. U.S. House Joint Resolution 433, 1920.

32. FO 371/43869/21.

CHAPTER SIX: THE GLITTERING DIPLOMAT

1. K. Scholder, *The Churches and the Third Reich*, Eng. trans, Vol. I (London, 1977), 65.

2. L. Volk, *Das Reichskonkordat* (Mainz, 1969), 11–13.

3. Scholder, *The Churches and the Third Reich*, Vol. I, 66.

4. Volk, *Reichskonkordat*, 18.

5. Scholder, *The Churches and the Third Reich*, Vol. I, 67.

6. *The Tablet*, February 18, 1939.
7. BelgFO, Allemagne, 17, Aspeslaugh to General de Guffory, Chief of the Belgian Delegation at the Inter-Allied Military Control Commission, July 12, 1923, cited Stehlin, 256.
8. Quoted in Scholder, *The Churches and the Third Reich*, Vol. I, 69.
9. Ibid.
10. DBFP, 1919–1939, Second Series, Vol. 5, 1933 (London, 1956), 525.
11. Quoted in A. Hatch and S. Walshe, *Crown of Glory: The Life of Pope Pius XII* (London, 1957), 83.
12. P. Lehnert, *Ich durfte Ihm dienen: Erinnerungen an Papst Pius XII* (Würzburg, 1982), 38.
13. A. Stahlberg, *Bounden Duty: Memoirs of a German Officer, 1932–45* (London, 1990), 36–37.
14. Scholder, *The Churches and the Third Reich*, Vol. I, 71.
15. For the text of the Prussian Concordat, see W. Weber, *Die Deutschen Konkordate und Kirchenverträge der Gegenwart* (Göttingen, 1962), 86–88.
16. Scholder, *The Churches and the Third Reich*, Vol. I, 72.
17. Quoted in Hatch and Walshe, *Crown of Glory*, 85.
18. *Teste*, 54.
19. Lehnert, *Ich durfte*, 42.

CHAPTER SEVEN: HITLER AND GERMAN CATHOLICISM

1. A. Hitler, *Mein Kampf*, trans. Ralph Manheim (London, 1992), 105–7.
2. See Paul Hoser, "Hitler und die Katholische Kirche," *Vierteljahrshefte für Zeitgeschichte*, July 1994, 483.
3. Quoted in F. Zipfel, *Kirchenkampf in Deutschland, 1933–45* (Berlin, 1965), 9, quoted in M. Housden, *Resistance and Conformity in the Third Reich* (London, 1997), 46.
4. See P. Hoser, "Hitler und die Katholische Kirche," 485ff.
5. For Catholic development in the 1920s, see E. C. Helmreich, *The German Churches under Hitler* (Detroit, 1979), 99f.
6. Helmreich, *The German Churches*, 100.
7. See O. Heilbroner, "The Disintegration of the Workers' Catholic Milieu," in *The Rise of National Socialism and the Working Classes in Weimar Germany*, ed. C. Fischer (1996), 217.
8. Quoted in T. Abel, *Why Hitler Came into Power* (Harvard, 1986), 98.
9. The correspondence appears, for example, in H. Müller, *Katholische Kirche und Nationalsozialismus, Dokumente, 1930–1935* (Munich, 1963), 13–15. Translation and discussion, K. Scholder, *The Churches and the Third Reich*, Eng. trans., Vol. I (London, 1977), 132–33.
10. Quoted in Scholder, *The Churches and the Third Reich*, Vol. I, 134.
11. Translation in ibid., 135.

12. *Teste*, 6ff.

13. See H. Daniel-Rops, *A Fight for God* (London, 1966), 326–27; Robert A. Graham, *The Vatican and Communism in World War II: What Really Happened?* (San Francisco, 1996), 48ff.

14. Daniel-Rops, *A Fight for God*, 327ff.

15. Quoted in J. D. Holmes, *The Papacy in the Modern World* (London, 1981), 80.

16. See L. Volk, *Reichskonkordat*, 45.

17. Ibid.

18. Scholder, *The Churches and the Third Reich*, Vol. I, 149.

19. Bergen to Foreign Office, June 2, 1930, Archive AA Bonn, *Botschaft Rom-Vatican*, Vol. 143, quoted in ibid.

20. G. A. Craig, *Germany, 1866–1945* (Oxford, 1981), 553.

21. W. Patch, *Heinrich Brüning and the Dissolution of the Weimar Republic* (Cambridge, 1998), 88–89ff.

22. See ibid., 2–4.

23. R. Morsey, "Die Deutsche Zentrumspartei," in *Das Ende der Parteien, 1933* ed. E. Matthias and R. Morsey (Düsseldorf, 1960), 301.

24. Heinrich Brüning, *Memoiren, 1918–1934* (Stuttgart, 1970), 358ff. Volk (see note 16 above), a Jesuit historian and personal admirer of Pacelli, finds it difficult to believe that Pacelli could have been so politically inept. Morsey (see note 23 above) extrapolates from occasional textual inaccuracies in the text as a whole to specific skepticism about the Pacelli meeting. My inclination, given his painstaking comparison of internal and external evidence, is to accept the judgment of Karl Scholder in *The Churches and the Third Reich*, Vol. I, 612n—"There cannot be any doubt that he indicates Pacelli's intentions correctly"—as against the qualifications of Volk in *Reichskonkordat*, 48ff, and R. Morsey's *Zur Entstehung, Authentizität und Kritik von Brünings Memoiren* (Opladen, 1975), 45ff. Morsey's scruples about the Pacelli-Brüning encounter are niggling and not entirely accurate. While Morsey's overall criticisms of the reliability of the memoir are not totally unfounded, the overwhelming probability is that a conversation such as Brüning describes actually took place.

25. Quoted in Scholder, *The Churches and the Third Reich*, Vol. I, 152.

26. Brüning, *Memoiren*, 358.

27. Scholder, *The Churches and the Third Reich*, Vol. I, 152.

28. I. Kershaw, *Hitler, 1889–1936* (London, 1998), 339.

29. Scholder, *The Churches and the Third Reich*, Vol. I, 152; Brüning, *Memoiren*, 358.

30. Brüning, *Memoiren*, 358.

31. Ibid., 359.

32. Scholder, *The Churches and the Third Reich*, Vol. I, 153; Brüning, *Memoiren*, 359.

33. Brüning, *Memoiren*, 359.

34. Ibid., 360.

35. Brüning manuscript, memoirs, 351–52: Harvard University Archive FP 93.4, quoted in Patch, *Heinrich Brüning*, 295–96.
36. Brüning, *Memoiren*, 361.
37. Quoted in Scholder, *The Churches and the Third Reich*, Vol. I, 153.
38. Report from Ritter to Munich, December 20, 1931, cited in Scholder, *The Churches and the Third Reich*, Vol. I, 154.
39. Ibid., 155.
40. Quoted in Scholder, *The Churches and the Third Reich*, Vol. 2, 157.
41. Quoted ibid., 157.
42. Ludwig Kaas, "Der Konkordatstyp des faschistischen Italien," *Zeitschrift für ausländisches öffentliches Recht und Völkerrecht, III.1, 1933*, 488–522.

CHAPTER EIGHT: HITLER AND PACELLI
1. Quoted in K. Scholder, *The Churches and the Third Reich*, Eng. trans., Vol. I (London, 1977), 406.
2. Quoted in W. Hofer, ed., *Der Nationalsozialismus Dokumente, 1933–1945* (Frankfurt am Main, 1957), 130.
3. Scholder, *The Churches and the Third Reich*, Vol. I, 240.
4. Quoted ibid., 243.
5. Quoted in L. Volk, ed., *Akten Kardinal Michael von Faulhaber, 1917–1945* (Mainz, 1975), 715.
6. Quoted in E. C. Helmreich, *The German Churches under Hitler* (Detroit, 1979), 237.
7. Quoted in Scholder, *The Churches and the Third Reich*, Vol. I, 244.
8. Quoted ibid., 246.
9. O. Chadwick, *Britain and the Vatican during the Second World War* (Cambridge, England, 1986), 86.
10. Scholder, *The Churches and the Third Reich*, Vol. I, 246.
11. Quoted ibid., 299.
12. Ibid., 299.
13. Quoted ibid., 247.
14. Quoted in Helmreich, *The German Churches under Hitler*, 239.
15. Quoted ibid., 239.
16. Quoted in Scholder, *The Churches and the Third Reich*, Vol. I, 253.
17. Quoted in W. L. Patch, Jr., *Heinrich Brüning and the Dissolution of the Weimar Republic* (Cambridge, England, 1998), 301.
18. Quoted in Scholder, *The Churches and the Third Reich*, Vol. I, 253.
19. S. Friedländer, *Nazi Germany and the Jews, Vol. 1: The Years of Persecution, 1933–39* (London, 1997), 42.
20. Quoted ibid.; 42; citing E. C. Helmreich, *The German Churches Under Hitler* (Detroit, 1979), 276–77.
21. Quoted in Scholder, *The Churches and the Third Reich*, Vol. I, 384.

22. P. Lehnert, *Ich durfte Ihm dienen: Erinnerungen an Papst Pius XII* (Würzburg, 1982), 28–31.
23. Scholder, *The Churches and the Third Reich*, Vol. I, 391.
24. Quoted ibid., 388.
25. Quoted ibid., 386.
26. Quoted ibid., 387.
27. Ibid., 393.
28. Quoted ibid., 394.
29. Quoted ibid., 395.
30. Quoted ibid.
31. Quoted ibid., 398.
32. Quoted in L. Volk, *Kirchliche Akten über die Reichskonkordatsverhandlungen, 1933* (Mainz, 1975), 82–85.
33. L. Volk, *Das Reichskonkordat vom 20. Juli 1933* (Mainz, 1972), 231.
34. Patch, *Brüning*, 302–3.
35. R. Leiber, "Reichskonkordat und Ende der Zentrumspartei," *Stimmen der Zeit*, 167, 1960–61, 220.
36. R. Leiber, "Pius XII As I Knew Him," *The Tablet*, December 27, 1958.
37. Attributed to Count Harry Kessler of Brüning, quoted in J.-G. Vaillancourt, *Papal Power* (Berkeley, 1980), 191.
38. Scholder, *The Churches and the Third Reich*, Vol. I, 402.
39. A. Kupper, *Staatliche Akten über die Reichskonkordatsverhandlungen, 1933* (Mainz, 1969), 166.
40. Ibid., 175.
41. Quoted in Scholder, *The Churches and the Third Reich*, Vol. I, 404.
42. Helmreich, *The German Churches under Hitler*, 245.
43. Quoted in Scholder, *The Churches and the Third Reich*, Vol. I, 404.
44. M. Burleigh and W. Wippermann, *The Racial State: Germany 1933–1945* (Cambridge, 1996), 138.
45. An English version of the Reich Concordat is printed in *British and Foreign State Papers*, Vol. 136, 697–705.
46. See D. J. Goldhagen, *Hitler's Willing Executioners* (New York, 1996).
47. G. Lewy, *The Catholic Church and Nazi Germany* (New York, 1964), 282, quoted ibid.
48. DBFP, 1919–1939, second series, Vol. 5, 1933 (London, 1956), 524.
49. Ibid., 525.

CHAPTER NINE: THE CONCORDAT IN PRACTICE

1. K. Scholder, *The Churches and the Third Reich*, Eng. trans., Vol. I (London, 1987), 495.
2. Quoted in E. C. Helmreich, *The German Churches under Hitler* (Detroit, 1979), 253.

3. Ibid., 254.

4. Quoted ibid.

5. Ibid., 257; Scholder, *The Churches and the Third Reich*, Vol. I, 411.

6. Quoted in Scholder, *The Churches and the Third Reich*, Vol. I, 502.

7. Quoted in Helmreich, *The German Churches under Hitler*, 259.

8. See also M. Faulhaber, *Judentum, Christentum, Germanentum. Adventspredigten, gehalten in St. Michael zu München, 1933* (Munich, 1934).

9. See Scholder, *The Churches and the Third Reich*, Vol. I, 518–19; S. Friedländer, *Nazi Germany and the Jews* (London, 1997), 47–48.

10. Quoted in Helmreich, *The German Churches under Hitler*, 262; see also D. J. Goldhagen, *Hitler's Willing Executioners* (London, 1996), 109.

11. Quoted in Scholder, *The Churches and the Third Reich*, Vol. I, 519.

12. Quoted in Helmreich, *The German Churches under Hitler*, 262.

13. Quoted ibid.; see also Scholder, *The Churches and the Third Reich*, Vol. I, 515.

14. Quoted in Helmreich, *The German Churches under Hitler*, 268.

15. Quoted in J. S. Conway, *The Nazi Persecution of the Churches, 1933–45* (London, 1968), 90–92.

16. Quoted ibid., 270.

17. Quoted in D. Tardini, *Pio XII* (Rome, 1959), 105.

18. See N. Padellaro, *Portrait of Pius XII*, Eng. trans. (London, 1956), 113.

19. C. Falconi, *Popes in the Twentieth Century*, Eng. trans. (London, 1967), 239.

20. P. Preston, *A Concise History of the Spanish Civil War* (London, 1986), 55.

21. Quoted in Padellaro, *Portrait of Pius XII*, 117.

22. A. Hatch and S. Walshe, *Crown of Glory* (London, 1957), 109.

23. Quoted in N. Perry and L. Echeverría, *Under the Heel of Mary* (London, 1988), 178.

24. Padellaro, *Portrait of Pius XII*, 122.

25. H. Daniel-Rops, *A Fight for God* (London, 1963), 425.

26. Padellaro, *Portrait of Pius XII*, 123.

27. Quoted ibid., 124; Hatch and Walshe, *Crown of Glory*, 121.

28. Quoted in S. Friedländer, *Pius XII and the Third Reich* (London, 1966), 7.

29. H. Daniel-Rops, *A Fight for God*, 332–35.

30. Quoted ibid., 333.

31. Quoted in J. Ridley, *Mussolini* (London, 1997), 263.

32. Quoted ibid., 263.

33. Hatch and Walshe, *Crown of Glory*, 115.

34. Spellman diary, December 22, 1936, quoted in J. Cooney, *The American Pope* (New York, 1984), 107.

CHAPTER TEN: PIUS XI SPEAKS OUT

1. Quoted in E. C. Helmreich, *The German Churches under Hitler* (Detroit, 1979), 276.

2. Quoted ibid., 279.

3. C. Falconi, *Popes of the Twentieth Century*, Eng. trans. (London, 1967), 228.

4. For Pacelli's involvement, see Helmreich, *The German Churches under Hitler*, 280, 526n; K. Scholder, *A Requiem for Hitler*, Eng. trans. (London, 1989), 112; S. Friedländer, *Pius XII and the Third Reich*, Eng. trans. (London, 1966), 6n; *L'Osservatore della Domenica*, June 28, 1964; Falconi, *Popes*, 228ff; A. Martini, "Il Cardinali Faulhaber e l'enciclica di Pio XI contro il nazismo," *Civiltà Cattolica*, December 5, 1964, passim.

5. I owe this information to Father Peter Gumpel, S.J., of the Jesuit Curia, who acted as a courier.

6. The English translation is to be found in *On the Condition of the Church in Germany*, published by the Catholic Truth Society (London, 1937), 36ff.

7. Quoted in Helmreich, *The German Churches under Hitler*, 281.

8. Quoted ibid., 280.

9. Quoted ibid., 282.

10. Quoted ibid.

11. *L'Osservatore Romano*, July 19–20, 1937.

12. Bergen to Berlin, July 23, 1937, *DGFP 1918–1945*, Series D, Vol. I, 990–92, quoted in S. Friedländer, *Pius XII*, 7.

13. Scholder, *A Requiem for Hitler*, 160.

14. Note by Weizsäcker April 8, 1938, quoted ibid., 161.

15. Quoted in N. Padellaro, *Portrait of Pius XII*, Eng. trans. (London, 1956), 128.

16. M. Y. Herczl, *Christianity and the Holocaust of Hungarian Jewry*, Eng. trans. (New York, 1993), 94.

17. Quoted in Helmreich, *The German Churches under Hitler*, 294.

18. S. Friedländer, *Nazi Germany and the Jews*, Vol. I: *The Years of Persecution, 1933–39* (London, 1997), 277.

19. Quoted in Padellaro, *Portrait of Pius XII*, 129.

20. For the details surrounding the commissioning of the encyclical *Humani generis unitas* and its texts, see G. Passelecq and B. Suchecky, *L'encyclique cachée de Pie XI: Une occasion manquée de l'Eglise face a l'antisemitisme* (Paris, 1995); R. Hill, "The Lost Encyclical," *The Tablet*, November 8, 1997; and S. Friedländer, *Nazi Germany and the Jews*, Vol. I, 250ff.

21. R. Hill, *The Tablet*, November 8, 1997, 1453.

22. Quoted in P. Lapide, *The Last Three Popes* (London, 1967), 114.

23. *Cité Nouvelle*, September 15, 1938.

24. See D. Kertzer, *The Kidnapping of Edgardo Mortara* (London, 1997).

CHAPTER ELEVEN: DARKNESS OVER EUROPE

1. For the Kulturkampf and comparisons with Catholic resistance to the Nazis, see D. Blackbourn, *The Marpingen Visions: Rationalism, Religion and the Rise*

of Modern Germany (London, 1995), passim, and especially 106ff. Also O. Chadwick, *A History of the Popes: 1830–1914* (Oxford, 1998), 254ff.

2. Blackbourn, *The Marpingen Visions*, 116.

3. Quoted ibid., 117.

4. Ibid., 270–71.

5. See N. Stoltzfus, *Resistance of the Heart* (London, 1996).

6. See J. P. Stern, *Hitler: The Führer and the People* (Los Angeles, 1975), 116; G. Lewy, *The Catholic Church and Nazi Germany* (New York, 1964).

7. See I. Kershaw, *Popular Opinion and Political Dissent in the Third Reich: Bavaria, 1933–1945* (Oxford and New York, 1983), 340ff.

8. Stoltzfus, *Resistance of the Heart*, 147.

9. Quoted ibid.

10. See M. Burleigh, *Death and Deliverance* (Cambridge, 1994), 176ff.

11. Lewy, *The Catholic Church and Nazi Germany*, 267.

12. N. Padellaro, *Portrait of Pius XII*, Eng. trans. (London, 1956), 1–5.

13. *Teste*, 12.

14. C. Falconi, *Popes in the Twentieth Century*, Eng. trans. (London, 1967), 215.

15. Ibid.

16. Quoted in E. C. Helmreich, *The German Churches under Hitler* (Detroit, 1979), 299.

17. See Padellaro, *Portrait of Pius XII*, 133. He cites the unsourced papal reflection *"avrebbero avuto rossore del proprio comportamento larvare."*

18. See N. Lo Bello, *Vatican Papers* (London, 1982), 70.

19. G. Ciano, diary, p. 28.

20. Quoted in Chadwick, *Britain and the Vatican during the Second World War* (Cambridge, England, 1986), 34.

CHAPTER TWELVE: TRIUMPH

1. See O. Chadwick, *Britain and the Vatican during the Second World War* (Cambridge, England, 1986), 34.

2. Quoted ibid., 42.

3. Ibid., 36.

4. Quoted ibid., 45.

5. Quoted ibid., 43.

6. G. Zizola, *Quale Papa?* (Rome, 1977), 145–47, cited in Chadwick, *Britain and the Vatican*, 47.

7. N. Padellaro, *Portrait of Pius XII*, Eng. trans. (London, 1956), 147; A. Spinosa, *L'Ultimo Papa* (Milan, 1994), 141.

8. F. Charles-Roux, *Huit ans au Vatican, 1932–1940* (Paris, 1947), 267.

9. Padellaro, *Portrait of Pius XII*, 147.

10. Quoted in Chadwick, *Britain and the Vatican*, 56.

11. ADSS, ii 420.

12. Ibid., 413–14.
13. K. Scholder, *A Requiem for Hitler*, Eng. trans. (London, 1989), 161.
14. Quoted ibid., 161.
15. A. Rhodes, *The Vatican in the Age of the Dictators, 1922–1945* (London, 1973), 229n.
16. H. Belloc, letter, March 22, 1939, quoted in A. N. Wilson, *Hilaire Belloc* (London, 1984), 358.
17. D. Woodruff in *The Tablet*, March 18, 1939, 345.
18. T. Driberg, *Ruling Passions* (London, 1977), 111.
19. I. Giordani, *Pio XII: Un Grande Papa* (Turin, 1961), 130.
20. *The Tablet*, March 11, 1939, 314.
21. D. Woodruff in *The Tablet*, March 18, 1939, 345.
22. H. Walpole, *Roman Fountain* (London, 1940), quoted in Driberg, *Ruling Passions*, 112–13.
23. Quoted in Chadwick, *Britain and the Vatican*, 47.
24. F. Charles-Roux to Bonnet, March 9, 1939.
25. Quoted in Chadwick, *Britain and the Vatican*, 48.

CHAPTER THIRTEEN: PACELLI, POPE OF PEACE

1. B. Wall, *Report on the Vatican* (London, 1958), 71ff.
2. Quoted in G. Craig, *Germany, 1866–1945* (Oxford, 1981), 709.
3. See AAS, Vol. 31, 1939, 130. The motto ran: "*Scutum coeruleum, quod in edio prae se ferat colore argenteo columbam tribus innixam montibus italicis e terra marique prodientibus. Columba autem prefata gestet rostello olivae ramum. Immineant scuto Claves decussatae ac Tiara de more.*"
4. Ibid., 149.
5. Ibid., 153–54.
6. FO, 371/23790/110.
7. O. Chadwick, *Britain and the Vatican during the Second World War* (Cambridge, England, 1986), 63.
8. See DGFP, Series D, vi, 426–28.
9. ADSS, i (English ed.), 120ff.
10. Ibid., 119.
11. FO, 372/23790/133–34.
12. D. Alvarez and R. A. Graham, *Nothing Sacred: Nazi Espionage Against the Vatican, 1939–1945* (London, 1997), 143.
13. Ibid., 149. See also D. Alvarez, "Faded Lustre: Vatican Cryptography, 1815–1920," *Cryptologia*, Vol. 20, no. 2 (April 1996), 97–131.
14. Alvarez and Graham, *Nothing Sacred*, 150.
15. Chadwick, *Britain and the Vatican*, 67.
16. Ibid., 70n.
17. FO, 371/23790/283.

18. Chadwick, *Britain and the Vatican*, 72.
19. ADSS, i, 197.
20. Chadwick, *Britain and the Vatican*, 73.
21. Quoted ibid., 74.
22. ADSS, i, 242–43.
23. *Oxford Companion to the Second World War*, 905–6.
24. ADSS, i, 262–63.
25. Quoted in Chadwick, *Britain and the Vatican*, 81.
26. FO, 371/23791/27.
27. AAS, Vol. 31 (1939), 413ff.
28. Chadwick, *Britain and the Vatican*, 84.
29. R. Graham, "Summi Pontificatus," *Civiltà Cattolica* (October 1984), 139–40.
30. For Pacelli's involvement in the 1939–40 anti-Hitler conspiracy, see H. Deutsch, *Conspiracy Against Hitler in the Twilight War* (Oxford, 1968); J. Fest, *Plotting Hitler's Death* (London, 1996); M. O'Carroll, *Pius XII: Greatness Dishonoured* (Dublin, 1980); Chadwick, *Britain and the Vatican*, 86ff; P. Ludlow, "Papst Pius XII, die britische Regierung und die deutsche Opposition im Winter 1939–40," in *Vierteljahreshefte für Zeitgeschichte* (1974), 229ff; and in FO and CAB papers, Jan.–Feb. 1940.
31. Deutsch, *The Conspiracy Against Hitler*, 115.
32. FO, 800/318/6.
33. Ibid./7.
34. CAB, 65/11/159.
35. FO, 800/318/25.
36. Ibid./27.
37. Ibid./34.
38. Ibid./36.
39. See J. S. Conway, "The Meeting Between Pope Pius XII and Ribbentrop," *Historical Papers of the Canadian Historical Association*, 1968, 215–27.
40. Quoted ibid., 222.
41. Quoted ibid., 224.
42. Quoted ibid., 225.
43. Chadwick, *Britain and the Vatican*, 98–99.

CHAPTER FOURTEEN: FRIEND OF CROATIA

1. O. Chadwick, *Britain and the Vatican during the Second World War* (Cambridge, England, 1986), 110.
2. ADSS, Vol. I, 442–47.
3. Chadwick, *Britain and the Vatican*, 111.
4. *Tablet*, August 30, 1941.
5. Chadwick, *Britain and the Vatican*, 114.

6. Information provided by J. F. Pollard in his paper, "The Vatican and the Wall Street Crash: Bernardino Nogara and Papal Finances in the Early 1930s."

7. Ibid., 117.

8. ADSS, iv, 63–65, 70.

9. Argument advanced by Chadwick in *Britain and the Vatican*, 223.

10. See Ciano's gratitude in ADSS, vii, 186.

11. Quoted in Chadwick, *Britain and the Vatican*, 227.

12. Quoted in C. Falconi, *The Silence of Pius XII*, Eng. trans. (London, 1970), 266.

13. J. Steinberg, *All or Nothing* (London, 1990), 179–80.

14. Quoted ibid., 276.

15. Ibid., 277–78.

16. C. Falconi, *Silence*. See also J. Morley, *Vatican Diplomacy and the Jews During the Holocaust* (New York, 1989), 147–65.

17. 308.

18. J. Steinberg, "Types of Genocide? Croatians, Serbs and Jews, 1941–45," in *The Final Solution*, ed. David Cesarini (London, 1996), 175. Steinberg bases his figures on a paper given in 1992 at the Twenty-second Annual Scholars Conference, Seattle, Washington.

19. Falconi, *Silence*, 273.

20. Quoted in J. Steinberg, *All or Nothing*, 181.

21. See Falconi, *Silence*, 298.

22. J. Steinberg, *All or Nothing*, 30.

23. Ibid., 132.

24. Falconi, *Silence*, 318.

25. Steinberg, *All or Nothing*, 133.

26. Quoted in H. Butler, *The Sub-Prefect Should Have Held His Tongue*, ed. R. F. Foster (London, 1990), 275.

27. Falconi, *Silence* , 303.

28. Ibid., 304.

29. ADSS, viii, 250ff.

30. Ibid., 259

31. Ibid., 307.

32. Quoted in Falconi, *Silence*, 333.

33. Quoted ibid., 334.

34. S. Friedländer, *Pius XII and the Third Reich: A Documentation*, Eng. trans. (London, 1966), 109.

35. G. Riegner, *Ne jamais désespérer* (Paris, 1998), 164–65.

36. Quoted in Falconi, *Silence*, 335.

37. Quoted ibid., 382.

38. Quoted ibid., 388.

39. Quoted ibid., 344–46.

40. Quoted in W. Purdy, *The Church on the Move* (London, 1965), 225.

41. Note of Counselor Hasso von Etzdorf of the Foreign Ministry, July 17, quoted in R. Graham, *The Vatican and Communism during World War II* (San Francisco, 1996), 122.

42. W. Jochmann, ed., *Adolf Hitler: Monologe im Führerhauptquartier, 1941–1944* (Hamburg, 1980), 41.

43. Ibid., 150.

44. Quoted in Graham, *The Vatican and Communism*, 121.

45. Falconi, *Silence*, 379.

46. Quoted in M. Carroll, *Greatness Dishonoured* (Dublin, 1980), 14.

47. Quoted in Falconi, *Silence*, 124.

48. Quoted ibid., 125–26.

49. J. Heenan, *Not the Whole Truth* (London, 1971), 101ff.

50. Graham, *The Vatican and Communism*, 134–35.

51. Quoted in Steinberg, "Types of Genocide," 178.

52. Pius XII, *Selected Encyclicals and Addresses* (New York, 1989), 166 and 153.

53. This section is based on the "Supplement to Preliminary Study on U.S. and Allied Efforts to Recover and Restore Gold and Other Assets Stolen or Hidden During World War II," prepared by William Slany, official historian at the U.S. Department of State. Published privately in 1998 by the Department of Economic, Business and Agricultural Affairs, the research had the participation of the CIA, six U.S. government departments, and the U.S. Holocaust Memorial Museum. The study will be cited as "Ustasha Treasury." The pages being unnumbered, references are to alphabetical section heads. For the opportunity to study this material I am indebted to Professor Jonathan Steinberg.

   See also M. Aarons and J. Loftus, *Unholy Trinity: How the Vatican's Nazi Networks Betrayed Western Intelligence to the Soviets* (New York, 1991), 88–119.

54. "Ustasha Treasury," D.

55. CIA Operational Files, October 11, 1946, cited ibid., D 28.

56. U.S. Department of Justice, Criminal Division, *Klaus Barbie and the U.S. Government: A Report to the Attorney General of the United States.*

57. CIA Operational Files, December 1958, cited in "Ustasha Treasury," D, n31.

58. G. Sereny, *Into That Darkness: An Examination of Conscience* (London, 1995), 273.

59. M. Linklater et al., *The Nazi Legacy: Klaus Barbie and the International Fascist Connection* (New York, 1984), 137–38.

CHAPTER FIFTEEN: THE HOLINESS OF PIUS XII

1. AAS, 1943, Vol. 35, 23. *"Questo voto l'umanità lo deve alle centinaia di migliaia di persone, le quali, senza veruna colpa propria, talora solo per ragione di nazionalità o di stirpe, sono distinate alla morte o ad un progressivo deperimento."*
2. Vatican Press Office bulletin, October 6, 1983, 2; quoted in P. Hebblethwaite, *Paul VI* (London, 1993), 181.
3. *Teste*, 31.
4. Quoted in Hebblethwaite, *Paul VI*, 159–60.
5. Quoted in M. Carroll, *Greatness Dishonoured*, 68.
6. L. Gedda, *18 Aprile 1948: Memorie inedite del'Artefice della Sconfitta del Fronte Popolare* (Milan, 1998), 74.
7. *Pastor Angelicus*, available in video by Filmoteca, Vatican City.
8. J. Guest, *Broken Images* (London, 1949), 192.
9. St. Malachy and his prophecies were the invention of the Benedictine monk Arnold Wion of Douai in the sixteenth century.
10. Quoted in R. Graham, *The Vatican and Communism during World War II* (San Francisco, 1996), 94.
11. W. Carr, *Angels and Principalities: Society for NT Studies*, No. 42 (Cambridge, 1981), 1–2.
12. See F. Kerr, "French Theology: Yves Congar and Henri de Lubac," in *The Modern Theologians*, ed. D. Ford (Oxford, 1997).
13. H. de Lubac, *Catholicisme: les aspects sociaux du dogme* (Paris, 1938).
14. H. de Lubac, *Corpus Mysticum: L'Eucharistie et l'Eglise au moyen age* (Paris, 1944).
15. For discussion of de Lubac's *Corpus Mysticum* and the historical shifts in the significance of the liturgy in the early Middle Ages, see Kerr, "French Theology," 110; and C. Pickstock, *After Writing* (Oxford, 1998), especially 158–64.
16. De Lubac argued that the continuity between the "mystical" and the "real" or the literal had been lost in the early Middle Ages, leading to harsh separations; that a rediscovery could lead to an opening up and deepening of connections. See Pickstock, *After Writing*, 159.
17. AAS, Vol. 35, 1943, 193ff.
18. Ibid., 203: *"Siquidem non omne admissum, etsi grave scelus, ejusmodi est ut—sicut schisma, vel haeresis, vel apostasia faciunt—suapte natura hominem ab Ecclesiae Corpore separet."*
19. Ibid., 239.

CHAPTER SIXTEEN: PACELLI AND THE HOLOCAUST

1. Quoted in L. Poliakov, *Harvest of Hate* (London, 1956), 17.
2. Guenter Lewy, "The Jewish Question," in *The Star and the Cross*, ed. C. T. Hargrove (Milwaukee, 1966), 162.
3. Quoted in M. Gilbert, *Final Journey* (London, 1979), 64.
4. Quoted in M. Gilbert, *Holocaust* (London, 1987), 281–82.

5. Quoted in J. Carroll, "The Silence," *The New Yorker*, April 7, 1997.

6. Y. Bauer, *Jews for Sale: Nazi Jewish Negotiations, 1933–1945* (Yale, 1994), 69.

7. F. Kerr, "French Theology: Yves Congar and Henri de Lubac," in D. Ford, ed., *The Modern Theologians* (Oxford, 1997), 112.

8. Osborne's diary quoted in O. Chadwick, *Britain and the Vatican during the Second World War* (Cambridge, England, 1986), 205.

9. S. Friedländer, *Pius XII and the Third Reich: A Documentation*, Eng. trans. (London, 1966), 104.

10. ADSS, viii, 457.

11. Letter Osborne to McEwan, April 21, 1942.

12. Letter Osborne to McEwan, June 11, 1942.

13. Osborne's diary quoted in Chadwick, *Britain and the Vatican*, 206.

14. Tittmann's papers cited in Chadwick, *Britain and the Vatican*, 207.

15. Chadwick, *Britain and the Vatican*, 208–9.

16. Letter Osborne to McEwan, July 31, 1942.

17. Letter Osborne to McEwan, August 25, 1942.

18. Letter Osborne to McEwan, September 18, 1942.

19. Letter Osborne to McEwan, July 1, 1943.

20. M. Marrus and R. Paxton, *Vichy France and the Jews*, Eng. trans. (Stanford, 1995), 250–51.

21. G. Lewy, *The Catholic Church and Nazi Germany* (New York, 1964), 303.

22. *Teste*, 85.

23. See Jonathan Lewis's documentary film for the "Reputations" series: "The Silence of Pius XII," BBC, 1996.

24. Gilbert, *Final Journey*, 159–60.

25. Ibid., 278.

26. Quoted in Chadwick, *Britain and the Vatican*, 213.

27. Letter Osborne to McEwan, September 18, 1942.

28. ADSS, v, 689.

29. Ibid., 685.

30. Quoted in Chadwick, *Britain and the Vatican*, 213.

31. ADSS, v, 721.

32. Ibid., 723.

33. FO, 380/86.

34. Quoted in Chadwick, *Britain and the Vatican*, 216.

35. Quoted ibid., 216.

36. See W. Laqueur, *The Terrible Secret* (London, 1980), 229.

37. Quoted in Chadwick, *Britain and the Vatican*, 217.

38. Ibid.

39. O. Chadwick, *The Tablet*, March 23, 1998, 401.

40. Official text in Italian, AAS, Vol. 35, 1943, 9ff.

41. For a discussion of the failings of Catholic social doctrine, from Leo XIII

to John Paul II, see J. Millbank, "Complex Space," in his *The World Made Strange* (Oxford, 1997), 268–85.

42. G. Ciano, *Diaries*, Eng. trans. (London, 1947), 538.

43. Chadwick, *Britain and the Vatican*, 219.

44. Ibid., 220; see also FO, 371/34363; M. Gilbert, *Auschwitz and the Allies* (London, 1981), 105.

45. Chadwick, quoting Tittmann to Cordell Hull, February 8, 1943, National Archives, Washington 866A/001/142.

46. Quoted in S. Shapiro, "Hearing the Testimony of Radical Negation," in *The Holocaust as Interruption* (Edinburgh, 1984), 3–4.

47. A. Cohen, *The Tremendum: A Theological Interpretation of the Holocaust* (New York, 1981), 37.

48. ADSS, ii, letter 53, 155ff.

49. AAS, Vol. 38, 1946, 323.

CHAPTER SEVENTEEN: THE JEWS OF ROME

1. For the historical sequence that follows I am indebted to P. J. Fitzpatrick, *In Breaking of Bread* (Cambridge, 1993), 274.

2. *L'Osservatore Romano*, September 8, 1943.

3. P. Blet, S.J., *Pie XII et la Seconde Guerre mondiale d'après les archives du Vatican* (Paris, 1997), 241.

4. For the details of the Jewish roundup and deportation I am indebted to R. Katz, *Black Sabbath* (London, 1969), which remains the most authoritative account.

5. Quoted ibid., 65.

6. Ibid., 85.

7. Ibid., 87.

8. O. Hacki, *Pius XII* (New York, 1951), 192.

9. Quoted ibid., 97.

10. See J. Steinberg, *All or Nothing* (London, 1990).

11. Blet, *Pie XII*, 243; see also J. Lewis, "The Silence of Pius XII," BBC documentary, 1996.

12. Quoted in Katz, *Black Sabbath*, 197.

13. Quoted ibid.

14. Quoted ibid., 198.

15. Telegram from Möllhausen to Ribbentrop, October 7, 1943, in *Inland II Geheim*, Doc. E421524—Documents of the German Foreign Ministry, 1920–1945 in National Archives, Washington, D.C.; quoted in Katz, *Black Sabbath*, 202.

16. ASS, Vol. 9, 505.

17. Ibid., 506. "Ho Risposto: La Santa Sede non vorrebbe essere messa nella necessità di dire la sua parola di disapprovazione."

18. "Volevo ricordargli che la Santa Sede è stata, come egli stesso ha rilevato, tanto prudente per non dare al popolo germanico l'impressione di aver fatto o voler fare contra la Germania la minima cosa durante una guerra terribile."
19. "... che la Santa Sede non deve essere messa nella necessità di protestare."
20. S. Wiesenthal, *Justice Not Vengeance* (London, 1989), 55.
21. Quoted in E. Möllhausen, *La Carta Perdente* (Rome, 1948), 117; cited and translated in Katz, *Black Sabbath*.
22. Telegram from Weizsäcker to Berlin, October 17, 1943, *Inland II Geheim*, quoted in Katz, *Black Sabbath*, 215.
23. ADSS, ix, 511.
24. Telegram from Tittmann to Secretary of State Hull, October 19, 1943, in Foreign Relations of the U.S., 1943, quoted in Katz, *Black Sabbath*, 259.
25. FO, 371/37571/R10995.
26. FO, 371/3725/19; O. Chadwick, *Britain and the Vatican during the Second World War* (Cambridge, England, 1986), 289.
27. ADSS, ix, 505.
28. Weizsäcker to Berlin, October 28, 1943, in *Inland II Geheim*, quoted and translated in Katz, *Black Sabbath*, 287.
29. Ibid., Docs. E421515; quoted in Katz, *Black Sabbath*, 288.
30. This material appears in the *Teste* manuscript, 822ff, in the keeping of the Jesuit Curia at the Borgo Santo Spirito in Rome.
31. *Teste*, 831.
32. Ibid., 832–33.
33. Ibid., 832.
34. Ibid., 834.
35. Ibid., 836–37.
36. Witness account in Lewis, "The Silence of Pius XII," BBC documentary.
37. Quoted in K. Scholder, *Requiem for Hitler: And Other New Perspectives on the German Church Struggle*, Eng. trans. (London, 1989), 166.
38. Account in Lewis, "The Silence of Pius XII," BBC documentary.

CHAPTER EIGHTEEN: SAVIOR OF ROME

1. FO, 371/43869/21; quoted in O. Chadwick, *Britain and the Vatican during the Second World War* (Cambridge, England, 1986), 290.
2. Interview with P. Gumpel, S.J., February 14, 1998.
3. Letter Osborne to McEwan, April 3, 1944.
4. ADSS, x, 190.
5. Quoted in R. Trevelyan, *Rome '44: The Battle for the Eternal City* (London, 1981), 227.
6. R. Graham, "La rappresaglia nazista alle Fosse Ardeatine: P. Pfeiffer, messaggero della carità di Pio XII," in *Civiltà Cattolica* 124 (1973), 4: 467ff.
7. M. Stern, *An American in Rome* (New York, 1964), 22–23.

8. *Sunday Times* (London), October 12, 1958.

9. O. Chadwick, *Britain and the Vatican*, 302.

10. H. Macmillan, *The Blast of War* (London, 1967), 555–56.

11. Quoted in D. Tardini, *Pio XII* (Rome, 1959), 79: *"Io non voglio collaboratori, ma esecutori."*

12. Ibid., 79.

13. J. Glorney Bolton, *Roman Century, 1870–1970* (London, 1970), 58.

14. *Teste*, 340.

15. R. Braham, *The Politics of Genocide: The Holocaust in Hungary*, Vol. 2 (New York, 1981), 1068.

16. Ibid., 1068–69, quoting H. Fein, *Accounting for Genocide* (New York, 1979), 110.

17. See ibid., 1070.

18. ADSS, x, 328.

19. P. Lapide, *The Last Three Popes and the Jews* (London, 1967), 153.

20. R. Braham, "The Holocaust in Hungary: A Retrospective Analysis," in *Genocide and Rescue: The Holocaust in Hungary, 1944*, ed. D. Cesarani (Oxford, 1997), 41.

21. Lapide, *The Last Three Popes*, 161.

22. Braham, *The Politics of Genocide*, 41.

23. D. Cesarani, introduction, in *Genocide and Rescue*, 5.

24. P. Preston, *Franco* (London, 1995), 622.

25. AAS, Vol. 37, 1945, 10–23.

26. See Leo XIII, encycl., *Libertas*, June 20, 1888.

27. S. Magister, *La politicà Vaticana e l'Italia* (Rome, 1979), 98.

28. *Vatican Pre-Election Activities:* Report from J. Graham Parsons to U.S. State Department, January 16, 1948 (865-001-2848A/VS).

29. Quoted in D. Keogh, "Ireland, the Vatican and the Cold War," paper for the Smithsonian Institution, Washington, D.C., April 1988, 21–22.

30. Ibid., 34.

31. L. Gedda, *18 Aprile 1948: Memorie inedite del'Artefice della Sconfitta del Fronte Popolare* (Milan, 1998), 131.

32. Ibid., 132.

33. P. Hebblethwaite, "Pope Pius XII: Chaplain of the Atlantic Alliance?" in *Italy and the Cold War: Politics, Culture and Society 1948–58*, eds. C. Duggan and C. Wagstaff (Oxford, 1995), 74.

34. See J. Cooney, *The American Pope* (New York, 1984), 213–14, 414n.

35. See *L'Osservatore Romano*, July 27, 1947.

36. J. Cooney, *The American Pope*, 214.

37. Ibid., 253.

38. A. Riccardi, "The Vatican of Pius XII and the Roman Party," *Concilium* 197 (1987): 47.

39. O. Chadwick, *The Christian Church in the Cold War* (London, 1993), 15–16.
40. J. Mindszenty, *Memoirs* (New York, 1974), 50.
41. Translated text, *The Tablet*, February 19, 1949.
42. Mindszenty, *Memoirs*, 50.
43. Quoted in O. Chadwick, *The Christian Church in the Cold War*, 71.

CHAPTER NINETEEN: CHURCH TRIUMPHANT

1. R. Leiber, "Pius XII As I Knew Him," *The Tablet*, December 13, 1958.
2. AAS, Vol. 42, 1950, 561–78.
3. Ibid., 567.
4. Ibid., 568; see also discussion in F. A. Sullivan, *Creative Fidelity* (Dublin, 1996), 22.
5. J. Aveling, *The Jesuits* (London, 1981), 360.
6. Quoted in F. du Plessix Gray, *Divine Disobedience* (New York, 1970), 70.
7. The story of the repression of the Dominicans is reported in Thomas O'Meara, "Raid on the Dominicans," *America*, February 5, 1994. (O'Meara draws extensively from F. Leprieur, *Quand Rome condamne* [Paris, 1989].)
8. Ibid., 9.
9. Quoted in M. Ward, ed., *France, Pagan?* (New York, 1949).
10. Quoted in O'Meara, "Raid on the Dominicans," 9.
11. H. Perrin, *Priest and Worker*, Eng. trans. (London, 1965), 235.
12. Quoted in Gray, *Divine Disobedience*, 70.
13. C. Davis, *A Question of Conscience* (London, 1967), 76.
14. AAS, Vol. 42, 1950, 753ff.
15. E. Schlink, "An Evangelical Opinion on the Proclamation of the Dogma of the Bodily Assumption of Mary," *Lutheran Quarterly* 3 (1951), 138; see also discussion in J. Pelikan, *Mary Through the Centuries* (Yale, 1996), 201ff.
16. *The Tablet*, October 20, 1951.
17. C. Staehlin, S.J., *Apariciones: Ensayo Crítico* (Madrid, 1954), 11.
18. Quoted in N. Perry and L. Echeverría, *Under the Heel of Mary* (London, 1988), 232.
19. Quoted ibid., 233.
20. AAS, Vol. 42, 1950, 581.

CHAPTER TWENTY: ABSOLUTE POWER

1. An observation made recently by Cardinal Franz König in "My Vision for the Church of the Future," in *The Tablet*, March 27, 1999, 426.
2. P. Ackroyd, *T. S. Eliot* (London, 1984), 286.
3. *Teste*, 102.
4. Ibid., 334.
5. D. Tardini, *Pio XII* (Vatican City, 1960), 137–38.
6. M. Amory, ed., *The Letters of Evelyn Waugh* (London, 1980), 202.

7. R. Leiber, "Pius XII As I Knew Him," *The Tablet*, December 13, 1958.
8. *Teste*, 89.
9. C. Pallenberg, *The Vatican from Within* (London, 1961), 33.
10. *Teste*, 219.
11. B. Leaming, *Orson Welles* (London, 1985), 351.
12. P. Hebblethwaite, *Paul VI* (London, 1993), 260–61.
13. *Teste*, 37.
14. Ibid., 249.
15. Ibid., 210.
16. I owe this item of information to Peter Gumpel, S.J.
17. CIC, 813/2.
18. AAS, Vol. 48, 1958, 658.
19. See R. Porter, *Greatest Benefit to Mankind* (London, 1997), 569–70.
20. Quoted in U. Ranke-Heinemann, *Eunuchs for Heaven: The Catholic Church and Sexuality* (London, 1990), 265.
21. Ibid., 265–66.
22. Hebblethwaite, *Paul VI*, 258.
23. *Teste*, 229ff.
24. An informant tells me that all the boys at the Benedictine monastic school of Fort August in Scotland were instructed to write "personal" letters of this kind to the Pontiff in 1953.
25. Pallenberg, *The Vatican from Within*, 35.
26. *Teste*, 276ff.
27. Ibid., 227.
28. A. Guinness, *Blessings in Disguise* (London, 1996), 45–46.
29. Loris Capovilla, ed., *Vent'Anni dalla elezione di Giovanni XXIII* (Rome, 1978), 13.
30. P. Lapide, *The Last Three Popes and the Jews* (London, 1967), 227.
31. *The Tablet*, October 18, 1958, 340.
32. P. Hofmann, *O Vatican* (New York, 1984), 25.

CHAPTER TWENTY-ONE: PIUS XII REDIVIVUS

1. Council decree, *Lumen gentium*. See A. Flannery, *Vatican Council II: Conciliar Documents*, 350ff.
2. Ibid., 912: "Pastoral Constitution of the Church in the Modern World," *Gaudium et spes*.
3. J. Cornwell, *A Thief in the Night* (London, 1989), 200.
4. A. Hastings, *The Shaping of Prophecy* (London, 1995), 105.

SOURCES, THE "SILENCE" DEBATE, AND SAINTHOOD

1. J. S. Conway, "How Shall the Nations Repent?," *The Journal of Ecclesiastical History*, Vol. 38, No. 4 (October 1987): 596.

2. John Paul II, "We Remember: Reflection on the *Shoah*" (Vatican, March 12, 1998); Joseph Nathan's tribute originally published in *L'Osservatore Romano*, September 8, 1945, 2.
3. R. Hochhuth, *Der Stellvertreter* (Hamburg, 1963).
4. Ibid., Act I, scene 1, 26.
5. According to Anthony Rhodes, *The Vatican in the Age of the Dictators* (London, 1973), 551–52, Hochhuth's sources were confined to the text of a lecture given by Cardinal Tardini in 1959, two articles by Father Leiber, and the biography of Pius XII by the notoriously untrustworthy Dr. Galeazzi-Lisi published in French in Paris because no Italian house would publish it. In addition, there were "confidences made to Hochhuth during a journey to Rome by a member of the Curia who had not wished his name to be revealed, being pledged to secrecy until his death."
6. E. Wiesel, *All Rivers Run to the Sea* (London, 1997), 329.
7. Author interview with P. Blet, S.J., at Gregorian University, Rome, May 21, 1997.
8. G. Riegner, *Ne jamais désespérer: Soixante années au service du people juif et des droits de l'homme* (Paris, 1998).
9. Ibid., 165.
10. ADSS, viii, 466n.
11. Riegner, *Ne jamais désespérer*, 166.
12. G. Lewy, *The Catholic Church and Nazi Germany* (New York, 1964), 180.
13. C. Falconi, *The Silence of Pius XII*, Eng. trans. (London, 1970).
14. Ibid., 14.
15. *Catholic Herald*, May 14, 1965, quoted in P. Lapide, *The Last Three Popes and the Jews* (London, 1967), 5.
16. Ibid., 353.
17. Ibid., 223.
18. W. Laqueur, *The Terrible Secret* (London, 1980), 55.
19. Ibid., 57n.
20. Ibid., 55.
21. *Times* (London), May 20, 1963, quoted in O. Chadwick, *Britain and the Vatican during the Second World War* (Cambridge, England, 1986), 316.
22. K. L. Woodward, *Making Saints* (New York, 1996), 287.
23. P. Gumpel, "Pius XII As He Really Was," *The Tablet*, February 12, 1999, 204.
24. Ibid.
25. Ibid., 206.

Select Bibliography

Actes et Documents du Saint Siège relatifs à la Seconde Guerre Mondiale, ed. Pierre Blet, Robert A. Graham, Angelo Martini, and Burkhart Schneider. 11 vols. in 12. Vatican City, 1965–81.

Alvarez, David, and Robert A. Graham. *Nothing Sacred: Nazi Espionage Against the Vatican, 1939–1945.* London, 1997.

Arendt, Hannah. *Eichmann in Jerusalem: A Report on the Banality of Evil.* New York, 1963.

Bea, Fernando. *Mezzo secolo della radio del Papa: Radiovaticana, 1931–1981.* Rome, 1981.

Blackbourn, David. *The Fontana History of Germany: 1780–1918, The Long Nineteenth Century.* London, 1997.

———. *The Marpingen Visions: Rationalism, Religion and the Rise of Modern Germany.* London, 1995.

Blanshard, Paul. *American Freedom and Catholic Power.* Boston, 1950.

Blet, Pierre, S.J. *Pie XII et la Seconde Guerre Mondiale d'après les archives du Vatican.* Paris, 1997.

Bull, George. *Inside the Vatican.* New York, 1982.

Burleigh, Michael. *Death and Deliverance: "Euthanasia" in Germany, c. 1900–1945.* Cambridge, England, 1994.

———. *Ethics and Extermination: Reflections on Nazi Genocide.* Cambridge, England, 1997.

Butler, Hubert. *The Sub-Prefect Should Have Held His Tongue, And Other Essays.* London, 1990.

Cardinale, Hyginus. *The Holy See and the International Order.* Gerrards Cross, 1976.

Cesarini, David, ed. *The Final Solution: Origins and Implementation.* London, 1994.

Chadwick, Owen. *Britain and the Vatican during the Second World War.* Cambridge, England, 1986.

———. *A History of the Popes: 1830–1914.* Oxford, 1998.

———. "Weizsäcker, the Vatican, and the Jews of Rome," *Journal of Ecclesiastical History,* 28: 2 (April 1977), 179ff.

Charles-Roux, François. *Huit ans au Vatican, 1932–1940.* Paris, 1947.

Chelini, Jean, et al. *Pie XII et la cité: La pensée et l'action politiques de Pie XII.* Marseille, 1988.

Cianfarra, C. M. *The War and the Vatican.* London, 1945.

Cohen, Philip J. *Serbia's Secret War: Propaganda and the Deceit of History.* College Station, Texas, 1996.

Collins, Paul. *Papal Power: A Proposal for Change in Catholicism's Third Millennium.* London, 1997.

Conway, J. S. "The Meeting Between Pope Pius XII and Ribbentrop," *Historical Papers of the Canadian Historical Association,* 1968, 103ff.

———. *The Nazi Persecution of the Churches, 1933–45.* London, 1968.

———. "Myron C. Taylor's Mission to the Vatican, 1940–1950," *Church History* 44:1 (1975), 85ff.

Dal-Gal, Hieronymo. *Pius X: The Life-Story of the Beatus.* Eng. trans. Dublin, 1953.

Daly, Gabriel. *Transcendence and Immanence: A Study in Catholic Modernism and Integralism.* Oxford, 1980.

Daniel-Rops, Henri. *The Church in an Age of Revolution: 1789–1870.* Eng. trans. London, 1965.

———. *A Fight for God: 1870–1939.* London, 1963.

Davis, Charles. *A Question of Conscience.* London, 1967.

Deutsch, Harold. *The Conspiracy Against Hitler in the Twilight War.* Oxford, 1968.

Di Nolfo, E. *Discorsi e radiomessagi di Sua Santità Pio XII,* 20 vols. Vatican City, 1955–59.

Duffy, Eamon. *Saints and Sinners: A History of the Popes.* New Haven, 1997.

Falconi, Carlo. *Popes in the Twentieth Century.* Eng. trans. London, 1967.

———. *The Silence of Pius XII.* Eng. trans. London, 1970.

FitzPatrick, P. J. *In Breaking of Bread: The Eucharist and Ritual.* Cambridge, England, 1993.

Fogarty, Gerald P. *The Vatican and the American Hierarchy from 1870 to 1965.* Wilmington, Delaware, 1985.

Friedländer, Saul. *Nazi Germany and the Jews, Vol. 1: The Years of Persecution, 1933–39.* London, 1997.

———. *Pius XII and the Third Reich: A Documentation.* Eng. trans. London, 1966.

Furlong, Paul, and David Curtis, eds. *The Church Faces the Modern World: "Rerum Novarum" and Its Impact.* Boston and Lincolnshire, 1994.

Garrone, Gabriel-Marie, et al. *Pio XII nel centenario della nascità.* Rome, 1979.

Ginsborg, Paul. *A History of Contemporary Italy: Society and Politics, 1943–1988.* London, 1990.

Giordani, Igino. *Pio XII: Un grande papa.* Turin, 1961.

Goldhagen, Daniel Jonah. *Hitler's Willing Executioners: Ordinary Germans and the Holocaust*. London, 1996.

Graham, Robert A. *The Vatican and Communism in World War II: What Really Happened?* San Francisco, 1996.

———. "La rappresaglia nazista alle Fosse Ardeatine: P. Pfeiffer, messaggero della carità di Pio XII," in *Civiltà Cattolica* 124:4 (1973), 467ff.

Hales, E. E. Y. *The Catholic Church in the Modern World: A Survey from the French Revolution to the Present*. London, 1958.

———. *Pio Nono: A Study in European Politics and Religion in the Nineteenth Century*. London, 1956.

Hanson, Eric O. *The Catholic Church in World Politics*. Princeton, 1987.

Hastings, Adrian. *Modern Catholicism: Vatican II and After*. London, 1991.

Hatch, Alden, and Seamus Walshe. *Crown of Glory: The Life of Pope Pius XII*. London, 1957.

Hebblethwaite, Peter. *John XXIII: Pope of the Council*. London, 1994.

———. *The Next Pope: An Enquiry*. London, 1995.

———. *Paul VI: The First Modern Pope*. London, 1993.

Helmreich, Ernst Christian. *The German Churches under Hitler: Background, Struggle and Epilogue*. Detroit, 1979.

Herczl, Moshe Y. *Christianity and the Holocaust of Hungarian Jewry*. Eng. trans. London, 1993.

Hofmann, Paul. *Anatomy of the Vatican: An Irreverent View of the Holy See*. London, 1985.

Holmes, J. Derek. *The Triumph of the Holy See: A Short History of the Papacy in the Nineteenth Century*. London, 1978.

Hughes, Philip. *Pope Pius the Eleventh*. London, 1937.

Johnston, Francis. *Fatima: The Great Sign*. Chulmleigh, Devon, 1980.

Katz, Robert. *Black Sabbath: A Journey Through a Crime Against Humanity*. London, 1969.

———. *Death in Rome*. London, 1967.

Kelly, J. N. D. *The Oxford Dictionary of Popes*. Oxford, 1987.

Kershaw, Ian. *Hitler, 1889–1936: Hubris*. London, 1998.

Kertzer, David I. *The Kidnapping of Edgardo Mortara*. London, 1997.

Kretzmann, Norman, and Eleonore Stump. *The Cambridge Companion to Aquinas*. Cambridge, England, 1993.

Küng, Hans. *Infallible? An Enquiry*. Eng. trans. London, 1971.

Kwitny, Jonathan. *Man of the Century: The Life and Times of Pope John Paul II*. London, 1997.

Laqueur, Walter. *The Terrible Secret: An Investigation into the Suppression of Information about Hitler's "Final Solution."* London, 1980.

Lehnert, Pasqualina. *Ich durfte Ihm dienen: Erinnerungen an Papst Pius XII*. Würzburg, 1982.

Leiber, Robert, S.J. "Pio XII e gli ebrei di Roma," in *Civiltà Cattolica*, 1961, I, 449ff.

McDermott, John M., ed. *The Thought of Pope John Paul II: A Collection of Essays and Studies*. Rome, 1993.

Marconi, Maria Cristina. *Mio marito Guglielmo*. Milan, 1995.

Marrus, Michael R., and Robert O. Paxton. *Vichy France and the Jews*. Eng. trans. Stanford, 1995.

Matheson, Peter, ed. *The Third Reich and the Christian Churches*. Edinburgh, 1981.

Milbank, John. *The Word Made Strange: Theology, Language, Culture*. Oxford, 1997.

Mommsen, Hans. *From Weimar to Auschwitz: Essays in German History*. Eng. trans. Cambridge, 1991.

———. *The Rise and Fall of Weimar Democracy*. Eng. trans. London, 1996.

Morley, John F. *Vatican Diplomacy and the Jews During the Holocaust, 1939–1943*. New York, 1980.

Muggeridge, Malcolm, ed. *Ciano's Diary: 1939–1943*. London, 1947.

Noel, Gerard. *The Anatomy of the Catholic Church*. London, 1980.

Padellaro, Nazareno. *Portrait of Pius XII*. Eng. trans. London, 1956.

Patch, William L., Jr. *Heinrich Brüning and the Dissolution of the Weimar Republic*. Cambridge, England, 1998.

Perry, Nicholas, and Loreto Echeverria. *Under the Heel of Mary*. London, 1988.

Peters, Walter H. *The Life of Benedict XV*. Milwaukee, 1959.

Pollard, John F. *The Unknown Pope: Benedict XV (1914–1922) and the Pursuit of Peace*. London, 1999.

———. *The Vatican and Italian Fascism, 1929–32*. Cambridge, 1985.

Preston, Paul. *A Concise History of the Spanish Civil War*. London, 1986.

Ratté, John. *Three Modernists: Alfred Loisy, George Tyrell, William L. Sullivan*. London, 1972.

Rhodes, A. *The Vatican in the Age of the Dictators, 1922–1945*. London, 1973.

Riccardi, Andrea, ed. *Le Chiese di Pio XII*. Bari, 1986.

Ridley, Jasper. *Mussolini*. London, 1997.

Scholder, Klaus. *The Churches and the Third Reich*. Translated by John Bowden. 2 vols. London, 1987, 1988.

———. *A Requiem for Hitler: And Other New Perspectives on the German Church Struggle*. Eng. trans. London, 1989.

Seidel, Gill. *The Holocaust Denial: Antisemitism, Racism and the New Right*. Leeds, 1986.

Smith, Denis Mack. *Modern Italy: A Political History*. London, 1997.

———. *Mussolini*. London, 1981.

Spinosa, Antonio. *Pio XII: L'ultimo papa*. Milan, 1992.

Stehlin, Stewart A. *Weimar and the Vatican, 1919–1933: German-Vatican Diplomatic Relations in the Interwar Years*. Princeton, 1983.

Steinberg, Jonathan. *All or Nothing: The Axis and the Holocaust, 1941–43*. London, 1990.

Stoltzfus, Nathan. *Resistance of the Heart: Intermarriage and the Rosenstrasse Protest in Nazi Germany*. London, 1996.

Sullivan, Francis A. *Creative Fidelity: Weighing and Interpreting Documents of the Magisterium*. Dublin, 1996.

————. *Magisterium: Teaching Authority in the Catholic Church*. Ramsey, N.J., 1983.

Sweeney, Garrett, ed., *Bishops and Writers: Aspects of the Evolution of Modern English Catholicism*. Wheathampstead, Hertfordshire, 1977.

Tardini, D. *Pio XII*. Vatican City, 1959.

Trevelyan, Raleigh. *Rome '44: The Battle for the Eternal City*. London, 1981.

Trinchese, Stefano. *La repubblica di Weimar e la Santa Sede tra Benedetto XV e Pio XI (1919–1922)*. Naples, 1994.

Vaillancourt, Jean-Guy. *Papal Power: A Study of Vatican Control over Lay Catholic Elites*. London, 1980.

Vidler, Alec R. *The Church in an Age of Revolution: 1789 to the Present Day*. London, 1961.

von Matt, Leonard, and Nello Vian. *St. Pius X: A Pictorial Biography*. Eng. trans. London, 1955.

Walsh, Michael. *John Paul II: A Biography*. London, 1994.

Woodward, Kenneth L. *Making Saints: How the Catholic Church Determines Who Becomes a Saint, Who Doesn't, and Why*. New York, 1990.

Zahn, Gordon C. *German Catholics and Hitler's Wars: A Study in Social Control*. South Bend, Ind., 1989.

Index

Abel, Theodor, 108
Accioly, Pinto, 284
Action française, L', 172
Adenauer, Konrad, 156, 328
Africa, 368
Albania, 223
Alexander, King, 170, 249
Alfieri, Dino, 239, 243
All or Nothing (Steinberg), 302
Americanism, 35–36, 38–39
Angriff, Der, 135
anti-Modernist campaign, 33, 35–40, 41,
    42, 43, 59, 337, 339, 342
Anti-Modernist Oath, 39, 41, 43, 59
anti-Semitism, 162, 172, 183, 187,
    189–90, 197, 203, 208, 295
    Catholicism and, 24–28, 280, 361
    Humani generis unitas and, 189–92, 203,
      295
    in Hungary, 185–86
    Pacelli and, 295–97
    see also Jews; Nazism
Aquinas, St. Thomas, 6, 21–22, 26, 30,
    35, 280
Arbeit, Die, 108
Arbeiterzeitung, 50

Argentina, 167–69
Ascherson, Neal, 267
Austria, 15, 171, 185, 218, 235
Austro-Hungarian Empire, 48, 49–50,
    52–58
Avenire d'Italia, 216
Aversa, Giuseppe, 61, 91
Axelrod, Towia, 74

Bacci, Antonio, 358
Baden Concordat, 117, 125–26
Badoglio, Pietro, 298, 299, 315
Bakotic, Luigi, 48, 49
Balaguer, Esrivá de, 370
Balasuriya, Tissa, 368
Balkans, 255
Ballerini, Raffaele, 24
Barbie, Klaus, 266–67
Bares, Nikolaus, 165
Batet, Domingo, 169–70
Baudrillart, Henri, 206
Bavaria, 147, 157–58, 160, 198
Bavarian Concordat, 87, 90–91, 92–93,
    100
Bea, Agostino, 270, 337
Beck, Ludwig, 235

Becker, Carl Heinrich, 97
Belgium, 15, 239, 242, 243
Belloc, Hilaire, 210, 215
Benedict XV, Pope (Giacomo della Chiesa),
    59–60, 61, 62–63, 65–66, 68,
    71–72, 73, 98, 211
Benigni, Umberto, 36–37, 38, 47, 59
Bergen, Diego von, 90, 117, 160, 175, 184,
    212, 234
Bernadini, Filippe, 258
Berning, Wilhelm, 144–45, 165
Berrigan, Daniel, 340, 342
Bertram, Adolf, 95, 97–98, 109, 134, 138,
    140, 142–43, 160, 165, 180, 181,
    183, 184, 201, 202, 208, 209, 317
Biddle, A. J. Drexel, 230
Bismarck, Otto von, 72, 86
    Kulturkampf persecutions of, 7, 14, 47,
        81, 97, 105, 133, 160, 186, 193–96,
        209, 364
Blackbourn, David, 193, 195
Black Nobles, 9
Black Shame, 94–95, 319–20
black troops, 94–95, 319–20
Blomberg, Werner von, 132
blood libel, 26, 28
Boelitz, Otto, 97
Bormann, Martin, 198, 262
Bossuet, Jacques-Bénigne, 20
Brady, Mrs. Nicholas, 178, 201
Braham, Randolph L., 325, 326
Braun, Otto, 102, 103
Britain, 205, 206, 217, 224, 225, 228–29,
    231, 232, 242, 244–47
Brüning, Heinrich, v, 118–24, 125, 126,
    135–36, 144, 148, 149–50, 155–56,
    218
Burleigh, Michael, 277
Butler, Hubert, 255
Buttmann, Rudolf, 150–51, 152, 159, 161,
    163, 164

Calles, Plutarco Elías, 113
canon law, 41, 167
    Code of, 6, 32, 41–45, 49, 54, 58, 59,
        60–61, 84, 88, 97, 100, 114, 128,
        129, 131, 144, 338–39, 362–63

Cardon, Denis, 48, 51–52, 53
Casaroli, Agostino, 332, 335
Casti connubii (Pius XI), 153
Caterini, Pietro, 9
Caterini, Prospero, 9
Catherine of Siena, Saint, 243
Catholic Action, 114–15, 122–23, 166,
    251, 270, 327, 329, 337, 368
Catholic Center Party, 47, 72, 75, 81,
    82–83, 92, 96, 105, 115–18, 120,
    122–26, 128, 131–39, 142–44, 147,
    148, 218, 327
    disbanding of, 149–50, 152, 327
Catholic Church and Nazi Germany, The (Lewy),
    199
censorship of books, 43–44, 59
centrists, 5–6
Cerejeira, Archbishop, 217
Cesarani, David, 326
Chadwick, Owen, 135, 229, 239, 242, 284,
    285
Chamberlain, Neville, 203, 222, 224, 235
Chambers, Whittaker, 331
Charles-Roux, François, 206–7, 208, 217,
    242, 244
Chenu, M.-D., 340
Christ, 274–75, 276
Christian Democrats, 327, 329, 330
Christianity and the Holocaust of Hungarian Jews
    (Herczl), 186
Churchill, Winston, 248, 323
Ciano, Galeazzo, 204, 212, 214, 217, 230,
    293
Cité Nouvelle, 190
Civiltà Cattolica, 24, 28, 45, 190, 192, 331
Claudel, Paul, 212
Code of Canon Law (1917), 6, 32, 41–45,
    49, 54, 58, 59, 60–61, 84, 88, 97,
    100, 114, 128, 129, 131, 144,
    338–39, 362–63
codes, 227–28
Cohen, Arthur A., 295
collegiality, 361, 362–63, 369, 370
Collins, Paul, 39
Combes, Émile, 46, 47
Communism, 7, 76, 112, 114, 116, 174,
    261, 263, 309, 316, 319, 320, 321,

322, 328, 336, 338, 339, 344, 364, 366, 367
  in Eastern Europe, 332–35
  Italian, Pacelli and, 326–32
  Nazis and, 127
concentration camps, 154, 188, 279, 284, 286, 310, 325, 326
concordats, 84–85, 167
  Baden, 117, 125–26
  Bavarian, 87, 90–91, 92–93, 100
  Prussian, 100, 102–3, 120
  Reich, 6–7, 84–87, 90–93, 96–98, 100, 103, 115, 117, 120–26, 130–31, 133–38, 141–55, 157–61, 166, 179, 183, 184, 186, 203, 205, 210, 218, 227, 296
  Serbian, 49–58, 131, 148, 256, 265
Congar, Yves, 340
Constantine, Emperor, 25
Cooney, John, 330–31
Corpus Mysticum (The Mystical Body) (de Lubac), 275
Cortesi, Filippo, 231
Coughlin, Charles, 176, 177
Croatia, 248–60, 262, 265–66, 279, 281
  gold of, 266
Croix, La, 45
Curran, Charles, 368
Czechoslovakia, 222, 235

D'Abernon, Lord, 101
Daily Telegraph, 245, 283
Daladier, Édouard, 233
Dalla Costa, Elia, 207
Daniel-Rops, H., 113, 174, 203
Dannecker, Theodor, 303, 308
"Darkness over the Earth" (Summi pontificatus) (Pius XII), 233–34, 273
Davis, Charles, 342
Death and Deliverance (Burleigh), 277
death camps, 154, 188, 279, 284, 286, 310, 325, 326
De Gasperi, Alcide, 327, 328
Delbrück, Richard, 92
della Chiesa, Giacomo, see Benedict XV, Pope
de Lubac, Henri, 274–76

Depression, Great, 180
Deputy, The (Hochhuth), vii
Desbuquois, Gustave, 189
Deutsch, Harold, 235–36
De Valera, Eamon, 212
Dimbleby, Richard, 358
Dirks, Walter, 108
Divino afflante spiritu (By the Inspiration of the Holy Spirit) (Pius XII), 337
Dollfuss, Engelbert, 166
Dominicans, 340, 342
Dragonovic, Krunoslav, 266, 267
Dreyfus, Alfred, 24, 45
Driberg, Tom, 213, 215
Duca, Francesco Borgongini, 257
Duchesne, Louis, 36, 339
Dulles, John Foster, 351

Eberhard, Bishop, 194
Ebert, Friedrich, 72, 73, 78, 92, 101, 136
Éclaireur de Nice, L', 51
Eden, Anthony, 290
Eggersdorfer, Franz, 143
Eichmann, Adolf, 279, 302, 303, 324, 326
Eisenhower, Dwight, 357
Eisner, Kurt, 73–74
Eliot, T. S., 349
Enabling Act, 92, 133, 134, 135–37
Enlightenment, 5
Ernst, Karl, 166
Erzberger, Matthias, 72, 82–83, 84, 85, 90, 91, 106, 119
Ethiopia, 171, 175–76

Falconi, Carlo, 47, 169, 173, 251, 254, 259, 262, 321, 352
Farinacci, Roberto, 241–42
Fascism, 114, 115, 123, 128–29, 133, 143, 171, 175, 205, 222, 229, 236, 241–42, 243, 272, 280, 298, 326, 327
Fátima, 61–62, 272–73, 344–45, 366
Faulhaber, Michael von, 83, 134, 137, 139, 140, 141, 143, 146–47, 157, 161–63, 180–81, 187, 208
Fein, Helen, 325

Final Solution (Holocaust), 24, 268–69,
    270, 275, 276–77, 278–97, 302–3
  Hungarian Jews and, 324–26
  Roman Jews and, 300–312, 316–18
First Vatican Council (Vatican I) (1870),
    5–6, 8, 12–13, 14, 41, 43, 193,
    338–39, 343, 361
Foa, Ugo, 300, 301
Fohr, Peter, 125, 126
Fourth Lateran Council, 25
France, 5, 15, 45–47, 49, 170–75, 205–7,
    217, 224, 225, 228–29, 231, 232,
    234, 239, 242–45, 281
  Black Shame and, 94–95
  deportation of Jews from, 285–86, 288
  Germany's territorial disputes with, 97,
    98, 99–100
Franco, Francisco, 170, 175, 223, 272,
    280, 327, 344, 345, 360
Franco-Prussian War, 13, 41
Franz Ferdinand, Archduke, 48, 51, 57
Franz Josef, Emperor, 11, 34, 50, 52–53
Friedländer, Saul, 140, 162, 188, 258–59
Fritz, Carl, 125
Fumagalli, Antonio, 35

Galeazzi, Enrico, 176, 200, 201, 350–51,
    354
Galeazzi-Lisi, Ricardo, 200, 354–55, 356,
    358
Galen, Clemens August von, 181, 197–99,
    277
Gasbarrini, Antonio, 355, 356
Gasparri, Pietro, 31, 38, 40, 41, 44, 46,
    54–56, 60, 61, 63–65, 67, 69–74,
    77, 78, 84, 88, 89, 91, 94, 95,
    99–100, 103, 114, 190
Gedda, Luigi, 270, 329, 330
George VI, King, 238
Gerade Weg, Der (The Straight Path), 110, 128,
    147, 166
Gerlich, Fritz, 110, 147, 166
Germany, 4, 6–7, 30, 45, 47, 48, 72–75,
    80–93, 103, 115, 118–29,
    157–66, 179–88, 206,
    217–18, 222–26, 229–31, 234,

    238–39, 241, 248, 299, 319–20,
    333, 364
  Black Shame and, 94–95
  Catholic Center Party in, 47, 72, 75, 81,
    82–83, 92, 96, 105, 115–18, 120,
    122–26, 128, 131–39, 142–44, 147,
    148, 218, 327
  Catholic Center Party disbanded in,
    149–50, 152, 327
  Catholic population of, 106–7, 133,
    142, 201, 215
  crucifixes banned in, 197–98
  euthanasia program in, 197, 198–99,
    277
  France's territorial disputes with, 97, 98,
    99–100
  Italy's pact with, 229
  Jews in, 70–71, 75, 82, 139–41,
    153–55, 158–60, 162, 180, 188,
    196–97; see also Jews
  Kulturkampf persecutions in, 7, 14, 47,
    81, 97, 105, 133, 160, 186, 193–96,
    209, 364
  Mit brennender Sorge and, 181–84, 205,
    296
  Nazi Party in, see Nazism
  Nuremberg Laws in, 154, 179–80
  plot against Hitler in, 234–40, 242
  Poland invaded by, 231–32
  Reich Concordat and, 6–7, 84–87,
    90–93, 96–98, 100, 103, 115, 117,
    120–26, 130–31, 133–38, 141–55,
    157–61, 166, 179, 183, 184, 186,
    203, 205, 210, 218, 227, 296
  Rosenstrasse protest in, 196
  socialist groups in, 73–75
  Soviet pact with, 230
  Soviet Union invaded by, 260–63, 264
  sterilization policy in, 153, 160
  in World War I, 61, 63–69, 71–72
  see also Hitler, Adolf
Gilbert, Martin, 287
Gladstone, William, 10
Glaise von Horstenau, Edmund, 253–54
Godfrey, William, 224
Goebbels, Joseph, 135, 183, 199, 279

gold ransom, 301–2, 308
Goretti, Maria, 346
Göring, Hermann, 132, 171, 183, 184
Gospel and the Church, The (Loisy), 36
Gött, Magnus, 106, 110
Great Britain, 205, 206, 217, 224, 225,
    228–29, 231, 232, 242, 244–47
Greece, 247, 248
Greene, Graham, 113, 347
Gröber, Konrad, 126, 144–46, 160, 163,
    165
Groener, Wilhelm, 118
Groer, Hans, 369
Guest, John, 271
Guinness, Alec, 355–56
Gumpel, Peter, v, 319–20
Gumpert, Gerhard, 306
Gundlach, Gustav, 189–90

Haas, Wolfgang, 368–69
Hácha, Emil, 222
Halifax, Edward Wood, Lord, 203, 218,
    224, 230, 235, 236, 237, 238
Hartmann, Felix von, 88
Hastings, Adrian, 8, 369
Heenan, John Carmel, 264
Hentrich, Guglielmo, 200, 349, 356
Herbigny, Michel d', 263
Herczl, Moshe Y., 186
Hertling, Georg Friedrich von, 63
Hewel, V., 224
Heydrich, Reinhard, 146, 157, 183, 262,
    263, 264, 278, 279, 282, 283
Hill, Roland, 189
Hilton, Isabel, 267
Himmler, Heinrich, 146, 157, 162, 185,
    301
Hindenburg, Paul von, 101, 104, 118, 126,
    127, 128, 131, 132, 134
Hinsley, Arthur, 206
Hitler, Adolf, 4, 47, 86, 92, 96–98,
    105–10, 112, 114–16, 118, 119,
    121–22, 124, 128, 130–55, 161,
    163–66, 170–71, 173, 179–81, 185,
    186, 188, 193, 195–96, 198–99,
    201–3, 205, 210, 218, 222, 224–26,

230, 231, 239–42, 247, 248, 252,
    260, 273, 280, 294, 299, 317, 333,
    364
    Enabling Act and, 92, 133, 134, 135–37
    Final Solution of, 24, 268–69, 270,
        275, 276–77, 278–97, 300–312,
        316–18, 324–26
    Mit brennender Sorge and, 181–82, 183
    Mussolini's pact with, 229
    and Night of the Long Knives, 165–66
    Pacelli kidnapping plan of, 313–15
    Pacelli's affirmation of, 208–9
    plot against, 234–40, 242
    Reich Concordat and, 6–7, 84, 85, 91,
        130–31, 133–38, 141–55, 160, 210,
        218, 296
    rise of, 131–39
    Via Rasella bombing and, 320–21
    see also Nazism
"Hitler and Catholicism" (Wild), 110
Hitler and Rome (Trossmann), 110
Hitler Youth, 163, 164, 186, 198
Hlond, August, 232–33, 234, 280
Hochhuth, Rolf, vii
Holland, 239, 242, 243
    deportation of Jews from, 285–86, 288
Holocaust (Final Solution), 24, 268–69,
    270, 275, 276–77, 278–97, 302–3
    Hungarian Jews and, 324–26
    Roman Jews and, 300–312, 316–18
Holy Year (1950), 1, 336–37
Horthy, Miklós, 185, 280, 325, 326
Hudal, Alois, 267, 306, 307
Hugenberg, Alfred, 132–33
Humanae vitae (Paul VI), 353, 363
Humani generis (Of the Human Race) (Pius
    XII), 191, 337–39
*Humani generis unitas (The Unity of the Human
    Race)*, 189–92, 203, 295
Hungary, 170, 185–86, 248, 281, 324–26,
    332, 333–35
Hunthausen, Raymond, 368

Ignatius Loyola, St., 20
Imitation of Christ (Thomas à Kempis),
    19–20, 269

Immortale Dei (Leo XIII), 30
Imrédy, Béla, 185
Innitzer, Theodor, 201–2, 206, 208
Innocent III, Pope, 25
Inter-racial Justice (LaFarge), 189
Into That Darkness (Sereny), 267
Italy, 114, 171, 207, 217, 218, 223, 224,
        225, 234, 238, 298–99
    Christian Democrats in, 327, 329, 330
    Communism in, 326–32
    Fascism in, 114, 115, 123, 128–29, 133,
        171, 175, 205, 236, 298, 326, 327
    Germany's pact with, 229
    Jews in, 203
    Lateran Treaty and, 114–15, 122, 123,
        127, 128, 133, 141, 143, 150, 177,
        205, 236, 241, 244, 327
    in World War I, 60
    in World War II, 238, 241–42, 244,
        245–48
    Yugoslavia and, 254
    see also Rome

Jesuits, 23–24, 45, 187, 189, 192, 193,
        227, 340
    cigarette smoking by, 352–53
Jesus Christ, 274–75, 276
Jews, 7, 24, 45, 130, 152–53, 183, 188,
        222, 258, 267
    blood libel against, 26, 28
    converts to Christianity, 140, 158, 159,
        160, 162, 164, 278, 279
    in Croatia, 249–54, 256–58, 265–66
    Final Solution and, 24, 268–69, 270,
        275, 276–77, 278–97, 300–312,
        316–18, 324–26
    in Germany, 70–71, 75, 82, 139–41,
        153–55, 158–60, 162, 180, 188,
        196–97; *see also* Germany
    in Hungary, 185–86, 324–26
    in Italy, 203
    Pacelli's statement on, 292–93, 297
    in Rome, 11, 297, 299–312, 316–18,
        320–21
    Rosenstrasse protest and, 196
    see also anti-Semitism

John Chrysostom, St., 24–25
John Damascene, 344
John of the Cross, St., 365
John Paul I, Pope, 363
John Paul II, Pope (Karol Wojtyla), ix, 8,
        82, 168, 272, 316, 332, 363–70
John XXIII, Pope (Angelo Giuseppe
        Roncalli), 7, 27, 30, 204, 273, 325,
        357, 361, 362
Joos, Joseph, 148
Judaism, Christianity and Germany (Faulhaber),
        162
Jung, Edgar, 166
Justo, Agustin Pedro, 168–69

Kaas, Ludwig, 96–97, 116–17, 120–22,
        124–29, 134–39, 141–44, 146,
        148, 149, 151, 163, 168, 200, 269,
        351, 352
    anti-Hitler plot and, 235, 236, 238
Kappler, Herbert, 301, 302, 303
Karski, Jan, 291
Katz, Robert, 308
Kerrl, Hans, 180, 183, 186
Kessel, Albrecht von, 304, 306
Kesselring, Albert, 299, 301, 321
Keteler, Wilhelm von, 194
Kirkpatrick, Ivone, 154–55
Klausner, Erich, 166
Klee, Eugen, 158, 159
Krol, John, 365
Kulturkampf persecutions, 7, 14, 47, 81,
        97, 105, 133, 160, 186, 193–96,
        209, 364
Küng, Hans, 368

LaFarge, John, 189, 190
Laghi, Pio, 369
Lais, Giuseppe, 18, 23
Lamentabili (Pius X), 38, 39
Lateran Treaty, 114–15, 122, 123, 127,
        128, 133, 141, 143, 150, 177, 205,
        236, 241, 244, 327
Latin America, 167–69, 267, 367
Laval, Pierre, 171
Ledochowski, Wladimir, 189, 192, 232

Lee, Belinda, 354

Lees-Milne, James, I

Lehnert, Pasqualina, *see* Pasqualina, Mother

Leiber, Robert, 20, 94, 142, 149, 200, 220, 235–36, 240, 336, 349, 350, 356

Leo X, Pope, 250

Leo XIII, Pope, 6, 20–22, 26, 28, 29–31, 33–34, 35–36, 45, 59, 81, 119, 167, 208–9, 211, 223, 233, 273

Levien, Max, 74, 75

Levine, Eugen, 74

Lewis, Jonathan, 287

Lewy, Guenter, 154, 197, 199, 286, 295

Lichtenberg, Bernhard, 187

Lichtheim, Richard, 281

Liguori, Alfonso, 13, 38

Linklater, Magnus, 267

Lobkowicz, Erwin, 258, 259, 260

Loisy, Alfred, 36, 339

Loubet, Émile-François, 46

Lourdes, 172–73

Lubac, Henri de, 340

Lucia, Sister, 272–73

Ludwig III, King, 63

Luther, Martin, 83

Luxemburg, 242, 243

McCarthy, Joe, 331

McEwan, Bridget, 282, 284–85, 320

Macmillan, Harold, 323, 357

Maglione, Luigi, 89, 207, 221, 226, 230, 231, 236, 245–46, 256–57, 259, 281–83, 289, 290, 303–5, 309–10, 320, 323

Manning, Henry, ix, 13, 15

Marchi, Giuseppe, 16–17, 26, 27

Marcone, Ramiro, 252, 256, 257–58

Marshall, George, 330–31

Marshall Plan, 330

Marx, Wilhelm, 96

Mary, 172, 269, 272, 273, 277, 343–45, 366, 370

    Assumption of, 343–44, 345

    Our Lady of Fátima, 61–62, 272–73, 344–45, 366

Massime eterne (*Eternal Principles*) (Liguori), 13

Mastai-Ferretti, Giovanni Maria, *see* Pius IX, Pope

Maurras, Charles, 172

Mayer, Rupert, 187

Mediator dei (*Mediator Between God and Men*) (Pius XII), 337

Meir, Golda, 357

Merry del Val, Rafael, 32, 46, 47, 49, 51–52, 54, 55, 59

Merton, Thomas, v

Mexico, 112, 113, 168, 263

Michaelis, Georg, 69

Mindszenty, József, 333–35

Mit brennender Sorge (Pius XI), 141, 181–84, 205, 280, 296

Modernism, campaign against, 33, 35–40, 41, 42, 43, 59, 337, 339, 342

Molinari, Paul, 313

Monti, Carlo, 61, 62–63

Montini, Giovanni Battista, *see* Paul VI, Pope

Mortara, Edgardo, 11, 27

Muckermann, Friedrich, 155, 156

Müller, Hermann, 90, 118

Müller, Josef, 235, 236, 238, 242

Mundelein, George, 183

Murri, Romolo, 40

Mussolini, Benito, 59, 114, 116, 120, 122–23, 128, 171, 175, 203–5, 212, 223–25, 229–31, 234, 236, 238, 239, 241–44, 246–49, 252, 280, 289, 293

    Hitler's pact with, 229

    voted out of office, 298–99

Mystici corporis (*Of the Mystical Body*) (Pius XII), 275–77

Myth of the Twentieth Century (Rosenberg), 164

Naab, Ingbert, 110

Napoleon I, Emperor, 5

Napoleon III, Emperor, 11

Napoleonic Code, 42

Nazi criminals, safe houses for, 267
Nazism (National Socialism), 7, 28, 47,
    63, 84, 85, 105–10, 112, 116, 118,
    119, 121, 123–28, 130–33, 137–40,
    144–47, 149–55, 157–62, 164, 166,
    174, 179–87, 189, 192, 194, 206,
    208, 212, 217–18, 222–23, 227,
    229, 234–35, 254–55, 261, 267,
    276–77, 306, 333, 360
  Catholic resistance to, 195–99
  Final Solution of, 24, 268–69, 270,
    275, 276–77, 278–97, 300–312,
    316–18, 324–26
  Jewish businesses boycotted by, 139–41
  Mit brennender Sorge and, 183
  Pacelli's statement on, 292–93, 297
  see also Germany; Hitler, Adolf
Ne jamais désespérer (Riegner), 259
Neurath, Konstantin von, 164
Newman, John Henry, 3
New Theology, 337, 338, 340, 360–61
New York Times, 11, 66, 283, 308
Niehans, Paul, 355, 356
Night of the Long Knives, 165–66
Noble, Andrew, 229
Non abbiamo bisogno (We Have No Need) (Pius
    XI), 123
Nuremberg Laws, 154, 179–80

O'Connell, William, 176, 207
ODESSA, 267
Opus Dei, 369, 370
Oreglia de San Stefano, Giuseppe, 28
Origen, 24
Ormesson, Wladimir d', 208, 244
Orsenigo, Cesare, 117, 183, 209, 224–26
Orsini, Filippo, 354
Osborne, Francis D'Arcy, 206, 217, 229,
    230, 233, 235–40, 242–47, 256,
    281–85, 288, 289, 290–91, 293,
    309–10, 319, 320
Osservatore Romano, L', 13, 80, 99, 116,
    122–23, 130, 137, 155, 190, 201–2,
    226, 227, 233, 241, 242, 243–44,
    287, 300, 311, 312, 320, 321, 330,
    357

Oster, Hans, 235, 242
Ottaviani, Alfredo, 331

Pacelli, Carlo (nephew), 200, 201, 350,
    354
Pacelli, Elisabetta (sister), 16, 17–18, 20,
    22, 23, 31, 94, 111–12, 200, 201
Pacelli, Ernesto (cousin), 32–33
Pacelli, Eugenio, *see* Pius XII, Pope
Pacelli, Filippo (father), 10, 13, 17, 18, 22,
    61, 294
Pacelli, Francesco (brother), 9, 16, 17, 61,
    111, 114, 115, 172, 200, 216
Pacelli, Giuseppina (sister), 16
Pacelli, Marcantonio (grandfather), 9–10,
    11, 13, 15, 27
Pacelli, Maria Teresa (cousin), 32–33
Pacelli, Virginia Graziosi (mother), 13, 17,
    18, 23, 61
Padellaro, Nazareno, 69, 172, 199–200
Papée, Kasimir, 293
Papen, Franz von, 126–27, 131, 132, 134,
    138, 141–42, 144, 146–49, 151,
    152, 160, 163, 261, 262
Pascendi (Pius X), 38, 39
Pasqualina, Mother, 76, 93–94, 101, 104,
    111–12, 142, 176, 200, 201, 206,
    207, 220, 271–72, 287, 351, 354
Pastor Angelicus, 270–71, 318, 329
Paul IV, Pope, 26
Paul VI, Pope (Giovanni Battista Montini),
    2–3, 168, 222, 230, 257, 258, 259,
    270, 287, 291, 298, 323, 330, 332,
    335, 352, 362, 363
  Humanae vitae, 353, 363
Pavelic, Ante, 248–53, 255, 258, 260, 265,
    266, 280
Petacci, Claretta, 204
Petacci, Francesco, 204
Peyton, Patrick, 345
Pfeiffer, Pankratius, 306, 321
Pignatelli-Aragona, Enza, 303
Pignatti, Count, 204
Pio Nono, *see* Pius IX, Pope
Pius VII, Pope, 5
Pius VIII, Pope, 5

Pius IX, Pope (Pio Nono; Giovanni Maria
      Mastai-Ferretti), 10, 11–13, 14, 15,
      26, 41, 85, 116, 172, 177, 209, 212,
      273, 298, 300, 344
    Quod nunquam, 195
    Syllabus of Errors, 11, 20–21, 177, 193
Pius X, Pope (Giuseppe Sarto), 22, 34–35,
      36, 37–40, 41, 42, 46–47, 56,
      57–58, 59, 106, 342
    canonization of, 40, 370
Pius XI, Pope (Achille Ratti), 7, 61, 81,
      98–99, 100, 106, 111, 113, 114,
      116, 120, 123–24, 125, 148, 150,
      151, 160–61, 163–68, 172, 174–76,
      180, 181, 184, 185, 188–90, 201,
      202, 206, 208, 209, 211, 217, 218,
      225, 263, 348, 353, 354
    Casti connubii, 153
    death of, 203–4, 205
    Humani generis unitas and, 189–92,
      203
    Mit brennender Sorge, 141, 181–84, 205,
      280, 296
    Non abbiamo bisogno, 123
    Quadragessimo anno, 119
    Quas primas, 167
Pius XII, Pope (Eugenio Pacelli):
    appointed Cardinal Secretary of State,
      104
    canonization of, 370
    childhood and youth of, 15–20
    Christmas broadcasts of, 291–93, 297,
      327–28
    consecrated archbishop, 61
    coronation of, 210–18
    death and burial of, 356–58
    Divino afflante spiritu, 337
    education of, 16–17, 18–19, 20,
      22–24
    elected to papacy, 207–8
    family of, 9, 13–14, 15–16
    Humani generis, 191, 337–39
    kidnapping plot against, 313–15
    Marian devotion of, 61–62, 269,
      272–73, 343–45
    Mediator dei, 337

Mystici corporis, 275–77
    statement of, on Nazi extermination of
      Jews, 292–93, 297
    Summi pontificatus ("Darkness over the
      Earth"), 233–34, 273
Pizzardo, Giuseppe, 151, 339, 340, 341
Poland, 97, 222, 223–25, 226, 229, 230,
      231, 234–35, 332, 363–64, 365,
      366
    Germany's invasion of, 231–32
Portugal, 217, 272, 360
Power and the Glory, The (Greene), 113, 347
Preysing, Konrad von, 145, 181, 184
Probst, Adalbert, 166
Prussia, 86, 87–90, 91, 93, 96, 97–98
Prussian Concordat, 100, 102–3, 120

Quadragessimo anno (Pius XI), 119
Quale Papa? (Zizola), 207
Quas primas (Pius XI), 167
Quod nunquam (Pius IX), 195

Rampolla del Tinaro, Mariano, 29, 30, 34,
      59
Ranke-Heinemann, Uta, 354
Rath, Ernst vom, 188
Ratti, Achille, *see* Pius XI, Pope
Red Brigade, 76–78, 263
Red Triangle, 112, 263
Reformation, 5, 26, 83
Reich Concordat, 6–7, 84–87, 90–93,
      96–98, 100, 103, 115, 117, 120–26,
      130–31, 133–38, 141–55, 157–61,
      166, 179, 183, 184, 186, 203, 205,
      210, 218, 227, 296
    ratification of, 158–60
Rerum novarum (Of New Things) (Leo XIII),
      21, 119
Resistance of the Heart (Stoltzfus), 196
Ribbentrop, Joachim von, 224, 225–26,
      229, 238–39, 300
Riegner, Gerhard, 259, 281
Ripa di Meana, Fulvia, 304
Ritter, Baron von, 117, 125, 128
Rock, John, 353
Röhm, Ernst, 166

Rome, 16, 319–20
  defense of, 244, 245–48, 290–91
  gold ransom and, 301–2, 308
  Jews in, 11, 297, 299–312, 316–18,
    320–21
  liberation of, 321–23
  Via Rasella bombing in, 320–21
Roncalli, Angelo Giuseppe, *see* John XXIII,
  Pope
Roosevelt, Franklin Delano, 176–77, 230,
  288, 325
Rosenberg, Alfred, 164, 262
Rosenstrasse protest, 196
Rossi, Pelligrino, 10
Rotta, Angelo, 324, 326
Rusinovic, Nicola, 258, 259–60
Russia, *see* Soviet Union

saints, 370
Salazar, Antonio, 272, 360
Sargent, Orme, 229
Sarto, Giuseppe, *see* Pius X, Pope
Scapinelli, Rafaele, 53, 55
Schachleitner, Alban, 110
Scheler, Max, 82, 83, 84, 85, 106, 119,
  140, 366
Schillebeeckx, Edward, 368
Schioppa, Monsignor, 63, 65, 66, 67, 68,
  73, 74, 75, 77–78
Schirach, Baldur von, 186
Schleicher, Kurt von, 118, 126, 127, 132,
  166
Scholder, Klaus, 91, 110, 149, 150, 184
Schulte, Cardinal, 89, 98, 137, 145, 181,
  208
Schuman, Robert, 328
Schuster, Ildefonso, 330
Sebastian, Ludwig, 145
Second Vatican Council (Vatican II)
  (1962), 7–8, 38, 361, 364–65,
  369
Seguic, Cherubino, 257
Senn, Wilhelm Maria, 110
Serbia, 4, 48–58
Serbian Concordat, 49–58, 131, 148, 256,
  265

Serbs, Croatian campaign against, 249,
  250–60, 266
Serenelli, Alessandro, 346
Sereny, Gitta, 267
sexual morality, Pacelli's views on, 352,
  353–54
Sheen, Fulton J., 331
Siri, Giuseppe, 269, 330
Slovakia, 262, 281, 332
socialism, 116, 328, 339
  in Germany, 73–75
South America, 167–69, 267, 367
Soviet Union, 112–13, 171, 248, 263–65,
  272, 296, 328, 331, 333, 345, 364
  Germany's invasion of, 260–63, 264
  Germany's pact with, 230
Spain, 30, 112, 169–70, 175, 217, 223,
  263, 272, 327, 344, 345, 360
  civil war in, 170, 180, 217
Spellman, Francis Joseph, 176, 177, 178,
  330–31
spinning sun, 61–62, 344–45, 350
Spiritual Exercises (Ignatius Loyola), 20
Spizzichino, Settimia, 310, 317–18
Stahel, Rainer, 306, 309
Stahlberg, Hans-Conrad, 102
Stangl, Franz, 267
Stefanori, Giovanni, 220, 350
Stein, Edith (Teresa Benedicta of the
  Cross), 140–41, 287
Steinberg, Jonathan, 252, 254, 302
Stepinac, Alojzije, 250, 253, 255, 256, 265
Stern, J. P., 197
Stern, Michael, 322
Stoltzfus, Nathan, 196–97
Stoppa, Mario, 220, 221
Story of a Soul (Thérèse), 174
Strasser, Gregor, 166
Stratman, Franziscus, 139
Stresemann, Gustav, 101, 103
Sturzo, Luigi, 190, 327
Stutz, Ulrich, 42
Suárez, Emmanuel, 340
Suhard, Emmanuel, 262, 288, 341
Summi pontificatus ("Darkness over the
  Earth") (Pius XII), 233–34, 273

sun, spinning, 61–62, 344–45, 350
Sweeney, Garrett, 44
Switzerland, 15
Syllabus of Errors (Pius IX), 11, 20–21, 177, 193

Tablet, The, 211
Tacchi Venturi, Pietro, 230–31
Tardini, Domenico, 167, 221, 230, 242, 247, 259, 289, 291, 323–24, 349, 351, 356
Tavelic, Nicola, 250
Taylor, Myron, 177, 288–90
Tedeschini, Federico, 345
Teilhard de Chardin, Pierre, 340
Temps, Le, 93
Teresa Benedicta of the Cross (Edith Stein), 140–41, 287
Thérèse, St., 174, 176
Thomas à Kempis, 19–20, 269
Thomas Aquinas, St., 6, 21–22, 26, 30, 35, 280
Thomism, 21–22, 280, 366
Thompson, Dorothy, 101
Thyssen, Fritz, 119
Time, 369
Times (London), 12–13, 203, 217
Tisserant, Eugène, 206–7, 259–61, 262, 263, 264–65, 329, 356–57
Tisserant Plan, 262, 263, 264–65
Tittmann, Harold, 282–83, 284, 293, 309, 316, 325
Togliatti, Palmiro, 328, 330
Treaty of London, 60
Treaty of Versailles, 80, 83, 224
Tromp, Sebastian, 274
Trossmann, Karl, 110

Ukraine, 261
ultramontanists, 5–6
United States, 367
enters World War II, 282
Italy aided by, 329, 331
Pacelli's view of, 328
Pacelli's visit to, 176–78
Ustashe, 249–54, 260, 266, 267

Vansittart, Robert, 154, 218, 247
Vatican I (First Vatican Council) (1870), 5–6, 8, 12–13, 14, 41, 43, 193, 338–39, 343, 361
Vatican II (Second Vatican Council) (1962), 7–8, 38, 361, 364–65, 369
Vatican Radio, 227–28, 232, 243
Versailles Treaty, 80, 83, 224
Vesnitch, Milenko, 49
Via Rasella bombing, 320–21
Virgin Mary, 172, 269, 272, 273, 277, 343–45, 366, 370
Assumption of, 343–44, 345
Our Lady of Fátima, 61–62, 272–73, 344–45, 366
Vittorio Emanuele II, King, 11, 14, 16, 46
Vittorio Emanuele III, King, 298
Volk, Ludwig, 138
Völkischer Beobachter, 105, 115, 202

Wagner, Adolf, 198
Waldeck-Rousseau, Pierre-Marie-René, 45
Wall, Bernard, 219–20, 350
Wall Street crash, 103, 118, 180, 244
Walpole, Hugh, 214–15
Walsh, Michael, 367
Walshe, Joseph, 329–30, 332
Waugh, Evelyn, 322, 350
Weizsäcker, Ernst von, 300–301, 303, 304–5, 306, 307, 309–10, 311–12, 314, 321, 322
Welles, Orson, 351
Wernz, Franz Xavier, 23
Wiesel, Elie, 294
Wild, Alfons, 110
Wilhelm II, Kaiser, 63, 65–69, 72, 91
Wilson, Woodrow, 68–69, 72
Wirth, Joseph, 97, 120, 136
Wojtyla, Karol, *see* John Paul II, Pope
Wolff, Karl Friedrich Otto, 313–15
Woodruff, Douglas, 211, 212, 213
worker-priests, 339, 340, 341, 342, 360
World War I, 4, 48, 58, 60, 61, 62, 63–69, 71–72, 80

World War II, 231–32, 233, 239, 241,
    242–48, 273, 274, 275, 276, 290,
    319–21
  Holocaust in, 24, 268–69, 270, 275,
    276–77, 278–97, 300–312, 316–18,
    324–26
  Rome defense in, 244, 245–48,
    290–91

Yugoslavia, 170, 171, 248, 249, 252, 254,
    255

Zeiger, Ivo, 314
Zeit, Die, 50, 57
Zizola, Giancarlo, 207
Zolli, Israel, 300, 301, 322
Zygilebojm, Shmuel, 283